We are in the midst of an extraordinary scientific revolution and this is a brilliant compilation of the latest discoveries and ideas from some of the leading minds leading the charge. Read this mind-blowing book and forever change your views of consciousness, yourself and your world.
Lynne McTaggart, internationally bestselling author of *The Field*, *The Intention Experiment* and *The Power of Eight*

As a method for studying and modeling the behavior of nature, science should be metaphysically agnostic. When particular views about what nature *is*—as opposed to how it *behaves*—are conflated with science, many legitimate avenues of investigation are left unexplored. In defiance to proper empiricism, intriguing observations are arbitrarily declared to be mistaken simply because, according to an *a priori* metaphysics, they *can't* be right. This has been the case for the past 200+ years, since the idiosyncratic notions of plausibility entailed by the metaphysics of materialism have come to dominate scientific thought. The present volume represents a desperately needed correction to this unfortunate state of affairs. Once scientists free themselves from the implicit but pernicious shackles of materialism, vast new horizons shall open up. Science shall then be able to return to its truly empirical roots, without arbitrary boundaries set by subjective biases or beliefs. I salute the authors of the many wonderful essays in this volume. The future shall recognize them as pioneers of a historical movement away from the demonstrably absurd and restricting materialist metaphysics.
Bernardo Kastrup, PhD, computer scientist and philosopher, author of *Why Materialism is Baloney* and *The Idea of the World*

An important summary of the defects of materialism, and a good beginning to understand postmaterialist theories of mind, body and health. The book touches, with much evidence, on the needed structures and functions of non-physical processes, maybe opening the way to seeing their substance and causal powers within a future comprehensive science.
Ian Thompson, PhD, physicist, Livermore, California, Fellow of Institute of Physics London and of American Physical Society

Science is undergoing fundamental change. Materialism, which has been its foundation for several centuries, is giving way to a new paradigm in which consciousness is understood to be causal and fundamental. *Expanding Science* is a benchmark in this process of change.
Stephan A. Schwartz, author of *The 8 Laws of Change* and *Opening to the Infinite*

EXPANDING SCIENCE

Visions of a Postmaterialist Paradigm

Volume II
Postmaterialist Sciences Series

Edited by
Mario Beauregard, PhD
Gary E. Schwartz, PhD
Natalie L. Dyer, PhD
Marjorie Woollacott, PhD

AAPS
Press

© copyright 2020 by The Academy for the Advancement of Post-materialist Sciences

AAPS Headquarters, Tucson, AZ.
AAPS Press and Information on AAPS,
P.O. Box 156,
Battle Ground, WA 98604

All rights reserved. No part of this book may be reproduced or utilized in any form of by any means, electronic or mechanical, including photocopying, recording, or by any information storage and retrieval system, without permission in writing from the publisher.

L.C. Cat. No.: 1-9172573111

ISBN-13: 978-1-7354491-2-8 print edition
ISBN-13: 978-1-7354491-3-5 e-book editions

This book was typeset in Baskerville.

The cover image is a portion of a Hubble Telescope photo, *Earth's Milky Way Neighborhood*. Credit: Robert Hurt, IPAC; Bill Saxton, *NRAO/AUI/NSF*

To send correspondence: aapsglobal@gmail.com

All matter originates and exists only by virtue of a force...
*We must assume behind this force the existence of a
   conscious and intelligent Mind.*
This Mind is the matrix of all matter.

Max Planck

Table of Contents

The Academy for the Advancement of Postmaterialist Sciences i

Preface to Advances in Postmaterialist Sciences Series ii

CHAPTER ONE 1
   The Next Great Scientific Revolution, Mario Beauregard, PhD

CHAPTER TWO 27
   Extraordinary Claims Require Extraordinary Evidence: The Case for Postmaterial Consciousness, Gary E. Schwartz, PhD

CHAPTER THREE 56
   Wave of Awakening: Support for a Postmaterialist Science and Society, Natalie L Dyer, PhD

CHAPTER FOUR 85
   The Reality of One (and Zero): Saving Science from Materialism, John H Spencer, PhD

CHAPTER FIVE 97
   Cosmic Connections: Towards a Postmaterialist Science of Self, Lorne Schussel, PhD, John H Spencer, PhD

CHAPTER SIX 117
   A Case for a New Scientific Paradigm: Toward Advancing the Knowledge Base, Emily R Hawken, PhD

CHAPTER SEVEN 133
   Setting Science Free From Materialism, Rupert Sheldrake, PhD

CHAPTER EIGHT 156
   Science within Consciousness: A Progress Report, Amit Goswami, PhD

CHAPTER NINE 187
   Beyond Gene Expression, Isabelle Goulet, PhD

CHAPTER TEN 203
   The Telecebo Response:
   Toward a Postmaterial Concept of Healing, Larry Dossey, MD
CHAPTER ELEVEN 240
   Near-death experience and the loss of brain function during
   cardiac arrest: A strong indication for non-local consciousness,
   Pim van Lommel, MD
CHAPTER TWELVE 286
   Consciousness and the brain: What does research on
   spiritual experiences tell us?, Alexander Moreira-Almeida, MD, PhD
CHAPTER THIRTEEN 312
   Reductive materialism explains everything, except for
   two small clouds, Dean Radin, PhD
CHAPTER FOURTEEN 331
   Reincarnation - Any Evidence For It?, Erlendur Haraldsson, PhD
CHAPTER FIFTEEN 350
   On the Psychological Need and Scientific Evidence for
   a Postmaterialist Expansion of Essential Science,
   Charles T. Tart, PhD
CHAPTER SIXTEEN 384
   Science, Soul, and Death,
   Marilyn Schlitz, PhD, John H Spencer, PhD
CHAPTER SEVENTEEN 399
   Towards a Postmaterialist Society (Back to Plato),
   Neal Grossman, PhD
CHAPTER EIGHTEEN 419
   Kundalini Awakenings: Expanding Science to Encompass a
   Postmaterialist Perspective, Marjorie Hines Woollacott, PhD

APPENDIX 440
   Expanding Matter: A New Postmaterialist take
   on Quantum Consciousness, Emmanuel Ransford
About the Authors 465
Index 472

Academy for the Advancement of Postmaterialist Sciences

The Academy for the Advancement of Postmaterialist Sciences (www.AAPSglobal.com) is a non-profit membership and education organization whose mission is to promote open-minded, rigorous and evidence-based enquiry into postmaterialist consciousness research. Our vision is to inspire scientists to investigate mind and consciousness as core elements of reality.

To achieve this paradigm changing mission, AAPS embraces the following values:

Support rigorous applications of the scientific method
Nurture curiosity and creativity in research
Encourage open-minded exploratory and confirmatory and investigations
Model integrity and honesty in communication and education
Value experimental and empirical data over dogma
Create safe settings for sharing theories, evidence, and experiences
Promote evidence-based innovation and positive societal change
Expand awareness of the interconnectedness of all things
Share postmaterialist evidence and understanding with the public

With these values in mind, AAPS is publishing an *Advances in Postmaterialist Sciences* book series to educate scientists, students, and science-minded readers about postmaterialist consciousness research and its applications. Our intent is that each volume combines rigor and creativity, expresses first person (inner experiences) as well as third person (external observations), and facilitates the betterment of humanity and the planet. Some volumes will address specific topics or themes, others will be wide ranging and diverse collections of research topics. Collectively they will help define and advance the evolution of postmaterialist theory, research and applications.

Preface

This volume is part of the AAPS book series Advances in Postmaterialist Sciences, created with the intent to educate scientists, students, and science-minded readers about postmaterialist consciousness research and its applications. Our intent is that each volume combines rigor and creativity, expresses first person (inner experiences) as well as third person (external observations), and facilitates the betterment of humanity and the planet. Some volumes will address specific topics or themes, others will be wide ranging and diverse collections of research topics. Collectively they will help define and advance the evolution of postmaterialist theory, research and applications.

Postmaterialism offers the potential for a new paradigm to emerge, one that can not only help science develop in novel ways, but also offers an important contribution to the ongoing transformation in human consciousness. The currently reigning paradigm, known as scientific materialism (or simply materialism), erroneously claims that everything is material (i.e. made up exclusively of physical matter) and that all phenomena are the result of purely material interactions. This worldview has more or less dominated science and the academic world for centuries, despite the fact that many of the leading pioneers in modern science have either implicitly or explicitly rejected it. At last, we are reaching a tipping point in the accumulation of evidence and deeper understanding, and the old materialist worldview has started to crumble. This anthology is a landmark publication, helping to light the way forward on this extraordinary journey toward a postmaterialist science and society.

In February 2014, during a meeting held at Canyon Ranch in Tucson, Arizona, the emergence of this new paradigm was discussed among a multidisciplinary group of scientists who shared a collective disillusionment with materialism. Titled the International Summit on Postmaterialist Science, Spirituality, and Society, this meeting was co-organized by two of the co-editors of this volume (Gary E. Schwartz of the University of Arizona and Mario Beauregard of the University of Arizona) and by research psychologist Lisa Miller of Columbia University. Its purpose was to advance the development of postmaterialist science and the emerging postmaterialist paradigm (PMP), for the betterment of science, spirituality, and society. Scientists spanning fields of expertise from biology and neuroscience to psychology, medicine, and psi research attended this watershed event.[1]

Following this event, the participants published the Manifesto for a Postmaterialist Science in the scientific journal Explore: The Journal of Science and Healing.[2] Since the publication of this groundbreaking manifesto, over 300 scientists and philosophers around the world have given their support to this movement by adding their signatures to this manifesto.

Out of the Summit was also born the Campaign for Open Science, and a website was created to share its message: opensciences.org. This website is a portal for open-minded scientific investigations that go beyond the dogmas dominating so much of mainstream science today. Visitors to the website will find cutting-edge materials on consciousness studies, alternative energy sources, integrative medicine and healing, postmaterialist approaches to science, and new discoveries in cosmology, physics, chemistry, and biology. Videos, books, journals, and links to the websites of open-minded scientific researchers and organizations, as well as a growing number of articles, are also to be found on this portal.

The term "postmaterialist" does not explicitly put forth a prescription for what a new theory (or theories) will be, but rather emphasizes the end of the era of materialism. We have selected this term intentionally, as it allows us to approach the future of science and society in a more expansive fashion, and inspires the vigorous pursuit of new ideas and systems of thinking. Indeed, not all the contributors are in agreement about everything related to postmaterialism, nor should they be. Science needs healthy and sometimes quite intense debate, and this new paradigm should not be constrained by dogmatic assumptions, as has been the case with materialism.

---

[1] *The summary report of this seminal meeting is available at* http://opensciences.org/files/pdfs/ISPMS-Summary-Report.pdf.
[2] *Available online at:* http://opensciences.org/about/manifesto-for-a-postmaterialist-science

During the Summit, one of us (Gary Schwartz) saw the value in producing an anthology of perspectives and evidence concerning the emergence of postmaterialist science, and invited Mario Beauregard and Dr. Natalie L. Dyer (née Trent) to co-edit an anthology devoted to this theme. Dr. Marjorie Woollacott was later invited to join the editorial team.

The majority of the contributors found in this volume are internationally known scientists and visionaries who are challenging the scientific status quo, and their viewpoints are, at times, markedly divergent from the mainstream. But, as it has been said before on numerous occasions, neither Copernicus, Galileo, nor Einstein were considered mainstream in their time. Of course, it does not follow that anyone who challenges the status quo is therefore necessarily right, but it also does not follow that something is necessarily true just because it is part of the assumptions of the status quo.

As editors of this anthology, we have encouraged the contributors to offer their personal perspectives on what the postmaterialist paradigm might be like. To do so, the contributors were free to discuss any empirical evidence they felt were relevant and important. In our view, this strategic approach that we used is part of this volume's strength. At the same time, it explains why similar evidence sometimes appears in various chapters, which can also help reinforce the ideas presented.

While this book is relevant to experts from various academic disciplines, it is also written for those with an interest in science, consciousness, mind-brain relationship, philosophy, and spirituality. It should also go without saying that some people who are thoroughly entrenched in materialism are not so likely to be enthusiastic about the general arguments and goals of this book, but some of these same people will demand evidence and yet refuse to see it when it is presented. Let us follow the true scientific spirit and keep an open mind.

We truly hope that the reader will find this anthology insightful, stimulating, and inspirational. We also trust that this book will succeed in illuminating the fact that we are riding on the cusp of what may be the greatest conceptual revolution in the history of humankind.

Mario Beauregard, Ph.D.
Gary E. Schwartz, Ph.D.
Natalie L. Dyer, Ph.D.
Marjorie Woollacott, Ph.D

Chapter One

The Next Great Scientific Revolution

Mario Beauregard, PhD[3]

Consciousness cannot be accounted for in physical terms.
For consciousness is absolutely fundamental.
It cannot be accounted for in terms of anything else.

Erwin Schrödinger

Introduction: The Failure of Materialism

Few scientists are aware that what has been called the "modern scientific worldview" is predicated on a number of metaphysical assumptions—i.e. hypotheses about the nature of reality—that were first proposed by some of the pre-Socratic philosophers (Burtt, 1949). These assumptions, which several centuries later became associated with classical physics, include materialism—the notion that matter is all that truly exists, i.e. everything in the universe is composed of collections of material/physical particles and fields (the terms 'materialism' and 'physicalism' are used interchangeably in this chapter)—and 'reductionism,' the idea that complex things can be understood by reducing them to the interactions of their parts, or to simpler or more fundamental things such as tiny material particles. Other assumptions include 'determinism,' the notion that future states of physical or biological systems can be predicted from current states, and 'mechanism,' the idea that the world works like a machine.

---

[3]*Laboratory for Advances in Consciousness and Health, Department of Psychology, The University of Arizona*

During the 19th century, these assumptions hardened, turned into dogmas, and coalesced into a belief system that came to be known as "scientific materialism" (Burtt, 1949; Sheldrake, 2012). This belief system implies that mind and consciousness—and all that we subjectively experience (e.g. our memories, emotions, goals, and spiritual epiphanies)—are identical with or can be reduced to electrical and chemical processes in the brain, and these brain processes are ultimately reducible to the interaction between basic physical elements. Another implication of this belief system is that our thoughts and intentions cannot have any effect upon our brains and bodies, our actions, and the physical world, since the mind cannot directly affect at a distance physical and biological systems. In other words, we human beings are nothing but complex biophysical machines. As a result, our consciousness and personality automatically vanish when we die.

The ideology of scientific materialism became dominant in academia during the 20th century—so dominant that a majority of scientists started to believe that it represented the only rational view of the world. This dominance has seriously constricted the sciences and hampered the development of the study of mind, consciousness, and spirituality. Furthermore, faith in this belief system as an exclusive explanatory framework for reality has compelled many scientists to neglect certain aspects of the subjective dimension of human experience. This has led to a severely distorted and impoverished understanding of ourselves and our place in nature (Beauregard and O'Leary, 2007; Nagel, 2012; Wallace, 2012).

Over a century ago, physicists discovered phenomena, at the atomic level, that could not be accounted for by classical physics. This led to the development of a revolutionary new branch of physics called quantum mechanics (QM). This "new physics" has convincingly refuted the metaphysical assumptions underlying scientific materialism. For example, QM has called into question the material foundations of the world by showing that atoms and subatomic particles are not really objects—they do not exist with certainty at definite spatial locations and definite times. Rather, they show "tendencies to exist," forming a world of potentialities within the quantum domain (Heisenberg, 1976). Moreover, physicists have discovered that particles being observed and the observer—the physicist and the method used for observation—are somehow linked, and the results of the observation seem to be influenced by the physicist's conscious intent. This phenomenon led towering figures of QM (such as Max Planck, Erwin Schrödinger, John von Neumann, and Eugene Wigner) to propose that the consciousness of the physicist is vital to the existence of the physical events being observed, and that mental events, such as intention, can affect the physical world. This interpretation of QM is supported by well-known living physicists (such as Freeman Dyson, Roger Penrose, Henry Stapp, Paul Davies, and Andrei Linde).

Although QM has invalidated the metaphysical assumptions associated with scientific materialism, several contemporary scientists and philosophers still hold this belief system and, therefore, adopt a very narrow view of what humans are and can be. They firmly believe that science is synonymous with methodological and philosophical materialism; further, they are convinced that the view that mind and consciousness are simply by-products of brain activity is an incontrovertible fact that has been demonstrated beyond reasonable doubt (Dossey, 2015).

Undoubtedly, scientific methods based upon materialistic philosophy have been highly successful, not only in increasing our understanding of nature but also in creating numerous benefits for the world, such as greater control and freedom through advances in technology. Nevertheless, science is, first and foremost, a non-dogmatic, open-minded method of acquiring knowledge about nature through the observation, experimental investigation, and theoretical explanation of phenomena. Science is not synonymous with materialism and should not be committed to any particular beliefs, dogmas, or ideologies.

Furthermore, materialist theories have utterly failed to explain how the brain could generate the mind and consciousness. Thus, these theories cannot solve the "hard problem" of consciousness, the problem of explaining how and why we have qualia or phenomenal experiences (Chalmers, 1995). In addition, these theories are unable to account for a plethora of empirical findings that are considered to be anomalous with regard to the materialist framework. This leads me to Thomas Kuhn's conception of scientific revolutions.

The Structure of Scientific Revolutions

In the 1960s, historian and philosopher of science Thomas Kuhn published a book titled *The Structure of Scientific Revolutions*, which became very influential in both academic and popular circles. In this book, Kuhn proposed that paradigms—theoretical frameworks of scientific disciplines within which theories are formulated and experiments performed—can and should change because sooner or later, they fail to explain observed phenomena. Importantly, Kuhn demonstrated that scientists are generally unable to acknowledge phenomena not allowed by the paradigm they are committed to:

"Can it conceivably be an accident, for example, that Western astronomers first saw change in the previously immutable heavens during the half-century after Copernicus' new paradigm was proposed? The Chinese, whose cosmological beliefs did not preclude celestial change, had recorded the appearance of many new stars in the heaven at a much earlier date" (Kuhn, 1970, p. 116).

According to Kuhn, when anomalies—experimental observations or other empirical evidence which violates the widely accepted theoretical framework—that the paradigm cannot accommodate accumulate, and persistent efforts by scientists fail to elucidate these anomalies, the scientific community begins to lose confidence in the dominant paradigm and a crisis period ensues. A new paradigm, competing with the old for supremacy, can now be entertained. This new paradigm is not just an extension of the old paradigm, but a completely different worldview.

The new paradigm is typically championed by bold scientists storming the bastions of accepted dogma. Unsurprisingly, as conservative scientists often believe that the anomalies will be resolved soon from within the old paradigm, they fight to salvage this theoretical framework. But if the new paradigm shows sufficient promise, i.e. if it is better able to account for anomalous observations, it then attracts a significant group of scientists away from the old paradigm, and a paradigm shift (or scientific revolution) occurs. Following this paradigm shift, scientists return to solving puzzles, but within the new paradigm.

A good example of a capital paradigm shift is the Copernican Revolution, the radical change of perspective from Ptolemy's geocentric model of the heavens to the heliocentric model with the Sun at the center of the solar system. It is noteworthy that Aristarchus had already laid the foundations of heliocentrism in the third century BC. However, as the power of the geocentric view was too strong, it took another 18 centuries before Copernicus proposed that the Earth moves around the sun and not vice versa (Kuhn, 1970). Another instance of a major paradigm shift in science was the development of QM between 1900 and 1930. This new physics began as mathematical explanations of certain anomalies, at the atomic level, that could not be accounted for by the predominant theories of classical physics.

Present day scientists working in the field of consciousness research and interested in the mind-brain problem find themselves in a situation similar to that of the physicists at the turn of the 20th century. Undeniably, they are confronted with an increasing amount of anomalous evidence that cannot be elucidated by materialist theories of the mind and consciousness. In the next section, I examine some of this evidence, guided by the radical empiricist view that we should study any human experience, no matter how unusual it may seem at first glance (James, 1904; In philosophy, empiricism is the view that all concepts originate in experience.).

Empirical Evidence Challenging Scientific Materialism

The various lines of empirical evidence examined in this section are grouped into three categories. Category I includes evidence for which a materialist explanation is often provided, but that could also be seen through a postmaterialist perspective. The phenomena described in this category demonstrate the enormous power of the mind to influence the brain and body. Category II contains evidence for which a materialist explanation, though commonly presented, is less adequate than a postmaterialist explanation. This category includes phenomena suggesting that mind is not limited to space or time. Category III contains evidence that is rejected outright by materialist theories of the mind, but is supportive of a postmaterialist perspective, since it is incongruent with the materialist perspective that mind and consciousness are produced solely by the brain.

Category I: The Power of the Mind to Influence Brain and Body

There are many instances in which mental activity—through intention, expectation, and will—has tremendous power over shaping our brain, body, and health. For example, several studies demonstrate that thoughts can causally affect behavioral outcomes via intentions that are translated into specific plans (Baumeister et al., 2011). In agreement with this, it is well established that the explanatory and predictive value of agentic factors (e.g., beliefs, goals, aspirations, and desires) is very high (Bandura, 2001). Moreover, there is now ample evidence that mental phenomena significantly influence the functioning of the brain.

This is exemplified by functional neuroimaging investigations of emotional self-regulation, which refers to the cognitive processes by which we can consciously and voluntarily affect which emotions we have, when we have them, and how we experience and express these emotions (Gross, 1999). Reappraisal—reinterpreting/transforming the meaning of the emotion-eliciting stimulus/event to change one's emotional response to it—and cognitive distancing—viewing a stimulus from the perspective of a detached and distant observer—are some of the cognitive strategies used to self-regulate emotion. Studies performed in my laboratory, at the University of Montreal, and in other labs have conclusively shown that the conscious and voluntary use of cognitive strategies specifically alters the activity of brain areas involved in emotion (e.g. the amygdala, hypothalamus, and insula). (For a review, see Beauregard, 2007.)

Additionally, a number of brain imaging studies suggest that the mental functions and processes implicated in various types of psychotherapy (e.g. cognitive-behavioral therapy and interpersonal psychotherapy) do exert a powerful influence on the functioning and plasticity of the brain (Beauregard, 2007).

Other lines of evidence in Category I include the placebo effect and psychosomatic influence. A placebo is a treatment (e.g., drugs, psychotherapy, and surgery) used for its ameliorative effect on a disease, but that is biologically inert (Shapiro & Shapiro, 1997). The physiological responses produced by placebos seem to reflect a mind/body interaction which is driven by subjective psychological factors (e.g. beliefs, expectations, meaning, and hope for improvement). To date, many neuroimaging studies have been carried out with respect to this phenomenon. Overall, their results strongly support the view that beliefs and expectations about placebo treatments can modulate neurophysiological and neurochemical activity in brain regions involved in various psychological functions (e.g., perception, movement, pain, and emotion).

The sphere of influence of the mind is not limited to the brain. Indeed, experimental investigations conducted in the field of psychoneuroimmunology—the study of the interactions between mental processes and the nervous and immune systems (Ray, 2004)—have revealed that chemical messengers produced by immune cells signal the brain, and the brain sends chemical signals to the immune system. Other studies have shown that the causes, development, and outcomes of an illness are determined by the interaction of psychological (e.g. thoughts, emotional feelings) and social factors with biochemical changes that influence the immune system, the endocrine system, and the cardiovascular system (Ray, 2004). In accordance with this, we now know that events and situations perceived as uncontrollable can lead to major disruptions of the immune and endocrine functions. For instance, immune responses are weakened during marital discord, and the levels of stress hormones increase in the spouse who experiences the greatest amount of stress and feelings of helplessness (Vitetta et al., 2005). In contrast, a positive emotional state can bolster the activity of the immune function.

Mental influence on the activity of the physiological systems connected to the brain is usually exerted unconsciously. However, there is some evidence that mental phenomena can also affect the body consciously and volitionally. In fact, it has been demonstrated that healthy volunteers can intentionally use mental imagery to positively impact their immune system, notably the activity of neutrophils, the most abundant type of white blood cells (Trakhtenberg, 2008).

Category II: Mind beyond Space and Time

This category contains various lines of evidence suggesting that mental functions and abilities are not constrained by space and time and the boundaries of the body. One of these lines of evidence relates to the so-called psi phenomena, which include extrasensory perception (ESP) and psychokinesis (PK). ESP denotes the acquisition of information about external events or objects by means other than the mediation of any known channel of sensory communication. It includes telepathy—the access to another person's thoughts without the use of any of our known sensory channels—clairvoyance—the apparent perception of events or objects that cannot be perceived by the known senses—and precognition—the knowledge of some future event that cannot be deduced from normally known data in the present. PK refers to the influence of mind on a physical system that cannot be totally explained by the mediation of any known physical means (Kugel, 2010). In this subsection, I will briefly examine the results of studies of several psi phenomena.

Since the 1970s, a large number of experiments have been performed to test telepathy using a sensory deprivation technique called the ganzfeld (for a description of this technique, please see Chapter 13, "Reductive Materialism Explains Everything, Except for Two Small Clouds" by Dr. Dean Radin). Several meta-analyses—statistical analyses of several separate but similar experiments/studies in order to test the pooled data for statistical significance—of ganzfeld telepathy studies have reported results significantly higher than expected by chance. (For a review of these meta-analyses, see Williams, 2011.)

During the last five decades, presentiment experiments have also been carried out to test whether it is possible to obtain specific, meaningful information in ways that transcend the usual limitations of time. These experiments often involve protocols where a series of emotionally laden stimuli are presented while participants have continuous physiological recordings, such as skin conductance, heart rate, pupil dilation, electroencephalography (EEG), and blood oxygenation level-dependent (BOLD) responses. In presentiment experiments, post-stimulus activity is predictive of pre-stimulus activity; that is, various aspects of human physiology respond to the stimulus before it is presented or known by the participants. A recent meta-analysis of 26 presentiment experiments between 1978 and 2010 was performed by Mossbridge and colleagues (2012). The physiological variables measured in these studies included electrodermal activity, heart rate, blood volume, pupil dilation, EEG activity, and BOLD activity. The results of this meta-analysis indicate a significant overall effect.

As for PK, researchers around the world have conducted laboratory experiments in this area for over a century to investigate the effects of mental intention on inanimate objects and physical systems (e.g. morphological changes in thin strips of metal, distribution of metallic and plastic balls, temperature changes in well-shielded environments, latencies in radioactive decay, and perturbations in sensitive magnetometers and interferometers). Several of these experiments have produced statistically significant results (see Radin & Nelson, 2003).

Electronic random number generators (RNGs) have frequently been used as physical targets in mind-matter interaction (MMI) experiments. Modern RNGs are circuits designed to produce electronic noise that is converted to random sequences of 0 and 1 bits. During a fixed group of successive trials, called a run, participants in these experiments are asked to mentally influence the outcome of a RNG so that it may produce, for example, a high number of 0s (i.e. greater than chance expectation), and then a low number of 0s (i.e. lower than chance expectation). In the control condition, the participants do not exert any intentional influence on the outcome. Typically participants in RNG experiments contribute several hundred runs. In 2003, Radin and Nelson published a meta-analysis which included 515 RNG experiments. The magnitude of the overall effect was small, but statistically very significant.

Psi researchers have also explored whether people can mentally influence living systems situated at a distance when shielded from all possible conventional influences. For instance, Braud and Schlitz (1991) conducted a series of experiments in which one person (the influencer) attempted to mentally influence the ongoing electrodermal activity (an index of emotional responses) of a distant target person (the influencee) using intentionality, focused attention, and imagery of desired outcomes. In these experiments, the influencee and the influencer were placed in separate, non-adjacent rooms, and the influencee's spontaneously fluctuating electrodermal activity was monitored while he/she made no deliberate attempts to relax or become more active. During series of 30-second electrodermal activity recording epochs, the influencer received instructions about what to do. Epochs were signalled to the influencer (through headphones) by special tones not audible to the influencee. During decreasing epochs, the influencer created and maintained a strong intention for the influencee to be calm and relaxed and to display little electrodermal activity; during non-influence (control) epochs, the influencer attempted not to think about the influencee or the experiment. Using this experimental protocol, Braud and Schlitz (1991) conducted 15 electrodermal influence experiments: in these experiments, a significant success rate was found, and the mean effect size compared favorably with effect sizes commonly reported in behavioral and biomedical studies.

Category III: Mind Beyond Brain: NDEs During Cardiac Arrest and Clinical Death

Near-death experiences (NDEs) are vivid, realistic, and often deeply life-changing experiences occurring to individuals who have been psychologically or physiologically close to death (Holden et al., 2009). A clear memory of the experience, enhanced mental activity, and a conviction that the experience is more real than ordinary waking consciousness are core features of NDEs (Greyson, 2011). Other typical features include an out-of-body experience (OBE), i.e. a sense of having left one's body and watching events going on around one's body and, occasionally, at some distant physical location; feelings of joy and peace; passage through a dark tunnel or a region of darkness; seeing an otherworldly realm of great beauty;

encountering deceased relatives and friends; seeing an unusually bright light, sometimes experienced as a "Being of Light" that radiates complete acceptance and unconditional love, and may communicate telepathically with the near-death experiencer (NDEr); seeing and reliving events of one's life, sometimes from the perspective of the other individuals involved; and returning to the physical body (often unwillingly).

NDEs are frequently evoked by cardiac arrest. When the heart stops, breathing stops as well, and blood flow and oxygen uptake in the brain are rapidly interrupted; the EEG becomes isoelectric (flat-line) within 10-20 seconds, and brainstem reflexes vanish (Clute & Levy, 1990); the individual having the cardiac arrest is then considered to be clinically dead. Because the brain structures supporting conscious experience and higher mental functions (e.g. perception, memory, and awareness) are dramatically impaired, cardiac arrest survivors are not expected to have clear and lucid mental experiences during the cardiac arrest period that will be remembered. Nonetheless, studies carried out in the United Kingdom (Parnia et al., 2001), the Netherlands (van Lommel et al., 2001), Belgium (Lallier et al., 2015), and the United States (Schwaninger et al., 2002; Greyson, 2003) have revealed that about 15 percent of cardiac arrest survivors do report some recollection from the time when they were clinically dead. In these studies, more than 100 cases of full-blown NDEs were reported. It is noteworthy that while they are clinically dead, NDErs sometimes report perceptions that coincide with reality.

Advocates of materialist theories of the mind object that even if the EEG is isoelectric, there may be some residual brain activity that goes undetected because of the limitations of scalp-EEG technology. This is possible, given that scalp-EEG technology measures mostly the activity of large populations of cortical neurons. However, the brain activity agreed upon by contemporary neuroscientists as the necessary condition of conscious experience is well detected via current EEG technology, and is clearly abolished by cardiac arrest (Greyson, 2011).

Proponents of materialist theories of the mind also argue that NDEs do not occur during the actual episodes of brain insult, but just before or just after the insult, when the brain is more or less functional (Saavedra-

Aguilar & Gómez-Jeria, 1989; Blackmore, 1993; Woerlee, 2004). The problem with this interpretation is that unconsciousness generated by cardiac arrest leaves patients amnesic and confused for events occurring immediately before and after such episodes (Aminoff et al., 1988; Parnia & Fenwick, 2002; van Lommel et al., 2001).

Reincarnation-Past Life Research

During the last 50 years, over 2,500 cases of young children who reported memories from ostensible previous lives have been studied (Haraldsson, 2012). The pioneer of this type of research was Dr. Ian Stevenson, a psychiatrist who worked at the University of Virginia. Today, other researchers, such as Erlendur Haraldsson and Jim Tucker, continue the research pioneered by Stevenson. Many cases have been verified. If the verified cases are indeed indicative of accurate memories from another life, these data challenge the materialist view that mind is what the brain does. Clearly, the fact that the brain of the deceased is no longer functional, and that the memories of the individual may still be accessible, seriously call into question what we know about memory and its dependence on cerebral activity (Haraldsson, 2012). (See Chapter 14, "Reincarnation: Any Evidence for It?" by Dr. Erlendur Haraldsson).

Most children experience ostensible past-life memories between the ages of two and five, and usually stop talking about these memories between five to seven years of age (Mills & Lynn, 2000). While most incidences occur in Eastern countries, where reincarnation is more culturally accepted, some cases also occur in Western countries (Stevenson, 2001). Approximately 80 percent of children's ostensible past-life memories are of violent deaths (Haraldsson, 2003). Common themes include claiming that their current parents are not their real parents, and that their homes are somewhere else. Many children have birthmarks that coincide with wounds reportedly associated with the previous life. Though not as common, there are multiple cases of children who present with xenoglossy, meaning they are able to communicate in a language, to various degrees of fluency, which they did not learn through any discernable means (Stevenson, 1976).

The investigations usually involve child and parent interviews, and any other person who has witnessed the child speaking of the memories. Then, it is important to rule out whether the child is speaking of events or experiences that he/she learned about from something or someone in his/her environment. After these steps, it is determined whether the case is worth investigating further. Often the witnesses are interviewed again for reliability. The next step, which is very important, is to determine if a deceased person can be traced whose life events correspond to the statements made by the child. Frequently, a person is found to whom the child is believed to be referring. The family of that person will then be interviewed, if possible, and all relevant documents obtained, such as birth and death certificates, postmortem reports, and any other relevant materials (Haraldsson, 2012).

Common materialist explanations for ostensible past-life memories include mere coincidence, child or parental fabrication, fantasies, and false memories or paramnesia (Haraldsson, 2003). Some have suggested that past-life memories may be a result of trauma in the current life, such as child abuse, but no evidence for this has been found (Haraldsson, 2003). However, these children may display post-traumatic stress disorder (PTSD) symptoms, such as fear, phobias, anxiety, and aggressiveness, though these behaviors may be related to the past life trauma rather than trauma from the current life (Haraldsson, 2003). These children could be actually remembering previous lives that they lived as they suggest, or they could be accessing information of a deceased individual through some unknown means (i.e. super-psi theory, also called super-ESP: the retrieval of information via a psychic channel).

Mediumship Research

The survival of consciousness hypothesis—the continued existence, separate from the physical body, of an individual's consciousness or personality after physical death—has been investigated for more than a century.

William James, the father of American psychology, was one of the early pioneers of mediumship research (see Gauld, 1983). James and the other pioneers in this field thought that investigating the information reported by mediums—individuals who report experiencing communication with deceased persons—could test the survival of consciousness hypothesis.

Contemporary research has been carried out mainly by Dr. Gary E. Schwartz in the Laboratory for Advances in Consciousness and Health (formally the Human Energy Systems Laboratory) at the University of Arizona. The early experimental designs were mostly single blinded, i.e. the medium was blind to the identity of the sitters (i.e. the living people who knew the deceased individuals) (e.g. Schwartz & Russek, 2001; Schwartz et al., 2001, 2002). Other exploratory experimental designs were double blinded, in that the medium was blind to the identity of the sitters, and the sitters were blind to the identity of their personal readings. In other experiments, the medium was blind to the identity of the sitters, and the experimenter was blind to the information about the sitter's deceased loved ones.

To determine whether accurate information about a sitter's deceased loved ones can be reliably obtained from research mediums, who are operating under highly controlled experimental conditions that effectively rule out conventional explanations, the most recent experimental designs were triple blinded (Beischel & Schwartz, 2007). Blinding was produced at three levels: (a) the mediums were blind to the identities of the sitters and their deceased loved ones, (b) the experimenter/proxy sitter interacting with the mediums was blind to the identities of the sitters and their deceased loved ones, and (c) the sitters rating the transcripts were blind to the origin of the readings (intended for the sitter vs. a matched control) during scoring.

Eight research mediums who had previously shown an ability to report accurate information in a laboratory setting performed the readings. Eight University of Arizona students served as sitters: four had experienced the death of a parent; the four others had experienced the death of a peer. Each deceased parent was paired with a same-gendered deceased peer to optimize potential identifiable differences between readings. Sitters were not present at the readings. The mediums each read two absent sitters and their paired deceased loved one; each pair of sitters was read by two mediums. Each blinded sitter then scored a pair of itemized transcripts (one was the reading intended for him/her; the other, the paired control reading) and chose the reading more applicable to him/her. The mediums performed the study readings over the phone at scheduled times in their homes to improve testing conditions. The audio-recorded phone readings took place long-distance; the medium was in a different city (if not state) than both the blinded absent sitter and the experimenter acting as the proxy sitter.

The results showed that the sitters were able to correctly identify above chance which of the two readings belonged to their paired deceased individuals. These findings provide evidence that under stringent triple blind conditions, certain mediums can receive accurate information about deceased individuals. The findings cannot discriminate between alternative hypotheses, such as the survival of consciousness or super-psi. However, the use of a blind proxy sitter condition eliminates telepathy (i.e., mind reading of the sitter) as a plausible explanation for the results.

Deathbed Communications

Deathbed communications (DBCs) constitute another source of evidence suggesting that consciousness and personality may not cease after bodily death. DBCs are any communication between the patient and deceased friends or relatives within 30 days of dying. These experiences have been reported across different cultures and throughout history (Fenwick et al., 2010). DBCs may encompass auditory, visual, and kinesthetic elements, and are often indicated by nonverbal processes (e.g. reaching out of the hands toward an invisible person or object) (Lawrence & Repede, 2012). One frequent type of DBC involves apparent encounters with deceased spirits who seem to welcome the experiencer to the afterlife and converse responsively with him/her (Greyson, 2010b). DBCs have a deep impact on the alleviation of physical, emotional, and existential distress at the end of life, and most of the people who have these experiences derive great meaning and comfort from them (Lawrence & Repede, 2012).

Research conducted with end-of-life nurses and physicians suggests that these experiences are not uncommon (Fenwick et al., 2010). The prevailing view among physicians is that DBCs are confusional-hallucinatory, drug induced (Fenwick et al., 2010), or due to expectation and wishful thinking (Greyson, 2010b). While this may sometimes be true, there are cases of DBCs which cannot be simply explained as hallucinations based on expectation: in these cases, the dying person apparently sees, and expresses surprise at seeing, a person whom he/she thought was living, but who had in fact recently died (Greyson, 2010b).

The Emerging Postmaterialist Paradigm

Taken together, the various lines of empirical evidence presented in the preceding section clearly show that the idea that the brain creates mind and consciousness is flawed and obsolete.

Materialists often claim that experimental evidence obtained using neuroscience techniques (e.g. recording, stimulation, and lesion) proves in a definite manner that the brain produces mind, much as the liver secretes bile. In fact, neuroscience studies only reveal that under normal conditions, mental activity is correlated with neuroelectrical and neurochemical activity. But correlations do not imply causation and identity, and the kinds of evidence obtained via these techniques do not necessarily validate the hypothesis that mind can be reduced solely to brain activity (for more on this topic, see Chapter 2, "Extraordinary claims require extraordinary evidence: The case for postmaterial consciousness" by Dr. Gary E. Schwartz).

Toward the end of the 19th century, William James proposed the idea that the brain may play a permissive and transmissive role regarding mental functions and consciousness (James, 1898). James further hypothesized that the brain may act as a filter that normally limits/constrains/restricts the access to extended forms of consciousness. This hypothesis, which was also defended by philosophers Ferdinand Schiller and Henri Bergson, implies that during transcendent experiences (e.g., NDEs, mystical experiences), the filter function of the brain is deactivated to various extents. Phenomenologically, such a deactivation can lead to an expansion of consciousness and the perception/experience of other domains of reality (Beauregard, 2012).

It is of paramount importance to realize that while the production hypothesis (i.e. that mind is produced by brain) cannot explain most of the empirical phenomena examined here, the transmission hypothesis provides a useful theoretical framework for understanding these phenomena, which appear anomalous only when seen through the lens of materialism.

Given that materialist theories of the mind cannot explain these phenomena, and have failed to elucidate how the brain could produce mental functions and consciousness, I posit that it is now time to free ourselves from the shackles and blinders of the old materialist paradigm, and enlarge our conception of the natural world.

Even though we do not have all the answers yet, it is nonetheless already possible to sketch out an outline of a postmaterialist paradigm (PMP), based on the various lines of empirical evidence presented in this chapter. From my perspective, here are some key elements of this new paradigm (the reader may also look at my Theory of Psychelementarity, Beauregard, 2014):

1. Mind is irreducible, and its ontological status is as primordial as that of matter, energy, and space-time. In addition, mind cannot be derived from matter and reduced to anything more basic. In regard to this question, philosopher David Chalmers (1996) and cosmologist Andrei Linde (1990) have both argued that consciousness is a fundamental constituent of the universe.

It seems plausible that mental processes/events, including subjective interiority, exist to different extents at every level of organization in the universe, and are not restricted to functioning brains or nervous systems (in line with this, see Chapter 7, "Setting Science Free from Materialism" by Dr. Rupert Sheldrake, and Chapter 13 by Dr. Dean Radin). With respect to this issue, physicist Freeman Dyson has proposed that, since atoms in the laboratory behave like active agents rather than inanimate matter, they must possess the reflective capacity to make choices (Dyson, 1988). Of course, this does not entail that, experientially, an atom has the same consciousness as a human being.

At the molecular level, there is evidence that molecules composed of only a few simple proteins have the capacity for complex interaction, as if they have a mind of their own (Cohen, 1997). Awareness and intentionality also appear to be present in primitive unicellular and multicellular species (Baluška & Mancuso, 2009). For instance, slime mold exists as a single-cell amoeba for most of its life. When it needs food, however, it transmits signals to others nearby until thousands of individual amoebas transform themselves into a much larger entity with new capacities, such as the ability to move across the forest floor. The members of the larger entity release spores from which new amoebas are formed when they reach a better feeding area (Cohen, 1997).

In this view, every level of organization comprises a physical aspect (an exterior) and a mental/experiential aspect (an interior).

2. As psi phenomena reveal, there is a deep interconnectedness between the mental world (psyche) and the physical world (physis), which are not really separated—they only appear to be separated. Actually, psyche and physis are deeply interconnected, since they are complementary aspects (or manifestations) arising out of a common ground. It is conceivable that this common ground is a transcendent level of mind/consciousness that constitutes the most fundamental principle underlying the whole of reality. I posit that the basic elements of physis—such as space-time, energy and matter—as well as singular expressions of the psyche (i.e. individual minds) emerge from this elemental level.

The deep interconnectedness between psyche and physis (the Greek word for nature) does not seem to rest on quantum entanglement. In fact, non-local connections between entangled particles do not implicate the transfer of information (Kafatos & Nadeau, 1999), whereas interaction at a distance between humans and physical/biological systems appears to involve a mental information transfer. Additionally, this type of interaction implicates different types of mental phenomena that are not accounted for by QM. In any case, physical/biological processes and mental events appear to be interconnected, probably through a non-local manner (i.e. beyond space and time). This suggests that we live in a participatory universe, and that nothing in the world is really separate. Stated otherwise, the universe is a colossal web of connections between all the various levels of organization.

3. The mind (will/intention) acts as a force, i.e. it can affect the state of the physical world, and operate in a nonlocal fashion. This implies that mind is not confined to specific points in space, such as brains and bodies, nor to specific points in time, such as the present.

The evidence succinctly reviewed in this chapter also indicates that mental phenomena do exert a causal influence on the functioning of the brain and body, as well as on behavior. In regard to this issue, I have proposed earlier (Beauregard, 2007) that conscious and unconscious mental events are specifically encoded by the brain—i.e. they are translated through a psychoneural transduction mechanism into different forms of information; that is, neural events at the various levels of brain organization (biophysical, molecular, chemical, neural circuits). In turn, the resulting neural events are translated into other forms of information, i.e. events in other physiological systems that are part of the psychosomatic network.

4. The brain acts as a transceiver of mental activity, i.e. the mind works through the brain, but is not produced by it. The fact that mental functions are disturbed when the brain is damaged does not prove that the brain generates mind and consciousness. Moreover, being non-physical, mental phenomena are not localized to the brain and the body, and cannot be reduced to physicochemical phenomena, since the mind can exert effects at a distance. Enhanced mental experiences and accurate OBE perception occurring at a time when cerebral activity is seemingly absent (e.g. during cardiac arrest) also accord with the view that mind and consciousness are not generated by the brain.

In line with the idea that the brain may be an interface for the mind, this organ may be compared to a television set. This device receives broadcast signals (electromagnetic waves) and converts them into image and sound. If we damage the electronic components within the TV, we may induce a distortion of the image on the screen and the sound, because the capacity of the TV to receive and decode the broadcast signals is impaired. But this does not mean that the broadcast signals (and the program) are actually produced by the TV. Likewise, damage to a specific region of the brain may disrupt the mental processes mediated by this cerebral structure, but such disruption does not entail that these mental processes are reducible to neural activity in this area of the brain.

Individually and collectively, the PMP has far-reaching implications. This paradigm re-enchants the world and profoundly alters the vision we have of ourselves, giving us back our dignity and power as human beings. The PMP also fosters positive values such as compassion, respect, care, love, and peace, because it makes us realize that the boundaries between self and others are permeable. In doing so, this paradigm promotes an awareness of the deep interconnection between ourselves and nature at large, including all levels of organization in the universe. These levels may encompass non-physical, spiritual realms. Concerning this topic, it should be noted here that the PMP acknowledges spiritual experiences, which relate to a fundamental dimension of human existence and are frequently reported across all cultures (Hardy, 1975): within the postmaterialist framework, these experiences are not considered a priori as fantasies or the symptoms of pathological processes. Finally, by emphasizing a deep connection between ourselves and nature, the PMP also promotes environmental awareness and the preservation of our biosphere. In that sense, the model of reality associated with the PMP may help humanity to create a sustainable civilization and to blossom.

Conclusion

The materialist worldview, which has dominated science and academia over the last few centuries, has run its course. At last the tired old materialist paradigm has started to crumble, and a new paradigm has begun to emerge.

As Thomas Kuhn insightfully noted, the history of science has been marked by a few special moments that were characterized by major conceptual breakthroughs. As previously mentioned, Kuhn called these breakthroughs paradigm shifts or changes (Kuhn, 1970). Pivotal paradigm changes include the shift in thinking that (a) the Earth was flat, to the Earth being spherical, that (b) the Sun revolved around the Earth, to the Earth revolving around the Sun, that (c) matter was solid and fixed (how we conventionally experience it), to matter being mostly "empty space" and dynamically probabilistic (as per QM) (see Schwartz, 2012).

It appears that we are now closing in on another crucial paradigm shift, namely the transition from materialist science to postmaterialist science. Holding great promise for science, this transition—which will lead us to the next great scientific revolution—will be of vital importance to the evolution of human civilization. I am convinced that this transition will be even more pivotal than that from geocentrism to heliocentrism.

References

Aminoff, M. J., Scheinman, M. M., Griffin, J. C., & Herre, J. M. (1988). Electrocerebral accompaniments of syncope associated with malignant ventricular arrhythmias. *Annals of Internal Medicine*, 108, 791–796.

Baluška, F., & Mancuso, S. (2009). Deep evolutionary origins of neurobiology. *Commun. Integrat. Biol*, 2:1-6.

Bandura, A. (2001). Social cognitive theory: An agentic perspective, *Annual Review of Psychology*, 52, 1–26.

Baumeister, R. F., Masicampo, E. J. & Vohs, K. D. (2011). Do conscious thoughts cause behavior?, *Annual Review of Psychology*, 62, 331–361.

Beauregard, M. (2007). Mind does really matter: Evidence from neuroimaging studies of emotional self-regulation, psychotherapy, and placebo effect, *Progress in Neurobiology*, 81(4), 218-236.

Beauregard, M. (2012). *Brain Wars*. New York: Harper Collins.

Beauregard, M. (2014). The primordial psyche. *Journal of Consciousness Studies*, 21, 132-157.

Beauregard, M. & O'Leary, D. (2007). *The Spiritual Brain*. New York: Harper Collins.

Beischel, J., & Schwartz, G. E. (2007). Anomalous information reception by research mediums demonstrated using a novel triple-blind protocol. *EXPLORE: The Journal of Science & Healing*, 3, 23–27.

Blackmore, S.J. (1993). *Dying to Live: Science and the Near- Death Experience*. London: Grafton.

Braud, W. G. & Schlitz, M. J. (1991). Consciousness interactions with remote biological systems: Anomalous intentionality effects. *Subtle Energies*, 2 (1), 1-46.

Burtt, E. A. (1949). *The Metaphysical Foundations of Modern Science*. London: Routledge.

Cohen, P. (1997, April 26). Can Protein Spring into Life? *New Scientist*.

Chalmers, D. J. (1995). Facing up to the problem of consciousness. *Journal of consciousness studies*, 2(3), 200-219.

Chalmers, D. J. (1996). *The conscious mind: In search of a fundamental theory*. New York: Oxford University Press.

Clute, H. L. & Levy, W. J. (1990). Electroencephalographic changes during brief cardiac arrest in humans. *Anesthesiology*, 73 (5), 821–825.

Dossey, L. (2015). http://opensciences.org/blogs/open-sciences-blog/232-consciousness-why-materialism-fails.

Dyson, F. (1988). *Infinite in All Directions*. New York: Harper & Row.

Fenwick, P., Lovelace, H., Brayne, S. (2010). Comfort for the dying: five year retrospective and one year prospective studies of end of life experiences. *Arch Gerontol Geriatr*, 51(2), 173-179.

Gauld, A. (1983). *Mediumship and Survival: A Century of Investigations*. Chicago: Academy Chicago Publishers.

Greyson, B. (2003). Incidence and correlates of near-death experiences in a cardiac care unit. *General Hospital Psychiatry*, 25 (4), 269-276.

Greyson, B. (2010a). Implications of near-death experiences for a post-materialist psychology. *Psychology of Religion and Spirituality*, 2 (1), 37-45.

Greyson, B. (2010b). Seeing Dead People Not Known to Have Died: "Peak in Darien" Experiences. *Anthropology and Humanism*, 35(2), 159-171.

Gross, J. J. (1999). Emotion regulation: past, present, future. *Cognition and Emotion*, 13 (5), 551-573.

Haraldsson, E. (2003). Children who speak of past-life experiences: Is there a psychological explanation? *Psychology and Psychotherapy: Theory, Research and Practice*, 76(1), 55-67.

Haraldsson, E. (2012). Cases of the reincarnation type and the mind–brain relationship. In *Exploring Frontiers of the Mind-Brain Relationship*. New York: Springer, pp. 215-231.

Hardy, A. (1975). *The Biology of God*. New York: Taplinger.

Heisenberg, W. (1976). *Physics and Philosophy: The Revolution in Modern Science*. New York: Harper and Row, p. 186.

Kuhn, T. S. (1970). *The structure of scientific revolutions*. Chicago: University of Chicago Press.

James, W. (1898). Human immortality: Two supposed objections to the doctrine. In: Murphy, G., Ballou, R.O. (Eds.), *William James on psychical research*. New York: Viking, pp. 279-308.

James, W. (1904). A world of pure experience. *The Journal of Philosophy, Psychology and Scientific Methods*, 1(20), 533-543.

Kafatos, M. & Nadeau, R. (1999). *The Conscious Universe: Parts and Wholes in Physical Reality*. New York: Springer.

Kugel, W. (2011). A faulty PK meta-analysis. *Journal of Scientific Exploration*, 25 (1), 47–62.

Lallier, F., Velly, G., & Leon, A. (2015). Near-death experiences in survivors of cardiac arrest: a study about demographic, medical, pharmacological and psychological context. *Critical Care*, 19 (Suppl 1), P421.

Lawrence, M. & Repede, E. (2012). The incidence of deathbed communications and their impact on the dying process. *American Journal of Hospice & Palliative Care*, 30 (7), 632-639.

Linde, A. (1990). *Particle Physics and Inflationary Cosmology*. Chur, Switzerland: Harwood Academic Publishers.

Mills, A., & Lynn, S. J. (2000). Past-life experiences. Cardeña, E., Lynn, S. J., Krippner, S. (Eds.), *Varieties of anomalous experience: Examining the scientific evidence.*, (pp. 283-313). Washington, DC, US: American Psychological Association, xi, 476 pp.

Nagel, T. (2012). *Mind and Cosmos: Why the Materialist Neo-Darwinian Conception of Nature Is Almost Certainly False*. New York: Oxford University Press.

Parnia, S., Waller, D. G., Yeates, R. & Fenwick, P. (2001) A qualitative and quantitative study of the incidence, features, and aetiology of near death experiences in cardiac arrest survivors. *Resuscitation*, 48 (2), 149–156.

Parnia, S., & Fenwick, P. (2002). Near death experiences in cardiac arrest. *Resuscitation*, 52, 5–11.

Radin, D., & Nelson, R. (2003). Research on mind–matter interactions (MMI): Individual intention. In: Jonas, W.B. & Crawford, C.C. (Eds.), *Healing, Intention and Energy Medicine: Research and Clinical Implications*. Edinburgh: Churchill Living stone, pp. 39–48.

Ray, O. (2004). The revolutionary health science of psychoendoneuroimmunology. *Annals of the New York Academy of Sciences*, 1032, 35–51.

Saavedra-Aguilar, J. C. & Gómez-Jeria, J. S. (1989). A neurobiological model for near-death experiences. *Journal of Near-Death Studies*, 7 (4), 205-222.

Schwaninger, J., Eisenberg, P. R., Schechtman, K. B. & Weiss, A. N. (2002). A prospective analysis of near-death experiences in cardiac arrest patients. *Journal of Near-Death Studies*, 20 (4), 215–232.

Schwartz, G. E. R., & Russek, L. G. S. (2001). Evidence of anomalous information retrieval between two mediums: Telepathy, network memory resonance, and continuance of consciousness. *Journal of the Society for Psychical Research*, 65, 257–275.

Schwartz, G. E. R., Russek, L. G. S., Nelson, L. A., & Barentsen, C. (2001). Accuracy and replicability of anomalous after-death communication across highly skilled mediums. *Journal of the Society for Psychical Research*, 65, 1–25.

Schwartz, G. E. R., Russek, L. G. S., & Barentsen, C. (2002). Accuracy and replicability of anomalous information retrieval: Replication and extension. *Journal of the Society for Psychical Research*, 66, 144–156.

Shapiro, A. K. & Shapiro, E. (1997). *The Powerful Placebo: From Ancient Priest to Modern Physician*. Baltimore, MD: Johns Hopkins University Press.

Sheldrake, R. (2012). *Science Set Free: 10 Paths to New Discovery*. New York: Random House.

Stevenson, I. (1976). A preliminary report of a new case of responsive xenoglossy: the case of Gretchen. *Journal of the Society for Psychical Research*, 70, 65-77.

Stevenson, I. (2001). *Children Who Remember Previous Lives* (rev. ed.). Jefferson, NC: McFarland & Company.

Trakhtenberg, E. C. (2008). The effects of guided imagery on the immune system: A critical review. *International Journal of Neuroscience*, 118 (6), 839-855.

van Lommel, P., van Wees, R., Meyers, V. & Elfferich, I. (2001). Near-death experience in survivors of cardiac arrest: A prospective study in the Netherlands. *Lancet*, 358 (9298), 2039–2045.

Vitetta, L., Anton, B., Cortizo, F. & Sali, A. (2005). Mind–body medicine: Stress and its impact on overall health and longevity. *Annals of the New York Academy of Sciences*, 1057, 492–505.

Wallace, B. A. (2012). *Meditations of a Buddhist Skeptic*. New York: Columbia University Press.

Woerlee, G. M. (2004). Cardiac arrest and near-death experiences. *Journal of Near-Death Studies*, 22, 235-249.

Chapter Two

Extraordinary claims require extraordinary evidence: The case for postmaterial consciousness[4]

Gary E. Schwartz, PhD

It doesn't matter how beautiful your theory is,
it doesn't matter how smart you are.
If it doesn't agree with experiment, it's wrong.

Richard P. Feynman, PhD

Extraordinary claims require extraordinary evidence.

Carl Sagan, PhD

Introduction

Few premises are as fundamentally important to science and society as the controversial hypothesis of survival of consciousness after physical death. Obtaining a definitive answer, positive or negative, would have deep significance for humanity.

Converging evidence from multiple research areas, including evidence from (1) near death experiences (e.g. van Lommel et al., 2001), (2) reincarnation in adults and children (e.g. Tucker & Nidiffer, 2014), and (3) multi-blinded mediumship experiments (e.g. Sarraf, Woodley, & Tressoldi, in press), each independently point to the plausibility of the survival of

---

[4] *In Expanding Science: Volume II AAPS. Portions of this paper were adopted from Schwartz (in press).*

consciousness hypothesis. However, none of the contributions of scientific evidence from these three research areas, <u>by themselves,</u> are sufficient to draw a definitive conclusion. It is the combination / consilience of the evidence that greatly strengthens, but does not establish, the conclusion (Beauregard, Trent, & Schwartz, 2018).

An emerging (fourth) area of scientific research investigating hypothesized discarnate presence and communication using state-of-the-art technology in controlled laboratory experiments (Schwartz 2010; 2011; in press) provides additional, and potentially definitive evidence, <u>especially when it is integrated with the other three areas of survival of consciousness research</u>. Unlike earlier explorations termed instrumental transcommunication which relied on uncontrolled, anecdotal observations (e.g. Macy, 2001), it is now possible to conduct multi-centered, multi-blinded, randomized controlled trials (RCTs) testing the discarnate presence and communication technology hypothesis Such research has the potential to serve as a "tipping point" in reaching a conclusion about the validity of the survival of consciousness hypothesis.

There is clearly a need for science to address the survival of consciousness hypothesis. The global public's interest in life beyond the earth (e.g. spanning astrobiology and spiritual psychology (Miller, 2013) may be more salient than at any time in human history.

Emphasis on evidence-based science

The emphasis in this paper is on experimental design and objective evidence, not underlying theoretical explanations per se. Some of the conceptual premises (as well as empirical observations) in survival of consciousness research "boggle the mind" (see King's comments at the end of this chapter). Theories and hypotheses that boggle the mind are unavoidably inherent in certain areas of contemporary science and technology. For example, although quantum mechanics provides precise mathematical formulas and explicit predictions that are consistently validated with objective evidence from laboratory experiments, conceptual understanding of the underlying phenomena is lacking. For example, despite the mathematics of particle and wave dynamics, physics currently lacks a deep conceptual understanding of how an invisible photon sometimes appears to be a "massless, miniscule point source / particle localized in space" and other times seems to be "a probabilistic, fluctuating wave function distributed in space."

One of the founders of quantum mechanics, Nobel laureate Niels Bohr is quoted as saying, "If quantum mechanics hasn't profoundly shocked you, you haven't understood it yet." And Nobel laureate Richard Feynman is quoted as saying, "If you think you understand quantum mechanics, you don't understand quantum mechanics." The skeptical reader is encouraged to resist the temptation to dismiss the replicated evidence obtained in controlled laboratory postmaterialist consciousness research because of the inherent mind-boggling nature of the phenomena under investigation.

Phases in biomedical research

The gold standard in biomedical research is the multi-center, multi-blinded, randomized control trial (RCT). According to National Institutes of Health (NIH) guidelines (https://www.nih.gov/health-information/nih-clinical-research-trials-you/basics), a Phase I trial involves testing a new drug or treatment "in a small group of people (20 – 80) for the first time. The purpose is to study the drug or treatment to learn about safety and identify side effects." A Phase II trial is where the new drug or treatment is given "to a larger group of people (100 – 300) to determine its effectiveness and further study its safety." Only after Phase I and II studies have been completed successfully is the new drug or treatment given "to large groups of people (1,000 – 3,000) to confirm its effectiveness, monitor side effects, compare it with standard or similar treatments, and collect information that will allow the new drug or treatment to be used safely." Concerning more than a century of research addressing the survival of consciousness, virtually all the published literature comes primarily from Phase I investigations (plus a few Phase II investigations). However, the validated RCT protocol described herein makes it possible to meet Phase III standards.

Phase I computer automated proof-of-concept experiments documenting apparent detection of presence of hypothesized postmaterial persons (HPPs) in the absence of physical experimenters have been reported (Schwartz 2011). The term *postmaterial* is used here to refer to the hypothesized continued existence of the consciousness and information (and associated energy) of individuals after physical death[5]. The term *presence* is used to refer to the potential hypothesized localization of the consciousness, information, and energy of the deceased person / discarnate (see Schwartz 2010, 2011, in press).

In two Phase I computer automated experiments (exploratory and confirmatory), a skeptical research assistant read a standardized script inviting two HPPs to come to the laboratory at 11 pm and to follow auditory and visual instructions presented by PowerPoint on a computer monitor. The experimental design involved a pre-experimental data collection baseline period, an HPP presence (in a light tight chamber) period, and a post-experimental baseline period. Each of these data collection periods was 30 minutes in duration.

Patterns of low-level light were recorded using a Princeton Instruments CCD camera thermoelectrically cooled to − 77 degrees C. A computer program was written that automated the administration of the instructions and the collection of the long exposure images. In addition, to examine possible false positive effects, no-participant control (sham) night sessions (hereafter referred to simply as control sessions) were run using the identical automated procedures when the HPPs were not invited. Replicated findings consistent with apparent discarnate detection were obtained even though no one was physically present when the data were collected.

<u>Given the absence of physical experimenters during the data collection and the inclusion of matched no discarnate control (NDC) sessions, the experimental design ruled out (1) experimenter presence, (2)</u>

---

[5] *Pitstick and Schwartz (2019) use the terms postmaterial persons or beings to refer to human postmaterial consciousness that survives physical death.*

experimenter conscious awareness, and (3) systematic methodological errors as plausible causes of the replicated effects. However, unconscious experimenter intention or retro-causal paranormal effects could not be excluded as speculative, alternative super psi explanations of the findings (e.g. see Palmer, 2017; Carenda, 2018).

Unfortunately, highly controlled research of this type has been extremely difficult for other interested investigators to replicate due to practical considerations such as funding for expensive equipment and staff, plus the availability of appropriately skilled research assistants. Recognizing this critical constraint in advancing the research, the author has developed an (1) automated, (2) no-cost (to collaborating investigators), (3) practical hardware and software system. This integrated system can produce replicable findings under carefully controlled laboratory conditions that minimize both false positive and false negative effects.

To understand the complex design, it is helpful to compare drug RCT's and HPP RCT's (adopted from Schwartz, in press) before discussing the present validation methods and findings. In a conventional drug RCT study, one (or more) drugs are compared to placebo controls. This is the primary independent variable. Using hypertension as an example, one or more purported antihypertensive drugs are administered to patients under conditions where (1) the patients are not informed whether they are receiving the hypothesized active medication or placebo pills, and (2) the physicians or nurses who are administering the pills do not know which patients are receiving the medications and which are receiving the placebos. Hence, both the patients and providers are blinded (i.e. double-blinded).

The selection of which patients receive the medications or placebos is determined randomly by experimenters (the keepers of the secret codes) who (1) are not providers, and (2) do not interact with the patients. Also, specific criteria are determined for selecting patients appropriate for the trial as well as the persons who are administering the pills.

The primary dependent variable is typically the standardized measurement of blood pressure. Multiple measurements are taken before, during, and after the drug trial to adequately quantify the effectiveness of the medications in lowering blood pressure. The measurements may (or may not) be taken by the providers. If the measurements are made by research assistants, then the research assistants are also kept blind to whether a given patient has received a medication or placebo.

In drug RCTs, the identical criteria for selecting patients and providers are used across the centers, and the identical protocols are used for measuring and quantifying changes in blood pressure. However, by necessity, different patients, providers and research assistants are employed across the collaborating centers.

An HPP RCT shares certain similarities, as well as important differences, with a drug RCT.

There are six primary similarities between HPP and drug RCTs:

1. One (or more) HPPs serve as the hypothesized independent variable(s) in HPP RCTs.

2. Just as the individual centers in drug RCTs do not create the standardized pills (the standardized pills are provided by the principle investigator of the drug RCT), the individual centers in HPP RCTs do not create the HPPs (i.e. the specific HPPs are provided by the principle investigator of the HPP RCT). These HPPs have been documented to have successfully participated in previous unblinded experiments (Schwartz, in press) plus the exploratory (Experiments 1 and 2) and confirmatory (Experiments 3 and 4) experiments reported here, that justified the validation of the HPP RCT protocol (Experiments 5 and 6).

3. Key HPP RCT personnel are blind to whether the HPPs are present or not for a given protocol of measurements. The HPP absent sessions serve as matched controls (sham sessions).

4. The presence or absence of the HPPs is determined randomly by specific experimenters who are keepers of the secret codes.

5. The dependent measurement protocol must be sensitive and sufficiently reliable for quantifying the predicted effects.

6. Conventional power analyses and statistics are used.

However, there are at least six differences between drug RCTs and HPP RCTs that are unique to an HPP RCT, and especially a completely computer automated HPP RCT:

1. There are no patients receiving medications or placebos in HPP RCTs. There are only measurement protocols used to detect the purported presence of the HPP(s) compared to no-treatment, matched control sessions of measurements.

2. Since no patients are required in HPP RCTs, there are no complications concerning balancing patient recruitment within and across centers.

3. Since there are no patients, there is no need for "providers."

4. Using a completely computer automated measurement protocol, it becomes possible in HPP RCTs to keep everyone associated with a given center blind to the presence or absence of the HPPs. Moreover, by collecting the measurements at night, when no one is physically present in the laboratory room housing the equipment, this can insure complete blinding (at least in terms of consciousness awareness) of the researchers and staff in the independent centers.

5. In order for the purported HPP(s) to know whether to go to a given center on a given night, carefully selected and validated research mediums are employed as the "experimenters" who follow the secret randomized codes. Their task is to instruct the collaborating HPP(s), nightly, as to when and where to go. To maximize multiple blinding conditions, even the principle investigator is kept blind to the actual HPPs schedules by employing a separate person (e.g. a true skeptic experimenter) who creates the secret codes and then (1) distributes them to the various experimenter mediums, or (2) runs a remote computer program in a separate laboratory room that instructs the HPP where to go on a given night (this addresses the experimenter psi hypothesis, Palmer, 2017).

6. Because the core research question involves the hypothesized existence of HPPs who are conscious, intelligent, volunteer participants, the systematic measurement protocol involves the careful design of tasks that require conscious cognitive information processing in order to successfully perform the tasks. The precise nature of these tasks is critical in evaluating the survival of consciousness hypothesis.

Practical requirements for conducting HPP technology RCTs

Given the highly controversial nature of the survival of consciousness hypothesis, there are numerous factors which mitigate definitive, large scale, Phase III research being conducted. These include:

1. conceptual factors (e.g. assumptions of falsity or impossibility, feelings of incredulity or unbelievability, difficulty in imagining or understanding the predictions),

2. personal factors (e.g. fundamental beliefs challenged, need to reevaluate foundational premises, emotional conflicts with aspects of early upbringing as well as academic education), and

3. social factors (e.g. rejection by colleagues, dismissal by mainstream editors and reviewers, lack of professional and financial support).

When additional practical factors inherent in technology-focused research are included (e.g. the expense of equipment, the need for special purpose software, the requirement of specialized research skills), the obstacles to responsible independent replication seem insurmountable.

However, thanks to advances in hardware and software, plus the author's success in obtaining funding from select private foundations, trusts, and individuals, it has become possible to create a computer automated and portable laboratory system that can be used by collaborating independent laboratories to replicate the research (Schwartz, in press). Five core goals have been specified and satisfied:

1. to use currently available, reliable, sensitive, and affordable technology (total hardware cost per system less than $4,000; these systems are loaned to collaborating laboratories)

2. to automate data collection and real-time analyses employing specially designed software

3. to only require a quiet space (used at night) in collaborating laboratories

4. to _not_ necessitate human subjects committee approvals at collaborating institutions (because the participants are hypothesized postmaterial persons), and

5. to enable international collaboration regardless of the investigator's personal beliefs about the hypothesis.

These five goals have dictated the selection of the hardware and the creation of the software. For example, the previous Schwartz (2011) computer-automated research required the use of a $40,000 low light CCD camera system housed in a light tight room operated at relatively cool temperatures (e.g. 60 degrees F). This system was neither affordable nor portable, and it required specialized training to operate and maintain. By contrast, the present computer-automated system is affordable and portable, it requires minimal training to setup and maintain, and it collect data under normal laboratory conditions.

The HPP RCT hardware

A simple hardware system that meets the above five goals involves the use of a high definition (HD) quality webcam to record the dynamics of light produced in a plasma globe (described below), a computer to automate the collection and analysis of the resulting video images, a light-tight enclosure to house the webcam and globe, and a secondary monitor to present the instructions to the HPPs.

In our research we have used industrial quality video cameras (https://www.jai.com/) as well as relatively inexpensive Logitech webcams (e.g. HD Pro C920s). It turns out that the latter are sufficiently stable and accurate to obtain reliable results for quantifying plasma globe dynamics.

Contemporary plasma globes are based on technology originally developed and patented by Nicola Tesla in 1881 (U.S. Patent No. 454,622) and developed into an artistic novelty item in the 1970s by Bill Parker, a student at MIT. Plasma globes (also called plasma balls and lamps) are spheres filled with a mixture of noble gases. The gasses are excited by a relatively high-frequency alternating current (e.g. 35k Hz, compared to the 60 Hz line power supply) at 2-5k volts (i.e. compared to 110 volts). Placing a fingertip directly on the glass creates an attractive spot for free electrons to flow. This is because the conductive human body is more easily polarized than the dielectric material around the electrode (i.e. the gas within

Expanding Science

the globe), which in turn provides an alternative discharge path having less resistance. Comparable electron attractive effects can be replicated with a robotic arm and hand (described below).

If the fingertip (or robotic finger) is placed on the top of the globe, the plasma stream is attracted to the top; if the fingertip (or robotic finger) is placed on the side of the globe, the plasma stream is attracted to the side. This "specificity of position" effect proves to be critical in documenting the predicted HPP effects on the globe.

The direct contact effect can be easily seen by the naked eye (e.g. see https://www.youtube.com/watch?v=RCi5rOy0Xnc for video recordings of live demonstrations of the classic effects). The plasma globe used in the present research was an AC powered Lebbeen Glass 5-inch plasma globe available from Amazon.com.

If a conductive object does *not* make direct contact with the globe, the dynamics of the plasma streams (including the specificity of position) will still change, but these *subtle changes* will *not* typically be apparent to the naked eye. However, using image averaging techniques, it becomes possible to quantify these effects via the means of multiple camera shots as well as other statistical methods (Schwartz, 2020 in press)

We reasoned that if (1) HPPs interacted with a plasma globe under controlled and replicated conditions, and that (2) HPPs had some sort of physical or quasi-physical presence, that (3) it might be possible using image averaging techniques to detect their interaction with the plasma globe, and therefore potentially employ a single globe as a sort of binary switch.

A subset of evidential research mediums report that they experience *seeing* specific HPPs in three-dimensional space. Moreover, the HPPs they report seeing not only have a recognizable anatomical (human) form, but they appear to move their arms and legs volitionally. Hundreds of hours of pilot experimentation with the collaboration of a skilled evidential research medium (and independently verified by four evidential mediums) indicates that HPPs can purportedly follow instructions and interact with the plasma globe using their apparent energy hands. Moreover, close analysis reveals that their patterned effects on the plasma dynamics often match the patterned effects observed with people physically interacting with the globes, albeit at much smaller magnitudes of effect.

Our working hypothesis is that HPPs consist of dynamically organized, historical, quantum and electromagnetic systems / bodies, and that like physical persons, they attract electrons in a plasma globe, albeit at much smaller magnitudes (since their electrical resistance is predicted to be substantially higher than physical persons). The reason for employing multiple HPPs is to establish the replicability of this hypothesis across HPPs.

A Windows 10 PC laptop with an Intel i7 processor, 16 gigabytes of ram, and a 1 terabyte hard drive, is sufficiently powerful to run the automated experiment and perform the image analyses. The complete system includes a high-quality black interior storage container (Bigso Black Woodgrain Storage Box, 15" x 2" 11-3/8" h). This enclosure creates a stable light tight environment for a Logitech Pro C920s HD webcam mounted on a sturdy miniature tripod (UBeesize Desktop Tripod, Tabletop Mini), plus the Lebbeen brand plasma globe. It also includes a secondary HD monitor for displaying information to the participants. The computer is connected to high speed wi-fi and controlled remotely with TeamViewer and Splash software.

A second PC laptop computer is used to provide video surveillance as well as collect environmental sound level, room temperature and humidity data using a LabQuest Mini interface and Logger Pro 3 software (https://www.vernier.com/).

The HPP RCT Software

With the collaboration of an optical sciences computer programmer and an optical camera specialist, the author has developed a general-purpose software system that we have dubbed AQUA (Automated Query and Analysis). AQUA makes it possible to completely automate data collection and analysis, not only in terms of presenting experimental conditions, but in performing image processing and summary graphs as well. One version of the software runs high-end video cameras (AQUA G), the other runs selected webcams (AQUA W). Though the AQUA system is currently designed for binary tasks, it can be expanded to accommodate multiple-choice tests.

A partial list of AQUA's fully automated features include:

1. Turn the globe on at the start of a session and off at the end of a session using a USB controlled power strip (http://www.pwrusb.com/)

2. Collect baseline (pre) and response (yes or no) periods per trial (e.g. "Is this a vehicle?").

3. Present prerecorded audio instructions using Verbose Text to Speech software for the baseline and response periods per trial

a. At the start of a baseline period, a standard aural instruction is: "This is a baseline. Please sit still with your hands in your lap."

b. At the start of a response period, depending upon the type of task, the instruction might be, "Are you ready? Here is the question. Is this a vehicle? Please answer yes or no."

4. Display visual slides for the baseline and response periods.

5. Vary the number, duration, and order of the baseline and response periods.

6. Vary the number of video frames collected per baseline and response period.

7. Calculate averaged (mean) images and standard deviation images per period per trial.

8. Calculate response minus baseline "delta" images, separately for yes and no response trials, and then display incremental averaged images for [(delta Yes) minus (delta No)] – i.e. "delta-delta" images (see column E in Figure 1).

9. At the end of the experiment, display multiple summary averaged means and standard deviations images for both deltas and delta-deltas.

10. Calculate values for specific "regions of interest" (ROIs) within the images, for subsequent statistical analyses across sessions and display them as bar or line graphs.

11. Enable remote running of multiple sessions in a batch mode (e.g. 16 different specified sessions, each session consisting of 24 trials, initiated every half hour).

The entire sequence is established through an extensive configuration file, and the sequence per session can be initiated remotely. The summary averaged delta and delta-delta images, as well as the ROI Excel files, are uploaded automatically via wi-fi to the cloud for storage and subsequent within and between center statistical analyses.

In our experiments, we have determined empirically that 10 second duration trial lengths for baseline and response periods, each period containing 280 to 300 images (at 30 images per second), and repeated for 20 to 24 trials, are enough to produce replicable averaged findings across sessions for physical person experiments. To control for unwanted sequential / order effects, we use a fixed ABBABAAB counterbalanced order design. Moreover, to test for possible systematic methodological error and false positive effects, we include matched no discarnate control (NDC) (sham / placebo) sessions employing the exact stimuli, counterbalanced order, etc.

Four Categories of Proof-of-Concept HPP Tests

To justify conducting a Phase III (NIH) HPP RCT, it is essential to employ carefully designed psychological tasks / tests that explicitly address the survival of consciousness hypothesis. The author has proposed that a <u>combination of four categories of tests can together provide an arguably definitive suite of tests for inferring HPP presence and communication</u>. The four types of tests are organized in a logical sequence:

Type I: Response Skills Tests: e.g. to determine if a given HPP can reliably make a specified yes or no response when requested (e.g. place their energy hands on the top versus sides of the globe). If positive findings are obtained, then

Type II: Cognitive Understanding Tests: e.g. to determine if a given HPP can recognize and discriminate between different classes of things such as vehicles versus animals, babies versus adults, red versus green colors, even versus odd numbers, etc. If positive findings are obtained, then

Type III: Personal Identification Tests: e.g. to determine if a given HPP can reliably identify himself or herself when presented with specific information such as names of parents and siblings, birth dates and birth places, occupations (e.g. physicist), dates and causes of death that fit or do not fit a given HPP. If positive findings are obtained, then

Type IV: Advanced Knowledge Tests: e.g. to determine if a given HPP is an expert physicist by providing specific formulas which are correct versus incorrect.

<u>If a program of research employs all four kinds of tests, and if the evidence from all four tests is positive, the consilience of the evidence rationally points to the probable, and arguably definitive, voluntary participation / presence of specific HPPs engaged in complex cognitive and communication tasks.</u> Moreover, <u>successfully performance in Type III (personal identification) and Type IV (advanced knowledge) tasks together minimize the possibility that the results could be achieved by potential hypothesized discarnate "imposters."</u>

Evidence Validating the HPP RCT Protocol

Schwartz (in press) has reviewed the findings from six small scale experiments demonstrating the HPP RCT protocol, and he has completed six large scale experiments validating the HPP RCT protocol (Schwartz, submitted for publication). The interested reader is encouraged to read the Schwartz (in press) paper. Though the large sample findings can not be presented here, a version of the abstract is included to summarize the research:

Abstract. The gold standard in biomedical research is the multi-center, multi-blinded, randomized control trial (RCT). An experimental randomized control method was devised to test for presence and communication with hypothesized discarnate intelligences. The method uses readily available laboratory equipment, automated data collection, and real-time analyses. A total of 1504 experimental sessions and 864 matched control sessions were run at two separate laboratories in the United States. Using a controlled binary personal identification test, replicated findings were obtained independent of investigators' beliefs about the presence of the discarnates, with experimental conditions associated with $p < .0001$, and control conditions associated with $p < .533$. The protocol involves an automated means of inviting discarnates to interact with high voltage electrical plasma contained within a sphere. The methodology minimizes false positive and false negative outcomes. Independent RCT replications are underway employing skeptical experimenters. If the current findings are replicated, the evidence for survival of human consciousness after death can be arguably interpreted as being definitive.

Evaluating extraordinary claims and evidence by true versus pseudo skeptical scientists

How do we discern when scientists engage in a disagreement about extraordinary claims and evidence whether they are engaging in what Dr. Marcello Truzzi (1987) calls "true skepticism" – an accurate, fair, and just form of unbiased questioning, versus "pseudo skepticism" – often an inaccurate, unfair, and unjust strategy of biased debunking?

To address this universal question in the context of survival of consciousness research, we will consider a real-life disagreement between two senior scientists that occurred in the summer of 2020 and use it as a teaching tool. We will then return to Truzzi's analysis and show how it helps us discern the difference between true-scientific thinking and pseudo-scientific thinking[6]. As you will see, I try to approach questions from the perspective of true skepticism, a philosophy that is a prerequisite for being a true scientist.

Below is an email written by a retired university professor and scientist in response to an invited virtual presentation I gave about survival of

---

[6] *It can be argued that some scientists are more accurately described as being "mixed" skeptics who (1) function as true skeptics when addressing certain topics, and (2) behave like pseudo-skeptics when addressing other topics (especially strongly emotionally charged topics). Interviews with notable skeptics like Carl Sagan, PhD and Neal deGrasse Tyson, PhD illustrate such mixed (and hypocritical) skeptical tendencies. This may also be the case for Dr. X.*

consciousness and HPP RCT research during the 2020 COVID-19 pandemic. To protect this distinguished professor's anonymity, I have blocked out virtually all his personal and professional identifying information. Save for these modifications in the first paragraph, the email is word-for-word what "Dr. X" shared with the residents in his exclusive retirement community.

As you read Dr. X's email, I encourage you to think about the judged credibility, accuracy, and honesty of Dr. Schwartz as perceived by Dr. X. Also note that there are many typographical errors and words left out in the email, which I have **not** corrected.

I would like to comment on Dr. Gary Schwartz' presentation yesterday, but first, what qualifies me to judge Dr. Schwartz? I have ScD in ... and a PhD in .... After eight years in industry and a postdoc at Oxford University, I took a job as Professor of ... at the University of Washington where I taught for ... years and was department chair for .... I received many research grants from industry and the National Science Foundation. My largest single grant was for ... M dollars. I have published dozens of papers on ..., science, and mathematics in internationally recognized, peer-reviewed journals, including Science. I am a Fellow of the American Academy for the Advancement of Science (AAAS). In short, by commonly accepted definitions, I am a scientist.

I would like to start by noting that Dr. Schwartz is a disarmingly engaging person, the sort of person you enjoy being with, for example at dinner. In short, a nice guy. That gives you confidence in what he has to say.

During the question period Dr. Schwartz gave an ad hominem attack on Michael Shermer for criticizing him. That was unfortunate. Michael Shermer is an American science writer, historian of science, founder of The Skeptics Society, and editor-in-chief of its magazine Skeptic, which is largely devoted to investigating pseudoscientific and supernatural claims. He is the author of several books. See https://en.wikipedia.org/wiki/Michael_Shermer#Published_works.

Dr. Schwartz has a PhD degree from Harvard, but I cannot find a publication based on his PhD, which is highly unusual. That maybe because shortly after, or perhaps earlier, he became interested in the paranormal, especially in mediums and life-after-death experiences. In the 1920s there was a famous woman medium in Boston, where she developed a reputation for her seances in the dark in which she was able to have long-dead relatives talk to one or more of the attendees. She was investigated by a team of scientist, including professors from MIT and found to be authentic. Then the famous magician Harry Houdini attended one of her seances and exposed her as a fake. He said that scientists were easily taken in by mediums and that only magicians had the knowledge and experience to be able to expose mediums. All of this was discussed in one of the Boston newspapers at the time. (Dr. Schwartz' wife is a medium.)

Dr. Schwartz' talk was entitled a "Scientific look Spirit Communication Technology." In it he described experiments that he designed and performed. Notably, these experiments were not vetted by other scientists, skeptical scientists in particular, nor have the reputed results been reproduced and published by any other scientist. (Maybe he could get them published in the annual Journal of Irreproducible Results.)

Dr. Schwartz claims to have heard the spirits of departed friends talk to him. I believe he thinks that actually happened, but I have never experienced that nor have I ever met anyone who has. Have you? How is that possible? Do spirits have vocal cords? How do they make sound?

I characterize Dr. Schwartz is a "tree believer" - the irrational persistence of an untenable belief. People who believe that we can establish regular communication with the dead use a variety of interesting phrases: "parallel dimensions," "voices from beyond," "out-of-body journey," "post materialist," "non-earthly being," "those who have crossed over," and "channeling. They talk about "Post-Materialist Science" and the "Ascended Masters."

Finally, Dr. Schwartz says he is working on a "soul phone," a piece of hardware that will enable anyone to talk to a deceased person. He says it will take about four years to design and build. Obviously, this is ripe for fraud. Do you believe that such a phone can be designed and built?

What do you is the likelihood that after you have as "chimney sweepers come to dust," that you will be able to talk to your living friends?

It has been said that "the devil in the details." Another way of saying this is that "discernment is in the details." To understand how pseudo-skeptics think, it is essential that we examine the details closely, making astute and wise discernments, and ideally learning lessons in the process. Honoring the writer's details, I will now requote each of Dr. X's statements and provide additional information. The purpose of sharing this example is not to defend the author but to better understand a compelling example of pseudo skeptical analysis of survival of consciousness research.

Twenty-one discernments

Dr. X: *I would like to comment on Dr. Gary Schwartz' presentation yesterday, but first, what qualifies me to judge Dr. Schwartz?*

Discernment: This is an interesting and meaningful first sentence. A true skeptic would focus on evaluating Dr. Schwartz's theory and evidence, not judging Dr. Schwartz per se. Since Dr. X's discipline (blocked out) is not these fields, common sense tells us that he would not have the detailed knowledge and expertise to judge theories and research in astronomy or psychology, for example, just as an astronomer or psychologist would not have the detailed knowledge and expertise to evaluate theories and research in his discipline. Psychologists are not invited to peer review Dr. X's articles just as scientists in his field are not invited to peer review astronomy or psychology articles. This fact will become important later.

Dr. X: *I have ScD in ... and a PhD in .... After ... years in industry and a postdoc at Oxford University, I took a job as Professor of ... at the University of Washington, where I taught for ... years and was department chair for .... I received many research grants from industry and the National Science Foundation. My largest single grant was for .. M dollars. I have published dozens of papers on ..., science, and mathematics in internationally recognized, peer-reviewed journals, including Science. I am a Fellow of the American Academy for the Advancement of Science (AAAS). In short, by commonly accepted definitions, I am a scientist.*

Discernment: Dr. X clearly has excellent credentials. His credentials are at least as excellent as Dr. Schwartz's (PhD from Harvard University, tenured professor at Yale University, many grants from the National Institutes of Health, the National Science Foundation, etc. published over 450 peer reviewed scientific papers, including six papers in the journal *Science*, director of multiple laboratories, etc.). Like Dr. Schwartz, Dr. X is a professional scientist respected in his field. However, does his stellar background justify his criticisms below?

Dr. X: *I would like to start by noting that Dr. Schwartz is a disarmingly engaging person, the sort of person you enjoy being with, for example at dinner. In short, a nice guy. That gives you confidence in what he has to say.*

Discernment: It is one thing to note that a speaker is engaging, it's another to claim that the person is "disarmingly" engaging. A common definition of disarming is "removing or capable of removing hostility, suspicion, etc., as by being charming: a disarming smile." (www.dictionary.com). Depending on its usage and intention, disarming can be a compliment or a criticism. Given the nature of the criticism below, Dr. X's starting with this comment implies that the listener might be disarmed by the speaker's charm, and therefore should be cautious of what the speaker is presenting.

Dr. X: *During the question period Dr. Schwartz gave an ad hominem attack on Michael Shermer for criticizing him. That was unfortunate.*

Discernment: Here Dr. X accuses Dr. Schwartz of an "ad hominem" attack on Michael Shermer. However, Dr. X. offers no evidence that Dr. Schwartz's criticism of Shermer's rejection of afterlife science was ad hominem. Ad hominem means "an argument or reaction directed against a person rather than the position they are maintaining." (from Oxford Languages). However, Dr. Schwartz's critique was of Shermer's techniques, not of Shermer as a person. Dr. X failed to mention that Dr. Schwartz's criticism addressed a question raised by an interested participant.

Dr. Schwartz illustrated some of the tactics Shermer uses to debunk afterlife science and explained why they were fallacious. For example, Dr. Schwartz explained that for over twenty years Shermer has claimed that all the evidence for laboratory mediumship research can be explained as sophisticated cheating techniques used by mediums, and that scientists like Dr. Schwartz are gullible. However, Dr. X failed to mention that Dr. Schwartz was aware of the existence of fraudulent mediums, and that to ensure that he and his colleagues would not be duped, that Dr. Schwartz learned how to become a fake medium himself. Moreover, Dr. X failed to mention that Dr. Schwartz and his colleagues, as well as scientists at other universities, designed controlled laboratory experiments that ruled out such fraudulent techniques as plausible explanations of the findings. Dr. X was not being a true scientist when he accused Dr. Schwartz, without any evidence, of making ad hominem arguments about Shermer the person.

Dr. X: *Michael Shermer is an American science writer, historian of science, founder of The Skeptics Society, and editor-in-chief of its magazine Skeptic, which is largely devoted to investigating pseudoscientific and supernatural claims. He is the author of several books. See https://en.wikipedia.org/wiki/Michael_Shermer#Published_works.*

Discernment: All of this is true. Dr. Schwartz regularly follows Shermer's and other skeptics' writings, including receiving a weekly newsletter from www.skeptic.com

Dr. X: *Dr. Schwartz has a PhD degree from Harvard, but I cannot find a publication based on his PhD, which is highly unusual.*

Discernment: Dr. X did not find Dr. Schwartz's published dissertation, and commented it is highly unusual (in certain disciplines more than others). The question is, how did he conduct his search? As it so happens, Dr. Schwartz's dissertation was published in the distinguished journal *Science*. The citation is Schwartz, G.E. (1972). Voluntary control of human cardiovascular integration and differentiation through feedback and reward. *Science, 174*, 90-93.

Dr. X: *That maybe because shortly after, or perhaps earlier, he became interested in the paranormal, especially in mediums and life-after-death experiences.*

Discernment: Because Dr. X is not an expert in this discipline (psychology) or the specific research area (afterlife science), he does not have the educational background to know the published literature. Hence, Dr. X made erroneous inferences based on a lack of knowledge. Dr. Schwartz has explained how he became interested in the possibility of mediumship and life-after-death experiences while he was a tenured professor of psychology and psychiatry at Yale University in the mid 1980's for professional reasons (based on an integration of electromagnetic theory, quantum physics theory, and general systems theory). And then he began formal research at the University of Arizona in the mid 1990s for personal reasons (e.g., it was begun at the request of a mature clinical psychologist who was grieving the death of her beloved father, Dr. Henry Russek, a distinguished cardiologist scientist, clinician, and teacher; this is discussed in Schwartz's book *The AfterLife Experiments,* 2002)[7].

Dr. X: *In the 1920s there was a famous woman medium in Boston, where she developed a reputation for her seances in the dark in which she was able to have long-dead relatives talk to one or more of the attendees. She was investigated by a team of scientist, including professors from MIT and found to be authentic. Then the famous magician Harry Houdini attended one of her seances and exposed her as a fake. He said that scientists were easily taken in by mediums and that only magicians had the knowledge and experience to be able to expose mediums. All of this was discussed in one of the Boston newspapers at the time.*

Discernment: The Boston account regarding the purported medium Mrs. Piper is mostly accurate. However, an implicit implication in Dr. X's comments is that Dr. Schwartz was either unaware of this history or chose to ignore it, and both would be incorrect. As explained above, Dr. Schwartz not only knew the early tainted history of mediumship, but he obtained the necessary expertise in fake mediumship to honor Houdini's efforts and develop the ability to discern the difference between fake and genuine mediums himself.

Dr. X: *(Dr. Schwartz' wife is a medium.)*

Discernment: Dr. Schwartz's wife, Rhonda Eklund Schwartz, is a skilled professional artist with a BFA and MA from Northern Illinois University. She retired from Federal Express where her last positions were (1) in quality assurance, and (2) as an international specialist. She then spontaneously developed mediumship skills after the death of her mother in 2001. However, she is not a professional medium; she is a selective evidential research medium who focuses on science and the afterlife. This

---

[7]*It is possible that Dr. X suggested that Dr. Schwartz's interest in the paranormal began "perhaps earlier" than his PhD training at Harvard University because Dr. X looked Dr. Schwartz up in Wikipedia. Dr. X would have read an erroneous claim that "having his [Dr. Schwartz's] life saved by a mysterious voice" when Dr. Schwartz was an undergraduate at Cornell University "prompted him to begin his research where that voice might have come from." The journal article cited in Wikipedia had nothing to do with that incident.*

information is discussed in detail in her book *Love Eternal: Breakthrough Personal and Scientific Evidence for Life After Death*, 2nd Edition (2017).

Dr. X: *Dr. Schwartz' talk was entitled a "Scientific look Spirit Communication Technology." In it he described experiments that he designed and performed. Notably, these experiments were not vetted by other scientists, skeptical scientists in particular:*

Discernment: The complete title was "A Scientific Look at Spirit Communication Technology." However, Dr. X's last sentence is another false claim made in the absence of expert knowledge. Dr. Schwartz's presentation clearly stated that three sets of experiments (Schwartz 2010; 2011; 2020) were published in the peer-reviewed biomedical journal *EXPLORE: The Journal of Science and Healing.* This journal prides itself on its commitment to honest, fair, and responsible peer-review by appropriate experts who can make knowledge-based evaluations. Moreover, Dr. Schwartz regularly invites (and acknowledges) true skeptics who critique his research studies prior to publication with the goal of improving their design, analysis, and interpretation.

Dr. X: *nor have the reputed results been reproduced and published by any other scientist.*

Discernment: This is true for the spirit communication technology research, not for the mediumship research. However, what Dr. X fails to mention is that the ongoing computer automated, multi-center, multi-blinded randomized control trials research was expressly designed to make it possible for independent investigators who lack the expert knowledge and funds to conduct such research to do so as part of a large scale collaborative research program. This is what true scientists do.

Dr. X: *(Maybe he could get them published in the annual Journal of Irreproducible Results.)*

Discernment: This remark is also sadly inaccurate. One would only submit an article to a journal like *Journal of Irreproducible Results* if the results are irreproducible. However, Dr. Schwartz's results <u>are</u> reproducible. That is why he gave the presentation in the first place.

Dr. X: *Dr. Schwartz claims to have heard the spirits of departed friends talk to him.*

Discernment: Again, this is a statement made by someone unknowledgeable in the field. Dr. Schwartz has indicated for more than twenty years that he is not a medium, and that he does not see nor hear purported spirits. In fact, one of his colleagues, Dr. Robert Stek, has called him "the Helen Keller of afterlife research." However, Dr. Schwartz has had numerous readings with more than a dozen evidential mediums in his laboratory. Dr. Schwartz has witnessed them report experiencing communication with members of his family and friends, providing details they could not have obtained by fraudulent means.

Dr. X: *I believe he thinks that actually happened,*

Discernment: Dr. Schwartz has video recorded many of these sessions as well as countless research sessions with such mediums. He does not "think" that this "actually happened," he knows that this has happened and has documented it. Any scientist who is knowledgeable about Dr. Schwartz's extensive research in this area knows this to be factually true.

Dr. X: *but I have never experienced that nor have I ever met anyone who has. Have you?*

Discernment: Is it logical and / or scientifically valid to claim that if (1) you have not experienced something, and if (2) the people you know have not experienced something, that therefore (3) peer reviewed scientific evidence should be disregarded or dismissed? This is an example of pseudo-skepticism (or pseudo-science), not true skepticism (or true science). True skepticism is a form of questioning and agnosticism (i.e. acknowledging lack of knowledge, one way or the other). Pseudo-skepticism involves dismissing specific hypotheses in the absence of evidence to justify the dismissal.

Dr X: *How is that possible? Do spirits have vocal cords? How do they make sound?*

Discernment: This is a good question that has been asked and addressed by serious researchers in the field. Dr. Schwartz and others have provided plausible scientific theories that explain how this is possible (e.g. see Schwartz 2020, in press).

Dr. X: *I characterize Dr. Schwartz is a "tree believer" - the irrational persistence of an untenable belief.*

Discernment: Another characteristic of pseudo-skeptics is that they often engage in the very actions that they attribute to others. Dr. X's statement that Dr. Schwartz is a "tree believer" is an "ad hominem" argument as well as a partially inaccurate one. One hypothesis is that "tree" was a typographical error and that Dr. X meant "true." Another possibility is that "tree believer" has some special poetic meaning to Dr. X. (e.g. see Dr. X quoting Shakespeare poetry at the end) and that he meant to write tree.

However, Dr. Schwartz's persistence in conducting afterlife research is not "irrational" unless we define "irrational" as "following replicated data where it takes us." One could argue that it is "irrational" for a scientist to claim that it is "irrational" to follow replicated evidence. True scientists follow evidence, and Dr. Schwartz describes himself as an evidence-based believer.

Dr. X: *People who believe that we can establish regular communication with the dead use a variety of interesting phrases: "parallel dimensions," "voices from beyond," "out-of-body journey," "post materialist," "non-earthly being," "those who have crossed over," and "channeling. They talk about "Post-Materialist Science" and the "Ascended Masters."*

Discernment: This collection of phrases is an accurate subset of interesting phrases used to attempt to describe afterlife phenomena.

Dr. X: *Finally, Dr. Schwartz says he is working on a "soul phone," a piece of hardware that will enable anyone to talk to a deceased person. He says it will take about four years to design and build.*

Discernment: Accuracy of communication is important. The details matter. What Dr. Schwartz has said is that the totality of evidence suggests that <u>if sufficient funding is available – and the key phrase is "if," then it is possible – and the key phrase is "possible," that a practical spirit communication device (i.e. texting on a cell phone) can be designed and built in four years.</u>

Dr. X: *Obviously, this is ripe for fraud.*

Discernment: Yes, such technology has the potential for fraud – from the people claiming to build it to the people potentially using it. However, is this a scientific argument about the theory or evidence for life-after-death or spirit communication technology? This is an ethical and moral prediction, one that serious scientists in this area pay close attention to. And the same potential for fraud applies to smart phones, computers, pharmaceuticals, tools, etc.

Dr. X: *Do you believe that such a phone can be designed and built?*

What do you is the likelihood that after you have as "chimney sweepers come to dust," that you will be able to talk to your living friends?

Discernment: Is this poetic use of a Shakespearean phrase an evidence-based scientific analysis or an opinion (personal bias) made in the absence of scientific evidence? What do you think? (another typing error is that Dr. X left out the word "think" in the second sentence).

Discerning the difference between true and pseudo skeptics

In a November 9, 2017 interview, the seasoned host Larry King asked the well-known astrophysicist and skeptic Neil deGrasse Tyson the following controversial question:

How could anybody know that there is a heaven? That they are going somewhere? That there is an afterlife? How can anyone know that? It boggles my mind.

Tyson replied,

They can believe they know…there is a difference between believing something and using the methods and tools of science to establish what is objectively true. And what is objectively true is something that is true outside of your belief system. That's what science is.

Most scientists (Dr. Schwartz included) and many lay persons agree (strongly) with Tyson concerning the role of science in establishing what is "objectively true." Most readers also probably agree with the distinguished astronomer and skeptic Carl Sagan who popularized the phrase, "Extraordinary claims require extraordinary evidence."

Sagan's scientific standard was previously expressed by an influential sociologist and skeptic Marcello Truzzi who said, "Extraordinary claims require extraordinary proof." Truzzi was a co-founder of the Committee for the Scientific Investigation of Claims of the Paranormal as well as the Society for Scientific Exploration.

Truzzi wrote:

In science, the burden of proof falls upon the claimant; and the more extraordinary a claim, the heavier is the burden of proof demanded. The true skeptic takes an agnostic position, one that says the claim is not proved rather than disproved. He asserts that the claimant has not borne the burden of proof and that science must continue to build its cognitive map of reality without incorporating the extraordinary claim as a new "fact." Since the true skeptic does not assert a claim, he has no burden to prove anything. He just goes on using the established theories of "conventional science" as usual. But if a critic asserts that there is evidence for disproof, that he has a negative hypothesis—saying, for instance, that a seeming psi[8] result was actually due to an artifact—he is making a claim and therefore also has to bear a burden of proof (1987).

As mentioned in footnote 1, Dr. Schwartz has pointed out that some scientists are more accurately described as being "mixed" skeptics who (1) function as true skeptics when addressing certain topics, and (2) act like pseudo-skeptics when addressing other topics (especially strongly emotionally charged topics. Dr. X. may be functioning as a mixed skeptic, at least concerning afterlife science.

In *The Case for Truth: Why and How to Seek Truth* (Bourey & Schwartz, 2020), the authors refer to such unconscious pseudo-skepticism as being instances of "notch filter blindness" where otherwise true skeptics unknowingly think and behave like pseudo-skeptics. This may be the case for Dr. X.

So, how can we discern whether a person is functioning as a true skeptic versus a pseudo-skeptic? Here are five pointers illustrated by Dr. X:

1. True skeptics focus primarily on theories and evidence (the messages), pseudo-skeptics often focus on the individual (the messenger) (e.g. "disarmingly engaging," a "tree believer" or a true believer).

2. True skeptics carefully discuss the theories and evidence, pseudo-skeptics either ignore the evidence or make false statements that do not

---

[8] Psi is the scientific term for controversial paranormal phenomena such as mind reading (telepathy), seeing the future in dreams (precognition), influencing physics objects with one's mind (psychokinesis), viewing distant objects with one's mind's eye (remote viewing). See Cardeña, E. (2018). The experimental evidence for parapsychological phenomena: A review. *American Psychologist, 73(5)*, 663–677.   https://doi.org/10.1037/amp0000236

speak to the evidence (e.g., Dr. X did not discuss any of the specific experiments; instead, he argued, for example, that Dr. Schwartz unfairly criticized Shermer as a person when in fact Dr. Schwartz criticized some of Shermer's strategies that ignored the experimental designs themselves.)

3. True skeptics are careful to qualify statements, pseudo-skeptics often make definitive, black or white (and inaccurate) statements without providing evidence that supports their claims (e.g. "these experiments were <u>not</u> vetted by other scientists").

4. True skeptics follow the evidence even if it challenges established theories and understandings; pseudo-skeptics ignore or dismiss the evidence if it challenges what they assume must be true.

5. True skeptics are careful to accurately present information, pseudo-skeptics often leave out important details in order to promote their position (e.g. Dr. X left out important details such as the requirement Dr. Schwartz emphasizes for increased funding to potentially build a working SoulPhone).

True skepticism lies at the heart of science. It lies at the heart of the statement made by Nobel laureate Dr. Richard Feynman that introduces this chapter. Do we have the courage to follow carefully collected evidence where it takes us, especially if the evidence challenges one of our fundamental theories or beliefs?

Here is how Carl Sagan explained it. I call this the Kepler Challenge:

When he [Johannes Kepler] found that his long-cherished beliefs did not agree with the most precise observations, he accepted the uncomfortable facts.

He preferred the hard truth to his dearest delusions, that is the heart of science.

One wonders how Dr. X might respond if he read this analysis of his skeptical email. Upon digesting this new information, and with this new education, would he able to meet the Kepler Challenge, practice the heart of science, and seriously consider the evidenced-based veracity of the afterlife hypothesis? I asked Mr. Leslie Klein, the person who invited me to give the presentation, whether he thought that Dr. might be interested in reading my analysis of his email. Here is Klein's email response: "Sensing that Dr. X had said all he wished to say on your presentation, I called him yesterday…I asked him if he wished to read your chapter X, he said no, a bad use of his time. I asked him what would change his mind. He said nothing will convince him until he actually witnessed the soul phone work."

Postmaterialist science challenges researchers and laymen alike to address the Kepler challenge and practice the heart of science in addressing extraordinary claims and evidence raised by advanced consciousness science.

References

Beauregard, M., Trent, N. L., & Schwartz, G. E. (2018). Toward a postmaterialist psychology: Theory, research, and applications. *New Ideas Psych.* 50, 21-33.

Cardeña, E. (2018). The experimental evidence for parapsychological phenomena: A review. *American Psychologist,* 73(5), 663–677. https://doi.org/10.1037/amp0000236.

Macy, M. H. (2001). Miracles in the Storm: Talking to the Other side with the New Technology of Spiritual Contact. New York: Berkley.

Miller, L. J. (Ed.) (2013). The Oxford Handbook of Psychology and Spirituality. New York: Oxford University Press.

Palmer, J. (2017). Experimenter Effects. *Psi Encyclopedia*. London: The Society for Psychical Research. https://psi-encyclopedia.spr.ac.uk/articles/experimenter-effects.

Pitstick, M., & Schwartz, G. E. (2019). Greater Reality Living. CreateSpace Independent Publishing Platform, Second Edition.

Radin, D., Michel, L., & Delorme, A. (2016). Psychophysical modulation of fringe visibility in a distant double-slit optical system. Physics Essays, 29(1), 14–22.

Sarraf, M. A., Woodley of Menie, M. A., & Tressoldi, P. (in press). Anomalous information reception by mediums: A meta-analysis of scientific evidence. EXPLORE: The Journal of Science & Healing.

Schwartz, G. E. (2010). Possible application of silicon photomultiplier technology to detect the presence of spirit and intention: three proof-of-concept experiments. EXPLORE: The Journal of Science and Healing, 6, 166-171.

Schwartz, G. E. (2011). Photonic measurement of apparent presence of spirit using a computer automated system. EXPLORE: The Journal of Science and H ealing, 7, 100-109.

Schwartz, G.E. (in press). A computer-automated, multi-center, randomized control trial evaluating hypothesized spirit presence and communication. EXPLORE: The Journal of Science and Healing.

Truzzi, M. (1987). On Pseudo-Skepticism. Zetetic Scholar, 12/13, 3-4.

Tucker, J. B., & Nidiffer, F. D. (2014). Psychological evaluation of American children who report memories of previous lives. Journal of Scientific Exploration, 28 (4), 583-594.

Van Lommel, P., Van Wees, R., Meyers, V., & Elfferich, I. (2001). Near-death experience in survivors of cardiac arrest: a prospective study in the Netherlands. The Lancet, 358, 2039-2045.

Walleczek, J., & von Stillfried, N. (2019). False-positive effect in the Radin double-slit experiment on observer consciousness as determined with the advanced meta-experimental protocol. Frontiers in Psychology, 22 August 2019, https://www.frontiersin.org/articles/10.3389/fpsyg.2019.01891/full.

Chapter Three

Wave of Awakening: Support for a Postmaterialist Science and Society

Natalie L. Dyer, PhD

> *Everyone who is seriously involved in the pursuit of science becomes convinced that a spirit is manifest in the laws of the Universe-a spirit vastly superior to that of man, and one in the face of which we with our modest powers must feel humble.*
> — Albert Einstein

Introduction: The Program is Changing

Programs are conditioned behavioral patterns, models, paradigms, and beliefs that guide behavior. Some we are born with through our genetics and are instinctual, but many programs we pick up throughout our lives. We are programmed into certain belief structures and behaviors at many levels and by many means: our parents, our education system, religious organizations, and the media, to name a few. Of course programming is necessary and has tremendous value. It allows us to develop habits and ways of being that can benefit us. But some programs can create incredible suffering, injustice, and prevent individual and collective growth. In fact, it can be stated that perhaps all world conflict is due to dogmas perpetuated by programming. Perhaps at one point in time the program may have served a valuable purpose, but at a later time it became harmful.

To create and maintain programs, different kinds of programmers are required: those who consciously program others, such as parents, policy makers or the media; those who repeat the program, such as educators or the church; and those who maintain the program and punish those who go against the program, such as law enforcement or the community. There is much overlap across types of programmers, and they are described here simply to generate a better understanding of the programming process. This programming dynamic has operated within mainstream science with the materialist program, confining most scientists to work within the belief that physical reality (i.e. matter) is all that exists.

The outdated materialist program has spawned a number of assumptions that are unscientific, yet persist largely through institutional and cultural programming reinforcement. Scientists who deviate from the materialist program often face punishment, risking career ostracization, lack of research funding, and social ridicule. There can be a large price to pay for being a postmaterialist scientist, with influential organizations such as TED (Technology, Entertainment, Design) and Wikipedia censoring or banning their talks and research. Some scientists have even been violently attacked. Because of the great risk involved, many scientists only reveal their true perspective in closed research meetings or in conversations among trusted colleagues. Fortunately, the tide is changing.

To change a program, we first need to receive new information about reality. This has been achieved through the principles of quantum mechanics (see Chapter 8, "Science Within Consciousness: A Progress Report" by Dr. Amit Goswami) and scientific evidence presented throughout this anthology. Second, and perhaps most importantly, we need to integrate this new information to modify our behavior and institutions, hopefully transforming society into a network of more accurate and beneficial systems. This second step is only just beginning, but it is gaining momentum. Humanity is transforming toward a postmaterialist perspective, and support for this shift is present in multiple spheres of influence in science and society, including education, research, medicine, and in the socio-political realm.

Maintaining the materialist program is detrimental to our collective progression as a species. It is time to make the transition toward a more open-minded science that is based in contemporary theory, research, and universal human experience that simultaneously relieves suffering and increases human flourishing. In this chapter, we will first look at some of the evidence against scientific materialism and how continuing to adhere to this paradigm is slowing scientific and societal progress. Second, we will follow the research suggesting that certain beliefs and practices incongruent with a materialist perspective can greatly enhance wellbeing on multiple levels. Third, we will explore the scientific and socio-political scaffolding being constructed by individuals and collaborative teams all over the world, all of which are supporting the shift to a postmaterialist science and society. Finally, we will explore how the aforementioned materialist programs are transformed by postmaterialism. Taken together, this perspective casts light on the path beyond materialism, one that guides us toward a postmaterialist science and society. My wish is that by the end of this chapter, you will feel hopeful, inspired, and optimistic about the future of humankind. Given the plethora of sociopolitical and environmental issues facing us today, postmaterialism provides a necessary new vision forward.

Beyond the Materialist Program

Maintaining old programs can hold back the progress and development of science, society, and the individual. Arguably, scientific materialism has impaired the advancement of humanity and our institutions through persistently imposing a false paradigm in which we are seen as largely powerless, finite, and separate from each other. However, many of psychology's founding fathers—including William James, Carl Jung, Sigmund Freud, and Abraham Maslow—were all oriented toward aspects of the human experience that are not possible within the materialist framework. James was deeply interested in topics of spirituality and religion, including mystical experiences (James, 1902/1985). Sigmund Freud even stated that if he were to live his life over again, he would devote it to psychical research rather than psychoanalysis (Jones, 1957, p. 392). From his lifelong study, Maslow arrived at the conclusion that spirituality is a distinct dimension and need of the human experience (Compton et al., 2001), and empirical studies support this claim (Hoffman, 1996; Piedmont, 1999). How have we veered away from these important universal aspects of the human experience in psychological science?

One of the main limitations to progress born out of scientific materialism is the assumption that consciousness is an emergent property of the brain, generated or produced by the brain, and not existing independent of the brain. This idea is discussed throughout this anthology because it is a key player of the materialist program in science. Not only does this assumption limit science—it alters the operation of society and our collective value system. Taking the approach that consciousness is produced by the brain, and is therefore annihilated upon death, is preventing progress toward a better understanding of how our consciousness, mind, brain, and body function and the extent of our potential. It has also generated the transhumanist 2045 Strategic Social Initiative, with the long-term goal of generating one's personality through a nonbiological, robotic, or holographic version of oneself (i.e. avatar) in order to be physically immortal. This plan is aimed for completion by 2045, as the name suggests. Clearly there are serious social and ethical considerations that accompany this kind of initiative, including redefining our idea of relationships, life, and free will, and socioeconomic disparities in who can become immortal and who cannot.

There are lines of evidence that suggest consciousness may operate much differently than the current view in mainstream science. These phenomena tend to involve consciousness and/or the mind transcending the boundaries of space and time, or functioning independent of the brain, thereby surviving the body after death. These lines of evidence are discussed throughout this anthology, and include near-death experiences (NDEs), out-of-body experiences (OBEs), past life memories, mediumship, psychical experiences, and the effect of the mind and heart on remote systems, both biological and non-biological. I will only be discussing these phenomena briefly in this chapter, because they are addressed in detail in other chapters.

The progression to postmaterialism allows for other possible relationships between consciousness, mind, and brain. To be clear, I define consciousness here as pure awareness, also referred to as the witness, the observer, or the 'I Am'; the mind as the contents of this awareness, including thoughts, emotions, beliefs, percepts; and the brain as the organ and its material components, including its nerve cells and electrochemical activity. Postmaterialism permits the possibility that consciousness may exist independent of the brain. It recognizes that we have evidence that this may be the case, and integrates ancient and contemporary theories and observations that consciousness may be fundamental (see Chapter 1, "The Next Great Scientific Revolution" by Dr. Mario Beauregard), and that the brain may act as a filter, a receiver/transmitter for consciousness instead of consciousness arising solely from the brain. The founder of American psychology William James (1842-1910) proposed at Harvard University that the brain might act as a filter, which restricts access to greater consciousness and a larger reality (James, 1989).

The great physicist and inventor Nikola Tesla (1856-1943) came to a similar perspective:

"My brain is only a receiver, in the Universe there is a core from which we obtain knowledge, strength and inspiration. I have not penetrated into the secrets of this core, but I know that it exists."

Philosopher and renowned author Aldous Huxley (1894-1963) stated the following, adapted from the work of philosopher C.D. Broad:

"To make biological survival possible, Mind at Large has to be funneled through the reducing valve of the brain and nervous system. What comes out at the other end is a measly trickle of the kind of consciousness which will help us to stay alive on the surface of this particular planet." (Huxley, 1954, p. 23)

And the pioneering educational psychologist Cyril Burt (1883-1971) concurred:

"Our sense organs and our brain operate as an intricate kind of filter which limits and directs the mind's clairvoyant powers, so that under normal conditions attention is concentrated on just those objects or situations that are of biological importance for the survival of the organism and its species." (Burt 1968, pp. 50, 58-59)

Perhaps, through our biological antennae, we are filtering a greater consciousness or reality, with each of us only perceiving a minuscule aspect of the whole. This filtering mechanism can be altered, in which case we can experience other aspects of reality not normally perceived. This alteration may be occurring during mystical experiences, psychedelic experience, mediumship, and other psychical phenomena. Perhaps we are also connected nonlocally through this one mind (Dossey, 2013) or "Mind at Large" as Aldous Huxley claimed (Huxley, 1954), remerging with it upon death. Postmaterialism re-opens these possibilities that have been prematurely shut out by materialism. Studies of ablation, stimulation, and disruption of the brain only provide evidence that the brain mediates different states of consciousness. We know that the brain is constantly filtering information, much of which never reaches our awareness. Information from both our external environment and internal mental environment is filtered, meaning we are only ever aware of a very small portion of reality at any given moment.

Many people claim to receive information from and perceive the energy of those who have died, often referred to as mediumship. It is not known how mediums access this information, but research suggests that some mediums do receive accurate information (Schwartz & Russek, 2001; Schwartz et al., 2001, 2002), including under triple blind protocols with moderate to large effect sizes (Beischel & Schwartz, 2007; Beischel et al., 2015a). The information obtained from mediums also helps individuals ameliorate the suffering associated with grieving their lost loved ones (Beischel et al., 2015b). This reason alone should justify more investigations into mediumship.

Mediums and psychics have been around since the dawn of recorded history, from shamans and medicine men and women, to the oracle at Delphi in ancient Greece, to modern day TV mediums and psychics. Of course the historical relevance and incidence of mediumship does not mean it is legitimate, but millions of people do derive great value from these abilities, and being open to the possibility of mediumship may serve society, especially considering its healing value and far-reaching implications regarding our understanding of relationships, consciousness, and the nature of reality. Importantly, a lack of investigation may promote the persistence of many fraudulent mediums, and scientific research can help to strengthen the legitimacy of accurate mediums, sometimes referred to as "research mediums."

Scientific materialism denies the possibility of communicating with the deceased because of the assumption that consciousness and mental activity, which includes the personality and memories of the deceased person, do not persist after the death of the brain. Postmaterialism re-opens the possibility of accurate mediumship because it does not assume that consciousness is dependent on the brain, nor does it assume that minds cannot communicate with each other without bodies or words. It also takes into account the evidence suggesting that some people are able to receive accurate information from or about those who have passed. Near-death experiences (NDEs) during cardiac arrest (see Chapter 11, "Near-Death Experience and the Loss of Brain Function During Cardiac Arrest: A Strong Indication for Non-Local Consciousness" by Dr. Pim van Lommel), mediumship, and validated past life memories (see Chapter 14, "Reincarnation: Any Evidence for It?" by Dr. Erlendur Haraldsson) provide some evidence that consciousness and aspects of the mind may transcend death and even re-emerge within another body at another time.

The denial of the possibility of life after death under the materialist paradigm has enabled fear and suffering surrounding death; everyone must die, and most everyone has suffered the devastating loss of a loved one. Connecting with spiritual or nonmaterial realities through NDEs, for example, or reuniting with the consciousness of loved ones through mediumship, have tremendous power to relieve fear of death and ease the grieving process. Instead, we tend to hide death, rushing off the deceased to morgues, covering them in makeup, and getting the funeral process done as quickly as possible, often at a very large price, literally. We also do not study death (apart from its prevention or postponement), nor do we talk deeply about death, or try to understand where we go when we die, if anywhere. We also assume death is bad or wrong, and that it should be prevented at all costs, to the point of keeping people connected to machines that breathe for them despite these individuals having no ability to communicate with others or live the kind of life they would find worth living.

It is apparent that we continue to be programmed by the media to value and seek materialistic goals and basic, primal needs and desires, such as money, power, and sex, turning a large profit for their corporate owners. Have we been systematically distracted from the deeper aspects of ourselves, the higher echelons on our hierarchy of needs, such as self-actualization and self-transcendence? Fortunately, there is a movement away from these programmed distractions toward deeper experiences, where evidence suggests that greater wellbeing is found. Next, we will explore the benefits of a postmaterialist perspective on psychological and physical health, personal transcendence, and transformation.

Seeking the Sacred: Spirituality, Health, and Transcendence

It is important that our practices and beliefs optimize health and wellness rather than create or enable suffering. It is also critical that these ways of being are supported, when possible, by scientific evidence. However, the vast majority of research in psychology and neuroscience, the two broad fields that deal with the mind, focuses on dysfunction of the mind and brain. We have only recently become interested in measuring the thriving human with the birth of positive psychology in the late 1990s. This bias is understandable, considering that dysfunction can cause great suffering and its pharmaceutical or surgical treatment can often save lives—while turning an enormous profit.

Identifying universal elements across different cultural belief systems provides insight into the fundamental characteristics of the human experience. Discovering our universality can promote pro-social behavior, and priming similarities between people has been shown to promote positive behaviors toward others and the self (Over & Carpenter, 2009; Rubin, 2011). Beliefs can heal (e.g., placebo), or harm (e.g., nocebo, a detrimental effect on health, such as from a false diagnosis or poor prognosis) and scientific research has revealed that certain beliefs are beneficial for our health and wellbeing compared to others.

The relationship between belief and health has been studied primarily through research on the placebo effect. Improved psychological and physical health has been repeatedly observed through belief in a treatment that is supposed to be ineffective, such as a sugar pill or sham surgery. The word "placebo" has been colloquially misused as being synonymous with "ineffective." This has enabled pseudoskeptics (those who are not true skeptics because they operate dogmatically within the materialist program) to claim that any healing methodology that falls outside the bounds of materialism works only through placebo. Yet, quite amusingly, at least 80% of the beneficial effect of antidepressants and 75% of pain medication is solely due to placebo (Kirsch & Sapirstein, 1998; Kirsch et al., 2002). The multibillion-dollar pharmaceutical industry does not want these data to be made available to the public, and they are quite comfortable with the materialist program.

Research into belief systems has revealed that beliefs oriented toward postmaterialist frameworks tend to come with many psychological, physical, and spiritual health benefits. Despite the materialist program, there has been an exponential increase in studies on religion, spirituality, and health between 1973 and 2010 (Koenig, 2014). A recent review of hundreds of quantitative original data-based research reports revealed that the majority of studies report that people who are spiritual or religious have better mental health and adapt more quickly to health problems compared to those who are not. This orientation improves physical health, reduces risk of disease, and influences response to treatment (Koenig, 2014). The author concludes that these results underscore the need to integrate spirituality into patient care and argues that spirituality is moving into the mainstream of healthcare. Similarly, others have reported that those who have goals around self-transcendence and spirituality have higher positive emotions, greater wellbeing, more concern for others, and better physical and mental health (Leak et al., 2007).

Despite the universality and benefit of spirituality, we have been slow to investigate spiritual experiences and practices, thereby preventing their integration into society and retaining their status as taboo. A brief visit into our past might shed some light on this puzzling neglect.

Spiritual Experience or Psychosis?

As a species, we have ridiculed, imprisoned, tortured, murdered, and vivisected the mentally ill. Throughout human history, many belief systems have held the view that humans who were mentally ill, especially those who had visions or hallucinations, were possessed or controlled by demons or some sort of evil force. Even the well-developed system of Tibetan medicine has roots in a form of shamanism known as Bon, in which it is believed that many diseases are caused by demonic forces (Waldau & Patton, 2009, p.224-229). Society has dealt with these alleged demon-inflicted people in a variety of ways depending on the religious or cultural program. They have been exorcised, burned to death, imprisoned, or hung. Even during the recent past in Western society, the mentally ill have been routinely imprisoned, tortured, lobotomized, and experimented on (Morrissey & Goldman, 1986; Fink, 1992). Today, we primarily use medication and psychotherapy to assist those who battle their figurative demons, but many mentally ill individuals are still locked up in prisons.

The horrendous acts of cruelty and stigmatization toward the mentally ill have programmed society into a fear of being "crazy" or of deviating from the norm, likely thwarting others from seeking altered states of consciousness or spiritual experiences. This program also likely contributes to the reason why today, psychiatric drugs are a multibillion-dollar industry in the United States alone (Greenslit & Kaptchuk, 2012). Most people can name multiple psychopharmaceuticals, and the use of antidepressants has doubled between 1999-2012 (Kantor et al., 2015). Despite the normality of psychopharmaceuticals, colloquially humiliating phrases such as "someone forgot to take their meds today" keep people in line and maintain the program of not acting outside of the norm.

Spiritual experiences have not always been demonized or ridiculed. In other programs or cultures, mystical and transcendent experiences are sacred gifts and mark an initiation into becoming a healer or spiritual teacher. After extensive study with indigenous peoples and those diagnosed with schizophrenia, the American anthropologist Julian Silverman at the National Institute of Mental Health wrote about the difference between schizophrenia in American culture and shamanism in indigenous cultures. He noted one major difference between the two cultures with regards to how life crises are resolved. In indigenous cultures, the abnormal experience (shamanism) is typically beneficial to the individual and he is regarded as being one with a greater consciousness. In a culture that does not provide guidelines for comprehending this kind of experience, the individual (perceived as schizophrenic) is likely to undergo further suffering over and above the original crisis (Silverman, 1967).

As religious historian Mircea Eliade (1907-1986) proclaims in *Birth and Rebirth*:

"...the shamanic vocation often implies a crisis so deep that it sometimes borders on madness. And since the youth cannot become a shaman until he has resolved this crisis, it plays the role of a mystical initiation" (Eliade, 1958, p. 89).

In contrast to the approach of other cultural programs, in the scientific materialist paradigm mystical experiences are often viewed as delusional and require intense, immediate treatment—most often a cocktail of antipsychotics, rather than initiation into a revered position or lineage. The materialist paradigm may be preventing and/or suppressing the need for individuals to process and integrate their mystical and spiritual experiences.

Understandably, given the materialist program, little attention is paid to whether someone's transcendent, mystical experiences or visions have any value to inform, create, heal, or reveal any truths. Instead, these types of experiences are greatly feared in Western society and usually result in immediate medication. Indeed, religious and spiritual ideas and experiences are common in hallucinations, even marking a characteristic of a symptom for psychotic and bipolar disorders (American Psychiatric Association, 2013). Another disorder, schizotypal personality disorder, is identified and diagnosed by a key symptom: odd beliefs or magical thinking (e.g. clairvoyance, telepathy, or a sixth sense) (American Psychiatric Association, 2013). In this case, merely believing in these phenomena is seen as pathological. In stark contrast to the pathologization of belief and mystical experience, 92% of the general U.S. population believes in a god or divinity (U.S. Religious Landscape Survey, 2008), and 59-72% of Americans have had a mystical or psychic experience at some point during their lives (Kennedy et al., 1994; Hood, 2005). In my own recent research it was revealed that 54% of Harvard psychology students "possibly, probably, or definitely" believe in a god or higher power, 65% believe that prayer can affect health, and 52% identify as spiritual or religious (Trent et al., 2019).

Are people who are mentally ill more likely to be spiritual? Based on an analysis of studies over the past 20 years, the opposite seems to be the case. Overall, people who were spiritually or religiously oriented were less likely to suffer from mental illness (Bonelli & Koenig, 2013). Because of the value of spirituality to mental health, a paradigm shift seems to be occurring in which spirituality is being integrated into psychotherapy (Sperry, 2012, p. 225).

Fortunately, both spiritual experiences and mental illness are becoming less taboo, and more people are using practices and forms of therapy that are not supported by the materialist paradigm. As evidence of this, there has been an exponential increase in both the practice of and research regarding many cross-cultural practices that have their origin in non-materialist paradigms, such as mindfulness, meditation, yoga, and energy medicine.

Research Regarding Spiritual Practices

Since we observe the value of seeking and experiencing the sacred to our wellbeing, it is in our best interest to further explore this dimension of the human experience. The operationalization of mindfulness meditation through mindfulness-based stress reduction (MBSR) by Jon Kabat-Zinn (1982) resulted in the generation of thousands of research studies investigating the benefits of mindfulness meditation on everything from stress to cancer to business. Mindfulness is defined in a few different ways, but in general, it refers to a process of focusing one's attention on the present moment without judgment or evaluation. This is a process whereby the contents of the mind, thoughts, and emotions, have less of a grasp on our state of being. In this practice, we are transcending the grip of our conditioned ways of being and behaving—our programs. Mindfulness research has grown exponentially in the past 10 years and has now permeated our culture, generating numerous mindfulness workshops, methods of therapy, and institutes all over the world.

Meditation or contemplative practices have their roots in being a means to unite with a higher aspect of self, a greater power, or divinity/god, through transcending and/or integrating the ego-self. These practices have a variety of goals, but one is *samadhi*, a state of pure awareness, and another is *metta*, or universal love, kindness, and compassion for all of existence (Buddharakkhita, 1989). Ultimately, contemplative practices lead us to transcend our programming to merge with a unitive, nondual state of being. When we pull the curtain back in this way, we connect with deeper truths and higher-level qualities of self, such as compassion and love. The spiritual experiences of others can become programs when religions form around them. This is not necessarily detrimental; the important point here is that we continue to mindfully re-assess our programs to discern whether they align with our beliefs, the evidence available to us, our experience, and whether they are beneficial or harmful.

Owing to the persistent problem of scientific materialism, spiritual and transcendent experiences are only just beginning to be scientifically evaluated, despite the widespread cross-cultural experience of transcendent states of being. In defense of the materialists, spiritual experiences are not necessarily easy to study—especially with rigorous methodology—and much of the phenomena cannot be directly measured, such as the divine being commonly encountered during near-death experiences. The research that does exist reveals that spiritual practices can increase social, cognitive, emotional, physical, and spiritual wellbeing, beneficially change brain function and structure, enhance immune function, and promote beneficial gene expression (Black & Slavich, 2016; Chang et al., 2013; Chu et al., 2016; Fox et al., 2014; Goyal et al., 2014; Hagen & Nayar, 2014; Kang et al., 2013; Lim & Cheong, 2015; Thrane & Cohen, 2014; Wang et al., 2014). In the last two decades, we have generated a collection of evidence suggesting that when people practice techniques and have experiences that are incompatible with the ideology of materialism, they experience profound benefits to their health and wellbeing. Over time, these practices change the structure and function of the brain in such a way that it becomes easier to maintain a peaceful mind, improve mood, and harness greater self-control, thereby positively reprogramming our physiology and psychology into homeostatic wellness.

The Rise of CAM and Energy Medicine

Energy medicine is incompatible with materialism in that it involves the use and manipulation of a nonlocal and infinite energy. Across many different religions, philosophies, and belief systems—from the concept of *chi* in China, to *ki* in Japan, *rlung* in Tibet, *prana* in India, holy spirit or the light in Christian traditions, to biofield energy in contemporary Western systems—there are numerous labels given to the same hypothesized life force energy on which energy medicine is based (Sperry, 2012; Hammerschlag et al., 2014). The practices corresponding to these labels operate under the theory that optimal health is achieved and maintained when this energy is flowing throughout and around the body in a balanced way.

The use of energy medicine-based practices is on the rise, as is the use of its higher order category: complementary and alternative medicine (CAM) (Kessler et al., 2001), although CAM has been absorbed by the term integrative medicine, which is essentially the use of evidence-based CAM combined with conventional care. This increase in CAM use has been observed in all 48 contiguous states of the U.S. (Kessler et al., 2001). Evidently, despite the materialist scientific program largely still present in medicine, the use of therapies such as Qigong and Reiki, whose theories are based in a postmaterialist perspective, are increasing. The tide is also changing in terms of the use and perception of CAM with science and medical students, a group who traditionally experience ample materialist programming. Approximately 59% of medical students and 73% of pharmacy students use some type of CAM (James et al., 2016). The integration of spirituality within medicine is on the rise, and as of 2014, more than 75% of medical schools offer spirituality–related courses to medical students (Putchalski et al., 2014).

While there is no scientific evidence for the existence of this energy, we have evidence for the effectiveness of these therapies. Important to the non-materialist aspect of these practices and theories, *chi* or life force operates nonlocally, and is manipulated across great distances (Jonas et al., 2012, p. 364). Jonas and Crawford (2004) examined 12 spiritual healing modalities and identified core characteristics between modalities. The most common healing techniques were the cultivating of love and good intentions for the other. Evidently, research into these types of CAM therapies is on the rise, but progress is limited by a shortage of funding. Despite this challenge, over 800 hospitals across the United States now offer Reiki to patients, because—to put it simply—it works.

To meet the research demand, the National Institutes of Health (NIH) has increased funding to CAM therapy research, and initiated the National Center for Complementary and Integrative Health (NCCIH), formally known as the National Center for Complementary and Alternative Medicine (NCCAM) in 1998, with the mission to "define, through rigorous scientific investigation, the usefulness and safety of complementary and integrative health interventions and their roles in improving health and health care." This includes funding research into spiritually-based practices, including Qigong, Reiki, meditation, and yoga.

The Importance of Experiencing the Sacred

Take a moment to feel the astonishing reality of your existence. Connect with the aspect of you that is the observer, the part of you that is behind all of your experiences, thoughts, and sensations—pure awareness itself. This aspect of you transcends space and time and is eternally present. This same awareness is in all others, though filtered through your unique experience, physiology, and psychology. If we were to discover that the same mind/awareness connected us all on a higher level, and that this was supported by scientific evidence, perhaps we would end up treating each other better. Much research suggests that this is indeed the case; we are connected to each other non-physically, and we may be a part of one mind or consciousness. Experiencing this pure awareness, interconnectivity, and higher levels of consciousness holds tremendous importance for how we perceive and relate to each other and the planet.

When it comes to the "search for the sacred," a phrase coined by positive psychology, humans have been oriented toward spirituality since prehistory, depicting and celebrating gods, goddesses, and spirit through art, dance, and medicine. Spiritual seeking and experiences are incredibly personal and have only recently been considered a serious topic for scientific inquiry. However, many prominent psychologists and other scientists from history—including William James, Sigmund Freud, Carl Jung, Nikola Tesla, and Albert Einstein—have all expressed a strong desire and need for scientists to focus on the nonmaterial aspect of the human experience.

Connecting with transcendent realities and experiencing the sacred often increases social and psychological wellbeing and relieves primal fears, like the fear of death (Greyson, 1992; van Lommel et al., 2001; Noyes et al., 2009). Direct experience is tremendously important for guiding our beliefs, and has the power to immediately override previous programs and frameworks for perceiving reality. Experiencing the afterlife or another aspect of reality is profoundly more effective at transforming one's perception than belief alone (Baruss, 2001). These other facets or dimensions of one underlying, unifying reality often feel more real than normal everyday reality, and involve unique perceptions such as colors which have never been seen in ordinary reality. Many materialists have had worldview-shattering experiences; Harvard neurosurgeon Eben Alexander was one such materialist who had a transformative NDE that instantly re-programmed him out of materialism:

"The brain itself does not produce consciousness. That it is, instead, a kind of reducing valve or filter, shifting the larger, nonphysical consciousness that we possess in the nonphysical worlds down into a more limited capacity for the duration of our mortal lives" (Alexander, 2012).

With the growing evidence against scientific materialism, together with the profound benefits of spiritually-based practices, many structures and systems—including educational and healthcare institutions—have been developed to support the transition toward a postmaterialist society.

Emerging Postmaterialist Systems

It is an exciting time for science and society. We are on the threshold of a transformation toward greater human potential, paired with an increased understanding of our interconnection. Technology is growing rapidly, communication across distance is instant, and we are sharing information on a scale which we have never previously seen. Science and spirituality are merging and are being shown not to be incompatible as previously thought. During his NDE, Eben Alexander also discovered that:

"Science—the science to which I've devoted so much of my life—doesn't contradict what I learned up there. But far, far too many people believe it does, because certain members of the scientific community, who are pledged to the materialist worldview, have insisted again and again that science and spirituality cannot coexist" (Alexander, 2012).

Declarations and Calls for Postmaterialism among Scientists, Philosophers, and Medical Practitioners

International teams of scientists are gathering to forge this new path for science. These collaborations have taken the form of declarations, societies, research institutes, institutional programs, scientific journals, and conferences.

In February 2014, a group of internationally renowned scientists from many different fields—many of whom are authors in this anthology—gathered for a meeting in Tucson, Arizona. Discussions and lectures centered on the impact of the materialist ideology on science, the need for a paradigm shift, and the emergence of a postmaterialist paradigm for science, spirituality, and society. From this meeting, the "Manifesto for a Postmaterialist Science" was created (Beauregard et al., 2014), a declaration comprised of 18 statements that demonstrate the need for a postmaterialist science and elucidate the implications of this paradigm shift. To date, the Manifesto for a Postmaterialist Science has been signed by over 300 scientists and philosophers, many of which are at top tier institutions. One of the statements (number 5) addresses the problem of programming:

"Some materialistically inclined scientists and philosophers refuse to acknowledge these phenomena because they are not consistent with their exclusive conception of the world. Rejection of postmaterialist investigation of nature or refusal to publish strong science findings supporting a postmaterialist framework are antithetical to the true spirit of scientific inquiry, which is that empirical data must always be adequately dealt with. Data which do not fit favored theories and beliefs cannot be dismissed a priori. Such dismissal is the realm of ideology, not science."

That same year, another declaration was published, "A Call for an Open, Informed Study of all Aspects of Consciousness," put forth by psychologist Etzel Cardeña (2014) and signed by 100 international scientists and professors. This article draws attention to the need for a non-dogmatic approach to the study of consciousness, and a recognition of parapsychological or psi research. They declare that dismissing empirical observations based on previous biases or theoretical assumptions impedes the ability of the scientific process to properly evaluate evidence. They further state that science is a non-dogmatic, open, critical process that requires thorough consideration of all evidence as well as skepticism toward both assumptions that are currently held and those that challenge them (Cardeña, 2014).

Healthcare professionals have sounded the alarm as well, with the publication of "Bringing Spiritually Oriented Psychotherapies into the Health Care Mainstream: A Call for Worldwide Collaboration" (Richards et al., 2015). The authors of this article introduce the Bridges system, a global collaboration network of scientists, educators, healthcare practitioners, and spiritual leaders, all with the common goal of bring spirituality into clinical practice based on the evidence for the benefits of spiritual practices to health and healing.

A somewhat recently released "Declaration for Integrative, Evidence-Based, End-of-Life Care that Incorporates Nonlocal Consciousness" (Schwartz et al., 2016), a declaration consisting of 11 statements aimed toward taking a postmaterialist perspective to end-of-life care. This declaration has also been signed by a number of scientists and healthcare practitioners. The final statement reads:

"We see nonlocal consciousness as existing within the broader context of the emergence of a new paradigm science, one which incorporates consciousness. We recognize, however, that acknowledging non-physiologically based consciousness has the potential to evoke emotional responses that challenge deeply held beliefs in both mainstream science and religions. It will take a commitment of courage, compassion, and integrity to address the wealth of implications and opportunities afforded by integrating the research findings supporting a consciousness inclusive model with end-of-life care—more accurately, end-of-physical-life care. Now is the time to advance this integration."

Co-Editors Mario Beauregard, Gary Schwartz and I have put forward a call for the field of psychology in our article titled "Toward a Postpostmaterialist Psychology: Theory, research, and Applications," published in New Ideas in Psychology (Beauregard et al., 2018). In this article we state:

"Despite the fact that quantum mechanism invalidated the metaphysical assumptions associated with scientific materialism, mainstream psychologists still adopt a reductive materialist stance of nature and the universe. They firmly believe that science is synonymous with methodological and philosophical materialism; further, they are convinced that the view that mind and consciousness are simply by-products of brain activity is an incontrovertible fact that has been demonstrated beyond reasonable doubt." (pg 22)

"If psychologists truly seek to make great strides concerning the scientific study of mind and consciousness, they need to consider all types of human experiences, not only a narrow range of phenomena; they also need to embrace a postmaterialist perspective that is compatible both with quantum mechanics and the evidence examined in this paper." (pg 30)

Within the design and execution of the scientific research itself, there have been calls for the development of new methodologies and technologies to study transcendental states of consciousness (Anderson & Braud, 2011) and for the need to improve scientific rigor (Rusek, 2007).

Research Institutes, Societies, and Conferences

Numerous research institutes now exist such as the Institute for Noetic Sciences, the Benson-Henry Institute of Mind-Body Medicine, the Osher Center for Integrative Medicine, the Mind and Life Institute, the Center for Reiki Research, and the Windbridge Institute. There are mind-body and integrative medicine centers being established in hospitals, and as of 2020, over 800 hospitals in the United States offered Reiki energy medicine (American Hospital Association). In a press release by the Benson-Henry Institute, it was reported that teaching patients mind-body approaches like meditation and yoga reduced their stress and improved overall physical health. The study found that patients had a 43% reduction in medical visits during the year following the programs at Benson-Henry (Stahl et al., 2015). Over the past three decades, the Princeton Engineering Anomalies Research (PEAR) center had studied "the interaction between human consciousness and physical devices to better understand the role of consciousness in the establishment of physical reality." Today, they have turned their attention to making such mind-matter interactive devices available to the public through their nonprofit associates.

Many academic research societies oriented toward postmaterialist science currently exist, and some have been around for over 100 years, such as the Society for Psychical Research, established in 1880. The Parapsychology Association began in 1957, the Academy for Spiritual and Consciousness Studies in the mid 1970s, and others, including the Society for Consciousness Studies, the Society for Scientific Exploration, the International Academy of Consciousness, and the International Society for the Study of Subtle Energies and Energy Medicine, were developed over the past 25 years. More recent societies include the Academy for the Advancement of Postmaterialist Sciences, formed in 2017, publisher of this series of volumes, and the Global Union of Scientists for Peace, formed in 2005 and led by physicist John Hagelin.

There are a variety of conferences to attend in any given year that support the presentation of postmaterialist-related research, including the

Science of Consciousness Conference, the Center for Consciousness Studies Conference, the Academy for Spiritual and Consciousness Studies Conference, the International Congress on Consciousness, the Science and Nonduality Conference, the International Congress for Integrative Medicine and Health, the Institute of Noetic Sciences Conference, the International Symposium for Contemplative Studies, and many more.

Postmaterialism is a growing movement in academia and medicine, but also in society in general. With the introduction of the Internet and social media elevating our access to information, false paradigms will begin to lose their grip.

The Influence of the Internet and Social Media

The Internet is a tool through which our interconnection is immensely enhanced, and through this new means of communicating, our expansion toward greater technological and scientific heights and understanding seems boundless. The Internet has allowed us to have access to an infinite library of information at our fingertips in only two decades. This wealth of easily searchable information enables an ordinary individual to have access to and to share paradigm-shattering information, if they so choose. A cultural shift is happening, influenced by the development of social media during the last decade. The impact of the ability to connect to anyone in the world and instantly share information is unprecedented. Humans have never communicated with and been exposed to so many diverse perspectives through near effortless global communication before. These networks have embedded themselves within our culture and have become a primary means of communication.

These are the new programming tools, but with them we are programming ourselves through seeking and sharing information, as opposed to being programmed by a few organizations, institutes, networks on television, or newspapers. With free access to information, dictatorships and perception manipulators can no longer be sustained. With the Internet, there is a greater likelihood for information to be unbiased; the Internet has created the ultimate freedom of the press and free speech. Emerging from this mass web of communication are independent social justice and political movements and organizations. Information spreads rapidly in this system, and as such, cannot be easily sequestered or controlled. New media groups have spawned online, many aimed at unbiased, non-corporate media that cannot be controlled by special interests. Hackers and secret digital information propagators abound, and are sometimes severely punished when caught. The terms "hacktivist" and "hacktivism" have emerged to describe hackers (hacktivists) who break into computer systems for socio-politically motivated purposes (hacktivism). These acts can alter the program by providing seemingly spontaneous new information to the public at large.

This global communication system is sprouting a fusion of multiple religious, scientific, and philosophical systems. Belief systems are cross-pollinating, where people are practicing yoga, attending church, and engaging in ayahuasca ceremonies. Spiritual seekers head to India and elsewhere in record numbers to gather at various gurus' ashrams. We have started to merge many of our previously separate religious programs into non-religious spiritual beliefs. What will be the result of this blend of perspectives, experiences, and ideas on our global society and human relationships, and what is the role of science in this transformation? It is important that science takes a central role in studying the effect, impact, and mechanisms of these experiences, practices, and beliefs.

Conclusion

In this chapter, we have taken a journey from the stagnant sea of materialism to the forefront of an enormous wave of postmaterialism sweeping across our planet. This wave brings new ways of perceiving reality and new ways of being in the world. Postmaterialism opens up vistas that were previously ignored or dismissed, and allows for the exploration of the bounds of human potential. Maybe we are a lot closer than we think to this global transformation; the wave is about to break and humanity will be forever changed. It is my hope that this is a tremendously positive change that results in a greater understanding of the universal aspects of humanity and our place in the cosmos.

With the fear-mongering mainstream media, high-stress society, increased non-communicable disease and psychiatric illness, and impending global financial crises, we absolutely must change our trajectory. What are we doing all this for? Why are we racing around, working overtime, not spending time with our families, living for the weekend, landing ourselves in massive amounts of debt, and being terribly unhappy? Materialism has trapped humanity into an externally driven, superficial way of being. Deeper inquiries into our existence come when we have the time to sit, think, and just be. But the Western world—and even the East—has us imprisoned in a debt-based economy with less time for the important higher aspects of living and deep connection. Filled with techno-gadgets and distracting media, in our spare time we turn from greater meaning and dive into our devices for games and shopping, to be quickly entertained and rewarded. In contrast, postmaterialism values the deeper, existential, immaterial aspects of the human experience, such as transcendent spiritual experiences, whereas materialism claims they do not exist, or worse—that they are dysfunctional, delusional, or simply wishful thinking.

Postmaterialism acknowledges our interconnection on deep, seemingly nonlocal levels, ultimately facilitating more kind and compassionate behaviors towards each other, other species, and the planet. Postmaterialism opens new fields of study that transcend the limits of materialism, many of which have yet to be imagined. May the hearts and minds of humanity open to this new paradigm.

References

Alexander, E. (2012). *Proof of Heaven: A Neurosurgeon's Journey Into the Afterlife.* New York: Simon and Schuster.

American Psychiatric Association. (2013). *Diagnostic and statistical manual of mental disorders (DSM-5®).* American Psychiatric Pub.

Anderson, R., & Braud, W. (2011). *Transforming self and others through research: Transpersonal research methods and skills for the human sciences and humanities.* Albany, NY: SUNY Press.

Baruss, I. (2001). The art of science: Science of the future in light of alterations of consciousness. *Journal of Scientific Exploration,* 15(1), 57-68.

Beauregard, M., Schwartz, G. E., Miller, L., Dossey, L., Moreira-Almeida, A., Schlitz, M., Sheldrake, R., & Tart, C. (2014). Manifesto for a postmaterialist science. *Explore: The Journal of Science and Healing,* 10(5), 272-274.

Beauregard, M., Trent, N. L., & Schwartz, G. E. (2018). Toward a postmaterialist psychology: Theory, research, and applications. *New Ideas in Psychology,* 50, 21-33.

Beischel, J., & Schwartz, G. E. (2007). Anomalous information reception by research mediums demonstrated using a novel triple-blind protocol. *Explore: The Journal of Science & Healing,* 3, 23–27.

Beischel, J., Boccuzzi, M., Biuso, M., & Rock, A. J. (2015a). Anomalous information reception by research mediums under blinded conditions II: replication and extension. *Explore: The Journal of Science and Healing,* 11(2), 136-142.

Beischel, J., Mosher, C., & Boccuzzi, M. (2015b). The possible effects on bereavement of assisted after-death communication during readings with psychic mediums: a continuing bonds perspective. *OMEGA-Journal of Death and Dying,* 70(2), 169-194.

Black, D. S., & Slavich, G. M. (2016). Mindfulness meditation and the immune system: a systematic review of randomized controlled trials. *Annals of the New York Academy of Sciences,* 1373(1), 13–24.

Bonelli, R. M., & Koenig, H. G. (2013). Mental disorders, religion and spirituality 1990 to 2010: a systematic evidence-based review. *Journal of religion and health,* 52(2), 657-673.

Buddharakkhita, A. (1989). *Metta--the philosophy and practice of universal love.* Wheel Publication. Kandy, Shri Lanka: Buddhist Publication Society.

Cardeña, E. (2014). A call for an open, informed study of all aspects of consciousness. *Frontiers in Human Neuroscience*, 8, 17.

Chan, J. S. M., Ng, S. M., Ho, R. T. H., Ziea, E. T. C., Ng, B. F. L., & Chan, C. L. W. (2013). Does Qigong shape body, mind and spiritual health for patients with chronic fatigue syndrome (CFS) in a RCT? *Annals of Behavioral Medicine*, 45 suppl. 2, S278.

Chu, P., Gotink, R. A., Yeh, G. Y., Goldie, S. J., & Hunink, M. M. (2016). The effectiveness of yoga in modifying risk factors for cardiovascular disease and metabolic syndrome: a systematic review and meta-analysis of randomized controlled trials. *European journal of preventive cardiology*, *23*(3), 291-307.

Compton, W. C. (2001). Toward a tripartite factor structure of mental health: Subjective well-being, personal growth, and religiosity. *The Journal of psychology*, 135(5), 486-500.

Dossey, L. (2013). *One mind.* Carlsbad, CA: Hay House.

Eliade, M. (1958). *Birth and rebirth.* New York: Harper.

Fink, P. J. (1992). *Stigma and mental illness.* American Psychiatric Pub.

Fox, K. C., Nijeboer, S., Dixon, M. L., Floman, J. L., Ellamil, M., Rumak, S. P., & Christoff, K. (2014). Is meditation associated with altered brain structure? A systematic review and meta-analysis of morphometric neuroimaging in meditation practitioners. *Neuroscience & Biobehavioral Reviews*, *43*, 48-73.

Goyal, M., Singh, S., Sibinga, E. M., Gould, N. F., Rowland-Seymour, A., Sharma, R., & Ranasinghe, P. D. (2014). Meditation programs for psychological stress and well-being: a systematic review and meta-analysis. *JAMA internal medicine*, *174*(3), 357-368.

Greenslit, N. P., & Kaptchuk, T. J. (2012). Antidepressants and Advertising: Psychopharmaceuticals in crisis. *Yale journal of biology and medicine*, 85(1), 153.

Greyson, B. (1992). Reduced death threat in near-death experiencers. *Death Studies*, 16(6), 523-536.

Hagen, I., & Nayar, U. S. (2014). Yoga for children and young people's mental health and well-being: research review and reflections on the mental health potentials of yoga. *Frontiers in psychiatry, 5*, 35.

Hammerschlag, R., Marx, B. L., & Aickin, M. (2014). Nontouch biofield therapy: a systematic review of human randomized controlled trials reporting use of only nonphysical contact treatment. *Journal of Alternative and Complementary Medicine, 20*(12), 881-892.

James, P. B., Bah, A. J., & Kondorvoh, I. M. (2016). Exploring self-use, attitude and interest to study complementary and alternative medicine (CAM) among final year undergraduate medical, pharmacy and nursing students in Sierra Leone: a comparative study. *BMC Complementary and Alternative Medicine, 16*(1), 1.

James W. (1898). Human immortality: Two supposed objections to the doctrine. In: G. Murphy & R.O. Ballou (Eds.), *William James on psychical research*. New York: Viking; pp. 279-308.

Jammer, M. (2011). *Einstein and religion: physics and theology*. Princeton: Princeton University Press.

Jonas, W.B., Fratts, M., Christopher, G., Jonas, M., & Jonas, S. (2012). Spirituality, Science, and the Human Body. In L. J Miller (Ed.). *The Oxford handbook of psychology and spirituality* (pp 361-378). Oxford University Press USA.

Jones, E. (1957). *The life and work of Sigmund Freud. Vol. 3. The last phase 1919-1939*. New York: Basic Books, Inc.

Kabat-Zinn, J. (1982). An outpatient program in behavioral medicine for chronic pain patients based on the practice of mindfulness meditation: Theoretical considerations and preliminary results. *General hospital psychiatry, 4*(1), 33-47.

Kang, D. H., Jo, H. J., Jung, W. H., Kim, S. H., Jung, Y. H., Choi, C. H., & Kwon, J. S. (2013). The effect of meditation on brain structure: cortical thickness mapping and diffusion tensor imaging. *Social cognitive and affective neuroscience, 8*(1), 27-33.

Kantor, E. D., Rehm, C. D., Haas, J. S., Chan, A. T., & Giovannucci, E. L. (2015). Trends in prescription drug use among adults in the United States from 1999-2012. *JAMA*, 314(17), 1818-1831.

Kessler, R. C., Davis, R. B., Foster, D. F., Van Rompay, M. I., Walters, E. E., Wilkey, S. A., ... & Eisenberg, D. M. (2001). Long-term trends in the use of complementary and alternative medical therapies in the United States. *Annals of internal medicine*, 135(4), 262-268.

Kirsch, I., & Sapirstein, G. (1998). Listening to Prozac but hearing placebo: A meta-analysis of antidepressant medication. *Prevention & Treatment*, 1(2), 2a.

Kirsch, I., Moore, T. J., Scoboria, A., & Nicholls, S. S. (2002). The emperor's new drugs: an analysis of antidepressant medication data submitted to the US Food and Drug Administration. *Prevention & Treatment*, 5(1), 23a.

Koenig, H. G. (2014). Religion, spirituality, and health: a review and update. *Advances in mind-body medicine*, 29(3), 19-26.

Lim, S. A., & Cheong, K. J. (2015). Regular yoga practice improves antioxidant status, immune function, and stress hormone releases in young healthy people: a randomized, double-blind, controlled pilot study. *The Journal of Alternative and Complementary Medicine*, 21(9), 530-538.

Morrissey, J. P., & Goldman, H. H. (1986). Care and treatment of the mentally ill in the United States: Historical developments and reforms. *Annals of the American Academy of Political and Social Science*, 484(1), 12-27.

Noyes, R., Fenwick, P., Holden, J. M., & Christian, S. R. (2009). Aftereffects of pleasurable Western adult near-death experiences. *The handbook of near-death experiences: Thirty years of investigation*, 41-62.

Over, H., & Carpenter, M. (2009). Eighteen-month-old infants show increased helping following priming with affiliation. *Psychological Science*, 20(10), 1189-1193.

Piedmont, R. L. (1999). Does spirituality represent the sixth factor of personality? Spiritual transcendence and the five-factor model. *Journal of personality*, 67(6), 985-1013.

Puchalski, C. M., Blatt, B., Kogan, M., & Butler, A. (2014). Spirituality and health: the development of a field. *Academic Medicine*, 89(1), 10-16.

Richards, P. S., Sanders, P. W., Lea, T., McBride, J. A., & Allen, G. E. (2015). Bringing spiritually oriented psychotherapies into the health care mainstream: A call for worldwide collaboration. *Spirituality in Clinical Practice*, 2(3), 169.

Rubin, M. (2011). Social affiliation cues prime help-seeking intentions. Canadian *Journal of Behavioural Science/Revue Canadienne desSsciences du Comportement*, 43(2), 138.

Ruzek, N. (2007). Transpersonal psychology in context: Perspectives from its founders and historians of American psychology. *Journal of Transpersonal Psychology*, 39(2), 153.

Schwartz, S. A., Schwartz, G. E., & Dossey, L. (2016). Declaration for Integrative, Evidence-Based, End-of-Life Care that Incorporates Nonlocal Consciousness. *Explore (New York, NY)*, 12(3), 162.

Silverman, J. (1967). Shamans and acute schizophrenia. *American anthropologist*, 69(1), 21-31.

Sperry, L. (2012). Spiritually Sensitive Psychotherapy: An Impending Paradigm Shift in Theory and Practice. In L. J. Miller (Ed.) *The Oxford handbook of psychology and spirituality* (pp. 223-233). Oxford University Press, USA.

Stahl, J. E., Dossett, M. L., LaJoie, A. S., Denninger, J. W., Mehta, D. H., Goldman, R., ... & Benson, H. (2015). Relaxation Response and Resiliency Training and Its Effect on Healthcare Resource Utilization. *PloS one*, 10(10), e0140212.

Thrane, S., & Cohen, S. M. (2014). Effect of Reiki therapy on pain and anxiety in adults: an in-depth literature review of randomized trials with effect size calculations. *Pain Management Nursing*, 15(4), 897-908.

Trent, N. L., Beauregard, M., & Schwartz, G. E. (2019). Preliminary development and validation of a scale to measure universal love. *Spirituality in Clinical Practice*.

Waldau, P., & Patton, K. (Eds.). (2009). *A communion of subjects: animals in religion, science, and ethics.* New York: Columbia University Press.

Wang, C. W., Chan, C. H., Ho, R. T., Chan, J. S., Ng, S. M., & Chan, C. L. (2014). Managing stress and anxiety through qigong exercise in healthy adults: a systematic review and meta-analysis of randomized controlled trials. *BMC complementary and alternative medicine, 14*(1), 8.

https://nccih.nih.gov/about/ataglancehttp://news.aha.org/article/more-hospitals-offering-cam-services-health-forum-reports

http://www.princeton.edu/~pear/

http://www.scientificamerican.com/article/is-consciousness-universal/
http://2045.com/ideology

Chapter Four

The Reality of One (and Zero): Saving Science from Materialism

John H Spencer, PhD

"Materialism is false." -Kurt Gödel

Why Bother?

Sometimes it feels pointless to expend any energy clarifying in detail how materialism is false. It is so obviously false that it is almost embarrassing to have to refute it at all, like trying to convince people that ice is cold.

Instead of evaluating counterevidence objectively, some materialists jump straight into derisive ridicule and attack the reputation of their opponents, accusing them of being peddlers of "woo-woo" and pseudoscience. Arguing against materialism can even cause you to lose your academic post or have your presentations censored. But when we say, "Hold on a minute: many of the key pioneering founders of modern physics rejected materialism and were often deeply mystical," some materialists either intensify their insults or do their best to continue ignoring the evidence. Why bother trying to reason with those who refuse to reason?

Too many academics seem not to know (or don't want to know) that one of the greatest logicians in history, Kurt Gödel, a close companion of Albert Einstein, unequivocally rejected materialism. Gödel also believed in a form of reincarnation, the existence of higher beings, and the objective realty of concepts (see Wang, 2001, p. 316). It is quite extraordinary that the established prejudice has been so pervasive that mainstream science can ignore such powerful and universally transformative ideas from one of humanity's greatest logicians.

While this anthology is offering hope that the lingering prejudice of materialism is beginning to crack and wane, it is still not likely to convince the resolute skeptic (at least not without something akin to divine intervention). But perhaps part of the importance of this volume lies in its ability to reach out to those many people who have unwittingly and unwillingly been indoctrinated into the materialist ideology. They may know intuitively that materialism can't be true, yet some part of their mind feels uneasy in admitting that reality includes *both* the physical *and* the non-physical. After all, the mainstream scientific discourse appears to be firmly entrenched in materialism. This anthology offers such people a way to resolve their cognitive dissonance between what they know or intuit to be true and what they believe they are supposed to accept unquestioningly as true. We can offer them a better chance to stand their ground when faced with the prejudice of materialism, regardless of whether such prejudice comes from another person or, worse, from somewhere buried deep within their own mind.

One thing is for certain: if materialism were true, then science would be a complete fiction—perhaps the greatest woo-woo on earth.

What is Materialism, and Why Does it Matter?

There are many complexities involved with the issues surrounding materialism, and it is not possible to discuss them all in such a short chapter, let alone do much more than briefly introduce a few of them. If you are interested in a more detailed examination of such topics and many more related issues, then you may wish to read my book *The Eternal Law: Ancient Greek Philosophy, Modern Physics, and Ultimate Reality*, on which much of the content of this chapter has been based (Spencer, 2012). Nevertheless, it is possible to offer here some relatively brief but powerful support for the rejection of materialism. First, however, we need to try to understand what *materialism* even means, and that also requires understanding what is meant (in this context) by the term *matter*.

Despite subtle variations which will not concern us here,[9] all materialists seem to adhere to the following basic definition of materialism given by theologian and philosopher Keith Ward: *materialism* says "that the only things that exist are material things in space" (Ward, 1996, p. 99). Since Ward is not a materialist, let us see if a materialist philosopher, such as Daniel Dennett, can define the concept any better: "there is only one sort of stuff, namely **matter** – the physical stuff of physics, chemistry, and psychology – and the mind is somehow nothing but a physical phenomenon" (Dennett, 1991, p. 33 (original emphasis). It is true that defining "matter" is not easy, but Dennett does not help, for all he is saying is that matter is physical stuff, and that physical stuff is matter.[10] This sort of circular reasoning is not something Dennett would tolerate from a theist arguing for the reality of God, so we have to wonder why he allows it for materialists such as himself. It is not so much that I think I can offer a better definition of materialism than Dennett; rather, I do not pretend that the issue is so simple.

Let us say that *matter* includes everything from rocks and chairs to planets, subatomic particles, and forces such as gravity. More broadly put: *matter* is anything that exists in space and time and thereby undergoes constant change of one sort or another (i.e., change in motion, size, quality, etc.). While we can certainly argue about the meanings of *time, space, motion*, etc., for our purposes here we can simplify the matter even further: if you are unwilling to let someone drop a 10,000 kilogram block of steel from a height of 100 meters directly onto your head, then you probably have a

---

[9] *For example, central state materialism says that "mental states are contingently identical with states of the central nervous system", but unlike logical behaviorism, it "does not imply that mental sentences can be translated into physical sentences" (McLaughlin in Audi, 2001, p. 687).*

[10] *Some philosophers use the words "physicalism" and "materialism" interchangeably, while others believe that there is a distinction. For example, physicalism tends to allow for forces such as gravity that may not fit the traditional definition of matter, which may be stated as being "an inert, senseless substance, in which extension, figure, and motion, do actually subsist" (Berkeley, 1992, p. 79, Of the Principles of Human Knowledge, Part 1, paragraph 9). (See also F. W. McConnell in Steinkraus, 1966, pp. 50-51, Daniel Stoljar, 2009, and Blackburn in Bunnin and Tsui-James, 2003, p. 65.) My definition of materialism includes forces.*

rough idea of what is meant by the word *matter*. You probably also have a basic idea of motion, and realize that a certain amount of time is required for the block of steel to fall on your head.

Materialism is often assumed to be a scientific fact, but this is completely false. Materialism is a metaphysical position, not a scientific one. *Metaphysics* is a technical term in philosophy that, in general, refers to our attempts to offer a comprehensive rational account of the most fundamental aspects of all reality. So materialism, which claims that only matter is real, is a philosophical position that is not empirically validated through science. And in principle it never could be validated empirically – how can you empirically prove that there is no non-empirical reality? On the contrary, experimental science can only empirically validate what it can measure (and even this presents its own deeper underlying problems), while theoretical science can postulate the reality of "things" beyond our current ability to measure them.

In any case, the question of whether or not anything can be real and also not be physical (or material, or made up of matter) is beyond the strict purview of both experimental and theoretical science. Nevertheless, many great scientists were also philosophers—and sometimes even mystics—and when they reflected more deeply about science, some of them were able to recognize that something beyond physicality must be real, and that this nonphysical realm must underpin all of physical reality. Many of the founders of modern science, going back four hundred years to the advent of quantum physics, have held such views, which have mostly been ignored by mainstream academia. It can be quite disheartening to enter university with the naïve assumption that such a place is there for the open pursuit of truth, only to discover that often it is nothing more than an indoctrination factory aiming to stifle the free inquiry into the nature of reality, an inquiry which is the very backbone of scientific progress and, indeed, of our civilization.

The more common usage of the term *materialist* would seem to be reserved for those who only care about money and expensive possessions, much like in Madonna's 1980's song "Material Girl." This colloquial usage, however, is underpinned by the deeper metaphysical meaning of materialism, and the irony about money is that it is actually an abstract concept connected to value, and *value* itself has no physicality.

We do need material things, because we are "living in a material world." But we are not *just* living in a material world. We are also connected to non-material reality. Indeed, each of us, and all of physicality, emerge out of the non-material. Some proponents of the New Age movement may assert a similar conclusion, but they may not always have the rational or scientific means to back up their claim, and that leaves them (and the whole movement) unnecessarily vulnerable to materialist criticism. It also forces those of us who are committed to the fullest expression of rationality to do a lot of extra work to clarify all the resultant confusion on both sides.

But saying that materialism is false does not mean that immaterialism is therefore true. *Immaterialism* denies that there are any physical objects in reality at all. It essentially says that all of reality is pure mind, or that all so-called material objects are nothing more than a collection of nonphysical qualities (see Pappas in Audi, 2001, p. 418). My view, however, which is rooted in what is known as *Platonic realism*, embraces and yet transcends both materialism and immaterialism. Mind and matter are both real, but mind is metaphysically prior to matter, and is therefore, in a certain sense, more real than matter. This idea very quickly becomes extremely complex, so I will note only that if universal mind were not prior to matter, then matter could never have come together in an orderly, intelligible, mindful way to form a brain (or anything else) in the first place. In fact, the very concept of order implies intelligibility, and the entire universe is pervaded by a nonphysical eternal order. One of the great pioneers in quantum physics, Wolfgang Pauli, put it this way: there is a "cosmic order independent of our choice and distinct from the world of phenomena" (Pauli in Jung & Pauli, 1955, p. 152).

What Pauli means by this is that there is some kind of cosmic order that exists independently of the physical universe, and which nevertheless guides the unfolding of all physical reality. When we understand the implications of his words, we have to admit that he does not sound so different from a medieval theologian describing the infinite intelligence and power of God. Einstein, too, was devoted to striving to "comprehend a portion, be it ever so tiny, of the Reason that manifests itself in nature" (Einstein, 1954, p. 11). Pauli and Einstein are saying that the cosmic order or universal reason—what the ancient philosophers would have called the *logos*—permeates the entire universe. In other words, there must be an inherent rationality to the universe that never changes, but always is just what it is.

If we could allow ourselves to view materiality as a necessary yet insufficient aspect of the totality of reality, and non-materiality as a necessary yet insufficient aspect of the totality of reality, then we would have the possibility of aiming for a far greater scientific understanding, and a much saner and more balanced way of life. Denying the need for at least some material things doesn't seem to make much sense, but it is easier to grasp because we are all familiar with materiality. Our normal experience, or common state of mind, is dominated by materiality in one form or another. But we cannot remain stuck at this level of mind or reality. We need to push our understanding significantly deeper, through rational reflection, scientific investigation, and direct personal experience.

Plato: Still Kicking Ass After Twenty-Five Centuries

This anthology could not have been produced without the prior creation of the relevant technology, which could not have been created without the relevant scientific understanding. Since science would be impossible if materialism were true, then the technology required for you to read this book would not have been created if materialism were true, rendering you unable to read this book. Therefore, since you are reading this book, materialism necessarily cannot be true. How can this be?

An essential point to understand is that the theoretical and metaphysical *foundations* of physics have never been congenial to materialism and have always aimed at unification, simplicity, and the abstract. My former PhD co-supervisor, physicist Peter Rowlands, once put it this way: "the truth is that simple facts are not concrete and concrete facts are not simple" (Rowlands, 1992, p. 21). In other words, a simple law of physics is not concrete, nor is it physical – and a concrete fact, such as a brick wall, is actually quite complex.

Mathematician and philosopher Alfred North Whitehead makes a similar point: "The history of seventeenth century science reads as though it were some vivid dream of Plato or Pythagoras…the paradox is now fully established that the utmost abstractions are the true weapons with which to control our thought of concrete fact" (Whitehead, 1953, p. 41).

There is no logical end to the scientific examination of any object, as we could always pursue ever greater, more detailed analysis. The level of complexity can soon become quite overwhelming, from the tangible qualities we experience through our senses when engaging with the object to the geometric chemical structures and subatomic particles/waves and quantum processes, which are themselves described in the language of mathematics. And it is mathematics that is the key here, as all of mathematics is based on numbers and, as we shall see, numbers are not quite what they seem.

Whitehead writes that "the Platonic world of ideas is the refined, revised form of the Pythagorean doctrine that number lies at the base of the real world." Therefore, "when Einstein and his followers proclaim that physical facts, such as gravitation, are to be construed as exhibitions of local peculiarities of spatio-temporal properties, they are following the pure Pythagorean tradition" (Whitehead, 1948, pp. 42-43). In a similar way as Werner Heisenberg, another one of the key founders of quantum physics, Whitehead also recognized the vital importance of Platonism for modern physics: "Plato and Pythagoras stand nearer to modern physical science than does Aristotle.... The popularity of Aristotelian Logic retarded the advance of physical science throughout the Middle Ages" (Whitehead, 1948, pp. 42-43).

And yes, Heisenberg, the great quantum pioneer, was a Platonist who rejected materialism, a cold, hard fact that has too often been ignored. Indeed, Heisenberg explicitly commends Plato and Pythagoras in opposition to the doctrine of materialism numerous times in his book *Across the Frontiers* (e.g., see Heisenberg, 1974, pp. 11, 22, 24, 26, 27, 105, 110, 116, 117, 118, 140, 171, 172, 173, 174, and 181).

After noting that the philosophy of materialism was developed in the ancient world by Leucippus and Democritus, Heisenberg offers the following observation: "The structure underlying the phenomena is not given by material objects like the atoms of Democritus but by the form that determines the material objects. The Ideas are more fundamental than the objects" (Heisenberg, 1974, pp. 110).

By "Ideas," Heisenberg is referring to *Platonic Ideas*, from the laws of physics to pure forms of beauty and symmetry, which are eternal and nonphysical. Thus, Heisenberg has clearly articulated his view that the nonphysical realm is more primary than the physical. There are so many such examples from great pioneering physicists and other scientists that it should be considered an intellectual embarrassment to continue mindlessly proclaiming the dogmatic falsehood that materialism is an incontrovertible scientific fact. The fact is, Platonism—or, more broadly stated, the perennial philosophy—and thus rational mysticism, is at the root of all science. It always has been, and it always will be.

But just because such great scientists have rejected materialism, this fact in itself does not necessarily mean that materialism is therefore false. But at the very least, materialists cannot simply ignore the fact that so many great pioneering scientists disagree with them. In the final section that follows, I offer my own argument to save science from materialism.

Look Out for Number One!

The number one is such a powerful and beautiful non-thing. And the pure absolute one, or what the ancient Platonic philosophers called *the One*, is the supreme head of all reality, beyond every and all description, law, or anything else. It is super-transcendent, and beyond even that. Heisenberg didn't go as far as the ancient philosophers in trying to clarify the nature of the One, but he did recognize its supreme position: he writes that "the search for the "one," for the ultimate source of all understanding, has doubtless played a similar role in the origin of both religion and science" (Heisenberg, 1974, p. 117).

Let's try this simple exercise by searching not for "the" one but "a" one. To begin, simply point to an object in front of you, such as a cup, and say aloud, "There is one cup." Then do the same thing for a few more objects (i.e. "There is one chair," "There is one table"). And then recognize that each one object itself is composed of several parts, and each part is itself another one part, and that each one part is composed of smaller parts, and each smaller part is itself one part—and so on, all the way down to subatomic particles/waves. When you think seriously about this, it is quite astonishing how a "one something," such as a cup, is actually composed of many "one somethings," and yet all these "one somethings" are unified in such a way as to make "one something else." In the words of the metaphysician, a whole is composed of many parts, where each part is itself a whole (which is also composed of many parts).

A few examples of significant concomitant questions would be: What is the ultimate unifying force underpinning and driving the unification of parts into greater wholes? How does each part, itself a whole, become an original whole? What limit, if any, is there in terms of the divisibility of wholes, i.e., is there infinite division into smaller and smaller parts? Can there be a whole without parts?

The question I wish to focus on here is the last one, and to help us further we will need to add another step to our simple exercise. After pointing at various objects and saying that there is "one something," drop the object in the sentence. Stop saying there is one chair, or one cup, or one table. Instead, simply say "There is one," and then point to the *one* that you are referring to. Don't point to one *something*, point *just to one*. At this point, someone is likely to draw the number "1" or spell "one" and point to that symbolization. But that doesn't work. I am not asking you to point to a symbol. I am asking you to point to what *the symbol actually represents*. The arrangement of letters that form the word "tree" gives us a symbol for something physical, while also referring to a universal idea of "tree" that is not any particular physical tree. But at least part of the meaning of the word "tree" in the sentence "There is a tree over there" refers to something physical in the world. I can point to the actual tree that is represented by the word "tree." So the word "one" or the mathematical symbol "1" are meant to represent something, whether in the world or somewhere else. But, as you may have noticed if you have done this fun experiment, it is impossible for you to point to anything that is physically represented by the symbol "one" or "1." In other words, a pure one, with no parts, cannot exist in physicality. There can be an infinity of relative "one somethings" in physicality, which are wholes made of parts, but a pure one, which is a whole without parts, cannot exist in physicality.

If a pure one were in space, it could be divided, and thus have parts, which would mean it was more than a pure one. If a pure one were in time, it could also be divided between past, present, and future, and thus have parts (of time), and therefore it would not be a pure one without any parts. So, a pure one, a whole without parts—can never be in space or time, and so can never be in physicality.

Now try the same exercise for zero. "There is zero cup," or "There are zero cups," or "There is a zero cup," whichever version you prefer. It won't matter, because *zero symbolizes nothing*. It means, in a mathematical context, that there is no one. So, zero has no physicality, and if you don't believe me, then you are welcome to go sit on all those zero chairs in your kitchen, or spend all the zero money in your bank account.

We are here unfolding in a very brief and simplified manner how materialism would spell the end of science if materialism were (somehow) actually true, and if this type of exercise were carried through to its fullest extent both intellectually and spiritually, we would also be aiming for ultimate reality itself. Indeed, this original approach is a simplified and revised form of what Plato offered in his dialogue called *The Parmenides*, a highly profound and intellectually challenging text.

But what about the number two or three and so on? Well, every number other than zero is, in one way or another, a multiplicity of one (or a part of one, which makes the part a one as well). So 2 just means two 1's, or $2 = 1 + 1$. There is no such thing as a two, or a three. There are only two ones and three ones. And zero, in one sense, is the absence of one.

What matters for us in this chapter is to realize that science ultimately rests upon the mathematical laws of physics. Something cannot happen in biology or chemistry that contradicts the laws of physics. Physics is foundational. And yet, all of the mathematical laws of physics ultimately rely upon the numbers zero and one, which we have already realized do not have any physicality. Here is the key question we should ask ourselves: are the numbers one and zero real or not real?

If the numbers one and zero are real, then we have to admit that something can be real and still not be physical, which in this case means that the foundational scientific laws of the universe are real but not physical, in turn meaning that materialism is false. However, if we refuse to accept that the laws of physics are real because we refuse to admit the falsity of materialism, then we have to say that the laws of physics are, in the end, unreal. And since all of science rests upon the laws of physics, which rely upon the numbers one and zero, which the materialist would say are unreal, then it follows that the whole foundation of science is unreal. But if science is unreal, then it could be no more than a fiction, and so we should all be able to make up any story about the laws of physics that we want. You can say that in your universe "$E = mc^2 + 7$ bananas," and you would be just as right as Einstein. Unfortunately, that would also spell the end of science, because this is not in fact the way physical reality operates.

While there are many further important details that I have had to leave aside in this brief chapter, enough has been said to show that if materialism were true, then that would necessarily mean the end of science.

References

Audi, R. (Ed.) (2001). *The Cambridge Dictionary of Philosophy* (2nd ed.). Cambridge University Press.

Berkeley, G. (1992). *Philosophical Works: including the works on vision* (Intro and Notes: M. R. Ayers). London: J. M Dent & Sons Ltd; Rutland, Vermont: Charles E. Turtle Co., Inc.

Bunnin, N. & Tsui-James, E. P. (Eds.) (2003). *The Blackwell Companion to Philosophy* (2nd ed.). Blackwell Publishing.

Dennett, D. C. (1991). *Consciousness Explained*. USA: Little, Brown & Company Limited.

Einstein, A. (Trans. 1954). *Ideas and Opinions* (Ed. C. Seelig) (Trans. S. Bargmann). London: Alvin Redman Limited.

Heisenberg, W. (Trans. 1974). *Across the Frontiers* (Trans. P. Heath). Harper & Row, Publishers.

Jung, C. G. & Pauli, W. (Trans. 1955). *The Interpretation of Nature and the Psyche* [Jung: 'Synchronicity: An Acausal Connecting Principle' (Trans. R. F. C. Hull); Pauli: 'The Influence of Archetypal Ideas on the Scientific Theories of Kepler' (Trans. P. Silz).] London: Routledge & Kegan Paul.

Rowlands, P. (1992). *Waves versus Corpuscles: The Revolution that Never Was*. Liverpool, UK: PD Publications.

Spencer, J. H. (2012). *The Eternal Law: Ancient Greek Philosophy, Modern Physics, and Ultimate Reality*. Vancouver: Param Media.

Steinkraus, W. E. (Ed.). (1966). *New Studies in Berkeley's Philosophy*. Holt, Rinehart and Winston, Inc.

Stoljar, D. (2009). 'Physicalism', *Stanford Encyclopedia of Philosophy*, First published Tue Feb 13, 2001; substantive revision Wed Sep 9, 2009. Retrieved from: http://plato.stanford.edu/entries/physicalism/ [Last accessed January 27, 2012.]

Wang, H. (2001). *A Logical Journey: From Gödel to Philosophy*. Cambridge: MIT Press.

Ward, K. (1996). *God, Chance & Necessity*. Oxford: Oneworld Publications.

Whitehead, A. N. (1948). *Essays in Science and Philosophy*. London: Rider and Company.

Whitehead, A. N. (1953). *Science and the Modern World*. Cambridge: Cambridge University Press.

Chapter Five

Cosmic Connections: Towards a Postmaterialist Science of Self

Lorne Schussel, PhD

John H Spencer, PhD[11]

The last four centuries of scientific innovation began with the emergence of the Copernican Revolution, a movement that redefined human perception and finally overturned the geocentric assumption that the earth was at the center of the universe. We now looked at the distant stars with a new sense of the unknown, wondering more deeply about our place in the far-reaching, seemingly inconceivable universe. However, there was also a feeling of isolation, as we were no longer the center of this vast cosmos.

The next scientific revolution came with quantum physics, which, in addition to ushering in extraordinary technological innovations, also helped us have a greater understanding of our cosmic connections. Among many astonishing aspects of quantum physics, one of the most important is quantum "entanglement," a term coined by the Nobel Prize winning physicist Erwin Schrödinger. The basic idea is that in quantum physics two entangled particles can only be described with reference to each other, regardless of the distance between them. In other words, there is some sort of nonlocal connection.

This revolutionary idea of entanglement was in apparent contradiction to the existing materialistic and deterministic paradigm, often referred to as the billiard ball universe. On this view, the universe is composed of entirely separate objects, and all interactions are purely mechanical, where

---

[11] *The authors would like to thank Dr. Lisa Miller at Columbia University for her helpful comments on Dr. Lorne Schussel's original draft.*

one object must strike another object for there to be any sort of causal relationship. That outdated view, however, has been challenged by modern physics, and that challenge has implications that reach far beyond physics, into our holistic connections to each other, the earth, and even to other aspects of ourselves, such as our own creativity.

Two other great pioneering thinkers recognized the holistically interconnected nature of this new paradigm – another Nobel Prize winning physicist Wolfgang Pauli and the ground-breaking psychoanalyst Carl Jung. However, their deeper recognition of our connected nature occurred not in a physics laboratory, as one might imagine, but in a therapy room.

Pauli had been struggling with the profound changes in his field of study, and initially the paradox of the new quantum revolution left him in a state of both awe and neurosis. At the time he humorously stated that, "physics is again terribly confused. In any case, it is too difficult for me, and I wish I had been a movie comedian or something of the sort and had never heard of physics" (Pauli, in Kuhn, 2012, p. 83).

In 1932, during both a personal and professional malaise, Pauli met with Jung for psychological healing. Despite his success in physics, Pauli had suffered a nervous breakdown following his divorce from his wife. After meeting with Jung for several years and undergoing the analysis of 400 of his dreams, the psychologically transformative process resulted in Jung's publishing *Psychology and Alchemy* (1954).

The extraordinary importance of their relationship should have been made well known and studied in great depth by philosophers, physicists, psychologists, psychiatrists, and sociologists (among others), but instead, it has mostly been ignored until relatively recently (and even now, it is still not receiving anything close to the kind of attention it deserves). Perhaps one of the reasons for not wanting to look deeply into this topic is because the evidence to be discovered in doing so strongly disavows materialism. Fortunately, things are starting to change.

Born of a "quantum mysticism," where *physic* meets *psyche*, the meeting of Pauli and Jung reflects the synthesis between the outer material and inner psychological worlds. It is an important metaphor for a postmaterialist science, which recognizes that both physical and nonphysical aspects of reality are real.

One important branch of postmaterialist science concerns the recognition that consciousness connects our inner experience with our outer experience. Indeed, everything is coordinated by a coherent and "entangled" universe, where all matter is necessarily intertwined, from physical states at a cosmological scale, to the way our inner minds are linked to the outside world. Erwin Schrödinger, another Nobel prize winning quantum pioneer, expanded on these initial ideas and imbued them with philosophical revelations about the nature of the self in relation to the universe. For example, he stated that:

"Hence this life of yours which you are living is not merely a piece of the entire existence, but is in a certain sense the whole... *Tat tvamasi*, this is you, I am in the east and in the west, I am below and above, I am this whole world" (Shrödinger, 1967, p. 22).

He also believed that the only task of science that really counts is the one that helps us answer the "one great philosophical question that embraces all others, the one that [third-century Platonic philosopher] Plotinus expressed by his brief [question]...*who are we*?" (Schrödinger's original emphasis) (Shrödinger, in Spencer, 2012, p. 13).

While it is fascinating to see Schrödinger make such comments about the nature of the self, is there any further scientific evidence that the universe is entangled? As we shall see below, there is.

An important mathematical explication, known as Bell's theorem, was famously conceived by John Bell in 1964 to explain how, based on electron spin, separated electrons could share the same properties even in a distant state. Bell suggested that one measuring device could influence the reading of another through a signal being instantaneously propagated.

Almost 20 years after the theorem was formulated, a French physicist named Alain Aspect and his research team were able to demonstrate the theorem experimentally using an excited calcium atom. During the experiment, the atom emits a pair of photons that travel in opposite directions along a fiberoptic cable (Aspect et al., 1982a,b). As the two photons move away from each other like cars moving in opposite directions, a special optical crystal alters the path of one of the photons, in order to divert it along a different path to another sensor. On the opposite side there is no crystal present, thus no possible way to divert the trajectory. The amazing discovery by Aspect and his team was that during the time the optical crystal was dropped down to affect the trajectory of the first photon, the second photon that was moving in the opposite direction also simultaneously exhibited a change in trajectory, mimicking the properties of the first photon (Blinder, 2004; Gill, 2003). This discovery verified Bell's theorem, and demonstrated the interconnected or entangled aspect of the fundamental nature of physical reality. Consequently, the assumed boundaries of physical reality had been forever altered.

Recently, Masahiroi Hotta of Tohoku University demonstrated that even energy could be teleported between the entangled photon pairs using squeezed vacuum states, theoretically allowing the procedure to work at any distance (Hotta et al., 2014; Verdon-Akzam et al., 2016). This emerging proof that energy and matter can be connected even at a distance could also intimate that the brain is more advanced than an isolated group of circuits, hinting at the inner and outer worlds being connected in ways not previously understood. (For further studies, see Kataoka et al., Bouwmeester et al., 1999; Sackett et al., 2000; Zhao et al., 2004; Lu et al., 2007; Prevedel et al., 2009; Häffner et al., 2005; Krauter et al., 2013; Li et al., 2016; Lee et al., 2011; Dolde et al., 2013; Hensen et al., 2015; Persinger et al., 2003).

75 years before the quantum entanglement experiments were conducted near the Danube river in Austria, Wolfgang Pauli's father, a lecturer at the University of Vienna, had numerous extramarital affairs that ended with Pauli's mother committing suicide. These events proved to have created a permanent impression on young Pauli's developing mind. The trauma of his youth manifested in deeply disturbing dreams that he reported as a grown man (Bair, 2003). As discussed at the beginning of this paper, in 1932 Pauli sought therapy from Jung and began treatment with the psychoanalyst. During their work together, Pauli helped propel Jung deeper into his understanding of the human psyche. Just as two photons can be connected at a distance, and two physically distant systems could

be related without the limit of time, Jung believed there was a similar connection between the psyche and matter (Conger, 2005; Jung, 1954).

For example, Jung had proposed that psyche and matter "ultimately rest on irrepresentable transcendental factors," and that "it is not only possible but even fairly probable that psyche and matter are two different aspects of one and the same thing" (Jung, 1954, para. 418).

However, to reconcile this perspective, the persisting view of consciousness would have to evolve beyond common mechanistic and reductionist assumptions. In other words, consciousness cannot be reduced to and confined by a group of moving parts.

Present theories of the brain posit that it is an isolated group of circuits with separation between the inner and outer world. This reductionist model of the brain, a permutation of the "neuronal doctrine" emerging from the work of Santiago Ramón y Cajal and Camillo Golgi, asserts that it is an electro-chemical computer, and that consciousness is isolated to space within the confined circuits of the brain (Shepherd, 1991; Simpkins, 2010).

Expanding beyond the theory of the brain as an isolated machine, a postmaterialist perspective proposes that the mind is analogous to a "quantum computer." The brain is part of a photonic information network connected to all parts of the world and the inner states of all human minds. Photons and electrons within the brain can wirelessly transmit information with other forms of matter in the outside world. Emerging scientific evidence has started to broach the suppositions synthesized in these theories, and evidence of photonic activity within biological processes, cellular signaling, and even within the brain itself have started to be experimentally demonstrated (Ives et al., 2014; Rattemeyer et al., 1981; Popp, 1986; Kataoka et al., 2001). While this may seem odd to those who cling, often unconsciously, to mechanistic, materialistic, and reductionist assumptions, something akin to this postmaterialist understanding is necessary to account for numerous unusual events, such as out-of-body experiences, telepathy, and so forth. There is also growing scientific evidence for these experiences.

For example, consider a bio-photon, which basically refers to the emission of weak light from varying biological sources. Innovations in cellular biology and biophysics have begun to touch upon the importance of bio-photons and their presence in different human physiological processes, and even the complexity of human consciousness.

Bio-photons have also been found in the central nervous system. In a landmark research paper by Yasushi Isojima, a direct relationship was found between the neural metabolic activity in a rat's brain and the emission of bio-photons, specifically in the hippocampus. Isojima's experiment was the first study to suggest that bio-photons could be related to the central nervous system and even memory function (Isojima et al., 1995). Masaki Kobayashi built on Isojima's work and also found the emission of bio-photons in the rat's cortex, with emission being correlated to both oxidative stress and neural metabolism (Kobayashi et al., 1999). The same fascinating line of research has even extended to human brain tissue, and directly linked to neural tissue oxidation (Kataoka, 2001).

Recently, István Bókkon, a Hungarian bioengineer, led a series of innovative studies, which found bio-photon emission to be present during activation of the visual cortex. During his experiments, Bokken asked participants to sit quietly and actively imagine white light. At the same time, the control group was asked to engage in mundane thoughts. When he compared the two groups, he found a significant change in the emission of bio-photons from the right hemisphere only in the group who were asked to imagine white light. He concluded that the active imagining condition could affect the nature of bio-photon behavior within human neural metabolic processes. The discovery suggested that even human cognition could influence photon emission (Bókkon, 2009; Bókkon et al., 2010; Kataoka et al., 2001) (15-17). (For further studies, see Dotta & Persinger, 2009, 2012; Burke et al., 2013; Scott et al., 2015; Berzhanskaya et al., 1995; Bókkon, 2005; Sun et al., 2013; Valone, 2012; Rusov et al., 2012; Tesla, 1982; Lindorff, 2004; Várlaki et al., 2008; Atmanspacher & Fuchs, 2014; Creath & Schwartz, 2005).

Neural Entanglement and the Global Connection

Emerging evidence has begun to support entanglement of groups of photons, physical structures, and even larger neural systems. There has been evidence of photon entanglement of two separated systems of photons ranging from three to six particles per system (Bouwmeester et al., 1999; Sackett et al., 2000; Zhao et al., 2004; Lu et al., 2007; Prevedel et al., 2009). Further research has shown that distally separated ions, and even a pair of rubidium atoms, could be entangled (Häffner et al., 2005; Hofmann, et al., 2012). Recently, clouds of cesium gas have exhibited the same entanglement properties as in the previous studies (Krauter et al., 2013). And even now, proposals of entanglement of a microorganism are emerging (Li & Yin, 2016).

In 2016, Tongcang Li and Zhang-Qi Yin expanded on this concept and proposed an experiment that would allow a microorganism to suspend between two different quantum states and be projected from one space to another. Taking the thought even further, they proposed a method for projecting an entire organism into another space in a way similar to what we think of as "teleportation." Amazingly, their work in the future could explain the experience of astral projection and remote viewing. In these phenomena, meditators claim to be able to project their mind, and even a simulated representation of their physical body, into another space, and have described lucid experiences of interacting in this alternate location. Projecting the quantum state of an organism into an alternate space might be the closest humanity has ever come to providing a possible method for "teleportation."

In further support of macro entanglement of two neural systems, there has been other experimental evidence linked to larger non-biological systems. The entanglement of separated diamonds at room temperature has recently been experimentally verified (Lee et al., 2011; Dolde et al., 2013). In 2011, Ian Walmsley and his colleagues at Oxford University aimed an optical pulse at the diamonds to induce a vibration, causing two diamonds to have their physical properties entangled. The initial experiment was a success, and has been replicated several times at different research laboratories throughout the world. In a recent experiment popularized in the New York Times, Ronald Hanson's research group at The Kavli Institute of Nanoscience, Delft, was able to produce the same entanglement effect at a distance of 1.3 km. This experiment, published in *Nature*, takes a significant step towards validating empirically the entanglement of larger scale systems (Dolde et al., 2013; Hensen et al., 2013).

Michael Persinger, a Professor at Laurentian University in Ontario, used EEG to monitor pairs of siblings who were separated into two different rooms. One sibling in the pair was asked to imagine or "feel the presence of the other sibling." Persinger measured EEG power during 20 seconds of "feeling projection." The results indicated that the corresponding sibling had a spike in parietal theta EEG power only during the moments of projected intention. It is interesting to note that parietal lesions have been associated with active out-of-body experiences, and this region of the brain could even be related to connectivity beyond the body (Brandt et al., 2005).

Persinger replicated the same study using strangers in one group and experimentally "entangled" pairs in another, and found the effect was stronger when pairs were "experimentally bonded." This "bonded" group refers to the participants that took part in the "feeling presence" exercise mentioned above (Persinger et al., 2003, 2008, 2010, Persinger & Lavallee, 2010; Dotta et al., 2009).

With some compelling initial research under his belt, Persinger and his team decided to take the experiment a step further and tested the experimental paradigm underlying human connectivity. He conducted a series of studies in which he connected pairs of individuals to head mounts with a rotating magnetic field and seated them in two separate, acoustically shielded rooms. However, instead of the "feeling presence" exercise used to bond the strangers in the previous experiment, in these experiments he hypothesized that the magnetic field itself would be enough to "bond" the pair. The results confirmed his hypothesis, and yielded a correlated change in EEG power during the light stimulus. As Persinger noted "the change in EEG power was not elicited when the shared magnetic fields were not generated." He also examined cerebral bio-photon emission and tested whether the same process would affect this even subtler process, and whether it could possibly be related to the "quantum effects" summarized in the previous research paradigm. The results did in fact confirm the hypothesis, and photon emission spiked in the separated partner's head despite receiving no light stimulus (Persinger & Lavallee, 2010; Persinger et al., 2003; Dotta et al., 2011).

These experiments were important in that they suggested that not only could "feeling presence" or a contemplative state connect individual subjects, but a larger scale force or magnetic field could possibly affect this connectivity. To further explore this notion, Persinger and Blake Dotta tested the process in vitro, looking exclusively at bio-photon emissions from two groups of carcinoma cells. After irradiating the cell groups with a magnetic field, the experimenter flashed a light to only one cell group, and tested for bio-photon emission in both groups. The results showed a significant spike in photon emission in the non-light flashed group that occurred when the other group received its light stimulus. This work has recently been replicated, and seems to suggest compelling evidence that an underlying magnetic field may be responsible for this experience of connectivity (Persinger et al., 2003; Dotta et al., 2012, 2014; Dotta & Persinger, 2012; Burke et al, 2013; Scott et al., 2015).[12]

The Mind and the Greater Field

The possibility of neural entanglement has emerged as a fascinating new line of research, and beckons questions about the nature of individual consciousness, as well as the connection of one's mind to a greater field. We already know that human intention can help the healing process of damaged leaves, and that two cancer cells can be coupled through a distant magnetic field. However, what consequences might this have for the way we interact with the world? How does the connection to a global field affect

---

[12] *See also Wackermann et al., 2003; Wackermann et al., 2004; Persinger et al., 2003; Standish et al., 2003; Richards et al., 2005; Dotta et al., 2009; Persinger et al., 2003, 2008, 2010; Persinger & Lavallee, 2010)*

all aspects of human existence, from human innovations, through psychological healing, to the recesses of our unconscious? Could the origins of this connectivity begin with the notion of a "quantum brain" as propagated via cerebral bio-photons?

Even though the relationship between bio-photon emission and a geo-magnetic field has not been extensively investigated, a direct relationship was found between geo-magnetic storms and photon emission, which increased over 300 percent during these global events, and became synchronized for measured intervals (Berzhanskaya et al., 1995). This discovery is significant, because it begins to establish a relationship between bio-photon emission, which is present during cerebral processes, and geo-magnetic behavior, which could even modulate connectivity (and cerebral function, to some degree). Istavan Bókkon suggested that "visual experiences, particularly dreams, may actually be awareness of a matrix or field of biophotons within the cerebrum," and first measured the bio-photonic activity during dream states (Bókkon, 2005; Dotta et al., 2011). This work was supported by Dotta and Persinger, who found that unconsciousness processes and human premonition may be related to geo-magnetic activity. They found correlations between brain generated bio-photons and geomagnetic influences (Dotta & Persinger, 2009).

However, the idea that the human mind, both conscious and unconscious, is connected directly to earth's magnetic field is not completely novel. Nikola Tesla suggested the concept when he first demonstrated the notion of wireless power transfer at a lecture at Columbia University in 1891 (Sun et al., 2013). He proposed that the transmission of energy and information could occur on a global level, and was even one of the earliest scientists to note the existence of the Schumann cavity (Valone, 2002). Schumann calculated that all electrical activity on earth resonated in a standing wave between the earth's crust and ionosphere averaged to 7.83 Hz (Rusov et al., 2012). Tesla observed this phenomenon when he was monitoring electrical magnetic radiations due to lightning discharges, and calculated a similar wavelength and frequency to Schumann of around 8 Hz (Valone, 2002). Due to the similarity of this frequency to the frequency range of deeply relaxed states, researchers have suggested a connection between Schumann's resonance and the ability of the human mind to interface within a global field. (See also Oschman, 2000). Furthermore, it may explain the source for dreams, visions, and other "otherworldly" experiences that appear subjectively to come from beyond the body. Jung referred to the information contained in this matrix of global energy as the "collective unconscious."

Tesla described being able to tune into this resonant field both unconsciously and consciously. He credited it as the basis for his discovery of the AC induction motor, a vision which appeared spontaneously before his eyes. According to Tesla's own autobiography, the image appeared in physical form as if made of "metal and stone," like a "flash of lightning." For Tesla, this was a supernatural experience of such significance that he compared it to Pygmalion's sculpture coming to life (Tesla, 1982).

Cosmic Order and the Cosmic Dream

Coming back to the intertwining experiences of Jung and Pauli, part of a breakthrough in Jung's treatment of Pauli occurred in 1938, after Pauli had dreamed of a "cosmic clock." The clock is referred to as "world" clock in several sources; however, it could be called a "cosmic clock" in that it appears to represent patterns of the universe on a greater cosmological scale. This may be similar to what Plato referred to as the "World Soul," which really meant the soul of the entire universe, the cosmic soul.

Jung interpreted the clock as bearing a resemblance to a "mandala" and attributed the dream to a deep "psychic transformational process." In the dream, the clock was divided into four sections, and surrounded by a golden ring with each hand emitting energetic pulses of a specific frequency. Jung compared the four sections to the four chambers of the human heart, and viewed the quaternity as part of the existence of an "archetypal god-image." From Pauli's perspective, the clock represented the pulses of the universe, and he understood it mathematically as being both infinite and infinitesimal at the same time. In its complexity, Pauli described the clock as evoking a state of "sublime harmony" (Lindorff, 2004).

As Jung continued the analysis of Pauli's dreams, he noted that they would often contain themes related to "numinous" or "archetypal images." At certain times, mathematical terms would spontaneously appear to explain the meaning of the dream metaphor as an explanation for a physical phenomenon. In the cosmic clock dream, the universe is represented as a greater cosmic rhythm, and also as a physical mathematical language that describes the structure of the atom (Lindorff, 2004; Várlaki et al., 2008; Atmanspacher & Fuchs, 2014).

In fact, Pauli believed that there is a "cosmic order independent of our choice and distinct from the world of phenomena." Since this cosmic order, what Einstein had called "Reason" (similar to what the ancient Greek philosophers called the "Logos") is distinct from the world, then it must not be physical. It is a universal that is independent of any particular, and yet it guides the unfolding of all particulars. It follows, therefore, that the cosmic order is not physical (since it is distinct from the world) and yet it is still real, and that necessarily implies that materialism is false. (See Spencer, 2012, p. 14 for Pauli reference and further discussion.)

Pauli's powerful cosmic clock vision reflects a manifestation of the connection between the inner state of the mind and the external physical world. He was able to receive information about the nature of the physical universe in both symbolic and mathematical terms, which appeared spontaneously to his inner psyche. And Pauli was not alone in this regard.

Fanchon Fröhlich, who had studied with Rudolph Carnap and was a friend of Schrödinger's (The Guardian, 2016), related a fascinating story about her late husband, Herbert Fröhlich, a highly acclaimed physicist at the University of Liverpool. His scientific contributions are extensive, including "providing the first successful explanation of superconductivity as the result of an electron-phonon interaction," and being "a pioneer in introducing quantum field theory into solid-state physics" (Hyland & Rowlands, 2006, quoted in Spencer, 2012, p. 63).

However, the foundation of Fröhlich's scientific genius was his direct mystical experience. F. Fröhlich relates how her husband believed "that there is an impersonal, non-individualistic path or Tao embedded both in the world and in the mind, and that at some deep level of insight they coalesce." He also regarded the role of abstract mathematics "as a source of wonder and mystery," and he often said that "in the creative process of thinking his mind goes out from his human frame and *becomes* the physical particle and field situation, feeling directly how they tend to behave." He would then use mathematical techniques "both to capture this unknown situation and as an anchor so the mind can return to his own brain or everyday personality" (Fröhlich in Hyland & Rowlands, 2006, original emphasis, quoted in Spencer, 2012).

Fröhlich's mind journeys into the subatomic realm were a vital part of his scientific endeavors, but it is this very sort of experience that is almost ubiquitously ignored because it does not fit the materialist's model of science being nothing more than collecting data and providing straightforward logical analysis. In fact, much to the consternation of materialists, Pauli, Fröhlich, Schrödinger, and many of the greatest pioneering theoretical physicists throughout history have held some sort of mystical view about the nature of reality, which is clarified in detail in Spencer's *The Eternal Law* (2012).

Both Pauli's cosmic dream and Fröhlich's mind journeys offer good examples of psyche and matter merging in a moment of time. And it is the branch of postmaterialist scientist that we have been discussing here that is necessary to explore further in order to help us understand this example of cosmic entanglement. But to do so, a much greater shift in our scientific focus must occur, one that goes beyond mere mechanistic materialism. We need to seek a postmaterialist framework to help us understand how our inner and outer experiences share a simultaneous reality.

As we enter a new era of scientific thought, we may be surprised to learn the nuances of how the inner and external world are intimately related through both psychological and quantum forces. Human innovation and invention will soon be attributed to a state of greater connectivity, as opposed to the triumph of individual ego. The self—our deepest, truest self—is cosmically connected with the entire universe.

Fröhlich and Pauli in their otherworldly states could access certain truths beyond the capacity of our ordinary limited sense of self, and thereby better understand the nature of reality from both psychological and physical perspectives. Towards the end of his life, Jung too had a vision where he found himself in the heavens above earth, and discovered that his true nature was beyond the limitations of persona or time—a state where he asserted: "past, present, and future are one" (Main, 2004). It is in the connected state that all invention and innovation are possible, a state beyond ego, and it is the task of a postmaterialist science to investigate such higher states so far as we are able.

References

Aspect, A., Dalibard, J., & Roger, G. (1982), Experimental Test of Bell's Inequalities Using Time-Varying Analyzers. *Physical review letters,* 49 (25), 1804.

Aspect, A., Grangier, P., & Roger, G. (1982). Experimental realization of Einstein-Podolsky-Rosen-Bohm Gedankenexperiment: a new violation of Bell's inequalities. *Physical review letters,* 49 (2), 91.

Atmanspacher, H., &. Fuchs, C. A. (2014). *The Pauli-Jung Conjecture and its impact today.* Andrews UK Limited.

Bair, D. (2003). *Jung: A Biography.* New York: Back Bay Books.

Berzhanskaya, L. Y., et al. (1995). Bacterial bioluminescent activity as a pointer to geomagnetic disturbances. *Biophysics,* 4.40, 761-764.

Blinder, S. M. (2004). *Introduction to quantum mechanics: in chemistry, materials science, and biology.* Academic Press.

Bókkon, I. (2005). Dreams and neuroholography: an interdisciplinary interpretation of development of homeotherm state in evolution. *Sleep and Hypnosis* 7.2, 47.

Bókkon, I., Salari, V., Tuszynski, J. A., & Antal, I. (2010). Estimation of the number of biophotons involved in the visual perception of a single-object image: Biophoton intensity can be considerably higher inside cells than outside. *Journal of Photochemistry and Photobiology B: Biology,* 100(3), 160-166.

Bókkon, I. (2009). Visual perception and imagery: a new molecular hypothesis. *BioSystems*, 96(2), 178-184.

Bouwmeester, D., et al. (1999). Observation of three-photon Greenberger-Horne-Zeilinger entanglement. *Physical Review Letters*, 82.7, 1345.

Brandt, C., Brechtelsbauer, D., Bien, C. G., & Reiners, K. (2005). [Out-of-body experience as possible seizure symptom in a patient with a right parietal lesion]. *Der Nervenarzt*, 76(10), 1259-1261.

Burke, R. C., et al. (2013). Experimental demonstration of potential entanglement of brain activity over 300 Km for pairs of subjects sharing the same circular rotating, angular accelerating Magnetic fields: verification by s_LORETA, QEEG measurements. *Journal of Consciousness Exploration & Research* 4.1, 35-44.

Conger, J. (2005). *Jung and Reich: The Body as Shadow*. North Atlantic Books.

Creath, K., & Schwartz, G. E. (2005). What biophoton images of plants can tell us about biofields and healing. *Journal of Scientific Exploration*, 19.4, 531-550.

Dolde, F., et al. (2013). Room-temperature entanglement between single defect spins in diamond. *Nature Physics*, 9.3, 139-143.

Dotta, B. T., & Persinger, M. A. (2009). Dreams, time distortion and the experience of future events: a relativistic, neuroquantal perspective. *Sleep and Hypnosis*, 11.2, 29.

Dotta, B. T., Mulligan, B. P., Hunter, M. D., & Persinger, M. A. (2009). Evidence of macroscopic quantum entanglement during double quantitative electroencephalographic measurements of friends vs strangers. *NeuroQuantology*, 7, 548-551.

Dotta, B. T., et al. (2011). Photon emissions from human brain and cell culture exposed to distally rotating magnetic fields shared by separate light-stimulated brains and cells. *Brain research*, 1388, 77-88.

Dotta, B. T., Saroka, K. S., &. Persinger, M. A. (2012). Increased photon emission from the head while imagining light in the dark is correlated with changes in electroencephalographic power: Support for Bókkon's Biophoton Hypothesis." *Neuroscience letters*, 513.2, 151-154.

Dotta, B. T., et al. (2014). Photon emission from melanoma cells during brief stimulation by patterned magnetic fields: is the source coupled to rotational diffusion within the membrane. *General Physiology and Biophysics*, 33, 63-73.

Dotta, B. T., & Persinger, M. A. (2012). "Doubling" of local photon emissions when two simultaneous, spatially-separated, chemiluminescent reactions share the same magnetic field configurations. *Journal of Biophysical Chemistry*, 3.01, 72.

Gill, R. D. (2003). Accardi contra Bell (cum mundi): The impossible coupling. In Moore, M., Froda, S., & Léger, C. (Eds.). *Mathematical Statistics and Applications: Festschrift for Constance van Eeden*, Vol. 42, pp. 133-154. Beachwood, Ohio: Institute of Mathematical Statistics.

Häffner, H., et al. (2005). Scalable multiparticle entanglement of trapped ions. *Nature*, 438, 643–646.

Hensen, B., et al. (2015). Experimental loophole-free violation of a Bell inequality using entangled electron spins separated by 1.3 km. *arXiv preprint* arXiv:1508.05949.

Hofmann, J., et al. (2012). Heralded entanglement between widely separated atoms. *Science*, 337.6090, 72-75.

Hotta, M., Matsumoto, J., & Yusa, G. (2014). Quantum energy teleportation without a limit of distance. *Physical Review A*, 89(1), 012311.

Isojima, Y., et al. (1995): Ultraweak biochem iluminescence detected from rat hippocampal slices. *NeuroReport*, 6.4, 658-660.

Ives, J. A., van Wijk, E. P., Bat, N., Crawford, C., Walter, A., Jonas, W. B., ... & van der Greef, J. (2014). Ultraweak photon emission as a non-invasive health assessment: a systematic review. *PloS one*, 9(2), e87401.

Jung, C. G. (1954). *The Collected Works of C. G. Jung. Volume 8, Structure & Dynamics of the Psyche*. London, UK: Routledge and Kegan Paul.

Kataoka, Y., Cui, Y., Yamagata, A., Niigaki, M., Hirohata, T., Oishi, N., & Watanabe, Y. (2001). Activity-dependent neural tissue oxidation emits intrinsic ultraweak photons. *Biochem Biophys Res Commun*, 285(4), 1007-11. doi:10.1006/bbrc.2001.5285. (http://www.greenmedinfo.com/article/activity-dependent-neural-tissue-oxidation-emits-intrinsic-ultraweak-photons)

Kobayashi, M., et al. (1999). In vivo imaging of spontaneous ultraweak photon emission from a rat's brain correlated with cerebral energy metabolism and oxidative stress. *Neuroscience research*, 34.2, 103-113.

Krauter, H., et al. (2013) Deterministic quantum teleportation between distant atomic objects. *Nature Physics*, 9.7, 400-404.

Lee, K. C., et al. (2011). Entangling macroscopic diamonds at room temperature. *Science*, 334.6060, 1253-1256.

Li, T., & Yin, Z-Q. (2016). Quantum superposition, entanglement, and state teleportation of a microorganism on an electromechanical oscillator. *Science Bulletin*, 61.2, 163-171.

Lindorff, D. (2004). *Pauli and Jung: The Meeting of Two Great Minds*. Wheaton, IL: Quest Books.

Lu, C-Y, et al. (2007). Experimental entanglement of six photons in graph states. *Nature Physics*, 3.2, 91-95.

Main, R. (2004). *The rupture of time: Synchronicity and Jung's critique of modern western culture*. Abingdon-on-Thames, UK: Routledge.

Oschman, J. L. (2000). *Energy medicine: the scientific basis*. NY: Churchill Livingstone.

Popp, F. A. (1986). On the coherence of ultraweak photon emission from living tissues. Disequilibrium and self-organization. In C. W. Kilmister (Ed.), *Disequilibrium and Self-Organization* (pp. 207-230). Dordrecht: D. Reidel Publishing Co.

Persinger, M. A., & Lavallee, C. F. (2010). Theoretical and experimental evidence of macroscopic entanglement between human brain activity and photon emissions: implications for quantum consciousness and future applications. *Journal of Consciousness Exploration & Research,* 1.7, 785-807.

Persinger, M. A., Koren, S. A, & Tsang, E. W. (2003). Enhanced power within a specific band of theta activity in one person while another receives circumcerebral pulsed magnetic fields: a mechanism of influence at a distance? *Perceptual and Motor Skills,* 97, 877-894.

Persinger, M. A., Saroka, K. S., Lavallee, C. F. Booth, J. N., Hunter, M. D., Mulligan, B. P., Koren, S. A., Wu, H. P., & Gang, N. (2010). Correlated cerebral events between physically and sensory isolated pairs of subjects exposed to yoked circumcerebral magnetic fields. *Neuroscience Letters,* 486 (3), 231–234.

Persinger, M. A., Tsang, E. W., Booth, J. N., & Koren, S. A. (2008). Enhanced power within a predicted narrow band of theta activity during stimulation of another by circum cerebral weak magnetic fields after weekly spatial proximity: evidence for macroscopic entanglement? *NeuroQuantology,* 6: 7-21.

Prevedel, R., et al. (2009). Experimental realization of Dicke states of up to six qubits for multiparty quantum networking. *Physical review letters,* 103.2, 020503.

Rattemeyer, M., Popp, F. A., & Nagl, W. (1981). Evidence of photon emission from DNA in living systems. *Naturwissenschaften,* 68(11), 572-573.

Richards, T. L., et al. (2005). Replicable functional magnetic resonance imaging evidence of correlated brain signals between physically and sensory isolated subjects. *Journal of Alternative & Complementary Medicine: Research on Paradigm, Practice, and Policy,* 11.6: 955-963.

Rusov, V. D., et al. (2012). Can Resonant Oscillations of the Earth Ionosphere Influence the Human Brain Biorhythm? *arXiv preprint* arXiv:1208.4970.

Sackett, C. A., et al. (2000). Experimental entanglement of four particles. *Nature,* 404.6775, 256-259.

Shrödinger E. (1964). *My View of the World*. Cambridge: Cambridge University Press.

Scott, M. A., et al. (2015). Experimental Production of Excess Correlation across the Atlantic Ocean of Right Hemispheric Theta-Gamma Power between Subject Pairs Sharing Circumcerebral Rotating Magnetic Fields (Part I). *Journal of Consciousness Exploration & Research*, 6.9, 658-684.

Shepard, G. (1991). *Foundations of The Neuronal Doctrine*. Oxford: Oxford University Press.

Simpkins, A. (2010). *The Dao of Neuroscience*. New York: Norton & Company.

Spencer, J. H. (2012). *The Eternal Law: Ancient Greek Philosophy, Modern Physics, and Ultimate Reality*. Vancouver: Param Media.

Standish, L. J., et al. (2003). Evidence of correlated functional magneticresonance imaging signals between distant human brains. *Alternative Therapies in Health and Medicine*, 9.1, 128-128.

Sun, T., Xie, X., & Wang, Z. (2013). *Wireless power transfer for medical microsystems*. New York: Springer.

Tesla, N. (1982). *My Inventions: The Autobiography of Nikola Tesla*. Williston, Vt: Hart Bros.

The Guardian, (2016). https://www.theguardian.com/artanddesign/2016/sep/08/fanchon-frohlich-obituary.

Valone, T. (2002). *Harnessing the wheelwork of nature: Tesla's science of energy*. Adventures Unlimited Press.

Várlaki, P., Nádai, L., & Bokor, J. (2008). Number archetypes and "background" control theory concerning the fine structure constant. *Acta Polytechnica Hungarica*, 5.2, 71-104.

Verdon-Akzam, G., Martín-Martínez, E., & Kempf, A. (2016). Asymptotically limitless quantum energy teleportation via qudit probes. *Physical Review, A* 93.2, 022308.

Wackermann, J., et al. (2003). Correlations between brain electrical activities of two spatially separated human subjects. *NeuroScience letters,* 336.1, 60-64.

Wackermann, J., Naranjo, J. R., & Pütz. (2004). Event-related correlations between electrical activities of separated human subjects: Preliminary results of a replication study. *Proceedings of the 47th Annual Convention of the Parapsychological Association.*

Zhao, Z., et al. (2004), Experimental demonstration of five-photon entanglement and open-destination teleportation. *Nature,* 430.6995, 54-58.

Chapter Six

A Case for a New Scientific Paradigm: Toward Advancing the Knowledge Base

Emily R Hawken, PhD

*"Science cannot pin down the mind or
the meaning of life…and the great mystery of death."*

Paul Kalanithi, When Breath Becomes Air

At this moment, you can bet that I am sitting in a lab designing my next set of experiments while intermittently interpreting some of the data I have recently collected. Such is the life of a modern-day neuroscientist. I came of age in the 1990s, a time declared by former US president George W. Bush Sr. the "Decade of the Brain," an interagency effort to educate people about brain discoveries. In an updated mandate, former US president Barack Obama recently launched the BRAIN initiative to figure out how the brain works through the support of development and application of new technologies. Part of the Grand Challenges (1980s US policies established to address fundamental problems in science), the BRAIN initiative focuses on revolutionizing our understanding of the human brain. This is how dedicated society is to knowing what the brain is. It may come as a surprise to some, but at the moment, we really have not figured it out.

The great mystery of the brain has captivated me throughout my life. Brain science is exciting because the brain remains largely undiscovered, like the Wild West once was, and represents to me a final frontier for scientific adventurers and explorers. Furthermore, I have been led to believe that knowing the brain will ultimately lead to understanding our human existence. The desire to understand our human nature is why I have returned again and again to brain research. I have dug deep into the basic make-up of the brain, looking for discoveries that I hope will unveil its secrets. Yet after 15 or so years of research, I am unsure if I have contributed much.

As part of the global brain-science team that has not yet figured out the brain, I am beginning to wonder: Am I doing it all wrong? Worse still, are we (the neuroscientists) doing it all wrong? Thoughts like this might seem ridiculous at first. How can it be possible to not know anything about the brain when seemingly so many advances in brain science have been made? Are these advances just a ruse, not actually representing real progress of our knowledge and understanding? It appears I am not the only neuroscientist asking these questions. As stated recently by a top neuroscientist to the New York Times, "…we have the tools…whether we have the intelligence to figure it out, I view that, at least in part, as a theory problem (Gorman, 2014)." But do we even have the tools? Given that our current tool-set has failed to unlock the brain's secrets, a reevaluation of everything we think we know to be true (i.e., our current scientific enterprise) is in order.

Our Current Scientific Paradigm

Normal science—or science as-we-know-it—starts with a question. Important questions like "why do objects fall to earth when dropped," or "what causes cancer," or "what is consciousness" have propelled science through the centuries. From these questions, scientists develop testable hypotheses. For instance, we have hypothesized that gravity carries objects to earth, that some cancer is caused by smoking, and that the brain creates our minds. Hypotheses arise from the collections of observations we have collectively agreed to define as "facts" and "knowledge." In order to determine if observations can be labelled as "fact," empirical evidence must be assessed critically via the process of induction. Through reasoning and inference, induction can derive a general theory from similarities in a group of observations. For instance, from consistent observations that smoking is associated with the prevalence of cancer, scientists have induced that smoking increases the odds of developing cancer. The process of deduction can be thought of as an inference made, but in the opposite direction: drawing conclusions about the nature of one observation by its resemblance to a set of accepted facts, for example, cigarettes cause cancer, therefore cigarettes are carcinogenic. Both reasoning tactics employ logic to solve problems and both are important for progressing science (Rothchild, 2006). "Facts" and "knowledge" derived via this logic build the framework of our current accepted understanding of how things work. The frameworks that are robust and commonly accepted become prevailing paradigms (Kuhn, 1962).

Kuhn (1962) defined these paradigms as conceptual frameworks or bodies of assumptions, beliefs, and related methods and techniques that are currently accepted and shared at a given time. The current prevailing paradigm of modern science has been called "reductionist" and "material": each observation or "thing" is a consequence and thus the sum of its physical material parts. Therefore, by breaking down every "thing" into its physical constituents and determining the function of each, we will learn something about its whole. In medicine, this approach is taken all the time, as we believe an illness to be caused by dysfunction of its biological parts, and through identification and understanding the role of what comprises that biology we will find the cause and cure of disease. In this way we hunt for the biomarkers and cures for all biological dysfunctions. Using this reductionist/materialist paradigm, many advances have been made in understanding both our human physiology as well as the world around us.

Brain Facts: What We Know, and What We Do Not Know

How has a material worldview impacted the understanding of the brain? Every day, the news is littered with the latest brain science discovery. With all of the advancing of brain recording and mapping technologies, we seem to know a lot about what the brain does. But let's take stock: What has science really taught us so far about the brain, what "facts" and "knowledge" have accumulated inside the reductionist/materialist paradigm?

We know what the brain looks like (a dark, convoluted jelly-like mass). We can describe the brain's smallest parts, consisting of microscopic brain cells that build highly networked structures. The functions of single neurons and even small neural circuits are fairly well understood (Hodgkin & Huxley, 1952). But how do larger circuits and networks work together to enable observations of experiences (the key features of the human mind), like rejoicing in a beautiful sunset or feeling a warm, wet shower? How do neurons firing allow us to move about with intention in the world, from satisfying a craving for a cup of coffee to planning a safe route across the street? We can stimulate the brain to make muscles twitch and experience sensations and feelings (Penfield, 1961). We have discovered that neurons use chemicals and electricity to communicate with each other (Donnerer & Lembeck, 2006). We can record these communications to make the brain light up in pictures (Attwell & Iadecola, 2002) when we think or move (Fox & Raichle, 2007).

Yet we do not know what a picture of a million firing neurons means. We can see when it becomes diseased and broken; we lose the abilities to function, to remember, to learn, and seemingly, we lose the very essence of self. Yet we have not been able to figure out the origin of thought disorders or much real evidence that thought disease is the result of actual brain disease. The best example is that scientists have not yet identified the etiology of schizophrenia, a disorder characterized by strange thought patterns and altered perceptions of reality, despite the persistent hunt to identify biological markers (in the brain or otherwise; Tandon et al., 2008; Lewis & Lieberman, 2000; Lewis & Anderson, 1995; Laruelle & Abi-Dargham, 1999). In fact, biological markers for most, if not all, mental illnesses remain elusive. Yet we know we need our brains to experience our inner and outer worlds, because when the brain stops, we stop. Or so we understand it to be.

Science also repeatedly tells us that we are our brains: where thought and action meet is intelligence or consciousness, and this meeting ground must be the physical brain (Gorman, 2014). In other words, based on how we believe everything in our material existence works, if we dissect and reduce enough, we will come to know where in the brain, the mind, and consciousness itself is found. Our scientific question formed from our current paradigm is summarized thus: "Where is the mind inside the brain?" We have induced (from our observations in a "material" world) that the brain generates the mind. But is this truly a "fact"? Science clearly has us believing that yes, indeed, this is *fact*. A "fact," by definition, is an indisputable thing. However, there is little evidence that the mind comes from the brain. Does a neuron that propagates an electrical signal produce a thought? There is not yet any proof that this is the case, even though a reductionist approach would suggest that a neuron is capable of such feats. From the current materialistic paradigm, this hypothesis (that the mind is in the brain) assumes that the physical generates everything, including consciousness, our reality, and our universe (and that to think otherwise is unscientific). Brain science is in the process of "catching up" to prove the brain-creates-mind hypothesis to be true. In philosophy, this is an example of circular reasoning (a common problem in science). Circular reasoning is a logical fallacy that begins with what the reasoner is trying to conclude; in our example here, since the brain creates the mind, if we look we will find the mind in the brain. As simplified by Wikipedia, this pragmatic fallacy highlights that the premise is often just as much in need of proof or evidence as the conclusion, and therefore the final position of the argument is weak and unconvincing. Thus, at this point in time it seems "the only thing that keeps alive the promise that the brain will one day explain consciousness is neuroscientists' blindness to any explanation other than the one assumed to be true in advance" (Chopra, 2014a).

We need paradigms to do science. A working framework or theory is necessary to generate a hypothesis and the interpretation of the observations made through the lens of the assumptions and framework within which it is postulated. Thus, paradigm constraints are unavoidable, placing limits on the types of questions we can ask, the methods and tools we can use, the interpretations made, and ultimately the conclusions drawn. In essence, objectivity is inherently lost as the bias of how we view nature is overlaid on the empirical observations made. For instance, while we have learned a lot about the brain using the materialist framework, it must still be remembered that the prevailing paradigm greatly dictates the type of "facts" and "knowledge" we are able to accumulate from this body of work. We have excelled at describing the brain; however, we can make very little comment on consciousness.

Despite the ardent pace with which brain science seems to advance, such "paradigm bias" will ultimately stall the progress toward truly identifying what the brain is. This is because the most we can ever learn is bound by our current worldview (aka paradigm) (Kuhn, 1972), regardless of the "truthiness" of the paradigm itself. According to our current view, we can only find consciousness inside the brain or in some other material construct; thus, we will keep looking there, possibly indefinitely, until we find it. But what if the truth is that the mind is elsewhere, not made of brain-matter? To consider this, we may need to change how we do science. We can only begin to question a prevailing paradigm by assessing its utility; paradigms exist as long as they continue to aid in our understanding. It is only when this utility begins to fade, when problems arise that cannot be solved by the current way of seeing the world, that we question if perhaps we need to adjust our perspective and devise a new set of rules for explaining the ways of nature. Because very different but equally true conclusions could be drawn from a single dataset depending on the paradigm used to interpret the data, tangible progress can be achieved through paradigm shifts. To understand the brain, are we in need of a paradigm shift?

How Does a New Paradigm Emerge to Create New Knowledge?

In order for a paradigm to rise to the forefront, a single theory of how things work to explain most of the presented facts must be defined. However, it does not need to explain all facts. Paradigms gain momentum and strength the more people accept the assumptions of the paradigm and come to share the same perspective. The more advocates, the more incontrovertible the assumptions may appear. Everyone believes that the mind is in the brain and all that is left is to find it. In time, evidence to suggest anything different may fail to accumulate as the paradigm supporters ignore its existence or discard it out of hand. Furthermore, little effort may be made to explore new phenomena that may exist outside of the paradigm. With confidence, scientists are busy solving the problems contained inside of the paradigm in order to justify, support, and understand the paradigm.

A paradigm begins to crumble when science produces new discoveries or identifies anomalies that do not make sense within the rules of the paradigm. Paradigms can withstand a certain amount of incongruence. In fact, rigorous adherence to the paradigm, following its rules and assumptions, is the best way to uncover new discoveries. New facts or observations found through scientific inquiry cause the paradigm to evolve, and assimilations of new information are made in a modified theory. However, a new theory or paradigm will begin to emerge when the current set of assumptions persistently fails to account for new observations. In other words, the revision required to accommodate the new discovery is too severe to be contained within the existing paradigm.

One of the last revolutionary scientific paradigm shifts occurred with the introduction of quantum mechanics and general relativity theory. In its time, classical physics, developed by Sir Isaac Newton, was very limited in the observations it could measure, confined to the empirical description of the most easily observed natural systems. However, observations from systems that deviated from the most obvious—for example, either systems that were considered very small (like atoms) or very large (like planets)—remained beyond the theory's mathematical capabilities. The limitations of Newtonian physics were relatively long known when Einstein and his colleagues came along and wrote a new set of rules that could encompass both the very small and the very big: quantum mechanics and relativity. Quantum mechanics gave us the ability to understand the tiniest essence of matter: the atom. This revolutionary theory of matter came complete with a new set of new tools to permit the quantitative understanding of molecules. At the time there were strong opponents to this theory, as it could not account for some very important observations, like gravity and everything that gravity governs. Relativity, however, was able to explain those observations that quantum mechanics could not. The rules of physics and reality itself had been rewritten into better, nearly all encompassing, theories. The success of the current theories of matter and relativity have occurred because the new framework made it possible to solve problems that stymied the previous intellectual regime. Even though our theories of the natural physical world have been radically rearranged, the rules still rest on two incompatible descriptions of reality: both quantum mechanics and relativity are correct, yet neither can be applied to each other. This highlights the fact that we still have not found the "theory of everything." Despite this, the above incongruence of theories does create a real space for discovery: as we continue to push to explain observations that breach our current paradigm, in this way will science and knowledge continue to progress.

How does consciousness and brain science fit into this? Consciousness continues to be a significant anomalous occurrence; in fact, it is so significant that it seems necessary for reality. Without consciousness, our experience of reality would not be what it is. For a real "theory of everything" to be true, then, it must be able to explain consciousness. At the moment, the theories that we have cannot do this. Like mathematically predicting gravity, we struggle to find proof that the mind can be predicted and explained by local quantum mechanics (Litt et al., 2006). Some have argued that the tiny substrates that constitute neurons may offer a milieu suitable to support quantum events (Hameroff, 1998; Kak, 1999; Nanopoulos 1995). However, little empirical evidence has been generated to support this theory. Thus, umbrellaed in the current paradigm, or set of science rules, the existence of consciousness may be as impossible to reconcile with the brain (and matter) as gravity is to quantum mechanics. In many scientific circles, such significant anomalies have begun to create tension.

As noted by Kuhn (1962), the emergence of new theories is generally preceded by a period of pronounced professional insecurity. The emergence of quantum mechanics, for example, began as a controversial set of mathematical explanations of experiments that the math of classical Newtonian mechanics could not explain. Have we reached a tipping point in neuroscience—or in all science—in which it is necessary for our scientific viewpoint to expand? Or are we stuck in the phase of ardently defending the old, with the vast majority of brain scientists still insisting that the mind is *in* the brain and that its discovery is imminent (Paller & Suzuki, 2014)? One could argue that perhaps all we need is more time to keep turning over the molecular rocks of the brain, looking for our minds. But if mind existed in brain, as a function of the basic rules of physics and matter, should it not have been found by now? After all, it has been a century since the laws of material nature have been updated to their current form. How much time should we take before we cut our collective losses and decide to look elsewhere for consciousness?

Chopra et al. (2014) recently distilled why the brain-as-mind model is falling apart into two basic problems: that the model is self-referential (the thing science is trying to define is also the thing doing the defining, or, put another way, "the eye cannot see itself"), and that consciousness is a stream of experiences that are immeasurable qualities and measurable "thing-like" observations (e.g., the wetness of water cannot be measured by breaking the water down into its fundamental parts). Physicist Richard Conn Henry (Henry, 2005) stated that "The only reality is mind and observations, but observations are not of things." If, ultimately, the substance of our experience cannot be predicted by the properties of the physical world, our matter-built view of reality cannot and will not ever find consciousness in the brain. Chopra et al. (2014) suggest that in order to challenge brain science we must get outside the brain. How in the world can science do this? Step one: change our perspective to that of one that may allow for it.

What is Next?

To "get outside the brain" as recommended by Chopra et al. (2014b), the first thing we must do is consider that the thing that creates our experience of consciousness and reality per se might not be in the brain at all. We know this is possible because there are several instances or anomalies of the mind existing separately from the brain. A non-exhaustive list includes the experience of conscious mental activity in clinical death (or "near-death experiences" Borjigin et al., 2013), mediums who claim an ability to communicate with the dead, and young children who have a full set of memories from a previous life (Tucker, 2008). Furthermore, science has reluctantly begun to recognize that the mind itself is able to influence both behavior and the activity and function of the brain (for example, mindfulness training and meditation [Tang et al., 2015]). If we allow our mind to be the creator of experience (and not the brain) then getting outside of the brain becomes easier. Accepting that the mind, and not the brain, is "running the show" requires us to consider a new set of rules for the nature of things. A growing number of scientists believe that it may require us to step outside of the current paradigm of science altogether if we truly wish to understand the mind, and ultimately human subjective experience.

A group of experts from around the world has recently generated support for a science that they dub "postmaterialist" (Beauregard et al., 2014). This is primarily based on the fact that materialist theories fail to elucidate how the brain generates the mind. Furthermore, quantum predictions that suggest observable consequences are carried by physical systems are at odds with the non-local influences on quantum systems (Gröblacher et al., 2007). These failures demarcate the need to expand our concept of the natural world and embrace a "something-other-than-material" basis of everything. Contrary to the fears and objections of some, a postmaterialist science (as argued in the Manifesto for a Postmaterialist Science) would not reject all of the evidence and advancement material-based science has collected and permitted. Rather, postmaterialism would be inclusive of matter in addition to being inclusive of mind—perhaps the two core constituents of the universe.

Historically, and as outlined above, a scientific revolution is defined in part by a non-cumulative developmental "burst into existence" of a new paradigm that replaces an old, incompatible one (Kuhn, 1962). Kuhn uses the analogy of choosing between two political parties in the advent of a political revolution. Political revolutions are instigated by a society when it begins to feel uneasy with the current political regime's ability to meet the needs of the people. Competing camps form, one supporting the old regime and others advocating for a new one, with those pushing for change reframing the structure of political institutions in ways that those institutions themselves prohibit. As the polarization deepens, political discourse fails and conflict resolution tactics resort to public persuasion. Kuhn argues further that, like the choice between political institutions, choosing between competing paradigms proves to be a choice between fundamentally incompatible ways of life. Because a successful new paradigm permits the prediction of new observations that are beyond those of its predecessor, it follows that the two paradigms are logically incompatible.

Thus, it is unlikely that a new scientific paradigm, like postmaterialism, will include matter as a substrate of reality. If the quantum mechanics of matter do not create our universe, then what does? In a postmaterial construct, we are able to consider consciousness as a creator and a "Mental Universe" becomes entirely possible (Chopra et al., 2015a, 2015b). From a materialist perspective, the derivative of everything is matter. But if we flip things on their head and look from the opposite direction, we have to ask ourselves: Could everything come from the mind?

Deepak Chopra and his colleagues remind us that the concept of a mental universe has been gaining momentum in scientific communities. In 2005, Professor Richard Conn Henry, a physicist from the Johns Hopkins University in Baltimore, Maryland, wrote an essay in the prestigious journal *Nature* entitled "The Mental Universe." He suggests that the "real science" behind the core observations of quantum mechanisms proves that "the Universe is immaterial – mental and spiritual." This "real science" consists of a few key quantum-based observations and paradoxes (Bell, 1987) that imply that mind is tightly coupled to the assumed matter-based phenomenon we observe.

One example that may prove the universe is mental is the observation of quantum entanglement. Quantum entanglement is a physical phenomenon. It occurs when particles are generated or interact in ways that do not allow their individual parts to be observed or characterized independently of one another; they can only be described as a whole. The paradoxical nature of this comes at the time of measurement or observation: two particles in a system are highly correlated, and by measuring one particle the nature of the second changes so that it is able to describe the entire system. For one, this disruption of the system due to observation is called the Heisenberg uncertainty principle. Thus, the observer (the conscious human participant) is only able to measure what it predicts it will observe (Kim et al., 2000), and that these observations are not the actual properties of the quantum system (Lapkiewicz et al., 2011). Thus, quantum objects appear to act differently when they are observed versus when they are unobserved (Feynman et al., 1965). An example of this is the role played by consciousness in the collapse of the quantum wave function. A wave function collapse is demonstrated in part as the result of measurement, and occurs when an initial wave function is shown to have a different final wave function. Using a classical double-slit optical system, Radin et al. (2012) performed several experiments to demonstrate simply paying attention to (or ignoring) a beam of light travelling through two small slits, could change the light wave that travelled through the double-slit. Furthermore, factors associated with consciousness (like meditation experience and electrocortical markers of focused attention) are highly correlated with changes in the double-slit wave pattern. Thus, as stated by Chopra et al. (2015b), "What we call physical things and events, as it turns out, do not exist independently of subjective experience."

Conclusion

If we can allow ourselves a novel perspective, a whole new world, or at least, a more unified underpinning reality, will open up for us, allowing for a real understanding of the essence of consciousness and our universe as we know it. But what will it take for a scientific revolution to happen? Will it be the slow and subtle persuasion achieved by a growing community of like-minded postmaterialists? Or will it happened more suddenly from flashes of genius? Change is hard and requires thinking in ways that might be entirely alien. As more of the world's great intellects adopt a new science (in mind and in practice), we will feel the strains of paradigm upheaval less and less. In the meantime, how do we scientists who sense change is in the wind proceed? For the time being, I will keep studying the brain using the tools I have in hand. However, I am only working toward a futile end if my ultimate goal as a neuroscientist is to find and understand the mind. While some might be discouraged by this insight, I am not. Like understanding how a radio works enables one to build a radio to receive a broadcast, learning about how the brain "works" will allow us to repair and fix it when its reception has been muddled by disease or dysfunction. With this objective I can move forward within the limitations dictated by my paradigm. However, I will stay tuned for true understanding, as I hope to witness (and participate in) the dawn of the next scientific revolution. In the search for knowledge, a completely new conceptualization of things as we know it is the only true way forward.

References

Attwell, D., & Iadecola, C. (2002). The neural basis of functional brain imaging signals. *TRENDS in Neuroscience*, 25, 621-625.

Beauregard, M., Dossey, L., Miller, L. J., Moreira-Almeida, A., Schltz, M., Schwartz, G., Sheldrake, R., & Tart, C. T. (2014). *Manifesto for postmaterialist science*, http://opensciences.org/about/manifesto-for-a-postmaterialist-science.

Bell, J. S. (1987). *Speakable and Unspeakable in Quantum Mechanics*. New York: Cambridge University Press.

Borjigin, J., Lee, U. C., Liu, T., Pal, D., Huff, S., Klarr, D., Sloboda, J., Hernandez, J., Wang, M. M., & Mashour, G. A. (2013). Surge of neurophysiological coherence and connectivity in the dying brain. PNAS, 110, 14432-14437.

Chopra, D., & Kastrup, B. (2014a). Getting real about brain science – a challenge to the current model. *SFGATE November 23*; http://www.sfgate.com/opinion/chopra/article/Getting-Real-About-Brain-Science-A-Challenge-to-5726540.php.

Chopra, D., Kastrup, B., Kafatos, M. C., & Tanzi, R. E. (2014b). Getting real about brain science – A challenge to the current model (Part 2). *SFGATE* November 9; http://www.sfgate.com/opinion/chopra/article/Getting-Real-About-Brain-Science-A-Challenge-to-5740774.php.

Chopra, D., Kafatos, M., Kastrup, B., & Tanzi, R. E. (2015a). Making a choice: is the universe mental or physical? *SFGATE* November 16; http://www.sfgate.com/opinion/chopra/article/Making-a-Choice-Is-the-Universe-Mental-or-6634743.php.

Chopra, D., Kafatos, M., Kastrup, B., & Tanzi, R. (2015b). Why a mental universe is the "Real" reality. *SFGATE* November 30, http://www.sfgate.com/opinion/chopra/article/Why-a-Mental-Universe-Is-the-Real-Reality-6657498.php

Donnerer, J., & Lembeck, F. (2006). *The Chemical Languages of the Nervous System.* Basel, Switzerland: Kager AG.

Feynman, R., Leighton, R., & Sands, M. (1965). *The Feynman Lectures on Physics.* New York: Assison-Wesley.

Fox, M. D., & Raichle, M. E. (2007). Spontaneous fluctuations in brain activity observed with functional magnetic resonance imaging. *Nature Reviews Neuroscience* 8, 700-711.

Gorman, J. (2014, November 10). Learning how little we know about the brain. *The New York Times* (online edition).

Gröblacher, S., Paterek, T., Kaltenbaek, R., Brukner, C., Zukowski, M., Aspelmeyer, M., & Zeilinger, A. (2007). An experimental test of non-local realism. *Nature*, 446, 871-875.

Hameroff, S. (1998). Quantum computation in brain microtubules? The Penrose-Hameroff "Orch OR" model of consciousness. *Philosophical Transactions of the Royal Society of London A*, 356, 1869-1896.

Henry, R. C. (2005). The Mental Universe. *Nature*, 436; 29.

Hodgkin, A. L., & Huxley, A. F. (1952). A quantitative description of membrane current and its application to conduction and excitation in nerve. *J Physiol*, 117: 500-544.

Kak, S. (1999). Quantum computing and AI. *IEEE Intelligence Systems*, 14, 9-16.

Kalanithi, P. (2016). *When Breath Becomes Air*. New York: Random House.

Kim, Y-H., Yu, R., Kulik, S. P., Shih, Y., & Scully, M. O. (2000). Delayed "choice" quantum easer. *Phys Rev Lett*, 84, 1-5.

Kuhn, T. S. (1962). *The Structure of Scientific Revolutions, 4th ed*. Chicago, IL: The University of Chicago Press.

Lapkiewicz, R., Peizhe, L., Schaeff, C., Langford, N.K., Ramelow, S., Wiesniak, M., & Zeilinger, A. (2011). Experimental non-classicality of an indivisible quantum system. *Nature*, 474, 490-493.

Lewis, D. A., & Anderson, S. A. (1995). The functional architecture of the prefrontal cortex and schizophrenia. *Psychol Med*, 25, 887-894.

Lewis, D. A., Lieberman, J. A. (2000). Catching up on schizophrenia: natural history and neurobiology. *Neuron*, 28, 325-334.

Litt, A., Eliasmith, C., Kroon, F. W., Weinstein, S., & Thagard, P. (2006). Is the brain a quantum computer? *Cognitive Science*, 30, 593-603.

Nanopoulos, D. V. (1995). Theory of brain function, quantum mechanics and superstrings. Retrieved 11 April 2016 from http://cds.cern.ch/record/282290/files/9505374.pdf

Paller, K. A., & Suzuki, S. (2014). The source of consciousness. *Trends in Cognitive Science*, 18, 387-388.

Penfield, W. (1961, April 27). Activation of the record of human experience. Summary of the Lister Oration delivered at the Royal College of Surgeons of England.

Radin, D., Michel, L., Galdamez, K., Wendland, P., Rickenbach, R., & Delorme, A. (2012). Consciousness and the double-slit interference pattern: Six experiments. *Physics Essays*, 25, 157-171.

Rothchild, I. (2006). Induction, deduction, and the scientific method. An eclectic overview of the practice of science. *The Society for the Study of Reproduction, Inc.* pp. 1-11.

Tandon, R., Keshavan, M. S., & Nasrallah, H. A. (2008). Schizophrenia, "just the facts" what we know in 2008. 2. Epidemiology and etiology. *Schizophr Res*, 102, 1-18.

Tang, Y.Y., Hölzel. B. K., Posner, M. I. (2015). The neuroscience of mindfulness meditation. *Nature Reviews Neuroscience*, 16, 213-225.

Tucker, J. B. (2008). *Life before Life*. New York: St. Martin's Griffin.

Chapter Seven

Setting Science Free From Materialism

Rupert Sheldrake, PhD

The "scientific worldview" is immensely influential because the sciences have been so successful. No one can fail to be awed by their achievements, which touch all our lives through technologies and through modern medicine. Our intellectual world has been transformed through an immense expansion of our knowledge, down into the most microscopic particles of matter and out into the vastness of space, with hundreds of billions of galaxies in an ever-expanding universe.

Yet now, when science and technology seem to be at the peak of the power, when their influence has spread all over the world and when their triumph seems indisputable, unexpected problems are disrupting the sciences from within. Most scientists take it for granted that these problems will eventually be solved by more research along established lines, but some, including myself, think that they are symptoms of a deeper malaise. Science is being held back by centuries-old assumptions that have hardened into dogmas. The sciences would be better off without them: freer, more interesting, and more fun.

The biggest scientific delusion of all is that science already knows the answers. The details still need working out, but the fundamental questions are settled, in principle.

Contemporary science is based on the claim that all reality is material or physical. There is no reality but material reality. Consciousness is a by-product of the physical activity of the brain. Matter is unconscious. Evolution is purposeless. God exists only as an idea in human minds, and hence in human heads.

These beliefs are powerful not because most scientists think about them critically, but because they don't. The facts of science are real enough, and so are the techniques that scientists use, and so are the technologies based on them. But the belief system that governs conventional scientific thinking is an act of faith, grounded in a 19th century ideology.

The Scientific Creed

Here are the 10 core beliefs that most scientists take for granted:
1. Everything is essentially mechanical. Dogs, for example, are complex mechanisms, rather than living organisms with goals of their own. Even people are machines, "lumbering robots," in Richard Dawkins' vivid phrase, with brains that are like genetically programmed computers.
2. All matter is unconscious. It has no inner life or subjectivity or point of view. Even human consciousness is an illusion produced by the material activities of brains.
3. The total amount of matter and energy is always the same (with the exception of the Big Bang, when all the matter and energy of the universe suddenly appeared).
4. The laws of nature are fixed. They are the same today as they were at the beginning, and they will stay the same forever.
5. Nature is purposeless, and evolution has no goal or direction.
6. All biological inheritance is material, carried in the genetic material, DNA, and in other material structures.
7. Minds are inside heads and are nothing but the activities of brains. When you look at a tree, the image of the tree you are seeing is not "out there," where it seems to be, but inside your brain.
8. Memories are stored as material traces in brains and are wiped out at death.
9. Unexplained phenomena like telepathy are illusory.
10. Mechanistic medicine is the only kind that really works.

Together, these beliefs make up the philosophy or ideology of materialism, whose central assumption is that everything is essentially material or physical, even minds. This belief system became dominant within science in the late 19th century, and is now taken for granted. Many scientists are unaware that materialism is an assumption; they simply think of it as science, or the scientific view of reality, or the scientific worldview. They are not actually taught about it, or given a chance to discuss it. They absorb it by a kind of intellectual osmosis.

In everyday usage, materialism refers to a way of life devoted entirely to material interests, a preoccupation with wealth, possessions, and luxury. These attitudes are no doubt encouraged by the materialist philosophy, which denies the existence of any spiritual realities or non-material goals, but I am here concerned with materialism's scientific claims, rather than its effects on lifestyles.

In the spirit of radical skepticism, each of these 10 doctrines can be turned into a question, as I show in my book *Science Set Free* (Sheldrake, 2012) (called *The Science Delusion* in the UK). Entirely new vistas open up when a widely accepted assumption is taken as the beginning of an enquiry, rather than as an unquestionable truth. For example, the assumption that nature is machine-like or mechanical becomes a question: "Is nature mechanical?" The assumption that matter is unconscious becomes "Is matter unconscious?" And so on.

The Credibility Crunch for the "Scientific Worldview"

For more than 200 years, materialists have promised that science will eventually explain everything in terms of physics and chemistry. Science will prove that living organisms are complex machines, minds are nothing but brain activity, and nature is purposeless. Believers are sustained by the faith that scientific discoveries will justify their beliefs. The philosopher of science Karl Popper called this stance "promissory materialism" because it depends on issuing promissory notes for discoveries not yet made (Popper & Eccles, 1977). Despite all the achievements of science and technology, materialism is now facing a credibility crunch that was unimaginable in the 20th century.

In 1963, when I was studying biochemistry at Cambridge University, I was invited to a series of private meetings with Francis Crick and Sydney Brenner in Brenner's rooms in King's College, along with a few of my classmates. Crick and Brenner had recently helped to "crack" the genetic code. Both were ardent materialists and Crick was also a militant atheist. They explained there were two major unsolved problems in biology: development and consciousness. They had not been solved because the people who worked on them were not molecular biologists—nor very bright. Crick and Brenner were going to find the answers within 10 years, or maybe 20. Brenner would take developmental biology, and Crick consciousness. They invited us to join them.

Both tried their best. Brenner was awarded the Nobel Prize in 2002 for his work on the development of a tiny worm, Caenorhabdytis elegans. Crick corrected the manuscript of his final paper on the brain the day before he died in 2004. At his funeral, his son Michael said that what made him tick was not the desire to be famous, wealthy, or popular, but "to knock the final nail into the coffin of vitalism." (Vitalism is the theory that living organisms are truly alive, and not explicable in terms of physics and chemistry alone.)

Crick and Brenner failed. The problems of development and consciousness remain unsolved. Many details have been discovered, dozens of genomes have been sequenced, and brain scans are ever more precise. But there is still no proof that life and minds can be explained by physics and chemistry alone.

The fundamental proposition of materialism is that matter is the only reality. Therefore, consciousness is nothing but brain activity. It is either like a shadow, an "epiphenomenon" that does nothing, or it is just another way of talking about brain activity. However, among contemporary researchers in neuroscience and consciousness studies there is no consensus about the nature of minds. Leading journals such as *Behavioral and Brain Sciences* and the *Journal of Consciousness Studies* publish many articles that reveal deep problems with the materialist doctrine. The philosopher David

Chalmers has called the very existence of subjective experience the "hard problem." It is hard because it defies explanation in terms of mechanisms. Even if we understand how eyes and brains respond to red light, the experience of redness is not accounted for.

In biology and psychology the credibility rating of materialism is falling. Can physics ride to the rescue? Some materialists prefer to call themselves physicalists, to emphasize that their hopes depend on modern physics, not 19th-century theories of matter. But physicalism's own credibility rating has been reduced by physics itself, for four reasons:

First, some physicists insist that quantum mechanics cannot be formulated without taking into account the minds of observers. They argue that minds cannot be reduced to physics because physics presupposes the minds of physicists (e.g., d'Espagnat, 1976).

Second, the most ambitious unified theories of physical reality, string and M-theories, with 10 and 11 dimensions respectively, take science into completely new territory. Strangely, as Stephen Hawking tells us in his book *The Grand Design* (2010), "No one seems to know what the 'M' stands for, but it may be 'master', 'miracle' or 'mystery'." According to what Hawking calls "model-dependent realism," different theories may have to be applied in different situations. "Each theory may have its own version of reality, but according to model-dependent realism, that is acceptable so long as the theories agree in their predictions whenever they overlap, that is, whenever they can both be applied" (Hawking & Mlodinow, 2010, p. 117).

String theories and M-theories are currently untestable, so "model-dependent realism" can only be judged by reference to other models, rather than by experiment. It also applies to countless other universes, none of which has ever been observed (Hawking & Mlodinow, 2010, pp. 118-119).

Some physicists are deeply sceptical about this entire approach, as the theoretical physicist Lee Smolin shows in his book *The Trouble With Physics: The Rise of String Theory, the Fall of a Science and What Comes Next* (Smolin, 2006). String theories, M-theories, and "model-dependent realism" are a shaky foundation for materialism or physicalism or any other belief system.

Third, since the beginning of the 21st century, it has become apparent that the known kinds of matter and energy make up only about 4% of the universe. The rest consists of "dark matter" and "dark energy." The nature of 96% of physical reality is literally obscure.

Fourth, the Cosmological Anthropic Principle asserts that if the laws and constants of nature had been slightly different at the moment of the Big Bang, biological life could never have emerged, and hence we would not be here to think about it. So did a divine mind fine-tune the laws and constants in the beginning? To avoid a creator God emerging in a new guise, most leading cosmologists prefer to believe that our universe is one of a vast, and perhaps infinite, number of parallel universes, all with different laws and constants, as M-theory also suggests. We just happen to exist in the one that has the right conditions for us (Carr, 2007; Greene, 2011).

This multiverse theory is the ultimate violation of Ockham's Razor, the philosophical principle that "entities must not be multiplied beyond necessity," or in other words that we should make as few assumptions as possible. It also has the major disadvantage of being untestable (Ellis, (2011). And it does not even succeed in getting rid of God. An infinite God could be the God of an infinite number of universes (Collins, 2007).

Materialism provided a seemingly simple, straightforward worldview in the late 19th century, but 21st century science has left it far behind. Its promises have not been fulfilled, and its promissory notes have been devalued by hyperinflation.

I am convinced that the sciences are being held back by assumptions that have hardened into dogmas, maintained by powerful taboos. These beliefs protect the citadel of established science, but act as barriers against open-minded thinking. Here, for example, I explore Dogma 2, the assumption that matter is unconscious.

Is Matter Unconscious?

The central doctrine of materialism is that matter is the only reality. Therefore consciousness ought not to exist. Materialism's biggest problem is that consciousness does exist. You are conscious now. The main opposing theory, dualism, accepts the reality of consciousness, but has no convincing explanation for its interaction with the body and the brain. Dualist-materialist arguments have gone on for centuries. But if we question the dogma that matter is unconscious, we can move forward from this sterile opposition.

Scientific materialism arose historically as a rejection of mechanistic dualism, which defined matter as unconscious and souls as immaterial, as I discuss below. One important motive for this rejection was the elimination of souls and God, leaving unconscious matter as the only reality. In short, materialists treated subjective experience as irrelevant; dualists accepted the reality of experience, but were unable to explain how minds affect brains.

The materialist philosopher Daniel Dennett wrote a book called *Consciousness Explained* (1991), in which he tried to explain away consciousness by arguing that subjective experience is illusory. He was forced to this conclusion because he rejected dualism as a matter of principle:

"I adopt the apparently dogmatic rule that dualism is to be avoided at all costs. It is not that I think I can give a knock-down proof that dualism, in all its forms, is false or incoherent, but that, given the way that dualism wallows in mystery, accepting dualism is giving up" (Dennett, 1991, p. 37).

This dogmatism of Dennett's rule is not merely apparent: the rule *is* dogmatic. By "giving up" and "wallowing in mystery", I suppose he means giving up science and reason and relapsing into religion and superstition. Materialism "at all costs" demands the denial of the reality of our own minds and personal experiences—including those of Daniel Dennett himself, although by putting forward arguments he hopes will be persuasive, he seems to make an exception for himself and for those who read his book.

Francis Crick devoted decades of his life to trying to explain consciousness mechanistically. He frankly admitted that the materialist theory was an "astonishing hypothesis" that flew in the face of common sense: "'You', your joys and your sorrows, your memories and your ambitions, your sense of personal identity and free will, are in fact no more than the behaviour of a vast assembly of nerve cells and their associated molecules" (Crick, 1994, p. 3). Presumably Crick included himself in this description, although he must have felt that there was more to his argument than the automatic activity of nerve cells.

One of the motives of materialists is to support an anti-religious worldview. Francis Crick was a militant atheist, as is Daniel Dennett. On the other hand, one of the traditional motives of dualists is to support the possibility of the soul's survival. If the human soul is immaterial, it may exist after bodily death.

Scientific orthodoxy has not always been materialist. The founders of mechanistic science in the 17th century were dualistic Christians. They downgraded matter, making it totally inanimate and mechanical, and at the same time upgraded human minds, making them completely different from unconscious matter. By creating an unbridgeable gulf between the two, they thought they were strengthening the argument for the human soul and its immortality, as well as increasing the separation between humans and other animals.

This mechanistic dualism is often called Cartesian dualism after Descartes. It saw the human mind as essentially immaterial and disembodied, and bodies as machines made of unconscious matter (Griffin, 1998). In practice, most people take a dualist view for granted, as long as they are not called upon to defend it. Almost everyone assumes that we have some degree of free will, and are responsible for our actions. Our educational and legal systems are based on this belief. And we experience ourselves as conscious beings, with some degree of free choice. Even to discuss consciousness presupposes that we are conscious ourselves. Nevertheless, since the 1920s, many leading scientists and philosophers in the English-speaking world have been materialists, in spite of all the problems this doctrine creates.

The strongest argument in favour of materialism is the failure of dualism to explain how immaterial minds work and how they interact with brains. The strongest argument in favour of dualism is the implausibility and self-contradictory nature of materialism.

The dualist-materialist dialectic has lasted for centuries. The soul-body or mind-brain problem has refused to go away. But before we can move forward, first we need to understand in more detail what materialists claim, since their belief system still dominates institutional science and medicine, and everyone is influenced by it.

Minds That Deny Their Own Reality

Most neuroscientists do not spend much time thinking about the logical problems that materialist beliefs entail. They just get on with the job of trying to understand how brains work, in the faith that more hard facts will eventually provide answers. They leave professional philosophers to defend the materialist or physicalist faith.

Physicalism means much the same as materialism, but rather than asserting that all reality is material, it asserts that it is physical—explicable in terms of physics—and hence including energy and fields as well as matter. In practice, this is what materialists believe, too. In the following discussion I use the more familiar word materialism to mean "materialism or physicalism."

Among materialist philosophers, there are several schools of thought. The most extreme position is called "eliminative materialism," which states that consciousness is just an "aspect" of the activity of the brain. Thoughts or sensations are just another way of talking about activity in particular regions of the cerebral cortex; they are the same things talked about in different ways.

Other materialists are "epiphenomenalists": they accept rather than deny the existence of consciousness, but see it as a functionless by-product of the activity of the brain, an "epiphenomenon," like a shadow. People might just as well be zombies, with no subjective experience, because all their behaviour is a result of brain activity alone. Conscious experience does nothing, and makes no difference to the physical world.

A recent form of materialism is "cognitive psychology," which dominated academic psychology in the English-speaking world in the late 20th century. It treats the brain as a computer and mental activity as information processing. Subjective experiences, like seeing green, or feeling pain, or enjoying music, are computational processes inside the brain, which are themselves unconscious.

Some philosophers, like John Searle, think that minds can emerge from matter by analogy with the way that physical properties can emerge at different levels of complexity, like the wetness of water emerging from the interactions of large numbers of water molecules. Many non-materialists would agree with Searle that consciousness is in some sense "emergent," but would argue that while mind and conscious agency originate in physical nature, they are qualitatively different from purely material or physical being.

Finally, some materialists hope that evolution can provide an answer. They propose that consciousness emerged as a result of natural selection through mindless processes from unconscious matter. Because minds evolved, they must have been favoured by natural selection and hence they must actually do something; they must make a difference. Many non-materialists would agree. But materialists want to have it both ways: emergent consciousness must do something if it has evolved as an evolutionary adaptation favoured by natural selection, but it cannot do anything if is just an epiphenomenon of brain activity, or another way of talking about brain mechanisms. In 2011, the psychologist Nicholas Humphrey tried to overcome this problem by suggesting that consciousness evolved because it helps humans survive and reproduce by making us feel "special and transcendent." But as a materialist, Humphrey does not agree that our minds have any agency—that is to say, they cannot affect our actions. Instead our consciousness is illusory: he describes it as "a magical mystery show that we stage for ourselves inside our own heads."[13] But to say that consciousness is an illusion does not explain consciousness: it presupposes it. Illusion is a mode of consciousness.

If all these theories sound unconvincing, that is because they are. They do not even convince other materialists, which is why there are so many rival theories. Searle has described the debate over the last 50 years as follows:

---

[13] *The most ingenious evolutionary arguments for the emergence of illusory consciousness are by Humphrey, N. Soul Dust: The Magic of Consciousness. London: Quercus; 2011.*

"A philosopher advances a materialist theory of the mind... He then encounters difficulties... Criticisms of the materialist theory usually take a more or less technical form, but, in fact, underlying the technical objections is a much deeper objection: the theory in question has left out some essential feature of the mind... And this leads to ever more frenzied attempts to stick with the materialist thesis" (Searle, 1992, p. 30).

The philosopher Galen Strawson, himself a materialist, is amazed by the willingness of so many of his fellow philosophers to deny the reality of their own experience:

"I think we should feel very sober, and a little afraid, at the power of human credulity, the capacity of human minds to be gripped by theory, by faith. For this particular denial is the strangest thing that has ever happened in the whole history of human thought, not just the whole history of philosophy" (Strawson, 2006, p. 5).

Francis Crick admitted that the "astonishing hypothesis" was not proved. He conceded that a dualist view might become more plausible. But, he added, "There is always a third possibility: that the facts support a new, alternative way of looking at the mind-brain problem that is significantly different from the rather crude materialistic view that many neuroscientists hold today and also from the religious point of view. Only time, and much further scientific work, will enable us to decide" (Crick, 1994, pp. 262-263). There is indeed a third way.

Panpsychist Alternatives

Galen Strawson shares the frustration of many contemporary philosophers with the seemingly intractable problems of materialism and of dualism. He has come to the conclusion that there is only one way out. He argues that a consistent materialism must imply panpsychism, namely the idea that even atoms and molecules have a primitive kind of mentality or experience. (The Greek word *pan* means "everywhere," and *psyche* means "soul" or "mind.") Panpsychism does not mean that atoms are conscious in the sense that we are, but only that some aspects of mentality or experience are present in the simplest physical systems. More complex forms of mind or experience emerge in more complex systems (Strawson, 2006).

In 2006, the *Journal of Consciousness Studies* published a special issue entitled "Does materialism entail panpsychism?" with a target article by Strawson, and responses by 17 other philosophers and scientists. Some of them rejected his suggestion in favour of more conventional kinds of materialism, but all admitted that their favoured kind of materialism was problematic.

Strawson made only a generalized, abstract case for panpsychism, with disappointingly few details as to how an electron or an atom could be said to have experiences. But like many other panpsychists he made an important distinction between aggregates of matter, like tables and rocks, and self-organizing systems like atoms, cells, and animals. He did not suggest that tables and rocks have any unified experience, though the atoms within them may have (Strawson, 2006). The reason for this distinction is that man-made objects like chairs or cars do not organize themselves, and do not have their own goals or purposes. They are designed by people and put together in factories. Likewise, rocks are made up of atoms and crystals that are self-organizing, but external forces shape the rock as a whole: for example, it may have been split from a larger rock as a boulder rolled down a mountain.

By contrast, in self-organizing systems, complex forms of experience emerge spontaneously. These systems are at the same time physical (non-experiential) and experiential; in other words they have experiences. As Strawson put it, "Once upon a time there was relatively unorganized matter with both experiential and non-experiential fundamental features. It organized into increasingly complex forms, both experiential and non-experiential, by many processes including evolution by natural selection" (Strawson, 2006, p. 27). Unlike Searle's attempt to explain consciousness by saying that it emerges from totally unconscious, insentient matter, Strawson's proposal is that more complex forms of experience emerge from less complex ones. There is a difference of degree, but not of kind.

The eminent American philosopher Thomas Nagel put forward a powerful argument for panpsychism in his book *Mind and Cosmos: Why the*

Materialist Neo-Darwinian Conception of Nature is Almost Certainly False (2012). He, too, frames it in an evolutionary context: "Each of our lives is a part of the lengthy process of the universe gradually waking up and becoming aware of itself" (Nagel, 2012, p. 85).

Panpsychism is not a new idea. Most people used to believe in it, and many still do. All over the world, traditional people saw the world around them as alive and in some sense conscious or aware: the planets, stars, the earth, plants, and animals all had spirits or souls. Ancient Greek philosophy grew up in this context, although some of the earliest philosophers were hylozoists rather than panpsychists; that is, they saw all things as in some degree alive, without necessarily supposing that they had sensations or experiences. In medieval Europe, philosophers and theologians took for granted that the world was full of animate beings. Plants and animals had souls, and stars and planets were governed by intelligences. Today, this attitude is usually rejected as "naïve," "primitive," or "superstitious." Searle described it as "absurd" (Searle, 1992, pp. 43-50).

In the United States, the pioneering psychologist William James (1842-1910) advocated a form of panpsychism in which individual minds and a hierarchy of lower- and higher-order minds constituted the reality of the cosmos (Searle, p. 31). The philosopher Charles Sanders Peirce (1839-1914) saw the physical and mental as different aspects of underlying reality: "All mind more or less partakes of the nature of matter… Viewing a thing from the outside… it appears as matter. Viewing it from the inside… it appears as consciousness" (Searle, p. 32).

In France, the philosopher Henri Bergson (1859-1941) took this tradition of thought to a new level by emphasizing the importance of memory. All physical events contain a memory of the past, which is what enables them to endure. The unconscious matter of mechanistic physics was assumed by Bergson's contemporaries to persist unchanged until acted on by external forces; matter lived in an eternal instant, and had no time within it. Bergson argued that mechanistic physics treated changes cinematographically, as if there were a series of static, frozen moments. But for Bergson, this kind of physics was an abstraction that left out the essential feature of living nature. "Duration is essentially a continuation of what no longer exists into what does exist. This is real time, perceived and lived... Duration therefore implies consciousness; and we place consciousness at the heart of things for the very reason that we credit them with a time that endures" (Searle, p. 33).

The leading panpsychist philosopher in the English-speaking world was Alfred North Whitehead (1861-1947), who started his career as a mathematician at Trinity College, Cambridge, where he taught Bertrand Russell. They co-authored *Principia Mathematica* (1910-1913), one of the most important works in 20th-century mathematical philosophy. Whitehead then developed a theory of relativity that made almost identical predictions to Einstein's, and both theories were confirmed by the same experiments.

Whitehead was probably the first philosopher to recognize the radical implications of quantum physics. He realized that the wave theory of matter destroyed the old idea of material bodies as essentially spatial, existing at points in time, but without any time within them. According to quantum physics, every primordial element of matter is "an organized system of vibratory streaming of energy" (Griffin, 1998, p. 49). A wave does not exist in an instant: it takes time, and its waves connect the past and the future. He thought of the physical world as made up not of material objects, but of actual entities or events. An event is a happening or a becoming. It has time within it. It is a process, not a thing. As Whitehead put it, "An event in realizing itself displays a pattern." The pattern "requires a duration involving a definite lapse of time, and not merely an instantaneous moment" (Griffin, 1998, p. 49).

As Whitehead made clear, physics itself was pointing to the conclusion that Bergson had already reached. There is no such thing as timeless matter. All physical objects are processes that have time within them—an inner duration. Quantum physics shows that there is a minimum time period for events, because everything is vibratory, and no vibration can be instantaneous. The fundamental units of nature, including photons and electrons, are temporal as well as spatial. There is no "nature at an instant" (Griffin, 1998, p. 113).

Perhaps the most astonishing and original feature of Whitehead's theory was his new perspective on the relationship between mind and body as a relationship in time. The usual way of conceiving this relationship is spatial: your mind is inside your body, while the physical world is outside. Your mind sees things from within; it has an inner life. Even from the materialist point of view, the mind is literally "inside"—inside the brain, insulated within the darkness of the skull. The rest of the body and the entire external world are "outside."

By contrast, for Whitehead, mind and matter are related as phases in a process. Time, not space, is the key to their relationship. Reality consists of moments in process, and one moment informs the next. The distinction between moments requires the experiencer to feel the difference between the moment of now and past or future moments. Every actuality is a moment of experience. As it expires and becomes a past moment, it is succeeded by a new moment of "now," a new subject of experience. Meanwhile, the moment that has just expired becomes a past object for the new subject—and an object for other subjects, too. Whitehead summed this up in the phrase, "Now subject, then object" (de Quincey, 2008). Experience is always "now," and matter is always "ago." The link from the past to the present is physical causality, as in ordinary physics, and from the present to the past is feeling, or, to use Whitehead's technical term, "prehension," meaning, literally, seizing or grasping.

According to Whitehead, every actual occasion is therefore both determined by physical causes from the past, and by the self-creative, self-renewing subject that both chooses its own past and chooses among its potential futures. Through its prehensions it selects what aspects of the past it brings into its own physical being in the present, and also chooses among the possibilities that determine its future. It is connected to its past by selective memories, and connected to its potential future through its choices. Even the smallest possible processes, like quantum events, are both physical and mental; they are oriented in time. The direction of physical causation is from the past to the present, but the direction of mental activity runs the other way, from the present into the past through prehensions, and from potential and futures into the present. There is thus a time-polarity between the mental and physical poles of an event: physical causation from past to present, and mental causation from present to past.

Whitehead was not proposing that atoms are conscious in the same way that we are, but that they have experiences and feelings. Feelings, emotions, and experiences are more fundamental than human consciousness, and every mental event is informed and causally conditioned by material events, which are themselves composed of expired experiences. Knowing can happen only because the past streams into the present, forming it and shaping it, and at the same time the subject chooses among the possibilities that help determine its future (de Quincey, 2008).

Whitehead's philosophy is notoriously difficult to follow, especially in his key book *Process and Reality* (1929), but his insights about the temporal relationship of mind and matter point to a way forward, and are well worth trying to understand, even if they are very abstract. One of his modern exponents, Christian de Quincey, has described his idea as follows:

"Think of reality as made up of countless gazillions of 'bubble moments', where each bubble is both physical and mental - a bubble or quantum of sentient energy.... Each bubble exists for a moment and then pops! and the resulting 'spray' is the objective 'stuff' that composes the physical pole of the next momentary bubble... Time is our experience of the ongoing succession of these momentary bubbles of being (or bubbles of becoming) popping in and out of the present moment of now. We feel this succession of moments as the flow of the present slipping into the past, always replenished by new moments of 'now' from an apparently inexhaustible source we objectify as the future... The future does not exist except as potentials or possibilities in the present moment – in experience – which is always conditioned by the objective pressure of the past (the physical world). Subjectivity (consciousness, awareness) is what-it-feels-like to experience these possibilities, and choosing from them to create the next new moment of experience" (de Quincey, 2008, p. 99).

Rupert Sheldrake

Conscious and Unconscious Minds

There are at least two senses of the word "unconscious." One means totally devoid of mind, experience, and feeling, and this is what materialists mean when they say matter is unconscious. Physicists and chemists treat the systems they study as unconscious in this absolute sense. But a very different meaning of "unconscious" is implied by the phrase "unconscious mind." Most of our own mental processes are unconscious, including most of our habits. When driving a car we can carry on a conversation while our perceptions of the road and other vehicles affect our responses, without our being consciously aware of all our movements and choices. When I come to a familiar road junction, I may turn right automatically, because this is my habitual route. I am choosing among possibilities, but choosing on the basis of habit. By contrast, if I am driving in an unfamiliar town and trying to find my way with the help of a map, my choice when I come to a junction depends on conscious deliberation. But only a small minority of our choices are conscious. Most of our behaviour is habitual, and habits by their very nature work unconsciously.

Like humans, animals are largely creatures of habit. Yet the fact that they are not conscious of most of their actions—as we are not conscious of most of our own—does not mean they are mindless machines. They have a mental aspect as well as a physical aspect, and their mental aspect is shaped by their habits, feelings, and potentialities, among which they choose, unconsciously or consciously.

It may not make much sense to suggest that electrons, atoms, and molecules make conscious choices, but they may make unconscious choices on the basis of habits, just as we do and animals do. According to quantum theory, even elementary particles like electrons have many alternative future possibilities. The calculation of their behaviour by physicists involves taking all their possible futures into account (Feynman, 1962). Electrons are physical in that they re-enact elements of their past; but they also have a mental pole in that they relate this re-enactment of the past to their future potentialities, which in some sense work backwards in time.

But can we meaningfully say that electrons have experiences, feelings, and motivations? Can they be attracted towards one possible future, or repelled by another? The answer is "yes." For a start, they are electrically charged; they "feel" the electric field around them; they are attracted towards positively charged bodies, and repelled by those with negative charges. Physicists model their behaviour mathematically without supposing that that their feelings, attractions, and repulsions are anything other than physical forces, or that their individually unpredictable behaviour is governed by anything other than chance and probability. Materialists would say that only by fanciful metaphors can they be seen to have feelings or experience. But some physicists think differently, like David Bohm and Freeman Dyson. Bohm observed, "The question is whether matter is rather crude and mechanical or whether it gets more and more subtle and becomes indistinguishable from what people have called mind" (quoted by Dossey, 1991, p. 12). Freeman Dyson wrote,

I think our consciousness is not just a passive epiphenomenon carried along by the chemical events in our brains, but is an active agent forcing the molecular complexes to make choices between one quantum state and another. In other words, mind is already inherent in every electron, and the processes of human consciousness differ only in degree but not in kind from the processes of choice between quantum states which we call 'chance' when they are made by an electron (Dyson, 1979, p. 249).

These are difficult questions, and raise all sorts of questions about the meaning of words like "feeling," "experience," and "attraction." Are they metaphorical when applied to quantum systems? Perhaps. But we do not have a choice between metaphorical and non-metaphorical thinking. There are no metaphor-free zones in science. The whole of science is suffused with legal metaphors, as in "laws of nature," materialist theories of mind in computer metaphors, and so on. But the issues are not merely literary or rhetorical; they are also scientific. As Bergson and Whitehead made clear, the mental and physical aspects of material bodies have different relationships to time and to causation.

Rupert Sheldrake

Minds Beyond Brains

If our minds are not just the activity of our brains, there is no need for them to be confined to the insides of our heads. As I argue in my book *Science Set Free* (2012) (called *The Science Delusion* in the UK), our minds are extended in every act of perception, reaching even as far as the stars. Vision involves a two-way process: the inward movement of light into the eyes, and the outward projection of images. What we see around us is in our minds but not in our brains. When we look at something, in a sense our mind touches it. This may help to explain the sense of being stared at. Most people say they have felt when someone was looking at them from behind, and most people also claim to have made people turn round by looking at them. This ability to detect stares seems to be real, as shown in many scientific tests, and even seems to work through closed circuit television.

Minds are extended beyond brains not only in space but also in time, and connect us to our own pasts through memory and to virtual futures, among which we choose. As discussed in *Science Set Free*, repeated failures to find memory traces fit well with the idea of memory as a resonant phenomenon, where similar patterns of activity in the past affect present activities in minds and brains. Individual and collective memory both depend on resonance, but self-resonance from an individual's own past is more specific and hence more effective. Animal and human learning may be transmitted by morphic resonance across space and time. The hypothesis of morphic resonance proposes that similar patterns of activity in self-organizing systems affect subsequent similar patterns across space and time. In its most general sense this hypothesis suggests that memory is inherent in nature and that the so-called laws of nature are more like habits. Each species has a kind of collective memory. The resonance theory helps account for the ability of memories to survive serious damage to brains, and is consistent with all known kinds of remembering. This theory predicts that if animals, say rats, learn a new trick in one place, say Harvard, rats all over the world should be able to learn it faster thereafter. There is already evidence that this actually happens. Similar principles apply to human learning. For example, if millions of people do standard tests, like IQ tests, they should become progressively easier, on average, for other people to do. Again, this seems to be what happens. Individual memory and collective memory are different aspects of the same phenomenon and differ in degree, not in kind.

And if minds are not confined to brains in space or in time, it becomes much easier to understand how psychic phenomena like telepathy might fit into an expanded, postmaterialist science.

Most people claim to have had telepathic experiences. Numerous statistical experiments have shown that information can be transmitted from person to person in a way that cannot be explained in terms of the normal senses. Telepathy typically happens between people who are closely bonded, like mothers and children, spouses, and close friends. Many nursing mothers seem to be able to detect when their babies are in distress when they are miles away. The commonest kind of telepathy in the modern world occurs in connection with telephone calls when people think of someone who then rings, or who just know who's calling. Numerous experimental tests have shown that this is a real phenomenon. It does not fall off with distance. Social animals seem to be able to keep in touch with members of their group at a distance telepathically, and domesticated animals like dogs, cats, horses, and parrots often pick up their owners' emotions and intentions at a distance, as shown in experiments with dogs and parrots.

Other psychic abilities include premonitions and precognitions, as shown by the anticipation of earthquakes, tsunamis, and other disasters by many species of animals. Human premonitions usually occur in dreams or through intuitions. In experimental research on human presentiments, future emotional events seem able to work "backwards" in time to produce detectable physiological effects.[14]

---

[14] *More details and references are given in my book Science Set Free (Sheldrake, 2012)*

Scientific Futures

The sciences are entering a new phase. The materialist ideology that has ruled them since the 19th century is out of date. All 10 of its essential doctrines have been superseded.

The sciences will have to change for another reason, too: they are now global. Mechanistic science and the materialist ideology grew up in Europe, and were strongly influenced by the religious disputes that obsessed Europeans from the 17th century onwards. But these preoccupations are alien to cultures and traditions in many other parts of the world.

In 2011, the worldwide expenditure on scientific and technological research and development was more than $1 trillion, of which China spent $100 billion (Royal Society, 2011). Asian countries, especially China and India, now produce enormous numbers of science and engineering graduates. In 2007, at the B.Sc. level there were 2.5 million science and engineering graduates in India and 1.5 million in China (Royal Society, 2011) compared with 515,000 in the US (US Census Data, 2011). In addition, many of those studying in the US and Europe are from other countries: in 2007, nearly a third of the graduate students in science and engineering in the US were from outside the country, with the majority being from India, China, and Korea (National Science Foundation, 2011).

Yet the sciences as taught in Asia, Africa, the Islamic countries, and elsewhere are still packaged in an ideology shaped by their European past. Materialism gains its persuasive power from the technological applications of science. But the successes of these applications do not prove that this ideology is true. Penicillin will go on killing bacteria, jet planes will keep on flying, and mobile telephones will still work if scientists move on to wider views of nature.

No one can foresee how the sciences will evolve, but I believe that by freeing the sciences from the ideology of materialism, new opportunities for debate and dialogue are opening up, and so are new possibilities for research.

References

Carr, B. (Ed.) (2007). *Universe or Multiverse?* Cambridge: Cambridge University Press.

Collins, R. (2007). The multiverse hypothesis: a theistic perspective. In Carr, B. (Ed.) *Universe or Multiverse?* Cambridge: Cambridge University Press, pp. 459-480.

Crick, F. (1994). *The Astonishing Hypothesis: The Scientific Search for the Soul.* London: Simon and Schuster;

Dennett, D. (1991). *Consciousness Explained.* Boston: Little, Brown and Co.

de Quincey, C. (2008). Reality bubbles. *Journal of Consciousness Studies,* 15, 94-101.

d'Espagnat, B. (1976). *Conceptual Foundations of Quantum Mechanics.* Reading, MA: Benjamin.

Dossey, L. (1991). *Meaning and Medicine.* New York: Bantam Books.

Dyson, F. (1979). *Disturbing the Universe.* Harper and Row, New York;

Ellis, G. (2011). The untestable multiverse. *Nature,* 469, 294-295.

Feynman, R. (1962). *Quantum Electrodynamics.* Reading, MA: Addison Wesley.

Greene, B. (2011). *The Hidden Reality: Parallel Universes and the Deep Laws of the Cosmos.* London: Allen Lane.

Griffin, D. R. (1998). *Unsnarling the World-Knot: Consciousness, Freedom and the Mind-Body Problem.* Eugene, OR: Wipf and Stock.

Hawking, S. & Mlodinow, L. (2010). *The Grand Design: New Answers to the Ultimate Questions of Life.* London: Bantam Press.

Nagel, T. (2012). *Mind and Cosmos: Why the Materialist Neo-Darwinian Conception of Nature is Almost Certainly False.* Oxford: Oxford University Press.

National Science Foundation, accessed June 2011: http://www.nsf.gov/statistics/infbrief/nsf09314/

Popper, K. R. & Eccles, J. C. (1977). *The Self and Its Brain.* Berlin: Springer International.

Royal Society (2011). *Knowledge, Networks and Nations: Global Scientific Collaboration in the 21st Century*, Policy Document 03/11. London: Royal Society.

Searle, J. (1992). *The Rediscovery of the Mind.* Cambridge, MA: MIT Press.

Sheldrake, R. (2009). *A New Science of Life* (3rd edition). London: Icon Books.

Sheldrake, R. (2012). *Science Set Free: 10 Paths to New Discovery.* New York: Random House.

Smolin, L. (2006). *The Trouble With Physics: The Rise of String Theory, The Fall of a Science, and What Comes Next.* London: Allen Lane.

Strawson, G. (2006). Realistic monism: why physicalism entails panpsychism. *Journal of Consciousness Studies*, 13, 3-31.

US Census data. (accessed June 2011). http://www.census.gov/compendia/statab/2011/tables/11s0807.pdf.

Chapter Eight

Science within Consciousness: A Progress Report

Amit Goswami, PhD[15]

It is well known that most scientists today like to work under a paradigmatic umbrella of a metaphysics called scientific materialism (SM), according to which every thing is a phenomenon of matter and material interactions in space and time. What is not generally well known, especially among nonphysicists, is that the latest physics—quantum physics—has established both theoretically and experimentally that there is a domain of reality beyond space and time (called a nonlocal domain, characterized by instant interconnection or signal-less communication), and therefore SM is not scientifically tenable.

The phenomenon that rules out SM in this definitive manner is fundamental to quantum physics—the wave-particle duality of all objects. Quantum objects are waves of possibility residing in an instantly interconnected domain of reality called the domain of potentiality. Only when an observer measures, the waves collapse instantly without going through space and time to localized particles. In other words, the collapse, too, is nonlocal; the causation behind it is nonmaterial, called downward causation. In contrast, material causation is upward causation as evident from the reductionistic nature of material interaction.

These things are not debatable; these are facts. Everyone, especially the practitioner of postmaterialist science, must come to terms with these facts when developing their theories.

[15] *Center for Quantum Activism, Eugene, OR 97402*

The important question that takes us to a science within consciousness (SWC) is the question of the role of the observer in quantum measurement: why is the observer needed for the collapse (Goswami, 1989, 1993, 1994)? Werner Heisenberg, the co-discoverer of quantum physics himself, gave us a hint: a quantum measurement is the change in our knowledge about the object. Before measurement, we only knew possibilities and probabilities; but after measurement, we know exactly where the object is. What is the vehicle through which we gather knowledge? Consciousness, of course. Quantum physics demands (von Neumann, 1955) that the collapsing consciousness is nonmaterial.

It took a while to find a paradox-free way to introduce nonmaterial consciousness into quantum physics, but eventually in 1985, I discovered that if consciousness is the ground of all being and matter exists as possibilities within consciousness for consciousness to choose from, all paradoxes are resolved (Goswami, 1989, 1993). The physicists Henry Stapp (1993) and Casey Blood (2001) reached virtually the same conclusion.

Controversy exists because scientific materialists maintain that alternative solutions to the quantum measurement problem must exist. Some scientists believe that such solutions already exist, such as the many worlds theory, although it has been pointed out by many physicists that this theory does not save SM, but instead leads us to an unverifiable arbitrary new metaphysics with incredible violation of the principle of parsimony (using the least possible number of unverifiable assumptions). Nevertheless, when a naïve reader, and a nonscientist to boot, is fed a table of various suggested solutions of the quantum measurement paradox, including the consciousness-based one to be sure, the impression is created that viable alternatives to the consciousness-based solution exists.

For developing a postmaterialist science, what is important is to realize that it is impossible to understand the latest model of physics—quantum physics—without positing consciousness as the ground of being. You can, of course, take the position of asking, "Why should we heed the lesson of physics to make our models of other fields?" But I think a vast amount of empirical data that already exists will change your mind.

Behold! The idea that consciousness is an essential aspect of reality is not new. All spiritual traditions for millennia have supported the idea, based on the codified experiences of great researchers who can be regarded as the founders of our civilization. In the tail end of the 19th century, the great Sigmund Freud rediscovered the causal efficacy of consciousness in human affairs in the form of what he called the unconscious. The idea of the unconscious is now on solid empirical ground (Goswami, 2008a). Quantum physics is really only the third in line to make the same claim, this time solidly based on objective scientific theory and data.

Scientific progress depends on making bold new assumptions that expand science into new arenas. In 1994, I made the bold new assumption that I call quantum psycho-physical parallelism, which expands science to the arena of the living and the conscious. Thus began the new postmaterialist paradigm of science within consciousness. So far, I have successfully applied the new science to biology (Goswami, 1994, 2008b), to medicine (Goswami, 2004), to economics (Goswami, 2015) and to psychology (Goswami and Pattani, in press).

Briefly, science within consciousness enables us to tackle the following hitherto difficult questions (not an exclusive list by any means):

- The ecology of the psyche
- The origin and nature of the self
- The nature of the unconscious
- The existence of the paranormal
- The nature and origin of life
- The nature of evolution in view of new controversies about the explanatory power of neo-Darwinism
- Is there purpose in all this?
- What is health?
- The science of alternative medicine practices
- The chakras and science of the heart
- Creativity and creative transformation
- Is there life after death?
- Quantum psychology and quantum psychotherapy
- What is enlightenment?

The Ecology of the Psyche and Quantum Psycho-Physical Parallelism

We have our sensory experiences which are external; everyone agrees about that. Not so for our internal experiences. They are controversial on several counts.

First, how many internal experiences are there, and second, are they physical or do they involve the nonphysical?

Amazingly, although today we debate, the East Indians gave us an answer three thousand years ago, an answer reached via meditation. Their answer is four: sensing (of the physical), feeling (vital energies), thinking (meaning), and intuiting (the Platonic archetypes such as truth and love).

Why meditation is needed to discern the internal experiences is that, at first look at the internal, all we find is thought, a property of the mind. This is the reason that the internal-external dichotomy problem is called even today the mind-body problem. But if you look closely, if you meditate on it, you find some thoughts come with a lot of energy; you can even trace the source of the energy to your body. These passionate thoughts we call emotion, and you now can discern that they consist of thought plus feeling of vital energies connected to the body's vitality.

Similarly, some thoughts are special because they come with some clarity or truth-value; we are bothered by them and call them intuitive thought—thinking plus intuiting. Thinking at its core value is about meaning, and intuition is about the archetypal context of meaning.

In modern times, the psychologist Carl Jung, from a study of his large number of case histories, empirically discovered four personality types—sensing, feeling, thinking, and intuiting. This agrees with there being four types of experiences; the dominant experience determines the personality type.

Are the internal experiences physical or nonphysical? If we say they are nonphysical (since they are internal and qualitatively different from external experiences, it is natural to perceive them as nonphysical), the materialist objects with one word: dualism. How do the dual—physical and nonphysical—interact? This is the mind-body or psyche-body problem. The materialist way out is to posit that these experiences are caused by the physical body—if they mean anything at all!

Materialists think the brain is a computer of sorts, which somehow produces what we call the mind. But as the philosophers John Searle (1994) and Roger Penrose (1991) have pointed out, mind also involves meaning, and computers cannot process meaning. So the dilemma is solved if mind is nonphysical.

Similarly, I have argued that feelings are our experiences of the movement of nonphysical morphogenetic fields, the fields consciousness uses for biological form-making (Goswami, 2008b; also see later).

It is easy to see that the laws of science are part of the archetype of truth; in other words, the archetype of truth sets the context for the laws of science and therefore could not possibly be of material origin. This, by the way, is the reason that materialists deny the existence of archetypes and intuition.

But what is the answer to dualism? The solution of SWC is: quantum psycho-physical parallelism. We posit that like matter, mind, the morphogenetic fields, and the archetypes (except truth, which is absolute; see Goswami and Pattani, in press) all are quantum possibilities for consciousness to choose from. When consciousness chooses, we have the corresponding experience.

In other words, we have four worlds of quantum possibilities: physical, vital, mental, and archetypal (also called supramental), from which come our experiences. What maintains the parallelism? Consciousness, of course, through its nonlocality which is signal-less communication; if there is no signal, there is no interaction, and no interaction dualism either.-

Implicitly we are assuming that thoughts, feelings, and intuitions, like matter, are quantum objects. Elsewhere I have cited good evidence for this (Goswami, 2008a) and also have demonstrated that the internal quality of the experiences of the psyche arises from the quantum nature of its objects. In contrast, matter in bulk—which is what we directly experience through our senses—is approximately Newtonian and deterministic; hence they appear to be objective and external.

It is imperative that we recognize the importance of the micro-makes-up-macro way the material world is built. The stability of macro-matter enables matter to make stable representations of the subtle energies behind our subtle experiences. In this way, the morphogenetic fields are represented by the body organs at the chakras (see below) and mind is represented in the brain. The supramental is yet to be represented en masse in the physical at this stage of our evolution, although certain individuals may already have been doing it (see later).

The Origin and Nature of the Self

The quantum measurement problem can be solved by accepting the primacy of consciousness. Since as early as 1989, I have been emphasizing that the biggest triumph of this solution is that it explains how our subject/self arises in connection with the brain along with the object (Goswami, 1989, 1993). In 1994, the philosopher David Chalmers became famous by calling the problem of the self the "hard problem" of neurophysiology, but he was being too kind. It is really an impossible problem for materialists, simply because if you start with objects, whatever conglomerate you make, it will always be an object! So either our self is false—that is, without causal efficacy—or SM is wrong. Quantum measurement theory shows the latter to be true.

The crucial element of the argument is that the brain has a tangled hierarchy—a causally circular hierarchy of two of its component apparatuses: the perception apparatus and the memory apparatus—built into it. Because of this circular hierarchy, when consciousness "enters" it in order to collapse a brain state, it gets trapped; it identifies with the brain and becomes the self (Goswami, 1993; Goswami and Pattani, in press).

This tangled hierarchical self I call the quantum self. This is not the end of the story of the self. Via reflection in the mirror of memory, the self acquires conditioning and personalities and becomes simple hierarchical. This latter is what we call the ego self—ego character plus ego-persona (Goswami and Pattani, in press).

In this way, SWC not only explains the dependent co-arising (with the collapsed object of experience) of the self, but also its twofold nature: a higher self, defined by tangled hierarchy and a lower self, defined by conditioning and simple hierarchy in agreement with spiritual traditions and transpersonal psychology.

Do we have causal efficacy? Or are we just an ornamental existence without any causal power as materialists propose? Do we have free will? Yes, we do, as exemplified by our creativity. Elsewhere I have shown (Goswami, 2014) how the ego and the quantum self work together via the creative process to access the power of downward causation, making creativity possible (also see later).

The Nature of the Unconscious

Downward causation collapses the brain with which we identify as the subject of an experience along with the object(s) of experience. Before collapse, the object and the brain are potentialities; after collapse we have the subject-object split that we call awareness. In contrast, the nonlocal consciousness from which the dependent co-arising takes place remains unconscious, without subject-object split awareness. In this way, what Freud called the unconscious is really consciousness without awareness.

However, the quantum vision of the unconscious is much wider than the Freudian personal unconscious, and even the later Jungian version of the collective unconscious. The personal unconscious consists of quantum possibilities arising mostly from suppressed and repressed childhood memory. Jung's collective unconscious similarly consists of quantum possibilities arising from suppressed memories from humanity's collective childhood. However, beyond all this we now have the quantum unconscious consisting of all the yet-unmanifest human potentiality. This extension of the concept of the unconscious is crucial for understanding the scope of human creativity (see later).

Extra-Sensory Perception

Whereas the role of nonlocal quantum consciousness is somewhat implicit in ordinary perception (you don't see the role without a lot of analysis as discussed above), in ESP—extra sensory perception--nonlocality is explicit; the only analysis we need is to demonstrate the role of consciousness.

Let's set the context by describing a typical distant viewing experiment pioneered by the physicists Russell Targ and Harold Puthoff (1974) and replicated many times ever since by many other researchers. One subject looks at a double blind selected scene or an object, and another (correlated) subject in a controlled laboratory at a distance draws a picture (or gives an oral description) of what his or her partner is looking at. What is viewed and the nonlocally received description of it are then compared. The experimenter looks for a matching rate that substantially beats the odds, and this this was found to be the case.

Is the nonlocality exhibited in distant viewing an example of quantum nonlocality? Parapsychologists hesitate to accept this idea because of Eberhard's theorem, which purports to have proved that no information can be transferred using quantum nonlocality. I have repeatedly pointed out (Goswami, 2001, 2004, 2008a) that, for information transfers between brains and minds in which consciousness is involved as the collapser of the synchronistic events that constitute the transfer of information, Eberhard's theorem does not apply. And of course, the proof of the pudding is in the eating; my theoretical idea has been verified by the replicated transferred potential experiments (Grinberg et al., 1994; Standish et al., 2004; Radin, 2009).

Let's discuss one of the experiments (Standish et al., 2004) that was designed much like a distant viewing, except that EEG machines were used to demonstrate a "physical" and objective transferred potential. Two subjects are chosen satisfying the following criteria: knowing each other well; having previous emotional and psychological connection; and experience in meditation and other introspective techniques. One person, called the "sender," is instructed to attempt sending an image or a thought, and the other, called the "receiver," is instructed to remain open to receive any image or thought from their partner during the duration of the experiment. The sender and receiver are put in sensorily isolated rooms 10 meters apart and their brains are connected to individual EEG machines. Now, the sender was alternately subjected to visual stimulation (stimulus on) and no visual stimulation (stimulus off). The receiver does not receive any light stimulation. In spite of this, the EEG of the receiver detected a signal whenever the sender's brain was stimulated by light.

The only explanation of the transferred potential is that consciousness collapses the similar events in correlated brains. In this kind of experiment, there is all the proof one needs of the violation of Eberhard's theorem, because information is transferred nonlocally between brains by virtue of quantum consciousness. By comparing a transferred potential with the very little brain potential you get for a control subject, you can tell that somebody is sending information and when.

So the same quantum nonlocality via quantum consciousness explanation should hold for mental telepathy as in distant viewing: consciousness collapses similar events of meaning in correlated minds.

The Nature and Origin of Life

Molecular biology can never answer the question, What is life? Just ponder: here is a living cell, and a moment later the same cell is dead. There is no change in molecular composition or dynamics. In this way it is easy to see, as the physicist Niels Bohr pointed out long ago, the molecular description of a living cell must be complemented by another complementary aspect that we are missing.

In SWC, this complementary aspect is recognized: it is consciousness. When consciousness is represented in the cell, it is alive; when consciousness withdraws, the cell is dead. And the key to the cell's ability to represent consciousness is, as elucidated above, a tangled hierarchy among the components of the cell.

To summarize, what characterizes a living cell is that two of its component apparatuses are acting tangled hierarchically; in the dead cell the tangled hierarchical dynamics cease to operate.

The collapse of the possibility state of the cell produces the subject-object split, an "I" of the cell experiencing itself separate from its environment. In this way, living cells have the propensity to maintain integrity; dead cells and inanimate matter do not.

It is easy to identify the tangled hierarchical components of a living cell; they are the DNA and the protein molecules. DNA has the genetic code to make proteins, and protein is needed to make the DNA (Hofstadter, 1980; Goswami, 1994, 2008a).

It is this tangled hierarchical dynamics of the making of the DNA-protein duo that makes it impossible to understand the origin of a living cell from molecular biology alone. Purely material interactions among molecules can only produce conglomerates step by step, simple hierarchy. But the tangled hierarchical DNA-protein combination, along with a cell wall confinement and cytoplasm and all that can evolve as a quantum possibility, that consciousness collapses. In this way, the origin of life can be explained.

Something else needs to be recognized here. Apart from the tangled hierarchical DNA-protein combination, the cell has a form which is also crucial for its existence. Molecular dynamics cannot explain form either; we need to postulate additional nonphysical form-making fields for that. Rupert Sheldrake (1981) calls these fields morphogenetic fields. Consciousness makes the form of the cell with the aid of these morphogenetic fields; think of them as intermediary blueprints for consciousness to make form.

What does the cell experience? Apart from the external experience of the world as separate from itself, it also experiences something internal—the movements of the morphogenetic field of form making. In other words, even single cells must have feelings. Materialists may think of this as an anachronism, but I think there is now a consensus among postmaterialist scientists that this is so! Animals—and all multicellular creatures—all feel, and the capacity for feeling extends all the way down to the single cell organism.

If Neo-Darwinism is Wrong, How Should We Explain Evolution?

Neo-Darwinism cannot explain the fossil gaps or the one-way-ness of biological evolution from simple to complex (Goswami, 2008b). If this is not enough, recent geological data is showing the impossibility for supporting a step-by-step gradual evolution theory like neo-Darwinism based on the fossil record. But of course, there is evolution. Then how should we build a theory of it?

Darwinism is based on the Newtonian worldview: define stasis, that is, the concept of species for a biologist, and then find a mechanism for change. For Darwin, that consists of environmental adaptation via the variation-natural selection dual mechanism.

But physics is replacing the Newtonian worldview with the quantum worldview, where consciousness plays the pivotal role. Matter makes representations of consciousness and its experiences. Evolution, then, must be looked upon as an evolution of consciousness and its experiences. Naturally, then, evolution proceeds first with developing more and more sophisticated representations of the morphogenetic fields, giving rise to more and more sophisticated biological forms for the experience of feelings. Then, with the evolution of the neocortex, the evolution of the mind begins. In this way, evolution is progressive; it proceeds from simplicity to complexity, explaining the one-way-ness of the fossil data.

It is easy to see progressive stages of mental evolution in the anthropological data. In the hunter-gatherer era, human beings gave meaning to the physical world because they were motivated by survival, and the mind that developed was the physical mind. With the development of garden agriculture, our ancestors settled down, and men and women started working together growing food in the backyard; their interactions produced the necessity of giving meaning to feelings. In this way, what developed was the vital mind. This did not last to maturity. With the development of heavy machinery agriculture, men and women became separated again and some men (the landowners and their associates) began giving meaning to the mind itself, creating the era of the rational mind.

We are still in the era of the rational mind; we have been so all through the progression of material technology from agriculture to industrial to technological.

We now can predict the next evolutionary era when mind, en masse, will begin giving meaning to the supramental archetypes and develop the intuitive mind. We can see the very beginnings of this era starting about three thousand years ago. Gradually, the material technology will give way progressively to subtle technology, humans will concentrate more toward the satisfaction of higher needs, and preparations will begin toward representing the supramental in the physical directly (Aurobindo, 1998; de Chardin, 1963; Wilber, 1981; Goswami, 2008b).

Incidentally, one important offshoot of invoking the quantum worldview to explain evolution is the scientific explanation of the two tempos of evolution, a slow and gradual tempo, and a fast tempo (Eldredge & Gould, 1972). The fast tempo is necessary to explain the fossil gaps: evolution is so rapid that there is no time to lay out fossils, hence the gap. The quantum explanation of the fast tempo is that they represent quantum leaps. Indeed, there is evidence of the whole creative process in action in biological evolution (Goswami, 2008b).

Is There Purpose in All This?

Scientific materialists believe there is no purpose in the world, simply because the Newtonian worldview is cause-based; there is no room for purpose. On the other hand, all postmaterialists recognize the importance of purpose in biological, and especially human, affairs. In this way, a big challenge of postmaterialist science is to include purpose in its theories.

Looking at evolution from the consciousness point of view solves the problem for SWC. A consciousness-based theory of evolution posits that evolution has the purpose of making better and better representations of its experiential potentialities. How does consciousness guarantee it? The purposiveness must be part and parcel of quantum collapse itself. We must postulate that consciousness chooses, but always with the purpose of evolution in mind.

This solves another discomfort that many people have with a science based on consciousness: the fear of subjectivity getting into affairs of the world that should be objective. Making quantum collapse purposive in this way also makes collapse objective.

In summary: yes, there is purpose in all this. Cosmologists struggle with the anthropic principle, which says that the universe is created in such way that its evolution proceeds in a manner that culminates with the creation of life or sentience. Indeed, there is compelling evidence of the fine-tuning of the physical parameters of the universe. Similarly, there is extreme fine-tuning in the origin of life (Davies, 1999); these fine tunings suggest purpose.

What is Health?

For materialists, health is absence of illness. Like life, materialists cannot define health in its own essence. Of course, etymologically, the word "health" comes from the Anglo-Saxon word *haelen* for wholeness. So philosophers have always known that health is the experience of wholeness. But then, what is wholeness?

For materialists, we are just our physical bodies, so to them, wholeness is the totality of our physical organs. But this locally communicable wholeness is not really a whole; for that, we need instant communication. And of course, there are illnesses in which all the organs are fine, and yet the patient feels disease—the absence of ease. A well-known example is chronic fatigue syndrome.

In SWC, we are consciousness—a nonlocal whole—and its potentialities—embodied and unembodied. There are four different worlds of potentialities; we can think of having a "body" in each of these worlds. That plus consciousness as a whole gives us five different bodies: the physical, the vital, the mental, the supramental, and the whole (called "bliss body" in the spiritual literature of the Hindu Upanishads, *anandamaya kosha* in Sanskrit). Health is when all the bodies, in their manifest and unmanifest aspects, work in harmony.

A Science for Alternative Medicine

Also, with five different bodies, there are five different sources of illness and five different systems of healing. Naturally, we have not only physical body medicine (conventionally called "modern medicine," in our judgment a misnomer; we will call it allopathy), vital body medicine, and the more recent mind-body medicine. The latter two are labeled "alternative medicine." Supramental body medicine and bliss body medicine are bunched together and called "spiritual medicine."

And now a theory for each force of alternative medicine can be given. First, let's consider vital body medicine. The organs, I have already said, are representations of the vital blueprints of form called morphogenetic fields. Each organ in this way is correlated with its own specific blueprint. So a physical organ is really a physical/vital correlated duo. A physical organ will pick up any defect of its correlated morphogenetic field. On the other hand, if a physical organ undergoes some degeneration, as for example with aging, the vital counterpart will have difficulty in maintaining correlation with it; this can lead to the feeling of pain and discomfort. Much of our chronic disease is in this way old-age disease. There is, of course, the auto-immune component of old age suffering: the immune system cannot distinguish a deteriorated organ as one of its own.

So what is the remedy for the second kind of disease—chronic disease, which takes up 75% of all our medical expenses? One remedy, of course, is organ transplant, which is not easily available. A second is to change the physical organ through drugs and bring its function into synch with its intended function, which then would reestablish the correlation with the vital body partner. This is what allopathic medicine tries to do. A third alternative is that of vital body medicine: trying to modify the vital body function to bring it more in synch with the deteriorated physical organ function.

Remember that the vital energies are subtle; it is much easier to creatively manipulate vital energies than the physical. Even hands off healing by simple hand movements and gestures with healing intention can do the job, such as in Reiki and Chi Gong. How does this work? Remember, vital energies are possibilities for consciousness to choose from. Through the

Expanding Science

healer's intention and hand movements, the existing possibilities are fed with new possibilities, which the old ones interact with, producing still new possibilities until a desirable gestalt is achieved via unconscious processing. This is part of the creative process. When the gestalt of possibilities of vital movement is reached, consciousness in synchrony with the healer's intention chooses the synchronized gestalt of possibilities of vital movement that correlates well with the diseased physical counterpart.

This kind of creativity we call situational creativity, and this is the dynamic basis of all vital body healing systems. In herbal practices such as Ayurveda and Traditional Chinese Medicine (TCM), remedial vital possibilities are injected through a potent herb, which is empirically found to be effective for the given symptoms. In acupuncture, the puncture is designed to introduce random possibilities into the game (compare with the action of a monkey wrench), again with the use of empiricism and communication between the healer and the healee.

However, some effective herbs are often poison to the physical body and can produce some side effects, although not as much as allopathy does. So in homeopathy, one administers only the vital energies by imprinting water (in a water-alcohol mixture) with them and eliminating the physical component of the medicine altogether.

I have given details of the three specific vital body medicine system—TCM, Ayurveda, and homeopathy—elsewhere (Goswami, 2004).

One problem of allopathic medicine is the assumption of homogeneity. But patients are not identical machines with identical diseases to be treated with the same medicine. Instead, biological systems are heterogeneous, not homogeneous, and every patient is an individual. Two patients with the same disease will have individuality that makes the same homogeneous treatment ineffective. Vital body medicine rectifies the homogeneity problem (see Goswami, 2004 for details).

The SWC approach not only explains the efficacy of the existing vital body medicinal systems but also expands its scope to new horizons. For example, creativity research shows that there are two kinds of creativity. Besides the situational, we also have fundamental creativity involving the archetype—in this case, the archetype of wholeness. Here we go for creatively replacing the old morphogenetic correlates of organs via a quantum leap; by the new ones leading to regeneration of the organ. We can creatively replace the old morphogenetic correlates of organs via a quantum leap, leading to regeneration of the organ. Research in this area is still in its infancy.

Readers will be familiar with the use of such creativity and quantum leaps in the spontaneous healing of mind-body disease such as cancer. Deepak Chopra (1990) called it quantum healing, and I recognized the role of the creative process in it that has made quantum healing tractable and available for everyone (Goswami, 2004).

The Chakras and a Science of the Heart

The physical organs pertaining to all our important biological functions are bunched in areas of our body that were recognized as the sites of the seven major chakras millennia ago. In this way, SWC provides a scientific explanation of the chakras (Goswami, 2001). Chakras are those points around which are bunched the physical-vital dual systems of our body. When the possibility waves of such a duo collapses, we experience the movement of the vital as feeling; we feel the vital energy of movement (change) of the vital counterpart of the duo. An important question is this: Is there an experience of pure feeling associated with the collapse of the possibility wave at a chakra?

When I first explored the subject, I thought consciousness indeed collapses the possibility waves of a relevant vital-physical duo at a chakra. Of course, for the lower three chakras, evolutionarily the brain enters the picture and then the mind, making the experience of pure feeling rather difficult.

But of course, as I have pointed out earlier in the article, collapse requires a tangled hierarchy. We know that consciousness identifies with the neocortex, with the brain. Similarly, can we say that consciousness identifies with these heart chakra organs? But then we have to find this tangled hierarchy. But a detailed search of the structures of the organs of the body has convinced me that the only tangled hierarchy in a normal human body is in the neocortex.

But recently, I looked at the problem again from a TCM point of view. In TCM, when they talk about organs having an influence on other organs, they are not talking about physical organs: they are talking about the vital correlates of the physical organs. They even have pathways for the interactions between the vital correlates. They call these pathways meridians. For example, there is a meridian from the vital correlate of the liver, a navel chakra organ, to the vital correlate of a heart chakra organ. When I looked carefully, I found that, indeed, the tangled hierarchy exists between the vital blueprints of the navel chakra organs and those of the heart chakra organs; the tangled hierarchy involves the vital body and two different chakras. This is not a tangled hierarchy that causes compulsory self-reference like that which occurs in the brain with the collapse of the possibility wave. For that, we need a tangled hierarchy in the physical. But if we identify, even at the vital level, with a tangled hierarchy, mightn't we develop the sense of a self, which can be called the heart self or the heart center of the body?

Is the heart here the same as that talked about in spiritual traditions? Is it the same connotation? I think so. Mystics see the heart as synonymous with love. Elsewhere I have explained why the heart chakra is the center of the feeling of romantic love. When I fall in love romantically with a partner and vice versa, there is no me-not me distinction between me and the other; the immune system (represented by the thymus gland at the heart chakra) function is suspended for both of us (Goswami, 2004). The same is true for all shades of love, including unconditional love.

Actually, it may even be possible to establish a physical tangled hierarchy associated with the vital one for the navel-heart combination. Maybe this occurs via the bioelectric body at the skin which is measured with Kirlian photography, and which some people even see as the aura—a bioelectric body that we have in addition to the biochemical body of which the organs are part.

In any case, with the bioelectric body contributing a physical tangled hierarchy to complement the tangled hierarchy in the vital that we can cultivate and identify with, there will be an ability to collapse feelings independently of the neocortex, independent of thinking. If the feelings at the tangled hierarchical combination of the two chakras—navel and heart—are truly autonomous, like thinking in the brain, what then follows? Our entire context of living can undergo radical change. Then we should be able to derive additional insight about how to attain emotional maturity.

Let me go over this hypothesis again. First of all, the navel chakra is where the body ego is located; our feelings of security, self-respect, and self-love come from there. The heart chakra is where love for the other is felt. And the heart chakra-associated bioelectric body together with the navel chakra-associated bioelectric body form a tangled hierarchy, and thus achieve self-referential collapse of feelings in this navel-heart system—both self-love and other-love.

Behold! All this has to start at the level of feelings. When I allow the feeling energies between these two chakras to become causally circular, when the feeling relationships between the body individuality versus the heart togetherness becomes tangled hierarchical, then I have developed this identity with the self of the navel-heart combination; let's call the latter the tangled hierarchical heart.

Feelings at the navel chakra are an expression of selfishness in terms of sexuality. Subjects I love become objects of sex when I identify with the body ego. Sex becomes a conquest. But unconditional love is the opposite of this; it is an expansion of consciousness. So when I realize that the selfishness is to give way to the expansion, that's the journey of discovering the self of the tangled hierarchical heart. And then, when we integrate the self of the heart, which is based on feeling, with the self of the brain, which is based on meaning or rationality, we have developed what is called emotional intelligence. Here, quantum physics is helping us to understand the dynamics involved with how romantic love can become unconditional love, where selfishness is transcended via the discovery of "the other," and then eventually can lead to emotional intelligence by integrating the self of the heart with the self of the brain.

There is controversy about this, but I really think males have better connection with their navel chakra; they likely have more self-love than other-love. On the other hand, a woman has more connection with her heart chakra; her love is more of the other-love variety.

I really think that's about it: that masculine-feminine imbalance is what is keeping humanity from experiencing the heart as a separate self and achieving emotional intelligence. I think our biological make-up contributes to the imbalance and the culture reinforces it. What is the remedy? How can you, as a person of self-love, develop other love? How can you, as a person of other-love, develop self-love defying biology, defying culture?

Elsewhere, I talk about the creative exploration of love (Goswami, 2014). If a person of self-love does it sincerely, he will end up with the discovery of the "otherness" of the other that he is trying to love unconditionally. This is the beginning of other-love. Then it is a question of harmonizing the two: self-love and other love.

What does a person of other love do? When she explores love the quantum way, she similarly discovers the otherness of the other, and doing that discovers herself as an individual worthy of her own love. Her navel chakra identity or self-respect becomes strong as a result. From that, establishing a tangled hierarchy is just a matter of harmonizing the two identities.

Creativity and Creative Transformation

Philosophy has two prongs: ontology and epistemology. The quantum worldview is based on the ontology that consciousness—the domain of quantum potentiality—is the ground of all being. But this domain is unconscious in us. The epistemological question is: How do we access the quantum unconscious—the previously unexplored part of the unconscious? The answer is: quantum creativity.

What is quantum creativity? The way materialists see it, all human phenomena are one level of space-time phenomenon, and creativity is no exception. Quantum creativity, keeping up with the quantum worldview, is two-level creativity: it uses not only conscious processing but also unconscious processing. Conscious processing is usually called divergent thinking; it consists of using as many ways of looking at the problem that we can think of and that we can find in other people's work, on the Internet, etc. Conscious processing primes the unconscious for processing possibilities created by divergent thinking. If we allow the unconscious waves of possibility to expand with collapsing them, they will expand like all waves do, creating bigger and bigger pools of possibility for consciousness to choose from. Other ways to expand the pool further is to 1) work with a collaborator. The collaborator acts like the famous "double slit," dividing and recombining the possibility waves of meaning into further proliferation (Goswami, 2014). 2) Creating conflict—thesis and antithesis. Unconscious processes conflict, creating new possibilities altogether that the conscious cannot do.

The net result of unconscious processing is a discontinuous insight that people of creativity call the "aha experience" and that quantum physicists call the quantum leap (also called convergent thinking by some researchers). The "aha" surprise is the proof of discontinuity of a creative thought from ordinary stream-of-consciousness thinking.

Empirical data amply show that the creative process consists of four stages (Briggs, 1990):

- Preparation
- Incubation
- Sudden insight
- Manifestation

Preparation is what I call conscious processing above, and incubation is unconscious processing. You can also see them as focused doing and relaxed being. In my own experiences in a long creative life, I have found that what works best is alternative doing and being, which I humorously call the do-be-do-be-do process. Do-be-do-be-do produces the quantum leap of "aha" insight. I have elaborated all this and much more elsewhere (Goswami, 2014).

Is There Life After Death?

I have spoken of purpose before; in SWC there is purpose. Collapse by nonlocal consciousness—downward causation—is purposive.

A related question is the meaning of life. If there is purposiveness in how consciousness collapses the possibilities in our lives, and the purposiveness consists of making better and better representations of the subtle—feeling, meaning, and archetypes—then it makes sense that there is meaning in our lives, and the best meanings realized are those that make better and better representations of the archetypes.

But archetypes have many facets; they are quantum objects, after all. In a particular creative act, we discover one facet. It takes many such acts to get a mastery over an archetype, and obviously much time. Human life is short; archetypal investigations are long. To solve this dilemma, the laws of SWC have given us the phenomenon of reincarnation. We die; a part of us survives after death. When a future being by design uses the part that survived after my death, that being is my reincarnation.

According to materialists, as my body dies, my "I" disappears. Is this correct? This is where we need to be clear what the "I" is. Remember, an "I" has two components: one we call storyline. Content of the I's brain, born so and so, taking on such and such a profession, proud of such and such accomplishments, victimized by this and that suffering, and then passing away. But at a deeper level, what defines the "I" is the character. This ego/character processes things in this particular way, like the way of a politician, say. That's the character.

The character consists of the habit patterns of conditioning or propensities that the mental ego acquires in the process of learning—stimulus, response, reinforcement. Conditioning takes place because the probabilities associated with certain mental responses gain more weight via reinforcement over other possibilities (Mitchel & Goswami, 1992). What is the root of this change of probability weighting? The root cause is the nonlinear modification of the quantum mathematics of movement. The laws of this modification are part of the potential world of our archetypes. These propensities, called karma by the Hindus, are a law-like inheritance; they are stored in the nonlocal domain of reality. If we call them memory, we must qualify this memory as nonlocal memory, memory stored outside space and time, not in the brain.

And what the new science is saying is that the character element is a deeper aspect of the ego than the personality and storylines, and this is the part that is stored non-locally, as non-local memory.

Let me at this point describe an experiment that suggests the distinction of content and character. In the 1950's, the neurophysiologist Karl Lashley was trying to find the location of memory in the brain when we learn a behavior. He taught rats how to find cheese in a Y-maze. In one branch of the Y there is cheese, and the other branch of the Y gives an electric shock. Of course, the rats very quickly learn how to find the cheese. In order to find the memory of where that learning is located, Lashley started chopping off parts of the rats' brains.

So if, after chopping, the memory is gone, then the conclusion is that the memory must have been in that chopped portion of the brain. But with 5% chopped off—and mind you, different rats lost different 5% portions of the brain—nothing happened. Basically, all the rats could still find the cheese. So then, Lashley started chopping off 10%, then 20%. Even with 50% of the brain chopped off, the rats could no longer see, could no longer walk, but they crawled and found the cheese. Lashley concluded that the memory of learning, the propensity of finding the cheese, must reside all over the brain. Of course, an equally valid conclusion would be that it is not in the brain at all. It is nowhere in the brain. The neurophysiologist Karl Pribram, Lashley's student, adopted Lashley's idea that memory of learning resides throughout the brain. Pribram gave us the holographic theory of the brain, a theory that enjoyed popularity for a time. Now, it really does not seem to be a very logical idea. Quantum memory, non-local memories, is the other idea that is supported by Lashley's experiment. Memory of that propensity of finding the cheese is nowhere in the brain. The brain memory consists of the individual episodes of learning—the content learned—but the propensity learned transcends brain memory and is stored non-locally.

If memory is nonlocal, reincarnation can be explained as follows. Your nonlocal memory can be inherited by an aborning baby in some other place at a future time. Similarly, you yourself may have been privy to nonlocal memory of a past life before you. In other words, you are part of "string of pearls," a chain of manifest reincarnations of an ongoing locus of accumulating propensities. Elsewhere (Goswami, 2001) I call this locus quantum monad.

The empirical evidence for survival after death consists of the vast data on near-death experiences, a part of which are experiences of autoscopic viewing (Sabom, 1982). The experiencer describes that he or she was hovering over the operating table, and gives such specific description of the surgery that took place that it is hard to deny that he or she was seeing the surgery nonlocally through distance viewing (Goswami, 2001).

The empirical evidence for reincarnation consists of 1) the data on babies as to whether they are born as tabula rasa or with already developed capacity to learn. Research confirms what any parent already knows: babies are born with an enormous amount of innate capacities that are triggered as their life experiences develop.

2) There is also evidence that geniuses are born with an innate ability for creativity, including ample motivation passed on to them from their previous incarnations. 3) There are also many cases of phobia associated with past life incidents (Stevenson, 1974, 1977, 1987).

Additionally, there is evidence that each one of us comes to this incarnation with a learning agenda that Easterners call by the Sanskrit word dharma. To fulfill our dharma, we even bring the right propensities acquired during many past incarnations. The past life regression therapist David Cliness has data that verify that we are not reborn with our entire accumulated propensities; instead, we bring the particular set that would be needed to follow our dharma. Unfortunately, sometimes the contingencies of this life take us astray and we forget. And sometimes a situation triggers the memory in us via what creativity researchers call a crystallization experience (Briggs, 1990).

Quantum Psychology and Creativity in Psychotherapy

In view of reincarnation, it is clear that the meaning of a human life is best served if 1) we become aware of our karmic load from our past lives that we bring to this life, 2) we attempt to fulfill our dharma, and 3) we move towards attaining more propensity toward fundamental creativity, so that we can pursue our dharma.

The quintessential question of course is how? How do we work towards attaining a higher level of consciousness that will result in more inner satisfaction? The challenge is that you are on your own individual journey, and therefore the key is to find what works for you. No singular method or set timeframe will be appropriate for everyone. However, the psychotherapist Sunita Pattani and I have formulated certain general principles for addressing the how question (Goswami and Pattani, in press).

1. Willingness and Intention

Being ready, willing, and committed means that you will have to put in constant intention, as real change takes dedication and patience.

Fundamental change requires that we observe, question, strip away our masks, and look at ourselves for who we really are. It may be uncomfortable in parts; at times you may have to face your vulnerability.

It is also worth remembering that the journey of fundamental healing will most likely be a life-long occurrence.

2. We are Dichotomous Beings

One of the fundamental factors in quantum psychology is that we are both an individual (immanent) consciousness as well as a transcendent consciousness, and hence it can be said that we are dichotomous beings from the get-go. This fundamental dichotomy is compounded by other dichotomies: inner-outer, creativity-conditioning, negative emotional-positive emotional, head-heart, male-female etc. Understanding, balancing, and harmonizing how these dichotomies play out in our lives lays the foundation for emotional healing.

3. The Quantum Psychology Spectrum of Consciousness

The Quantum Psychology Spectrum of Consciousness is a five-fold classification of the level of awareness that we live: Levels 0 and 1 are classified as psychopathology—psychosis and neurosis. There are various factors, including genetic issues and childhood trauma, that may lead to the experience of these lower levels.

Level 2 is classified as "normal." We recognize that the term "normal" is a subjective term, as it means different things to different people. However, in quantum psychology we use the term "normal" to represent people who can cope with their neurosis in most situations, with the help of some occasional therapy if the going gets really tough. The objective of "normal" mental health is to enjoy a balanced psyche without too many ups and downs. Balancing the dichotomies mentioned above is helpful.

Level 3 is "positive mental health." At this level, we are consciously engaging in our personal growth and self-enhancement. We are fully exploring our human potential and are both working on and embodying and expressing the Platonic archetypes.

Level 4 is "enlightenment," which is experiencing a profound state of consciousness where we surpass ordinary states of consciousness and live the reality of who we really are (see below).

It is important to remember that this is a spectrum of consciousness, which means that we move between the different levels.

We are human beings with the capacity to experience a whole range of emotions, hence there will be times where our neurotic and negative emotional side will get the better of us. The Quantum Psychology Spectrum of Consciousness serves as a loose guide to help us reflect upon where we are along our own personal journey. It also helps us to grow so we can come out of the grips of the unconscious quicker. Indeed, this question of "how much time it takes you to get out of a negative episode" can be used as a measure for your particular level of awareness (Sperry, 2012).

4. The Four Worlds of Quantum Possibilities

At its very core, consciousness is undivided. This undivided state has four worlds of quantum possibilities: material, vital, mental, and archetypal/supramental. In quantum psychology, we seek to work with and explore and harmonize these four worlds of quantum possibilities within us: we aim to nourish the body and use our physical senses to experience the present moment; we work to balance our vital energies and release emotions that no longer serve us. We also work towards mastering our thoughts and realigning ourselves with the movement of consciousness. And finally, we strengthen our intuition so that we are able to better express the supramental archetypes, which is the purpose of our being.

5. The Iceberg of the Human Condition

One of the central tenets of quantum psychology is that consciousness is the ground of all being. In other words, ultimately there is nothing but consciousness, which can exist in a number of different ways—some unconscious and some conscious. In quantum psychology we call this the Iceberg of Human Condition, which includes the four major states of consciousness: the self, the subconscious, the collective unconscious, and the quantum unconscious.

As you can see, the self is our conscious awareness, which means that we have direct experience with it. There are three sublevels: the quantum self, ego-character, and ego-persona.

The quantum self is the "unconditioned you," or the "immediate you" when the collapse first occurs. In other words, in each new moment we have access to our unconditioned self if we choose to identify with it.

All therapy processes ultimately work towards helping one to align with this quantum self-aspect of themselves, and as a result make different choices that signify real change. Real "free choice" can only be made when we utilize this aspect of ourselves. Quite often what is happening is that we are continuously receiving stimulus through our five physical senses, and at this point our memory is kicking in and playing out conditioned responses. We have to actively train ourselves to slow our minds down and create space between our thoughts, so that we can experience our quantum self and make a decision outside of our past conditioning.

The creative process is our enabler here. In this way, we are proposing that most conventional therapies are really situational creativity and the healing is tentative. Fundamental healing can only be achieved through fundamental creativity engaging all four stages of the creative process.

What is Enlightenment?

Some of the enlightened people throughout history have reported states of consciousness that sure sound like the unqualified ground of being that consciousness is. If this is scientifically plausible or verifiable, then we have literally a verification of the basic premise of SWC.

In many spiritual traditions, the idea of enlightenment means having a sudden experience in which the nature of the self is revealed. Elsewhere (Goswami, 2014), I have argued that the enlightenment experience is part of a creative process for the exploration of the self archetype; it is the quantum leap from the ego to the quantum self when the quantum self-nature of the self is revealed. Some confusion exists in the spiritual literature which all can be resolved when we realize that the creative process has one more stage after the quantum leap—namely, manifestation. Manifestation consists of transformation to a "perfected" being, to an identity with the quantum self.

In Hinduism, the enlightenment experience is called Samadhi. Hindus then ask the question, "What is beyond Samadhi, beyond experience?" Well, beyond experience is the unconscious. For example, in deep sleep, we don't have any experience. But ordinary deep sleep is not particularly transformative. After sleep, when we wake up, we haven't changed. It is easy to understand why that is. In normal sleep, we continue to process, albeit unconsciously, the same kind of repressed emotions and suppressed thoughts that we have a problem with in waking life. This is why most of our dreams are "day-residue" dreams.

When the ego identity begins to fall away in the manifestation stage after the Samadhi experience, then the attachment to the suppression-repression dynamic also begins to fall away. The quality of sleep becomes different along with the quality of dreams. In sleep now, when we are one with the totality, we no longer process only the suppression-repression dynamic. In their place, some of the time we process wonderful new possibilities of consciousness. And when we wake up from this kind of "super" sleep or "creative" sleep, we enjoy profuse happiness instead of that suppression-repression dynamic that produces the mood swings that often happen upon waking up from ordinary sleep. In Hindu spirituality, the emphasis on the manifestation stage of creativity is on developing the capacity of such creative sleep, which the tradition calls by another name—Nirvikalpa Samadhi—Samadhi without separateness.

There are two kinds of this Nirvikalpa Samadhi that the experiential literature refers to. In Samadhi without separateness of the first kind, there is still a little bit of tendency to identify with the supramental possibilities, the archetypal values. In other words, there is a little bit of qualification still left to give to the self-identity. And then, in the very final stage, all possibilities are allowed. There is not even that little distinction that this is a heavenly possibility and that is an earthly possibility. There is no preference.

Most importantly, we now have a positive answer to the question: can one directly verify that consciousness is the ground of all being? Yes, one can verify experientially via the Nirvikalpa Samadhi of the second kind.

Some scientists may still object because any experience is subjective. There are two ways to deal with this. If we have such reports from more than one person, and we do, then the reports pass the test of weak objectivity—subjective but invariant when you go from one subject to another subject. The other way is to look for brain wave correlates of such exalted states. There is some recent data suggesting that there are brain wave correlates of such states and we have found them!

I hope I have amply demonstrated the versatility of science within consciousness, but this last item is a cinch. It would prove empirically that the individual self is indeed a representation of the cosmic Oneness.

References

Aurobindo, S. (1996). *The Life Divine*. Pondicherry, India: Sri Aurobindo Ashram.

Blood, C. (2001). *Science, Sense, and Soul*. L.A.: Ranaissance Books.

Briggs, J. (1990). *Fire in the Crucible*. L.A.: Tarcher/Penguine.

Chopra, D. (1990). *Quantum Healing*. N.Y.: Bantam-Doubleday.

Davies, P. (1999). *The Fifth Miracle: The Search for the Origin and Meaning of Life*. N. Y.: Simon & Schuster.

Dossey, L. (1991). *Meaning and Medicine*. N.Y: Bantam.

Eldrege, N. & Gould, S. J. (1972). "punctuated equilibria: an alternative to phyletic gradualiam." In *Models of Paleontology*. T. J. M. Schopf (Ed.), pp. 82-115. San Francisco: Freeman.

Goswami, A. (1989). The Idealistic interpretation of quantum mechanics. *Physics Essays*, 2, 385-400.

Goswami, A. (1993). *The Self-Aware Universe: How Consciousness Creates the Material World*. N.Y.: Tarcher/Putnam.

Goswami, A. (1994). *Science within Consciousness: a monograph*. Petaluma, CA: Institute of Noetic Sciences.

Goswami, A. (2001). *Physics of the Soul*. Charlottesville, VA: Hampton Roads.

Goswami, A. (2004). *The Quantum Doctor*. Charlottesville, VA: Hampton Roads.

Goswami, A. (2008a). *God is not Dead*. Charlottesville, VA: Hampton Roads.

Goswami, A. (2008b). *Creative Evolution*. Wheaton, IL: Theosophical Publishing House.

Goswami, A. (2011). *How Quantum Activism Can Save Civilization*. Charlottesville, VA: Hampton Roads.

Goswami, A. (2014). *Quantum Creativity: Think Quantum, Be Creative*. N. Y.: Hay House.

Goswami, A. (2015). *Quantum Economics*. Faber, VA: Rainbow Ridge Books.

Grinberg, J., Delaflor, M., Attie, L., & Goswami, A. (1994). Einstein Podolsky Rosen paradox in the human brain: The transferred potential. *Physics Essays*, 7, 422-28.

Hofstadter, D. (1980). *Goedel, Escher, Bach: an Eternal Golden Braid*. N.Y.: Basic Books.

Mitchel, M. & Goswami, A. (1992). Quantum mechanics for observer systems. *Physics Essays*, 5, 525-29.

Penrose, R. (1991). *The Emperor's New Mind*. N.Y.: Penguin.

Pert, C. (1997). *Molecules of Emotion*. N.Y.: Scribner.

Radin, D. (2009). *The Noetic Universe*. London: Transworld Publishers.

Sabom, M. (1982). *Recollections of Death: a Medical Report*. N. Y.: Harper & Row.

Searle, J. (1994). *The Rediscovery of the Mind*. Cambridge, MA: MIT Press.

Sheldrake, R. (1981). *A New Science of Life*. L.A.: Tarcher.

Sperry, L. (2012). Spiritually sensitive psychotherapy: an impending paradigm shift in theory and practice. In *The Oxford Handbook of Psychology and Spirituality*, L. Miller (Ed.), pp. 223-233. Oxford: Oxford University Press.

Standish, L. J., Kozak, L., Clark Johnson, L., & Richards, T. (2004). Electroencephalographic evidence of correlated event-related signals between the brains of spatially and sensory isolated human subjects. *Journal of Alternative and Complementary Medicine*, 10, 307-314.

Stapp, H. P. (1993). *Mind, Matter, and Quantum mechanics.* N.Y.: Springer.

Stevenson, I. (1974). *Twenty Cases Suggestive of Reincarnation.* Charlottesville: The University Press of Virginia.

Stevenson, I. (1977). Research into the evidence of man's survival after death. *Journal of Nervous and Mental Disease,* 165, 153-183.

Stevenson, I. (1987). *Children Who Remember Previous Lives: A Question of Reincarnation.* Charlottesville, VA: The University Press of Virginia.

Targ, R. & Puthoff, H. (1974). Information transfer under conditions of sensory shielding. *Nature,* 252, 602-07.

Teilhard de Chardin, P. (1961). *The Phenomenon of Man.* N.Y.: Harper & Row.

Wilber, K. (1981). *Up from Eden.* Garden City, N.Y: Anchor/Doubleday.

Chapter Nine

Beyond Gene Expression

Isabelle Goulet, PhD[16]

A deep-rooted belief in the mind of the general public, and amongst many scientists, is that we are victims of our genes.[17] They form a fixed blueprint that dictates everything: our physical attributes, our behavior, and our overall health status. Predetermined by our genes, our destiny is inescapable: "we are who we are and we do what we do, because we were simply 'born that way'" (Wright, 1999; Dawson, 2008). Therefore, any efforts to change our genetic fate is useless.

On the bright side, this belief makes human nature utterly simple: tell me what genes you are made of and I will tell you who you are. This was the primary motive to launch the Human Genome Project in the early 1990s. By sequencing the human DNA and mapping out all of its genes and their functions, we could predict what genes have in store for us—e.g. how long we would live and which diseases we would have. We could, for once, be proactive instead of reactive in the face of a threat of developing an illness. We could replace the defective genes with normal ones, through genetic therapy, to ensure a longer and healthier life. 12 years after the completion of the Project and many more years of associated research, it turns out our DNA does have lots in store for us, but not necessarily what

---

[16] *SCIENTIVE, 11 New Street, Newboro, Canada, Website: scientive.ca. Email: isabelle@scientive.ca*

[17] *A gene is the basic physical and functional unit of heredity. Genes are made of DNA (desoxyribonucleic acid) and act as instructions to make molecules called proteins (Genetics Home Reference.,2016a).*

we had initially anticipated. This chapter discusses the limitations of a gene-focused understanding of our life experience and health outcomes.

Genes Do Not Dictate Our Destiny

Identical twins are as close as ones can get in terms of sharing nearly identical copies of the same genetic material. If genes define most of our characteristics and experiences throughout life, we would expect twins to develop the same illnesses over time. Yet, twins who were born with similar genes often experience very different life outcomes as they get older. Several studies have confirmed that there are only moderate chances of both individuals in a pair of identical twins having the same disease, even if the disease in question is thought to have a genetic component. A study of 45,000 pairs of twins showed that there is no more than 20% probability that twins develop the same type of cancer (Lichtenstein et al., 2000). Another study found that for all male pairs where one twin has Alzheimer's Disease, only 45% of the healthy twins may develop the disease (Gatz et al., 2006). If one identical twin gets Type 2 diabetes, there is a 34% chance that the other one will as well, while the figure for Type 1 diabetes is only about 23% (Kaprio et al., 1992). This probability hovers around 40% for heart diseases (Tarnoki et al., 2014), 17% for inflammatory bowel disease (Thompson et al., 1996), and 15% for rheumatoid arthritis (Svendsen et al., 2013). The fact that most pairs of twins are discordant for illnesses suggests that the risk of developing diseases is only moderately influenced by heritable genetic factors. It is the non-genetic factors that seem to play a more prominent role in disease occurrence.

Another study, assessing genetic and environmental influences on adult mortality, found that genetic background has little impact on premature death from cancer (Sorensen et al., 1988). The death of a biological parent from cancer has no significant influence on the risk of death of its child who has been placed in an adoptive family. However, the risk of death from cancer of the adoptee is five times greater when one of the adoptive parent dies from cancer (Boukaram, 2011). Adoptive parents and adoptees do not share similar genetic material, but do share similar social-environmental contexts, which suggests that contextual factors may have more influence on the causation of cancer than genetic ones.

Collectively, these findings show that while heritable genetic factors do affect the risk of disease onset, they are not absolute indicators. Even individuals with similar genes experience different life outcomes. If genes were to dictate who we are, how can the same genes generate different outcomes?

The Gene: a 'Field of Possibilities'

At the beginning of the Human Genome Project, it was thought that the more complex the organism, the more genes it would take to carry all the information required to create and operate it. Based on this assumption, it was estimated it would take at least 100,000 genes to provide the instructions to manufacture all the proteins[18] required to run a human body. Scientists were baffled to find out that it is not the case. While the genome[19] of a rice cell contains 50,000 genes, the human genome contains only 20,000 of them! And even more puzzling is the discovery that these 20,000 genes are contained in only 2% of the whole human genome! How can all the information needed to build and maintain a human being be contained in such a small number of genes?

Scientists discovered that contrary to what was once widely assumed, a single gene can produce many different gene products through mechanisms such as alternative splicing. When a gene is expressed, it allows the synthesis of a RNA (ribonucleic acid) molecule, called a 'messenger' RNA or mRNA. This process is called transcription because the mRNA is a replica of the gene. During its transcription, parts of an mRNA can be alternatively spliced—i.e. added, multiplied, or removed—to create different transcripts from the same gene. Even genes located on different chromosomes can be brought into close physical proximity to each other, where their mRNA transcripts can be joined together to generate a hybrid

---

[18] *Proteins are the 'workhorses' of the cells. They perform most of the tasks that make life possible.*

[19] *A genome is an organism's complete set of DNA, including all of its genes (Genetics Home Reference, 2016b).*

transcript. Each one of these transcripts provides the instructions for the fabrication of a different protein.

But all possible transcripts are not produced at the same time in our cells. Whether the access to a gene is 'opened' or 'closed' for expression—or production of transcripts—and which one of the possible transcripts is produced are mainly the result of intricate networks of hundreds of proteins and RNAs of various types interacting in many possible ways with the genome itself, RNA transcripts, and other proteins. Each possible combination of these elements in the vicinity of or on a given gene determines a specific 'expression state' for the gene—i.e. whether it is expressed or not and if so, the amount of RNA transcripts produced and proteins made from them, as well as the timing of its expression.

Non-coding DNA sequences, located either in close proximity to or distant from the 'fundamental' portion of a gene, also often play an important role in its expression. 'Non-coding DNA sequences' refer to DNA sequences that are not 'genes' as we currently define them, because they do not contain instructions to manufacture proteins. What is intriguing is the fact that 98% of our DNA is not 'coding' for proteins. The function(s) of the non-coding portion of our genome is still largely unknown, but scientists are slowly discovering that it may contain some instructions making up an additional repertoire of information that shapes and regulates the different 'expression states' genes can take.

In light of these findings, genes can no longer be viewed as static entities, having clear-cut boundaries, and operating as default programs. The elements that make up our genome—DNA, proteins, and RNAs—interact with our genes in multiple ways to create as many different 'expression states' dictating how and when our genes are expressed. Therefore, it may be more accurate to view genes as 'fields of possibilities' (Jorgensen, 2011), capable of adopting various configurations to provide the instructions to make a variety of different products from the same DNA sequences—e.g. to make 100,000 proteins to run a human body from only 20,000 genes.

However, not all 100,000 proteins are produced at the same time in all of our cells. For example, specific proteins may be required during cell division, but not during cell growth, and some cells may require specific proteins to function that are not required by other cells (e.g. cardiac cells versus skin cells). If all proteins are produced from a limited number of genes, the question then becomes: how do our genes 'know' which configuration to select from their 'field of possibilities' to make the appropriate proteins required for specific functions?

Gene Expression Is Largely Influenced by the Context

Supporting the findings from the twin studies, researchers discovered that the selection of the different possible configurations or 'expression states' for a given gene mostly depends on the circumstances or cues the cell, the organ, and the organism encounter. Through a complex network of interactions between a number of biological molecules, signals from the cellular environment are translated into the expression of specific genes to create a particular response to a situation or a cellular context. A context is the result of both tangible and intangible circumstances. Examples of tangible circumstances include but are not limited to the presence of growth hormones, drugs, nutrients, and harmful bacteria in the cellular environment, while intangible circumstances may include thoughts, intentions, emotions, stress, and social interactions.

Since an organism can encounter many possible circumstances, the number of possible genetic 'expression states' and their corresponding outcomes are likely to be very large. To use an analogy, 10 individuals provided with the same selection, quality, and amount of ingredients to make soup are likely to create 10 different varieties of soup since they all have different skill levels, experience, personal taste, time to allocate to the preparation, etc. Even if each individual starts with the same ingredients, the end result can range anywhere from delectable to inedible. It is not only the ingredients that make the soup, but also the circumstances surrounding its preparation. Likewise, it is not only the genes themselves that create a human being's experience, but also the context in which they are expressed. We may be born with a particular set of genes, but it is mainly our context that determines how our genes are expressed to produce our physiological states and health outcomes.

Can We Predict Outcomes From Gene Expression?

If it is not only the genes themselves, but also how and when they are expressed that influence our destiny, then perhaps a more suitable approach to predict what genes have in store for us would be to determine all of the different possible genetic expression states or configurations that can lead to the development of health conditions or diseases. Because the expression state of a given gene is dictated by its interaction with the genome itself, RNAs, and proteins, uncovering the configurations that lead to a particular outcome would mean to know all of the molecular variables affecting its expression.

If most diseases were the results of changes in the expression of only a few genes, such a task could be conceivable. But instead of finding only a few genes involved in common conditions such as anxiety, obesity, osteoporosis, and cancer, scientists found hundreds to thousands of them! While many of these genes are commonly expressed between individuals with a similar condition, they may not be expressed at the same level—i.e. they may not produce the same amount of RNAs and proteins made from it. In some cases, genes may even be expressed or shut off in an opposite manner between individuals afflicted with a similar condition. Even cancerous tumors which appear to be structurally and histologically similar often show remarkable heterogeneity at the molecular level (Rivenbark et al., 2013). Since life circumstances influence gene expression, such molecular heterogeneity between individuals should come as no surprise, because there are many possible contexts. Different expression levels of many different genes thus form a personalized 'molecular soup' tailored to fulfill a person's specific needs in response to their context. And if various expression states of many different genes can lead to the development of comparable health conditions, one can only imagine how herculean the task of defining a precise 'molecular signature' for each condition becomes. "While we [may] be able to learn a lot about a given gene [or condition using this approach], we can never know what we do not know about it, i.e., its complete 'field of possibilities' [may] not be determinable simply because it will be impossible to anticipate for every gene every circumstance that an organism may encounter" (Jorgensen, 2011).

Therefore, a gene-focused or even a genome-focused approach to predict health outcomes with accuracy may be neither realistic nor sufficient. "We tend to see everything as simple cause and effect, reproducible and mechanistic" (Ryan, 2014), while our genes and entire genome are highly dynamic, malleable, and responsive to their context. Our genome is a complex system in constant interaction with its environment and its functions emerge from these interactions, not the other way around. Could it be conceivable that we may be trying to predict our life experience and health outcomes from looking at the wrong organization level?

Complex Systems

A complex system, as proposed by Ladyman and colleagues, "is an ensemble of many elements which are interacting in a disordered way, resulting in robust organization and memory" (Ladyman et al., 2012). A migrating flock of geese is a good example of a complex system that is easily understandable. Many geese resting in a field may go about their business in a disordered manner, but through constant interactions with one another, they can take flight in an organized V-shaped formation in a matter of seconds. Memory is also an important aspect, because it allows geese to assemble in such a stable flight pattern without apparent leadership. They not only remember optimal flight formation from their individual and collective past experience, but also where they are going!

In and of itself, this complex system seems 'simple' enough. Put into its natural context, however, a migrating flock of geese is no longer as simple as it looks. It is part of a hierarchical structure made up of many more complex systems: many cells forming organs and tissues, many organs and tissues forming geese, many geese forming a flock, many flocks of birds forming bird migration, many types of animal migration forming migration ecology, etc. Each one of these systems does not function in isolation, but rather in constant interaction with one another to create a coherent whole: life on planet Earth. It is this interaction, the continuous exchange of energy, matter, and information between systems, that makes an already complex system even more complicated. Influenced by so many intrinsic and extrinsic variables, the behavior of the system becomes extremely difficult to predict.

Let's take geese migration patterns as an example to illustrate this concept. Migration patterns cannot be predicted only by looking at goose body parts. Neither can they be predicted by looking at each of the next levels of organization, such as a goose or a flock of geese in a V formation. Geese migration patterns emerge from the interactions of all levels. Mild weather and prolonged availability of food sources may delay migration. Inversely, exceptionally cold weather may trigger an early departure. Weather conditions may cause delays or an itinerary change. A shortage of food or changes in the landscape may cause a change of destination the following year, and so on and so forth. A migrating flock of geese is in constant interaction with its surroundings; it responds and adapts to it. Geese migration patterns are governed by many interactions or variables. Only when all the variables of the all-encompassing level of organization are known can geese migration patterns be predicted. Otherwise, only their probability can be estimated.

Cracking the Code of Life: Have We Bitten off More Than We Can Chew?

Like a goose, the human body is made up of a network of networks exchanging information all the time: from its genome to the proteins and cells that make up its organs and all the way out to the physical body itself, its social network, and so on (Institute for Systems Biology, 2016). The human body is a complex system within a hierarchy of many complex systems in constant interaction. It is from the interaction—the exchange of energy, matter, and information—between all of these networks or systems that the human body's biological functions and health outcomes emerge.

It is the understanding that health outcomes are emergent properties resulting from the interactions between the various networks forming a human body that led scientists to create holistic models of its biological systems. If we could get to know 'enough' of the many interactions giving rise to biological functions, cells, and tissues, surely we could predict outcomes with better accuracy and learn how to take control over the system to influence these outcomes. To this end, biologists started to collect data from many levels of networks to build integrative computational, mathematical, and statistical models to predict how biological systems react over time, as a whole, to varying conditions (Institute for Systems Biology, 2016). But if gene expression itself emerges from the interaction of hundreds of genes, their RNA transcripts, and the proteins made from them, one can only imagine the amount of data, let alone of programming code, the modeling of various cellular functions or of a single organ require.

In fact, with the advent of high-throughput biological data collection, biologists are now struggling with massive data sets that are, as Andreas Sundquist points out, "larger than the tools used to analyse them" (Marx, 2013). By 'massive,' they mean many petabytes of data and the amount keeps growing at an exponential rate every year. One petabyte is equivalent to 10^{15} bytes. "If we were to count using standard definition TV episodes, then 1 petabyte would amount to around 10,000 hours of TV programming" (Lee, 2012). It would take a person over a year of non-stop viewing to watch it all. From such a perspective, one can easily understand how the storage, handling, processing, and interpretation of such large data repositories come with significant challenges. This is especially true for biological data. They are complex to analyse because they are heterogenous. They come from varied sources: genetic sequences, pools of RNA transcripts and their expression levels, protein interaction maps, or entries from medical records. Neither the current technology nor the human resources available can keep up with the task of making sense of all this data. And as Lawrence Hunter points out in an interview with Vivien Marx: "getting the most from the data requires interpreting them in light of all the relevant prior knowledge" (Marx, 2013). Personally, I would add that getting the most from the data is nearly impossible without interpreting them in light of what we do not know about them.

Models are instrumental to understand our world, but they cannot be an accurate representation of reality in all its complexity. Interactions in complex systems are non-linear, which means the behavior of the system cannot be calculated or predicted by the simple addition of the responses caused by each individual interaction. Therefore, where "there are a lot of simultaneous, non-linear interactions, it soon becomes impossible to keep track of causal relationships between components" (Cilliers, 2001). In addition, complex systems are historical in nature, i.e. they have a memory of previous experiences and they use it to inform their present behavior. These properties are extremely difficult to model and to avoid getting lost within such complexity:

"Models have to reduce this complexity in order to generate some understanding. In the process something is obviously lost. [...] However, we have no way of predicting the importance of that which is not considered. In a non-linear world where we cannot track a clear causal chain, something that may appear to be unimportant now, may turn out to be vitally important later. Or vice versa, of course. Our models have to 'frame' the problem in a certain way, and this framing will inevitably introduce distortions (Cilliers, 2001)."

What is more is that we cannot know what we do not know about a system. Only the parameters that are known and measurable are incorporated into its modelling. What we do know about the human genome so far is mostly contained in only 2% of it—i.e. the portion of the genome that contains the genes coding for proteins. We are just at the dawn of breaking the code of the remaining 98% of the genome, most of which remains largely unknown to this day. To illustrate this point, researchers at the J. Craig Venter Institute have attempted "using all available genomic knowledge" to piece together the minimal set of genes that would sustain the life of a microorganism, but they failed (Service, 2016). When they used trial and error, however, they succeeded in engineering a synthetic bacterium capable of surviving and reproducing with the smallest-yet genome (Hutchison et al., 2016). The new organism has only 473 genes. So few genes, but still, a third of these genes have no known biological functions (Hutchison et al., 2016). Such a finding only underscores how little we know about life's genetic makeup. As Dr. Venter rightly concluded: "it is clear that our current knowledge of biology is not sufficient to sit down and design a living organism and build it" (Service, 2016). If so, how can we possibly model the dynamics of the human genome or predict health outcomes with any degree of accuracy?

Furthermore, our perception and understanding of the world, including our physical body, is largely based on what we can consciously see with our eyes. Even when something is too small to be visible to the naked eye, we develop the appropriate technology to make it visible. To see is to believe. Visible light is what we humans experience as 'color,' as visible forms, as tangible objects. It is the portion of the electromagnetic spectrum that our eyes can see (from 700 to 400 nanometers). But the range of frequencies of electromagnetic radiation runs from zero in one direction to infinity in the other. So really, on a logarithmic scale of frequency, visible light only represents 2% of the entire electromagnetic spectrum (Link, 2007). Most of it is invisible to us. A huge part of our world is intangible (e.g. magnetic fields, sound waves, brain waves). Yet, most biologists still turn a blind eye to it and do not acknowledge its influence on living systems, let alone factor these variables into their equations or models.

I certainly do not intend to imply that models of complex systems are useless; quite the contrary. Models are crucial to improve our understanding of the structures or mechanisms involved in the expression of specific genes and to identify general trends leading to particular physiological states or health outcomes. These general principles, however, are usually difficult to apply to all individual cases. If they were simple, a treatment or remedy to correct a molecular anomaly would have the same effect and efficacy on each individual. But we are all well aware that not everyone responds to treatments in the same way. This is especially evident in the case of cancer patients. A general model cannot capture the subtleties and singularities brought about by an individual's specific history and conditions in a specific context (Cilliers, 2001).

"[And if we were to succeed in repeating] the complexity of a system in another medium, [...] one should remember that we now have a 'model' that is as complex as the system being modelled. It will be as difficult to understand as the system itself, and its behavior will be as unpredictable. If the history of the model and the history of the system is not kept identical [...], the two will soon become uncorrelated. My conclusion is that it is impossible to have a perfect model of a complex system" (Cilliers, 2001).

Towards a Contextual Approach

Similar to a hard drive, our genome may contain a lot of information to run our body, but at any given time, we are utilizing only parts of this information. Which parts are in use—i.e. which genes are expressed (turned on) or not (turned off)—is mainly influenced by our experiences—our inner and outer contexts—and the meaning we assign to them (Dawson, 2008). Our genetic profile is therefore a snapshot at a particular point in time of all the molecular mechanisms involved in translating cues from our contexts into the expression of specific genes to create a particular physiological state or response—an outcome. Our genome thus acts as "a system to convert environmental information into molecular resources" (Cole, 2014) to respond to and evolve through our subjective experience.

Under the constant influence of our past and present life circumstances, it becomes difficult to develop a general model of gene expression to explain, let alone predict, individual health outcomes. But in a world largely defined by physical concepts, our natural tendency is to look for ways to control a system's outcomes through the understanding and manipulation of its physical parts. For example, if we keep driving our car over potholes, chances are our car's suspension will eventually get damaged (geese and potholes: can you tell I am Canadian?). Our natural reaction is to replace our suspension with a higher-quality brand. But if we do not change our driving habits and keep driving our car over potholes, there is a risk our car's suspension will break again. If not its suspension, then the tires will get damaged, or the rims will bend, or the wheel alignment will go out of whack. Similarly, making any 'corrections' to the mechanics of our gene expression may bring temporary relief or delay the onset of a disease, but if they do not address our history and life context—the ultimate orchestrators of genetic expression—it is very unlikely that the health issue will be permanently resolved. Since our genome is dynamic and many different combinations of expression states can lead to similar conditions, our genome eventually finds another way to respond and adapt to its context. Not unlike changing our driving habits to avoid costly repairs, fixing detrimental aspects of our lifestyle may be more efficient in achieving personal well-being than fixing the mechanical parts of our gene expression's machinery.

Our lifestyles or contexts are the result of interactions within ourselves, our social networks, and our environment. It is from these interactions—the exchange of information between systems—that our life and health outcomes emerge. As such, an approach focused on the interactions themselves rather than our genetic makeup has the potential to provide us with deeper insights into the etiology of diseases and the strategies to prevent them. "[W]e have to look at the whole picture, [...] if we are to understand a more full set of forces in play" (Gazaniga, 2011). To get the 'whole picture,' however, both tangible and intangible aspects of our interactions must be considered. For quite some time already, scientists have been on the lookout for 'risk factors' or other commonalities between individuals affected by or recovering from similar health conditions. But if they still cannot predict health outcomes with better accuracy, it is because concepts that fall outside of what is generally accepted by the scientific community have been generally excluded from these studies. This is especially true with regard to concepts of mind-body interactions, i.e. the influence of mental states and processes on the person's physiological states or those of another person. I firmly believe that many of the answers we are seeking are hidden in plain sight, within the subtle fabric of our experiences and our interactions within our networks and communities. To retrieve them, however, we need to start asking ourselves the right questions.

What is Next?

Combining the knowledge and wisdom of both materialistic and postmaterialistic sciences - of both the physical and the non-physical [metaphysical] - my colleagues and I are currently developing a theoretical model of the powerful interactions between body, mind, and spirit. This model will provide us with key leads into how these interactions can affect a person's biology and overall health, whether it is through alterations in gene expression or not. The model will also help us define new well-rounded scientific questions to explore as well as propose new approaches to study the influence of both physical and non-physical concepts on human nature and reality.

References

Boukaram, C. (2011). *Le pouvoir anticancer des émotions*. Montréal, Québec: Les Editions de L'Homme.

Cilliers, P. (2001). Boundaries, Hierarchies and Networks in Complex Systems. *International Journal of Innovation Management*, 5, 135-147.

Cole, S. W. (2014). Human social genomics. *PLoS Genet* 10, e1004601.

Dawson, C. (2008). *The genie in your genes: epigenetic medicine and the new biology of intention*. Santa Rosa, California: Energy Psychology Press.

Gatz, M., Reynolds, C. A., Fratiglioni, L., Johansson, B., Mortimer, J. A., Berg, S., Fiske, A. & Pedersen, N. L. (2006). Role of genes and environments for explaining Alzheimer disease. *Arch Gen Psychiatry*, 63, 168-74.

Gazzaniga, M. S. (2011). *Who's in charge? Free will and the science of the brain*. New York: Harper Collins.

Genetics Home Reference. (2016a). What is a gene? *Genetics Home Reference*. Retrieved from: https://ghr.nlm.nih.gov/primer/basics/gene.

Genetics Home Reference. (2016b). What is a genome? Genetics Home Reference. https://ghr.nlm.nih.gov/primer/hgp/genome.

Hutchison, C. A., 3rd, Chuang, R. Y., Noskov, V. N., Assad-Garcia, N., Deerinck, T. J., Ellisman, M. H., Gill, J., Kannan, K., Karas, B. J., Ma, L., Pelletier, J. F., Qi, Z. Q., Richter, R. A., Strychalski, E. A., Sun, L., Suzuki, Y., Tsvetanova, B., Wise, K. S., Smith, H. O., Glass, J. I., Merryman, C., Gibson, D. G. & Venter, J. C. (2016). Design and synthesis of a minimal bacterial genome. *Science*, 351, aad6253.

Institute for Systems Biology. (2016). Retrieved from: https://www.systemsbiology.org/about/what-is-systems-biology/.

Jorgensen, R. A. (2011). Epigenetics: Biology's Quantum Mechanics. *Front Plant Sci*, 2, 10.

Kaprio, J., Tuomilehto, J., Koskenvuo, M., Romanov, K., Reunanen, A., Eriksson, J., Stengard, J. & Kesaniemi, Y. A. (1992). Concordance for type 1 (insulin-dependent) and type 2 (non-insulin-dependent) diabetes mellitus in a population-based cohort of twins in Finland. *Diabetologia*, 35, 1060-1067.

Ladyman, J., Lambert, J. & Wiesner, K. (2012). What is a complex system? *European Journal for Philosophy of Science*, 3, 33-67.

Lee, J. (2012). Memory Sizes Explained. MakeUseOf. Retrieved from: http://www.makeuseof.com/tag/memory-sizes-gigabytes-terabytes-petabytes/.

Lichtenstein, P., Holm, N. V., Verkasalo, P. K., Iliadou, A., Kaprio, J., Koskenvuo, M., Pukkala, E., Skythe, A. & Hemminki, K. (2000). Environmental and heritable factors in the causation of cancer--analyses of cohorts of twins from Sweden, Denmark, and Finland. *N Engl J Med*, 343, 78-85.

Link, J. (2007). What percentage of the electromagnetic spectrum is visible light? *Mad Sci Network*. Retrieved from: www.madsci.org/posts/archives/2007-08/1188407794.Ph.r.html.

Marx, V. (2013). Biology: The big challenges of big data. *Nature*, 498, 255-60.

Rivenbark, A. G., O'Connor, S. M. & Coleman, W. B. (2013). Molecular and cellular heterogeneity in breast cancer: challenges for personalized medicine. *Am J Pathol*, 183, 1113-24.

Ryan, J. G. (2014). *The Missing Pill.* John G Ryan MPC.

Service, R. F. (2016). SYNTHETIC BIOLOGY. Synthetic microbe has fewest genes, but many mysteries. *Science. United States*: pp. 1380-1.

Sorensen, T. I., Nielsen, G. G., Andersen, P. K. & Teasdale, T. W. (1988). Genetic and environmental influences on premature death in adult adoptees. *N Engl J Med*, 318, 727-32.

Svendsen, A. J., Kyvik, K. O., Houen, G., Junker, P., Christensen, K., Christiansen, L., Nielsen, C., Skytthe, A. & Hjelmborg, J. V. (2013). On the origin of rheumatoid arthritis: the impact of environment and genes--a population based twin study. *PLoS One*, 8, e57304.

Tarnoki, A. D., Tarnoki, D. L. & Molnar, A. A. (2014). Past, present and future of cardiovascular twin studies. *Cor et Vasa*, 56, 486-493.

Thompson, N. P., Driscoll, R., Pounder, R. E. & Wakefield, A. J. (1996). Genetics versus environment in inflammatory bowel disease: results of a British twin study. *BMJ*, 312, 95-96.

Wright, W. (1999). *Born that way: genes, behavior, personality*. London: Routledge

Chapter 10

The Telecebo Response:
Toward a Postmaterial Concept of Healing

Larry Dossey, MD

In 1909 two titans of modern psychology, Sigmund Freud (1856-1939) and Carl Gustav Jung (1875-1961), met in Freud's home in Vienna. As Jung writes in his autobiography, *Memories, Dreams, Reflections,* he wanted to know more about Freud's views on extrasensory perception or ESP, an area that fascinated Jung and toward which he was quite open. Although Freud later changed his position in favor of ESP, on this particular occasion he dismissed Jung's views with such shallowness, Jung said, "I had difficulty in checking the sharp retort on the tip of my tongue." As Freud continued to disparage ESP, Jung began to sense "a curious sensation. It was as if my diaphragm were made of iron and were becoming red-hot—a glowing vault. And at that moment there was such a loud report in the bookcase, which stood right next to us, that we both started up in alarm, fearing the thing was going to topple over on us. I said to Freud: 'There, that is an example of a so-called catalytic exteriorization phenomenon.'"

"Oh come," Freud protested. "That is sheer bosh."

"It is not," Jung replied. "You are mistaken, Herr Professor. And to prove my point I now predict that in a moment there will be another such loud report!" No sooner had Jung made this prediction than the same loud detonation occurred in the bookcase. Freud simply stared aghast at him.

Jung was baffled about what gave him this certainty, but he knew "beyond all doubt" that the phenomenon would occur again. Jung sensed that the incident aroused Freud's mistrust, and Jung felt he had "done something against him." Jung never discussed the event afterward with him (Jung, 1965, p. 155-156).

Many interpretations have been offered to explain (or explain away) the close temporal sequence of Jung's internal feelings and the successive exploding sounds from the nearby bookcase. Among them are (1) random, accidental, unrelated happenings, "just one of those things"; (2) faulty observations (the sounds might have come from gunshots down the street); (3) synchronicity, an acausal connection of events that are highly meaningful to the individual involved; (4) precognition, the awareness of future events; and (5) psychokinesis, the causal influence of thought, feeling, and intention on the physical world. The first two possibilities reflect Freud's view that any connection between the detonations and emotion, thought, or intention was imaginary. Jung believed his interior feelings had somehow exteriorized and were connected with physical events outside his body.

Jung was no stranger to these curious happenings. Similar events had occurred previously in the Jung household. In 1898, while Jung was sitting in his room studying his textbooks, an event occurred that influenced him profoundly:

"In the adjoining room, the door to which stood ajar, my mother was knitting. That was our dining room, where the round walnut dining table stood…about seventy years old…. Suddenly there sounded a report like a pistol shot. I jumped up and rushed into the room from which the noise of the explosion had come. My mother was sitting flabbergasted in her armchair, the knitting fallen from her hands…. The table top had split from the rim to beyond the center, and not along any point: the split ran right though the solid wood. I was thunderstruck. How could such a thing happen? A table of solid walnut that had dried out for seventy years—how could it split on a summer day in the relatively high degree of humidity characteristic of our climate?" (Jung, 1965, p. 104-105)

A few weeks later Jung arrived home at six o'clock in the evening and found the household—his mother, his fourteen-year-old sister, and the maid—greatly agitated. About an hour previously there had been another deafening sound, this time from the direction of the sideboard, a heavy piece of furniture dating from the 18th century. By the time Jung arrived, the other household members had inspected it thoroughly, as well as the surrounding area, and could find no evidence of a split in the wood. Jung repeated their inspection, again finding nothing. Then he looked inside. In the area containing the breadbasket he found a loaf of bread, with the bread knife beside it. As he describes:

"The greater part of the blade had snapped off in several pieces. The handle lay in one corner of the rectangular basket, and in each of the other corners lay a piece of the blade. The knife had been used shortly before at four-o'clock tea, and afterward put away. Since then no one had gone to the sideboard." (Jung, 1965, p.104-106)

The next day Jung took the shattered knife to one of the best cutlers in the city. The expert examined the knife with a magnifying glass and said, "The knife is perfectly sound. There is no fault in the steel. Someone must have deliberately broken it piece by piece. It could be done, for instance, by sticking the blade into the crack of the drawer and breaking off a piece at a time. Or else it might have been dropped on stone from a great height. But good steel can't explode. Someone has been pulling your leg."

For Jung, the suggestion that the shattered knife was faked was inadequate, and the notion that Freud's noisy bookcase and Jung's split dining table were just a coincidence "went much too far"—like saying that "the Rhine would flow backward just once, by mere chance...."

Mind, Interior and Exterior

The basic premise underlying mind-body medicine is that a patient's thoughts and emotions matter clinically, often greatly. As the mind-body field has evolved, the mind has become thoroughly *interiorized* inside a patient's body as a variable factor in perhaps all illnesses (Olshansky, 2015).

Jung, however, was suggesting a more extensive role for the mind. He believed that mental-emotional events can become *exteriorized*—that is, they can escape an individual's body and act outside it, somehow "catalyzing" distant physical events. Today, however, as in Jung's time, this idea is often considered occult nonsense—Freud's "sheer bosh." Those who want to keep the mind safely interiorized inside an individual's cranium often respond to Jung's suggestion with mouth-foaming denunciation, as if science itself is under attack by demon-haunted, dark forces of unreason (Sagan,

1997). This includes disciples of the moribund ideology of materialism, which asserts that consciousness is produced by the brain and is confined and limited to a single individual's brain and body (Dossey, 2015; 2016; Kelly et al., 2015; Tart, 2009). Nowhere is this issue more crucial than in the perennial debates surrounding the placebo response and the nature of healing.

The Placebo Effect

"Placebo" is Latin for "I shall please." The term expresses a long-accepted goal in medicine. As Ambroise Paré, France's great surgeon of the 16th century said, the duty of the physician is "to cure occasionally, relieve often, console always" (Paré, 2015). In service of this duty, placebos were widely used in medicine as necessary deceptions in relieving and consoling patients until the 20th century, when their use took on a derogatory quality (de Craen et al., 1999).

The placebo effect is traditionally defined as the positive therapeutic results that arise following the administration of a harmless, inert substance or ineffectual treatment for a medical, surgical, or other condition. These results are customarily attributed to suggestion, expectation, and positive thinking on the part of the patient, which are enhanced by his or her faith and trust in the clinician who is involved (Johnson, 2013). Adverse, negative results called nocebo responses are the dark twin of placebo effects (Sanderson et al., 2013). They reflect a patient's negative beliefs, anxieties, and expectations of harm.

More sophisticated views of the placebo effect are being offered (Benedetti, 2009). Miller, Colloca, and Kaptchuk view the placebo effect as "interpersonal healing" that takes place in the clinical encounter between clinician and patient. Interpersonal healing may be activated by diverse behaviors, symbols, and rituals in the clinical encounter, through which a patient finds hope, trust, meaning, support, and empathy. This can result in therapeutic benefit by modifying the perceptions and experience of illness symptoms such as pain, anxiety, and fatigue, rather than by modifying the pathophysiology of disease. However, the placebo effect is not "all in the mind." Many studies show that placebo effects can elicit quantifiable changes in neurotransmitters, hormones, and immune regulators. Interpersonal healing is distinct from spontaneous natural healing, as well as from technological healing dependent on active pharmaceuticals or procedures (Miller et al., 2009).

Placebos have been used for centuries (Jütte, 2013). In 1807 Thomas Jefferson wrote that "one of the most successful physicians I have ever known has assured me that he used more bread pills, drops of colored water, and powders of hickory ashes, than of all other medicines put together" (Jefferson, 1898). About a century later Richard Cabot, a distinguished physician of Harvard Medical School, described how he "was brought up, as I suppose every physician is, to use placebo, bread pills, water subcutaneously, and other devices" (Cabot, 1903).

Even though placebos were acknowledged to bring comfort to patients, it was assumed they had no actual impact on pathophysiology (Kaptchuk & Miller, 2015; Handfield-Jones, 1953). Moreover, they were believed to be more effective on the weak-minded (Kaptchuk, 1998). As de Craen and colleagues report in their historical review of placebos and their effects, "The value of placebo was thought inversely related to the intelligence of the patient; the use of a medical ritual was more effective and necessary for 'unintelligent, neurotic, or inadequate patients" (de Craen et al., 1999).

Secrecy and obfuscation have often been used by physicians to hide the use of placebos. A hospital pharmacist once told me that one of the most popular medications in his hospital was Lipragus—"sugar pill" spelled backward. Obecalp, "placebo" spelled backward, has also been used (http://www.wsoctv.com). (To find out if your medications are real medicine, go to a federal database of approved drugs: https://www.accessdata.fda.gov/scripts/cder/daf/).

In recent years several authorities have vigorously defended the use of placebos in clinical practice. As physician-ethicist Howard Brody stated in 1982 in a seminal article, "The Lie That Heals: The Ethics of Giving Placebos" (Brody, 1982):

"The 170-year-long debate in the medical literature about the ethics of prescribing placebos in medical therapeutics needs to be reevaluated in light of recent placebo research and improved understanding of the placebo effect as an integral part of the doctor-patient relationship. It has traditionally been assumed that deception is an indispensable component of successful placebo use. Therefore, placebos have been attacked because they are deceptive, and defended on the grounds that the deception is illusory or that the beneficent intentions of the physician justify the deception. However, a proper understanding of the placebo effect shows that deception need play no essential role in eliciting this powerful therapeutic modality; physicians can use nondeceptive means to promote a positive placebo response in their patients" (Brody, 1982).

The Telecebo Effect

Both placebo and nocebo effects are considered limited to an individual patient, simply because mental effects are regarded as originating in, and confined to, the brain and body of the individual experiencing them. In other words, my thoughts cannot directly affect your body, and your thoughts cannot directly affect mine.

This view of placebo responses is incomplete. Abundant evidence requires a place for what I wish to call the *telecebo* effect.

"Telecebo" is a neologism formed by combining the Greek *tele*, meaning "far" or "distant," with the fragment *cebo* from "placebo." Telecebo effects are not generated by a patient; they are an exteriorization of a clinician's, nurse's, therapist's, or healer's intentions and thoughts for a patient's welfare. These mental efforts can directly influence a patient, no matter how distant, creating effects that can merge seamlessly with a patient's own self-generated placebo responses in a cascade toward healing.

"Telecebo" expresses both kinship with, and difference from, the placebo response—kinship, in that both telecebo and placebo effects arise from intentions, thoughts, and emotions; difference, in that placebo responses arise from a patient, while telecebo effects originate from a clinician.

The telecebo phenomenon can be completely invisible to both clinician and patient, if both of them accept the taboo that these effects are forbidden in science and cannot exist. In this case, the clinician may misinterpret telecebo effects as placebo responses originating within a patient's own body, or perhaps dismiss them as the nonspecific results of her empathy, compassion, or simply good bedside manner.

Even if a clinician is aware that telecebo effects exist, they can still be elusive, because in any given clinician-patient interaction it may be impossible to distinguish them from placebo responses originating in the patient.

So how do we know telecebo effects exist? We know because we can tease telecebo effects apart from placebo responses, as in hundreds of experiments and reports involving both humans and nonhumans, as we shall see. The data from experiments involving nonhumans is especially revealing. As far as we know, nonhumans don't think positively or engage in symbolic meaning to the degree of humans, so that if healing intentions are effective in nonhuman animals, plants, microbes, or chemical reactions, the results are presumably not due to placebo effects but to the results of telecebo intentions from the healer.

This generalization requires qualification. There is abundant evidence that nonhuman animals can manifest placebo effects through operant conditioning. For example, Ader and Cohen paired an immunosuppressive drug (cyclophosphamide) with a neutral stimulus (a saccharine solution) in mice with a lupus-like disease. When only the neutral stimulus was later given, the result was immunosuppression, suggestive of a placebo response (Ader & Cohen, 1982; Siegel, 2002).

Moreover, there is a substantial body of research demonstrating healthy effects in animals from visual and tactile contact from a human, involving rabbits, dogs, horses, dairy cows, and sows. In humans, placebo effects are believed to be mediated by the empathy, compassion, likeability, and trustworthiness manifested by a physician. Thus, veterinarian and placebo researcher F. D. McMillan states, "To the extent that animals form such perceptions…it is reasonable to posit a similar influence of placebo effects in animal health care" (McMillan, 1999).

How, then, can placebo responses be differentiated from our hypothesized telecebo effects? The reasons are straightforward. Many of the relevant studies do not involve animals at all, but cells, tissues, plants, microbes, and chemical reactions. Moreover, telecebo effects do not depend on proximity to a subject. Many of the experiments suggesting telecebo effects have been done remotely, beyond sensory contact. This suggests that a *nonlocal* phenomenon is at play, as opposed to the *local*, sensory-mediated mechanisms believed to underlie placebo responses in humans and higher animals. Therefore, if animals are not involved as test subjects, and if sensory-mediated contact is bypassed, placebo effects would appear to have been eliminated.

A comparison of placebo, nocebo, and telecebo responses are represented at the end of this chapter.

The Exteriorization of Intentions: the Achterberg fMRI Study

What is the evidence that one's thoughts can exteriorize and affect a distant patient? There is an old folk saying: "If you want to hide the treasure, put it in plain sight. Then nobody will see it." Telecebo effects are like that. Evidence supporting them has long been in plain sight, but we have been slow to notice.

Researcher Jeanne Achterberg, who was well known for her decades-long research in imagery, visualization, and healing intentions, moved to the Big Island of Hawaii in the early 2000s to investigate healing (Achterberg, 1985; Achterberg et al., 1984). She spent two years integrating with the community of native healers, who accepted her and shared their methods. After gaining their trust, she and her colleagues recruited 11 healers. Each healer was asked to select a person they had worked with previously with distant intentionality (DI), and with whom they felt an empathic, compassionate bond. The healers were not casually interested in healing; they had pursued their healing tradition for an average of 23 years. They described their healing efforts variously—prayer, sending energy or good intentions, or wishing for the subject the highest good. Each recipient was placed in a functional MRI (fMRI) scanner and was isolated from all forms of sensory contact with the healer. The healers sent forms of DI related to their own healing practices at two-minute random intervals that could not be anticipated by the recipient. Significant differences in the subjects' brain function between the experimental ("send") and control ("no send") conditions were found; there was less than approximately one chance in 10,000 that the results could be explained by chance happenings ($p = 0.000127$). The areas of the brain that were activated during the "send" periods included the anterior and middle cingulate areas, the precuneus, and frontal areas. This study suggests that remote, compassionate, healing intentions can be exteriorized from one individual to another to exert measurable effects on the recipient, and that an empathic, trusting connection between the healer and the recipient may be a vital part of the process (Achterberg et al., 2005).

Achterberg's experiment is not a one-off. Many similar studies utilizing simultaneous electroencephalographic (EEG) or fMRI recordings of distant individuals who are emotionally close show that when one person's brain is stimulated, the distant individual's brain often responds similarly at the same time. References to the relevant experiments in this field can be found in the comprehensive book *Entangled Minds* (Radin, 2006) by consciousness researcher Dean Radin, Chief Scientist at California's Institute of Noetic Sciences, and on his blog site at http://deanradin.blogspot.com/2010/03/brain-correlation-experiments.html.

Further Evidence

In a 2003 systematic analysis of healing intentions in general, Jonas and Crawford found

"…over 2200 published reports, including books, articles, dissertations, abstracts and other writings on spiritual healing, energy medicine, and mental intention effects. This included 122 laboratory studies, 80 randomized controlled trials, 128 summaries or reviews, 95 reports of observational studies and nonrandomized trials, 271 descriptive studies, case reports, and surveys, 1286 other writings including opinions, claims, anecdotes, letters to editors, commentaries, critiques and meeting reports, and 259 selected books" (Jonas, 2003, pp.xv-xix).

How good are the clinical and laboratory studies? Using strict CONSORT criteria (Consolidated Standards of Reporting Trials) (http://www.consort-statement.org.), Jonas and Crawford gave an "A," the highest possible grade, to studies involving the effects of intentions on inanimate objects such as sophisticated random number generators. They gave a "B" to the healing intention studies involving humans (which often took the form of intercessory prayer). A "B" was also given to laboratory experiments involving nonhumans such as animals, cells, and plants.

Many additional systematic and meta-analyses of healing intentions with positive findings have been published in peer-reviewed literature (Schmidt, 2004, 2012; Roe et al. 2012; Hodge, 2007; Astin et al., 2000; Abbot, 2000; Braud & Schlitz, 1989; Jonas, 2001).

Scores of clinical trials have been published in the past few decades assessing the possible impact of a healer's intentions on patients. Here are some examples involving humans—not a comprehensive survey, but intended only to convey what these experiments generally look like.

In 2009, Tsubono, Thomlinson, and Shealy conducted a randomized controlled trial that assessed the ability of a healer to relieve chronic pain. The researchers concluded, "The results showed that the treatment group was significantly improved compared to the control group even though both groups were kept blind to their group assignment. Moreover, many subjects in the treatment group were relieved of chronic pain after only two months of healing. This suggests that healing can take place even from a distance, and distant healing can be a very effective treatment for chronic pain" (Tsubono et al., 2009).

In 2013, Kuwada reported a double blind, randomized study evaluating the effect of Distant Intentionality Healing (DIH) on narcotic analgesic use. The author wanted to determine if there was any difference between the control group and the group receiving DIH on the total number of narcotic analgesics taken after foot and ankle surgery for three weeks post-op. The study found that there was on average seven fewer narcotic analgesics taken by the DIH group than the control group. Analysis revealed a significant difference between the control group and the group receiving DIH at the $P = .01$ level (Kuwada, 2013).

In 2010 Brown, Mory, and McClymond evaluated the influence of intercessory prayer on auditory and visual impairments in 24 consecutive rural Mozambican subjects in a prospective study. They measured significant improvements in both auditory ($P = <0.003$) and visual ($P = <0.02$) functions following healing intentions in the form of prayer (Brown et al., 2010).

In a phase-1 pilot study, researchers assessed the influence of shamanic "journeying" and other shamanic healing techniques in 23 female patients with temporomandibular joint dysfunction and pain. Pain improved significantly and results were highly significant. At the end of the study, only four of the 23 patients merited the original diagnosis (Vuckovich et al., 2007).

Distant Mental Interactions With Living Systems (DMILS)

In addition to studies in humans, telecebo effects are further supported by a body of research known as DMILS—*d*istant *m*ental *i*nteractions with *l*iving *s*ystems. These experiments involve a wide variety of entities such as organs, tissues, microbes, plants, and animals. In these studies, individuals have used their intentions to influence the growth rates of bacteria and fungi in test tubes and Petri dishes, the rate of wound healing in mice, the healing of transplanted cancers in mice, the function of cells in tissue cultures, the germination rates of seeds, the growth rates of seedlings, and many other phenomena. Two examples follow.

Gronowicz and colleagues assessed the effect of Therapeutic Touch (TT) on the proliferation of normal human cells in culture, compared to sham and no-treatment controls. This non-touch technique, which emphasizes healing intentions, was administered twice a week for 2 weeks. Compared to untreated controls, TT significantly stimulated proliferation of fibroblasts (cells that produce collagen and are important in wound healing), tenocytes (tendon cells), and osteoblasts (bone cells) in culture ($P = $

0.04, 0.01, and 0.01, respectively). These data were obtained by sophisticated techniques such as immunocytochemical staining for proliferating cell nuclear antigen (PCNA). The researchers concluded, "A specific pattern of TT treatment produced a significant increase in proliferation of fibroblasts, osteoblasts, and tenocytes in culture. Therefore, TT may affect normal cells by stimulating cell proliferation" (Gronowicz et al., 2008).

In 10 controlled experiments, Bengston tested the effect of "healing with intent" on laboratory mice. In eight of these experiments, mice were injected with mammary adenocarcinoma (breast cancer) cells. In two experiments, mice with methylcholanthrene-induced sarcomas were used. The fatality rate for both cancers in mice, if untreated, is 100%. The healers were faculty and student volunteers. Although they had no previous experience or belief in healing with intent and were often skeptical of such, they were drilled extensively in the healing technique. Treatment length was from 30 to 60 minutes, delivered daily to weekly until the mice were cured or died. They were successful in producing full cures in approximately 90% of the mice. When mammary adenocarcinoma cells were reinjected into cured mice, the cancer would not take, suggesting that an immune response had been stimulated during treatment. The proximity of the volunteer healers to the cages of the mice varied from on site to approximately 600 miles. Thus, Bengston notes, "[T]hese effects were at times brought about from a distance that defies conventional understanding," suggesting that a nonlocal process was at work. This series of studies, conducted at several academic centers, suggests that healing through intent can be predictable, reliable, and replicable (Bengston, 2010, 2012; Bengston & Krinsley, 2000; Bengtson & Moga, 2007).

The DMILS field is too extensive to be reviewed here. These studies are described and summarized in readily available sources (Benor, 2002; Kelly et al., 2007, 2015; Radin, 1997, 2006; Jonas, 2003; Dossey, 1999; Schwartz, 2007; Schwartz & Dossey, 2010; Bengston, 2000; Sheldrake, 1999).

Studies in nonhumans permit us to differentiate between telecebo effects and placebo responses, as already mentioned. To reiterate, nonhumans such as cells, plants, microbes, and biochemical reactions presumably do not think positively or symbolically and are therefore not subject to suggestion and expectation. If in controlled experiments these entities respond to intentions, presumably the placebo response is not responsible and telecebo effects are likely at work, reflecting the influence of the thoughts and intentions of the healer.

Exteriorization in Time

Evidence further suggests that intentions can act not only at a distance in space, but also at a distance in time, outside the present. Many of these studies suggest retro-temporal phenomena, in which thought and intention appear to function in the past. Consciousness researcher William Braud reviewed 24 positive experiments involving apparent retro-temporal influence on biological and inanimate systems (Braud, 2000).

The possibility of retro-temporal influence or backward causation is being taken seriously in certain areas within science. The theoretical and experimental evidence for such has been the subject of two symposia at the University of San Diego, part of the annual regional meetings of the American Association for the Advancement of Science (Sheehan, 2006).

One peer-reviewed study suggests the influence of healing intentions on past medical events, even though these events are presumed already to have happened. In this randomized, controlled experiment, healing intentions in the form of intercessory prayer were offered to over 3,000 patients with sepsis four to 10 years *after* they were hospitalized. The prayed-for group had a statistically better course regarding length of stay and the course of fever (Leibovici, 2001; Olshansky & Dossey, 2003).

Moreover, dozens of so-called presentiment experiments from various laboratories suggest that individuals can unconsciously anticipate and respond physiologically to future events, especially if such events are emotionally provocative. Some researchers suggest that this ability would confer a Darwinian advantage via the anticipation and avoidance of future threats.

Overall, these retro-temporal and presentiment studies suggest that the mind can exteriorize not only with respect to space, but to time as well

(Schwartz, 2007; Mossbridge et al., 2012, 2014; Bierman & Radin, 1997, 1998; Radin, 2004).

Extrasensory Perception Revisited

Since Freud and Jung clashed over ESP, the experimental landscape surrounding this area has changed dramatically. In 2010 in the journal *NeuroQuantology*, consciousness researchers Patricio Tressoldi, Lance Storm, and Dean Radin analyzed the experimental database for extrasensory perception (Tressoldi, et al., 2010). They state:

"The possibility that information can be acquired at a distance without the use of the ordinary senses, that is by "extrasensory perception" (ESP), is not easily accommodated by conventional neuroscientific assumptions or by traditional theories underlying our understanding of perception and cognition.

"The lack of theoretical support has marginalized the study of ESP, but experiments investigating these phenomena have been conducted since the mid-19th century, and the empirical database has been slowly accumulating. Today, using modern experimental methods and meta-analytical techniques, a persuasive case can be made that, neuroscience assumptions notwithstanding, ESP does exist. We justify this conclusion through discussion of one class of homogeneous experiments reported in 108 publications and conducted from 1974 through 2008 by laboratories around the world. Subsets of these data have been subjected to six meta-analyses, and each shows significantly positive effects. The overall results now provide unambiguous evidence for an independently repeatable ESP effect. This indicates that traditional cognitive and neuroscience models, which are largely based on classical physical concepts, are incomplete. We speculate that more comprehensive models will require new principles based on a more comprehensive physics. The current candidate is quantum mechanics."

The "unambiguous evidence" that is referred to by these researchers deals with the correlation of subjective impressions between distant individuals (in the vernacular, "telepathy"). Equally significant is evidence supporting the ability to acquire information beyond the reach of the senses, commonly called ESP or clairvoyance. But as we've seen, robust evidence also supports our query, the ability to *insert* information *into* the environment at a distance, as the healers in the Achterberg experiment were apparently able to do. Taken together, both vectors—the acquisition of information from the environment and the insertion of information into the environment—affirm the emerging concept of *nonlocal mind*—mind unconfined to specific points in space, such as individual brains and bodies, and mind unlimited to specific points in time, such as the present (Dossey, 1989).

Telecebo effects between a clinician and a patient are examples of nonlocal phenomena because they demonstrate the three essential features that characterize all nonlocal happenings: they are *unmediated* (by any known form of energy), *unmitigated* (their strength does not diminish with increasing distance), and *immediate* (instantaneous) (Herbert, 1987; Markoff, 2015).

Intrinsic Connectedness

You are me, and I am you.
Isn't it obvious that we "inter-are"?
— Thich Nhat Hanh (2009), "Interrelationship"

What makes telecebo effects possible? Emerging evidence suggests that living creatures are intimately connected in astonishing, nonclassical ways. This intrinsic connectedness permits information exchanges within and between distant organisms, bypassing conventional mechanisms, previously thought impossible.

Quantum entanglement, the key phenomenon that demonstrates nonlocality, is a term coined by Nobel Prize-winning physicist Erwin Schrödinger in 1935 to describe an intimate connectedness between distant subatomic particles (Schrödinger, 1935; Darling 2015). This time and space-spanning intimacy has been confirmed to also exist in macroscopic systems as well. As physicist Vlatko Vedral reports in a seminal article in *Scientific American* in 2011:

"The quintessential quantum effect, entanglement, can occur in large systems...including living organisms.... These effects are more pervasive than anyone ever suspected. They may operate in the cells of our body.... The entanglements are primary" (Vedral, 2011).

Consciousness researcher Dean Radin, already mentioned, emphasizes the scope of these applications. He states, ["M]inds are entangled with the universe, so in principle minds can nonlocally influence anything, including a collection of other minds or physical systems." Radin's view is fully compatible with telecebo effects (Radin, 2006).

A similar view is expressed by the eminent theoretical physicist Henry P. Stapp of the University of California-Berkeley:

"The new physics presents prima facie evidence that our human thoughts are linked to nature by nonlocal connections: what a person chooses to do in one region seems immediately to affect what is true elsewhere in the universe....[O]ur thoughts... DO something (emphasis in original)" (Stapp, 2001, p.8).

Evidence for an intrinsic, distant connectedness at the cellular level in humans continues to mount (Dossey, 2013). In a series of experiments at DiBit Laboratories in Milan, Italy, researcher Rita Pizzi and her colleagues placed two batches of human neurons or neural stem cells in distant containers that were shielded to prevent any communication between them. When one group of cells was stimulated with laser light, the distant group of cells registered the same changes, although both were completely shielded. The researchers stated, "[O]ur experimental data seem to strongly suggest that biological systems present non-local properties not explainable by classical models" (Pizzi et al., 2004).

In a laboratory experiment at Chicago's Rush University Medical Center, physician-researcher Ashkan Farhadi and his colleagues separated two groups of human epithelial cells in such a way that they could not communicate by any known physical means. When they damaged the "inducer" group of cells with hydrogen peroxide, the distant "detector" cells were damaged in a similar way (Farhadi et al., 2007).

Researcher Victor V. Chaban and his colleagues at the UCLA School of Medicine have demonstrated that neuroblastoma cancer cells can communicate with normal neurons when both are shielded, bypassing any known means of communication (Chaban et al., 2013).

Why has this distant connectivity arisen in humans? What purpose might it serve? Johann Summhammer, of the Atom Institute at the Vienna University of Technology, believes it may assist in our biological evolution and survival:

"Entanglement would lead to a Darwinian advantage.... [It] could coordinate the behaviors of members of a species, because it is independent of distance and requires no physical link.... [Or]... between members of different species, and even between living systems and the inanimate world" (Summhammer, 2006).

Unpacking the Resistance

Often in science the reaction to a new finding is directly proportional to the strength of the dogma it overturns. People are still in denial of the theory of relativity, too.
— *Elias Zerhouni, former director,*
National Institutes of Health (2002, p. 42).

This is the sort of thing I would not believe, even if it really happened.
— *Skeptical scientist*
(Targ & Putoff, 1977, p.169; Editorial, 1976, p. 291).

Why do the above studies evoke such sharp criticism, as in the tense interchange between Freud and Jung? It's an article of faith in most scientific circles that the brain produces human consciousness, and that its effects are confined to the brain and body of an individual and to the present, as mentioned. Thus, it is widely assumed that conscious intentions cannot, in principle, be exteriorized and act remotely in space and time beyond the confines of the corporeal brain and body. The above studies evoke vigorous objections because they violate this prohibition.

Unfortunately, the depth and breadth of healing research remains little known among health care professionals, as well as many of those outside of medicine—biologists, physicists, psychologists—who have offered critiques and analyses of it. These examinations are almost never comprehensive. Literature searches are piecemeal. Key studies are commonly omitted. Some critics identify one or two studies that are problematic, ignore the rest, and generalize to condemn this entire field of research. Crucial evidence from nonhuman studies is almost always ignored as if it is irrelevant or does not exist.

Critics often resort to philosophical speculation about whether healing intentions *ought* to work remotely or not. They often insist that these studies involve the supernatural because they seem to invoke a transcendent, metaphysical agency or higher power, which places them outside the domain of empirical science. This is a straw-man argument, because researchers in this field do not make assertions about gods or metaphysical agents in interpreting their findings. They are merely recording correlations between intentions and observable effects in the world. They usually defer on the question of mechanism, which is an accepted procedure in science when empirical knowledge runs ahead of theoretical models. And in any case, if these phenomena occur in nature, they are necessarily natural, and not supernatural.

Another frequent criticism of healing studies involves theoretical plausibility. Critics commonly maintain that these studies so radically violate the accepted canons of science and the known laws of nature that this places them completely off the scientific map. Therefore, these experiments are so wrongheaded they don't deserve consideration and should not even be done.

Eminent scientists say otherwise. Gerald Feinberg, the prominent Columbia University physicist, observed, "If such phenomena [so-called paranormal events] indeed occur, no change in the fundamental equations of physics would be needed to describe them" (Feinberg, 1975). Henry Margenau, the esteemed Yale University physicist and member of Princeton University's Institute for Advanced Study, agreed. Speaking of so-called paranormal events, he said, "Strangely, it does not seem possible to find the scientific laws or principles violated by the existence of [these phenomena]. We can find contradictions between [their occurrence] and our culturally accepted view of reality—but not—as many of us have believed—between [their occurrence] and the scientific laws that have been so laboriously developed" (Margenau, 1987, p. 118). The eminent physicist Olivier Costa de Beauregard similarly observed: "Today's physics allows for the existence of 'paranormal' phenomena of telepathy, precognition, and psychokinesis.... The whole concept of 'nonlocality' in contemporary physics requires this possibility" (de Beauregard, 1998). And, "Far from being 'irrational,' *the paranormal is postulated by today's physics*" [emphasis in original] (de Beauregard, 2002).

Throughout the history of science, plausibility-based verdicts regarding new ideas and developments have often backfired. Many currently accepted concepts in medicine and the physical sciences, such as the circulation of the blood, the importance of hand washing and sterile technique, and continental drift were initially condemned by authorities because of their perceived implausibility, only later to be embraced as scientific theories advanced (Hellman, 1998; 2001).

There are no inviolable laws of consciousness. As Sir John Maddox, the former editor of *Nature*, has said, "What consciousness consists of . . . is . . . a puzzle. Despite the marvelous successes of neuroscience in the past century . . . we seem as far from understanding cognitive process as we were a century ago" (Maddox, 1999). Donald D. Hoffman, a respected cognitive scientist at the University of California, Irvine, states: "The scientific study of consciousness is in the embarrassing position of having no scientific theory of consciousness" (Hoffman, 2008). Distant healing effects violate not laws of nature or consciousness but, it often seems, challenge deep-seated prejudices.

We can be certain that we have not exhausted nature's inventory, which means that even currently accepted scientific views always exist in a state of "Until Further Notice." This may even apply to the so-called "ironclad laws of nature." As one physicist said, "When I hear the word 'ironclad,' I want to get my acetylene torch." And as Nobel laureate and physicist Max Planck, the founder of quantum physics, said, "We have no right to assume that any physical laws exist, or if they have existed up to now, that they will continue to exist in a similar manner in the future" (Planck, 2015). This is not a rationale for "anything goes" or playing fast and loose with the limitations of science, but a caution against a hide-bound, inflexible ideology.

Dossey and Hufford have offered a critique of the most common objections directed toward the field of healing intentions (Dossey & Hufford 2005; Dossey, 2008).

C. D. Broad, the eminent Cambridge University philosopher of science, unleashed a weaponized salvo against the critics of so-called paranormal phenomena at mid-20th century. Though harsh, his words still apply:

"Anyone who should nowadays start to investigate these subjects, without first mastering the relevant parts of that literature, would be acting very unwisely, laying up trouble for himself which he might have avoided.... And anyone who at the present day expresses confident opinions, whether positive or negative, on ostensibly paranormal phenomena, without making himself thoroughly acquainted with the main methods and results of the careful and long-continued work may be dismissed without further ceremony as a conceited ignoramus" (Broad, 2010, p. 6).

Anyone who researches the nonlocal manifestations of consciousness learns soon enough that uninformed critics such as those described by Broad still abound. How should one respond to them? As a general principle, we ought to seriously consider the approach suggested by Jung: "I shall not commit the fashionable stupidity of regarding everything I cannot explain as a fraud" (Jung, 1960). On a lighter note, J. B. Priestley, the British playwright-philosopher, in his important book *Man & Time*, offers facetious advice that may sometimes be appropriate: "[O]f course if a man, with his theory at stake, makes up his mind not to *be* shown that queer things are happening, little can be done except to make a face at him and a rude noise" (Priestley, 1978, p. 68).

Using Telecebo Effects Consciously

Evolving evidence requires an image of consciousness that is nonlocal in space and time, in which the effects of intention, thought, and emotion can exteriorize from a clinician's or therapist's mind to influence a patient. This view of consciousness transcends our usual notion of the limited, confined self, which Buddhist scholar Alan Watts satirized as the "skin-encapsulated ego" (Antares, 2009).

I've called certain nonlocal mental actions telecebo effects because they commonly crop up in interactions between healthcare providers and patients, and because they have long been lumped together with placebo responses. However, the distinctions between telecebo and placebo are important. If we understand the differences between these categories, physicians, nurses, and other healthcare providers might lay claim to the telecebo effect and use it consciously, as healers throughout human history have always done. The consensus of shamans and medicine men and women was that intention, hope, meaning, and purpose can be exteriorized via a healer's intentions, sometimes impacting a patient decisively, either positively or negatively. Thus the deliberate use of telecebo effects is an affirmation of the universal human endeavor called healing, which always employs compassionate intentions on behalf of someone who is sick and in need.

But in truth, employing telecebo effects is not optional, but obligatory. Doctor-patient interchanges are seldom emotionally neutral, because physicians are not emotion-free automatons. Therefore, we clinicians *will* use telecebo effects for good or ill with our patients, either consciously or unconsciously.

The materialistic straightjacket with which we have shackled consciousness should be removed. Some of the eminent founders of modern science have already done so, but their views have been largely ignored (Dossey, 2016). Many of them believed that the popular view that consciousness is an entity that is produced by the material brain, is limited to it, and perishes with it, is simply wrong. They believed, rather, that consciousness is fundamental, that it cannot be derived from anything more basic, and that it can affect matter—an underlying premise of telecebo effects. None of these great scientists was more emphatic on this score than Max Planck:

"I regard consciousness as fundamental. I regard matter as derivative from consciousness. We cannot get behind consciousness. Everything that we talk about, everything that we regard as existing, postulates consciousness" (Planck, 1931).

Nobel Prize-winning physicist Erwin Schrödinger, whose wave equations are at the heart of quantum physics, agreed (Schrödinger, 1960):

"Although I think that life may be the result of an accident, I do not think that of consciousness. Consciousness cannot be accounted for in physical terms. For consciousness is absolutely fundamental. It cannot be accounted for in terms of anything else.... If we have to decide to have only one sphere, it has got to be the psychic one, since that exists anyway." (Schrödinger, 1994, p 181).

In view of the evidence we've examined, should we not consider using telecebo effects deliberately? If not, why not? Because they are old-fashioned? Because there is no billing code for such a service? Because our colleagues might accuse us of "going mystic"? Because the materialistic worldview with which we were dragooned in our educational years continues to persuade us that these phenomena cannot happen? Because of our willful blindness toward the abundant, replicated, biologically relevant, empirical evidence for the exteriorized actions of consciousness? Because we think it is "more prudent to keep quiet, to be a moderate defender of orthodoxy, or to maintain that all is doubtful, sit on the fence, and wait in statesmanlike ambiguity for more data...."? (Bullard, 1990, p. 184; Dossey, 2015).

Opening to the centrality of consciousness recognized by Planck, Schrödinger, and other towering giants in science might assist us in removing our blinders, so that telecebo effects can emerge in full view and take their place alongside placebo responses as co-factors in healing (Dossey, 2015).

The Everyday

From the foregoing, it may appear that the exteriorization of intention and thought manifests mainly in medical environments, but as the emotion-charged exchange between Freud and Jung demonstrated, this is not always the case. These phenomena can erupt in everyday life when emotional intensity is high, as in the following account reported by author Bill Sweet:

"During the 1970s draft for the Vietnam War, my friend Richard got a notice to appear for a physical for the army draft. He hypnotized himself to get sick. It worked. He got out of the army draft temporarily for two months.

"Richard joined the Navy Reserve. He did everything he could to communicate that he would not kill if so ordered. The sergeant sent him to the company psychiatrist. The psychiatrist determined that he was not potentially good material for the military and sent him to a counselor to see what could be done.

"Before seeing the counselor, Richard decided he would tell her the truth—how nervous, anxious, fearful, disgusted, neurotic, worried, and freaked out he was about the prospect of learning to use a rifle to kill people. Richard walked into the counselor's office in a deplorable state of mind. The session lasted about forty-five minutes.

"On the counselor's desk was a plant with large leaves. As soon as the session began, the plant began to droop. The counselor and Richard couldn't help notice it sagging. As Richard continued with his negative thoughts, the plant kept wilting. By the end of the session, the leaves of the plant had bent over to half their original height.

"The drooping plant freaked out the counselor. Her eyes followed it down, but she didn't say anything. Richard acted like he didn't notice it going down but inside thought it was really neat because the plant's descent, he thought, was obviously a reaction to his negative state of mind.

"The counselor was sympathetic. Richard was released from his obligation to serve in the military" (Sweet, 2007, 2015).

Did Richard's thoughts exteriorize to negatively influence the plant, or was its collapse just a cute coincidence, "just one of those things?" I think I know what Jung would have said. But you decide. As you do, bear in mind the laboratory experiments in which individuals have demonstrated the ability to harm living organisms through negative intentions (Barry, 1968; Nash, 1982; Tedder & Monty, 1981; Dossey, 1997).

Vienna Revisited

Although Freud vigorously disagreed with Jung about ESP in their Vienna confrontation, his opposition was not to last. Late in life he sanctioned Jung's view, stating, "I am not an out and out sceptic.... If I had my life to live over again, I would devote myself to psychical research rather than to psychoanalysis" (Freud, 1996, p. 128). As Frank McLynn, one of Jung's biographers, explains,

"Freud was always interested in telepathy but feared it could be used for reactionary and superstitious purposes rather than to advance the understanding of the unconscious. It was for purely prudential reasons that he did not publish until late in his career the many strange cases of thought-transference he had come across; he simply feared that until psychoanalysis was established beyond risk of destruction by ridicule, to exhibit open-mindedness was to hand enemies a weapon. In 1932 he wrote that he used to fear that science might be overwhelmed by spiritualism or mysticism if parts of the occultist canon were proved true, but he no longer felt like that and was, indeed, convinced that thought-transference was a fact" (McLynn, 1996, pp. 127-128).

We may never know for certain why Freud's bookcase erupted twice with noisy detonations in Jung's presence, why Jung's old walnut dining table tore its guts out, or why his flawless steel bread knife committed suicide by exploding into several pieces. We can conclude, however, in view of abundant evidence, that in the main Jung got it right: emotions, thoughts, and intentions can exteriorize to affect the outside world. In the domain of medicine and healing, this can manifest not as exploding furniture and cutlery, but as the telecebo effect.

Neither Freud nor Jung could have known the extent to which empirical evidence would eventually support the impact of exteriorized thought and intention. Our world is different than theirs: we know more; we have more data points. As a consequence, empirical and ethical considerations require, I believe, that we cultivate and employ telecebo effects consciously, alongside the dazzling modern advances in the healing arts, and always toward the end that Paré articulated five centuries ago: "to cure occasionally, relieve often, console always."

A new era of healing is upon us, in which our tools include our mind in ways we have been hesitant to acknowledge. There is no going back (Cardeña, 2014; Penraeth, 2014; Beauregard et al., 2014). As novelist Arundhati Roy says, "Another world is not only possible, she's on the way and, on a quiet day, if you listen very carefully you can hear her breathe" (https://www.goodreads.com/author/quotes/6134.Arundhati_ Roy).

Placebo, Nocebo, and Telecebo Effects: A Taxonomy

	Placebo	**Nocebo**	**Telecebo**
Space-Time Characteristic	Local (effects confined or localized to specific points in space and time)	Local (effects confined or localized to specific points in space and time)	Nonlocal (effects *not* confined or localized to specific points in space and time)
Psychological Characteristic	Intrapersonal/ interpersonal	Intrapersonal/ interpersonal	Interpersonal/ transpersonal

Expanding Science

Description	Placebo effects are the *positive* actions of an individual's thoughts and intentions on his/her body following the administration of a harmless, inert substance. They may be activated by the interpersonal clinician-patient encounter, as a result of perceived trust, comfort, support, empathy, and compassion manifested by a clinician. These effects are often considered a result of positive thinking, suggestion, or expectation. Placebo interventions can evoke quantifiable fluxes in neurotransmitters, hormones, and immune regulators. There is little reliable evidence that placebos can actually cure disease by modifying pathophysiology. Most authorities believe that placebos have the power to ameliorate illness by relieving symptoms such as pain, anxiety, and fear, thereby helping patients cope with illness and suffering.	Nocebo effects are the *negative* actions of an individual's thoughts and intentions on his/her own body following the administration of a harmless, inert substance. In addition, these effects can result from a *negative* interpersonal encounter between a clinician and patient. They can be triggered, e.g., by dire predictions such as a dismal prognosis or careless language. These effects can be largely understood through the neural, biochemical, and humoral actions that are recognized as the body's response to perceived fear, dread, anxiety, and stress.	"Telecebo" is a neologism formed by combining the Greek *tele*, meaning "far" or "distant," with the fragment *cebo* from "placebo." Telecebo effects represent an *exteriorization* of the intentions, thoughts, or emotions of a clinician toward a patient. They may be positive or negative. Telecebo effects can be initiated *de novo* by intention alone. They do not depend on the intermediary influence of a harmless, inert substance. These effects occur beyond the reach of the physical senses and are inexplicable by conventional exchanges of matter/energy. These effects have been demonstrated in a variety of subjects including humans, human tissue and cells, animals,

			microorganisms, plants, and chemical reactions. Telecebo effects demonstrate three essential characteristics of nonlocal phenomena: they are *unmediated* (by any known form of energy), *unmitigated* (their strength does not diminish with increasing distance), and *immediate* (instantaneous).

References

Abbot, N. C. (2000). Healing as a therapy for human disease: a systematic review. *Journal of Alternative and Complementary Medicine*, 6(2), 159-169.

Achterberg, J. (1985). *Imagery in Healing*. Boston, MA: Shambhala.

Achterberg, J., Dossey, B., & Kolkmeier, L. (1984). *Rituals of Healing*. New York, NY: Bantam.

Achterberg, J., Cooke., K., Richards, T., Standish, L., Kozak. L., & Lake, J. (2005) Evidence for correlations between distant intentionality and brain function in recipients: a functional magnetic resonance imaging analysis. *Journal of Alternative and Complementary Medicine*, 11(6), 965-971.

Ader, R. & Cohen, N. (1982). Behaviorally conditioned immunosuppression and murine systemic lupus erythematosus. *Science*, 215(4539), 1534-36.

Antares. (2009). Alan Watts and the skin-encapsulated ego. Retrieved from http://www.magickriver.org/2009/06/alan-watts-and-skin-encapsulated-ego.html. 3 April, 2015. Accessed 25 September, 2015.

Astin, J. E., Harkness, E., & Ernst, E. (2000). The efficacy of "distant healing": a systematic review of randomized trials. *Annals of Internal Medicine*, 132, 903-910.

Barry, J. (1968). General and comparative study of the psychokinetic effect on a fungus culture. *Journal of Parapsychology*, 1968; 32, 237-43.

Beauregard, M., Schwartz, G., & Miller, L. (2014). Manifesto for a postmaterialist science. Opensciences.org. http://opensciences.org/about/manifesto-for-a-postmaterialist-science.

de Beauregard, O. C. (1998). The paranormal is not excluded from physics. *Journal of Scientific Exploration*, 1998;12(2), 315-320.

de Beauregard, O. C. (2002). Wavelike coherence and CPT invariance: Sesames of the paranormal. *Journal of Scientific Exploration*, 16(4), 651-54.

Benedetti, F. (2009). *Placebo Effects: Understanding the Mechanisms in Health and Disease*. Oxford, UK: Oxford University Press.

Bengston, W. (2010). *The Energy Cure: Unraveling the Mystery of Hands-on Healing*. Louisville, CO: Sounds True Publishing.

Bengston, W. F. (2012). Spirituality, connection, and healing with intent: reflections on cancer experiments on laboratory mice. In Miller, L. J. (Ed.), *The Oxford Handbook of Psychology and Spirituality*. New York, NY: Oxford University Press, pp. 548-577.

Bengston, W. F., & Krinsley, D. (2000). The effect of the laying-on of hands on transplanted breast cancer in mice. *Journal of Scientific Exploration*. 14(3), 353-364.

Bengston, W. F., & Moga, M. (2007). Resonance, placebo effects, and type II errors: some implications from healing research for experimental methods. *Journal of Alternative and Complementary Medicine*, 13(3), 317-327.

Benor, D. J. (2002). Healing Research, Vol. 1. Southfield, MI: Vision.

Benor, D. J. (2002). Distant healing. *Subtle Energies and Energy Medicine.* 11(3), 249-264.

Bierman, D. J. & Radin, D. I. (1997). Anomalous anticipatory response on randomized future conditions. *Perceptual and Motor Skills,* 84, 689-690.

Bierman, D. J. & Radin, D. I. (1998). Conscious and anomalous non-conscious emotional processes: A reversal of the arrow time? *Toward a Science of Consciousness, Tucson III.* Cambridge, MA: MIT Press, pp. 367-386.

Braud, W. (2000). Wellness implications of retroactive intentional influence: exploring an outrageous hypothesis. *Alternative Therapies in Health & Medicine,* 6(1), 37-48. http://www.integral-inquiry.com/docs/649/wellness.pdf

Braud, W., & Schlitz, M. (1989). A methodology for the objective study of transpersonal imagery, *Journal of Scientific Exploration,* 3(1), 43-63.

Broad, C. D. (2010). *Lectures in Psychical Research: Incorporating the Perrott Lectures Given in Cambridge University in 1959 and 1960.* Routledge Revival edition. London, UK: Routledge, p. 6.

Brody, H. (1982). The lie that heals: the ethics of giving placebos. *Ann Intern Med,* 97(1),112-118. Doi:10.7326/0003-4819-97-1-112.

Brown, C. G., Mory, S. C., Williams, R., & McClymond, M. J. (2010). Study of the therapeutic effects of proximal intercessory prayer (STEPP) on auditory and visual impairments in rural Mozambique. *South Med J,* 103(9), 864-9.

Bullard, E. (1975). Quoted in: John A. Steward. *Drifting Continents & Colliding Paradigms: Perspectives on the Geoscience Revolution.* Bloomington, IN: Indiana University Press; 1990:184. Original quotation in: Bullard, E.C. (1975). The emergence of plate tectonics: A personal view. *Annual Review of Earth and Planetary Sciences,* 3, p. 5.

Cabot, R. C. (1903). The use of truth and falsehood in medicine: an experimental study. *Am Med,* 5, 344-349.

Cardeña, E. (2014). A call for an open, informed study of all aspects of consciousness. *Frontiers in Human Neuroscience,* 2014; 8(17).

http://journal.frontiersin.org/article/10.3389/fnhum.2014.00017/full. http://dx.doi.org/10.3389/fnhum.2014.00017. Accessed 7 November, 2015.

Chaban, V. V., Cho, T., Reid, C. B., & Norris, K. C. (2013). Physically disconnected non-diffusable cell-to-cell communication between neuroblastoma SH-SY5Y and DRG sensory neurons. *Am. J. Translational Research*, 5(1), 69-79.

Consort. Retrieved from: http://www.consort-statement.org. Accessed 11 October, 2015.

de Craen, A. J., Kaptchuk, T. J., Tijssen, J. G., & Kleijnen, J. (1999). Placebos and placebo effects in medicine: historical review. *J R Soc Med*, 92 (10), 511–515.

Darling, D. Quantum entanglement. Daviddarling.info. Retrieved from: http://www.daviddarling.info/encyclopedia/Q/quantum_entanglement.html. Accessed 5 October, 2015.

Dossey, L. (1989). *Recovering the Soul*. New York, NY: Bantam, pp.1-11.

Dossey, L. (1997). *Be Careful What You Pray For*. San Francisco, CA: HarperSanFrancisco, pp. 168-170.

Dossey, L. (1999). *Reinventing Medicine*. San Francisco, CA: HarperSanFrancisco, pp. 37-84.

Dossey, L. (2008). Healing research: what we know and don't know. *Explore (NY)*, 4(5), 341-352.

Dossey, L. (2013). *One Mind: How Our Individual Mind Is Part of a Greater Consciousness and Why It Matters*. Carlsbad, CA: Hay House.

Dossey, L. (2015). Something higher: lessons from *Beyond Physicalism*. *Explore* (NY), 1(4), 261-272.

Dossey, L. (2016). Consciousness is eternal, infinite, and one. In: Laszlo, E. (Ed.), *What Is Consciousness?* New York, NY: Select Books, pp. 33-95.

Dossey, L., & Hufford, D. J. (2005). Are prayer experiments legitimate? Twenty criticisms. *Explore (NY)*, 1(2), 109-117.

Editorial. (1976, March). Scanning the issue. *Proceedings of the IEEE*, LXIV(3), 291.

Farhadi, A., Forsyth, C., Banan, A., Shaikh, M., Engen, P., Fields, J. Z., & Keshavarzian, A. (2007). Evidence for non-chemical, non-electrical intercellular signaling in intestinal epithelial cells. *Bioelectrochemistry*, 71 (2), 142-148.

Feinberg, G. (1975). Precognition — a memory of things future. In Oteri, L. (Ed.), *Quantum Physics and Parapsychology*. New York, NY: Parapsychology Foundation, pp. 54-73.

Freud, S. (1996). Quoted in Frank McLynn, *Carl Gustav Jung*. New York, NY: St. Martin's Press; p. 128.

Gronowicz, G. A., Jhaveri, A., Clarke, L. W., Aronow, M. S., & Smith, T. H. (2008). Therapeutic Touch stimulates the proliferation of human cells in culture. *The Journal of Alternative and Complementary Medicine*, 14(3), 233-239. doi:10.1089/acm.2007.7163.

Handfield-Jones, R. C. P. (1953). A bottle of medicine from the doctor. *Lancet*, ii: 823-825.

Hanh, T. N. (2009). *Call Me by My True Names: The Collected Poems*. Berkeley, CA: Parallax Press, p. 154.

Hellman, H. (2001). *Great Feuds in Medicine*. New York, NY: John Wiley.

Hellman, H. (1998). *Great Feuds in Science*. New York, NY: John Wiley.

Herbert, N. (1987). *Quantum Reality*. Garden City, NY: Anchor/Doubleday, p. 214.

Hodge, D. R. (2007). A systematic review of the empirical literature on intercessory prayer. *Research on Social Work Practice*, 17(2), 174-187.

Hoffman, D. (2008). Consciousness and the mind-body problem. *Mind & Matter*, 6(1), 87-121.

Jefferson, T. (1898). *The Writings of Thomas Jefferson*. Ford, P.L. (Ed.), Version 9. New York, NY: G. P. Putnam's.

Johnson, N. (2013, January 18). Forget the placebo effect: it's the 'care effect' that matters. Wired. http://www.wired.com/2013/01/dr-feel-good/ Accessed 25 September, 2015.

Jonas, W. B. (2001). The middle way: Realistic randomized controlled trials for the evaluation of spiritual healing. *The Journal of Alternative and Complementary Medicine*, 7(1),5-7.

Jonas, W. B. (2003). Crawford CC (eds). *Healing, Intention and Energy Medicine*. New York, NY: Churchill Livingstone, pp. xv-xix.

Jung, C. G. (1960). *The Collected Works of C. G. Jung, Volume 8: The Structure and Dynamics of the Psyche* (2nd ed.) (R. F. C. Hull, trans.). Princeton University Press/Bollingen Series XX, pp. 301-318.

Jung, C. G. (1965). *Memories, Dreams, Reflections*. Jaffé, A. (Ed.), New York, NY: Vintage.

Jütte, R. (2013). The early history of the placebo. *Complement Ther Med*, 21(2), 94-7. Accessed 30 December, 2015.

Kaptchuk, T. J. (1998). Powerful placebo: the dark side of the randomized controlled trial. *Lancet*, 351, 1722-1725.

Kaptchuk, T.J., & Miller, F. G. (2015). Placebo effects in medicine. *New England Journal of Medicine*, 373 (1), 8-9.

Kelly, E. F., Kelly E. W., Crabtree, A., Gauld, A., Grosso, M., & Greyson, B. (2007). *Irreducible Mind: Toward a Psychology for the 21st Century*. Lanham, MD: Rowman and Littlefield.

Kelly, E. F., Crabtree, A., & Marshall, P. (Eds.). (2015). *Beyond Physicalism: Toward Reconciliation of Science and Spirituality*. Lanham, MD: Rowman & Littlefield.

Kuwada, G. (2013). Distant intentionality healing and its effects on post-operative pain and narcotic usage after foot and ankle surgery. *The Foot and Ankle Online Journal*, 6 (9), 1.

Leibovici, L. (2001). Effects of remote, retroactive intercessory prayer on outcomes in patients with bloodstream infection: a randomized controlled trial. *British Medical Journal*, 323, 1450-1451.

Maddox, J. (1999). The unexpected science to come. *Scientific American*, 281(6), 62-7.

Margenau, H. (1987). Quoted in: Lawrence LeShan, *The Science of the Paranormal*. Northamptonshire, UK: Aquarian Press, p. 118.

Markoff, J. (2015). Sorry, Einstein. Quantum study suggests 'spooky action' is real. Retrieved from: NYtimes.com.http://www.nytimes.com/2015/10/22/science/quantum-theory-experiment-said-to-prove-spooky-interactions.html?emc=eta1. Accessed 22 October, 2015.

McLynn, F. (1996). *Carl Gustav Jung*. New York, NY: St. Martin's Press, pp. 127-128.

McMillan, F. D. (1999). The placebo effect in animals. *J Am Vet Med Assoc*, 215(7), 992-9.

Miller, F. G., Colloca, L., & Kaptchuk, T. J. (2009). The placebo effect: illness and interpersonal healing. *Perspectives in Biology and Medicine*, 52(4), 518-539. Retrieved from: http://www.ncbi.nlm.nih.gov/pubmed/19855122. Accessed 26 October, 2015.

Mossbridge, J., Tressoldi, P. & Utts, J. (2012). Predictive physiological anticipation preceding seemingly unpredictable stimuli: a meta-analysis. *Frontiers in Psychology*, 3,390. doi: 10.3389/fpsyg.2012.00390. Retrieved from:http://www.frontiersin.org/Perception_Science/10.3389/fpsyg.2012.00390/full. Accessed 2 October, 2015.

Mossbridge, J. A., Tressoldi, P., Utts, J., Ives, J. A., Radin, D., & Jonas, W. B. (2014, March 25). Predicting the unpredictable: critical analysis and practical implications of predictive anticipatory activity. *Frontiers in Human Neuroscience*, Retrieved from: http://dx.doi.org/10.3389/fnhum.2014.00146. Accessed 2 October, 2015.

Nash, C. B. (1982). Psychokinetic control of bacterial growth. *Journal of the American Society for Psychical Research*, 51, 217-221.

Olshansky, B. (2007). Placebo and nocebo in cardiovascular health: implications for healthcare, research, and the doctor-patient relationship. *J Am Coll Cardiol,* 49(4), 415-21. Retrieved from: http://www.ncbi.nlm.nih.gov/pubmed/17258086. Accessed 23 September 2015.

Olshansky, B., & Dossey, L. (2003, December 20). Retroactive prayer: A preposterous hypothesis? *British Medical Journal*, 327, 1465-68.

Paré, A. (2009). Quoted in: Balakrishnan V. The making of a physician. *Mens Sana Monographs.* 2009; 7(1): 184–188. Retrieved from: http://www.ncbi.nlm.nih.gov/pmc/articles/PMC3151448/. Accessed 30 December, 2015.

Penraeth, S. (2014, November 5). 100 notable scientists call for open study of consciousness. Opensciences.org. Retrieved from: http://opensciences.org/blogs/open-sciences-blog/199-100-notable-scientists-call-for-open-study-of-consciousness. Accessed 10November, 2015.

Pizzi, R., Fantasia, A., Gelain, F., Rossetti, D., & Vescovi, A. (2004). Non-local correlation between separated human neural networks. In: Donkor, E., Pirick, A.R., & Brandt, H.E. (Eds.), *Quantum Information and Computation II.* Proceedings of SPIE5436. 2004:107-117. Abstract retrieved from: http://adsabs.harvard.edu/abs/2004SPIE.5436..107P. Accessed 25 September, 2015. Also available at: Smithsonian/NASA Astrophysics Data System.

Planck, M. (1931, January 25). *The Observer*. London, UK.

Planck, M. Wikiquote. Retrieved from:
http://en.wiiquote.org/wiki/Max_Planck. Accessed 28 September, 2015.

Priestley, J. B. (1978). *Man & Time*. Reprint edition. London, UK: W. H. Allen & Co., p. 68.

Radin, D. (1997). *The Conscious Universe*. San Francisco: HarperSanFrancisco.

Radin, D. I. (2004). Electrodermal presentiments of future emotions. *Journal of Scientific Exploration*, 18(2), 253-274.

Radin, D. (2006). *Entangled Minds*. New York, NY: Paraview, pp. 136-141.

Roe, C. A., Sonnex, C., & Roxburgh, E. (2012). Two meta-analyses of distant healing studies. *Journal of Parapsychology*, 76(2), 223-224.

Roy, A. Quoted in: Goodreads.com. https://www.goodreads.com/author/quotes/6134.Arundhati_Roy. Acc

Sagan, C. (1997). *The Demon-Haunted World: Science As a Candle in the Dark.* Reprint edition. New York, NY: Ballantine.

Sanderson, C., Hardy, J., Spruyt, O., & Currow, D. C. (2013). Placebo and nocebo effects in randomized controlled trials: the implications for research and practice. *Journal of Pain and Symptom Management*, 46(5), 722-730. doi: 10.1016/j.jpainsymman.2012.12.005.

Schlitz, M., & Braud, W. (1997). Distant intentionality and healing: assessing the evidence, *Alternative Therapies in Health and Medicine*, 3(6), 62-73.

Schmidt, S. (2012). Can we help by good intentions? A meta-analysis of experiments on distant intention effects. *Journal of Alternative and Complementary Medicine*, 18(6), 529-533.

Schmidt, S., Schneider, R., Utts, J., & Walach, H. (2004). Distant intentionality and the feeling of being stared at — two meta-analyses. *British Journal of Psychology*, 95 (2), 235-247.

Schrödinger, E. (1935). Discussion of probability relations between separated systems. *Proceedings of the Cambridge Philosophical Society*, 31, 555-563.

Schrödinger, E. (1960). *My View of the World*. Cambridge: Cambridge University Press, p. 62.

Schrödinger, E. (1994). Quoted in: Walter Moore. *A Life of Erwin Schrödinger*. Canto edition. Cambridge, UK: Cambridge University Press, p. 181.

Schwartz, S. A. (2007). *Opening to the Infinite: The Art and Science of Nonlocal Awareness*. Buda, Texas: Nemoseen.

Schwartz, S. A., & Dossey, L. (2010). Nonlocality, intention, and observer effects in healing studies: laying a foundation for the future. *Explore (NY)*, 6(5), 295-307.

Sheehan, D. P. (2006). *Frontiers of Time: Retrocausation—Experiment and Theory*. Melville, NY: American Institute of Physics.

Sheldrake, R. (1999). *Dogs That Know When Their Owners Are Coming Home: And Other Unexplained Powers of Animals*. New York, NY: Crown.

Siegel, S. (2002). Explanatory mechanisms for placebo effects: Pavlovian conditioning. In Guess, H.A., (Ed.), *The Science of the Placebo: Toward an Interdisciplinary Research Agenda*. London, UK: BMJ Books, pp.133-157.

Stapp, H. P. (2001, February). Harnessing science and religion: Implications of the new scientific conception of human beings. *Science & Theology News*, 1(6), 8.

Summhammer, J. (2006). Quoted in: Radin D. *Entangled Minds*. New York, NY: Paraview/Simon & Schuster; pp. 16-17.

Sweet, B. (2015, October 5). Adapted from personal communication from Bill Sweet to Larry Dossey. Used with permission.

Sweet, B. (2007). *A Journey into Prayer*. Bloomington, IN: Xlibris.

Targ, R., & Puthoff, H. (1977). *Mind-Reach. Scientists Look at Psychic Ability*. New York, NY: Delta, p. 169.

Tart, C. T. (2009). *The End of Materialism: How Evidence of the Paranormal is Bringing Science and Spirit Together*. Oakland, CA: New Harbinger.

Tedder, W., & Monty, M. (1981). Exploration of long-distance PK: A conceptual replication of the influence on a biological system. In Roll, W.G. et al. (Eds.), *Research in Parapsychology 1980*. Metuchen, NJ: Scarecrow Press, pp. 90-93.

Tressoldi, P. E., Storm, L., & Radin, D. (2010). Extrasensory and quantum models of cognition. Studies related to brain activity correlation at a distance. Supplement Issue 1. *Neuroquantology*, 8(4), 581-587.

Tsubono, K., Thomlinson, P., & Shealy, N. (2009). The effects of distant healing performed by a spiritual healer on chronic pain: A randomized controlled trial. *Alternative Therapies in Health and Medicine*, 15 (3), 30-34.

Vedral, V. (2011). Living in a quantum world. *Scientific American*, 304 (6), 38-43.

Vuckovich, N. H., Gullion, C. M., Williams, L. A., Ramirez, M., & Schneider, J. (2007). Feasibility and short-term outcomes of a shamanic treatment for temporomandibular joint disorders. *Alternative Therapies in Health and Medicine*, 12(6), 18-29.

Wsoctv.com. (2006). Gulf war veteran gets placebos instead of real medicine. Wsoctv.com. http://www.wsoctv.com/news/news/gulf-war-veteran-gets-placebos-instead-of-real-med/nG8ws/. 23 February, 2006. Accessed 24 September, 2015.

Zerhouni, E. (2002, November 18). Quoted in: Amanda Spake. The menopausal marketplace *US News & World Report*, 133 (19), 42.

Chapter Eleven

Near-Death Experience and the Loss of Brain Function During Cardiac Arrest: A Strong Indication for Non-Local Consciousness

Pim van Lommel, MD[20]

'To study the abnormal is the best way of understanding the normal.'
William James (1842-1910, American philosopher, psychologist)

Introduction

Scientific research on near-death experiences (NDEs) during cardiac arrest questions the purely materialistic paradigm in science. In four recently published prospective studies on NDEs in survivors of cardiac arrest (van Lommel et al., 2001; Greyson, 2003; Parnia et al., 2001; Sartori, 2006), between 10 and 20% of the 562 included patients reported an experience of enhanced consciousness during the period of unconsciousness, during clinical death, during a transient functional loss of the cortex and the brainstem. An NDE seems to be an authentic experience which cannot be reduced to oxygen deficiency, imagination, fear of death, hallucination, psychosis, or the use of drugs. People appear to be permanently changed by an NDE during a cardiac arrest, despite lasting for only a few minutes. Because of occasional and verifiable out-of-body experiences (OBEs), we know that NDEs with all the reported elements happen during the period of unconsciousness, and not in the first or last seconds of cardiac arrest. But how could a clear consciousness outside one's body be experienced at

---

[20] *Department of Cardiology, Rijnstate Hospital, Arnhem, The Netherlands.*

the moment that the brain no longer functions during clinical death? A clear sensorium and complex perceptual processes during such a period of impaired cerebral perfusion challenges the concept that consciousness is localized exclusively in the brain. Complex experiences such as those reported during NDEs should not arise in the first place, nor be retained in memory.

Scientific study of NDEs pushes us to the limits of our medical and neurophysiological ideas about the range of human consciousness and the mind-brain relationship. The concept thus far assumed but never scientifically proven, that consciousness and memories are produced by large groups of neurons and are localized in the brain should be questioned. For decades, extensive research has been done to localize consciousness and memories inside the brain, so far without success. Although providing evidence for the role of neuronal networks as an intermediary for the manifestation of thoughts (neural correlates), those studies do not necessarily imply that those cells also produce the thoughts. Direct evidence of how neurons or neuronal networks could possibly produce the subjective essence of the mind is currently lacking. Despite our modern neuroimaging techniques like EEG, fMRI, and PET-scan, we cannot measure nor scientifically and objectively prove what we think or feel: we just measure changing neural activation.

Since the publication of these four prospective studies on NDEs in survivors of cardiac arrest (van Lommel et al., 2001; Greyson, 2003; Parnia et al., 2001; Sartori, 2006), with strikingly similar results and conclusions, the phenomenon of the NDE can no longer be scientifically ignored. According to these aforementioned empirical studies on NDEs and to neurophysiological studies in cardiac arrest, the current materialistic view of the relationship between the brain and consciousness held by most physicians, philosophers, and psychologists seems too restricted for a proper understanding of this phenomenon. By making a scientific case for consciousness as a nonlocal and thus ubiquitous phenomenon, this view can contribute to new ideas about the relationship between consciousness and the brain. There are now good reasons to assume that our consciousness does not always coincide with the functioning of our brain: enhanced consciousness with unaltered self-identity and with the possibility of perception can apparently be experienced independently from the lifeless body. Studies on NDEs seem to suggest that our consciousness does not reside in our brain and is not limited to our brain, because our consciousness has nonlocal properties, and according to this hypothesis our brain seems to have a facilitating function and not a producing function to experience consciousness. It seems inevitable that we need new ways of thinking and a new kind of postmaterialist science to study consciousness and to reconsider the relationship between consciousness and the brain.

What Is an NDE?

A near-death experience is a form of non-ordinary mental expression, and can be defined as the reported memory of a range of impressions during a special state of consciousness, including a number of special and universal reported elements such as an out-of-body experience, pleasant feelings, seeing a tunnel, a light, deceased relatives, a life review, and a conscious return into the body. Many circumstances are described during which NDEs are reported, such as cardiac arrest (clinical death), shock after loss of blood (childbirth), coma caused by traumatic brain injury or stroke, near-drowning (mostly children) or asphyxia, but also in serious diseases that are not immediately life-threatening, during isolation, depression, or meditation, or without any obvious reason. Similar experiences to near-death ones can occur during the terminal phase of illness, and are called deathbed visions or end-of-life experiences. Furthermore, so-called "fear-death" experiences are mainly reported after situations in which death seemed unavoidable, like serious traffic or mountaineering accidents. The NDE is usually transformational, causing enhanced intuitive sensitivity, profound changes of life-insight, and the loss of fear of death. The content of an NDE and the effects on patients seem similar worldwide, across all cultures and all times. However, the subjective nature and absence of a frame of reference for this ineffable experience lead to individual, cultural, and religious factors determining the vocabulary used to describe and interpret this experience.

Near-death experiences occur with increasing frequency because of improved survival rates resulting from modern techniques of resuscitation, and from new therapies for patients with cerebral trauma. According to a recent random poll in the US and in Germany, about 4% of the total population in the western world has experienced an NDE (Gallup & Proctor, 1982; Schmied et al., 1999). Thus, about 9 million people in the US, about 2 million people in the UK, and about 20 million people in Europe should have had this extraordinary conscious experience. An NDE seems to be a relatively regularly occurring—and, to many physicians, an inexplicable—phenomenon, and hence an often ignored result of survival in a critical medical situation. For most physicians the phenomenon of near-death experience raises a number of fundamental questions, like how and why does an NDE occur? Or how does the content of an NDE come about? And why does a person's life change so radically after an NDE? After all, according to current medical knowledge it is impossible to experience consciousness during cardiac arrest or deep coma.

In order to answer these aforementioned questions, we need a better understanding of the relationship between brain function and consciousness. We will start by examining whether there is any indication that consciousness can be experienced during cardiac arrest, or clinical death. Clinical death is defined as the period of unconsciousness caused by a total lack of oxygen in the brain (anoxia) because of the arrest of circulation and breathing, as caused by cardiac arrest in patients with an acute myocardial infarction. If in this situation no resuscitation is initiated within five to ten minutes, the brain cells will be irreversibly damaged and the patient will always die. If, indeed, consciousness is experienced during such a cardiac arrest, we should look for scientific explanations and scrutinize the relationship between brain function and consciousness in this period of clinical death. Until quite recently there was no prospective and scientifically designed study to explain the cause and content of an NDE. All studies had been retrospective and very selective with respect to patients. Based on these incomplete retrospective studies, some believed the experience could be caused by physiological changes in the brain as a result of lack of oxygen (cerebral anoxia). Other theories assume a psychological reaction to approaching death, hallucinations, side effects of drugs, dreams, or even false memories. Properly designed prospective studies in survivors of cardiac arrest are necessary in order to obtain more reliable data to corroborate or refute the existing theories on the cause and content of NDEs. We need to know if there could be a physiological, pharmacological, psychological, or demographic explanation for why people experience enhanced consciousness during a period of cardiac arrest.

Four Recent Prospective Studies on NDEs

'All science is empirical science, all theory is subordinate to perception;
a single fact can overturn an entire system'.
Frederik van Eeden (1860-1932, Dutch MD, Author)

In four recently published prospective studies on NDEs in survivors of cardiac arrest (van Lommel et al., 2001; Greyson, 2003; Parnia et al., 2001; Sartori, 2006), with identical study design, between 10 and 20% of the 562 included patients reported an experience of enhanced consciousness during the period of unconsciousness, during clinical death, during a transient functional loss of the cortex and the brainstem.

1. The Dutch Prospective Study on NDEs in Survivors of Cardiac Arrest

In 1988 a prospective study was initiated in the Netherlands (van Lommel et al., 2001). At that point, no large-scale prospective study into NDEs had been undertaken anywhere in the world. And until now, only the Dutch study allowed for statistical analysis of the factors that may determine whether or not an NDE could occur. Our study aimed to include all consecutive patients who had survived a cardiac arrest in one of the 10 participating Dutch hospitals. In other words, this prospective study would only be carried out among patients with a proven life-threatening crisis. All these patients were in the first stage of the process of dying, and would have died if resuscitation had not been initiated. This kind of design also creates a control group of patients who have survived a cardiac arrest but who have no recollection of the period of unconsciousness. In a prospective study, such patients are asked, within a few days of their resuscitation, whether they have any recollection of the period of their cardiac arrest, i.e. of the period of their unconsciousness. All patients' medical and other data are carefully recorded before, during, and after their resuscitation. The advantage of this prospective study design was that all procedures were defined in advance so no selection bias could occur. Within four years, between 1988 and 1992, 344 successive patients who had undergone a total of 509 successful resuscitations were included in the study. If patients reported memories from the period of unconsciousness, the experiences were scored according to a certain index, the WCEI, or 'weighted core experience index' (Ring, 1980). The higher the number of elements reported, the higher the score and the deeper the NDE. Because of the prospective design of our study, we also included patients with NDEs with a low score, also in the American and British prospective studies that are mentioned later in this chapter, because we found in our longitudinal study that all patients with a low NDE score—with only one or two typical elements of an NDE—showed the same transformation as patients with NDEs with a higher score. The WCEI by Ring and the NDE Scale by Greyson (1983) were only based on retrospective studies, and in these retrospective studies patients with a score of less than 6 were excluded.

The Dutch study was published in *The Lancet* in December 2001 (van Lommel et al., 2001). Our study found that 282 patients (82%) had no recollection of the period of their unconsciousness, whereas 62 patients— 18% of the 344 patients—reported an NDE. Of the 62 patients with memories, 21 patients (6%) had some recollection; having experienced only some typical elements, they had a superficial NDE with a low score of less than 6. A core experience was reported by 41 patients (12%), where the following elements were reported: half of the patients with an NDE were aware of being dead and had positive emotions; 30% had a tunnel experience, observed a celestial landscape, or met with deceased persons; approximately 25% had an out-of-body experience, communication with 'the light' or perception of colours; 13% had a life review; and 8%

experienced the presence of a border. In other words, all the familiar elements of an NDE were reported in our study, with the exception of a frightening or negative NDE.

Were there any reasons why some people do but most people do not recollect the period of their unconsciousness? In order to answer this question, we compared the recorded data of the 62 patients with an NDE to the data of the 282 patients without an NDE. To our surprise, we could rule out the aforementioned possible physiological, psychological, and pharmacological explanations for the occurrence of an NDE. The degree or gravity of the lack of oxygen in the brain (anoxia) appeared to be irrelevant, because we failed to identify any differences between the patients with a very long or a very brief cardiac arrest. We did not identify any significant differences in the duration of the cardiac arrest, no differences in the duration of unconsciousness, and no differences in whether or not intubation was necessary for artificial respiration in seriously ill patients who remained in a coma for days or weeks after a complicated resuscitation. It was also established that medication could play no role. A psychological cause such as fear of death did not affect the occurrence of an NDE either, although it did affect the depth of the experience. Whether or not patients had heard or read anything about NDEs in the past (foreknowledge) made no difference either. Any kind of religious belief, or indeed its absence in non-religious people or atheists, was irrelevant. The same was true for the standard of education reached. We found that patients who had reported an NDE in the past reported significantly more frequent NDEs in our study. A complicated resuscitation can result in a long coma and most patients who have been unconscious on a respirator for days or weeks are more likely to suffer short-term memory defects as a result of persistent brain damage. These patients reported significantly fewer NDEs in our study, and this suggests that a good short-term memory is important for remembering an NDE. It is important to mention here that in the years 1988 to 1992 we did not yet apply local cerebral hypothermia in patients with post-anoxic coma. Cerebral hypothermia is induced by cooling the head of a patient in coma after surviving a cardiac arrest, and it is performed to improve the neurologic outcome of the patient.

We were particularly surprised to find no medical explanation for the occurrence of an NDE. All patients in our study had been clinically dead and only a small percentage reported an enhanced consciousness with lucid thoughts, emotions, memories, and sometimes perception from a position outside and above their lifeless body while doctors and nursing staff were carrying out resuscitation. If there were a physiological explanation such as a lack of oxygen in the brain (anoxia) for the occurrence of this enhanced consciousness, one might have expected all patients to have reported an NDE. They had all been unconscious as a result of their cardiac arrest, which always caused the loss of blood pressure, the cessation of breathing and the loss of all body and brain stem reflexes. And it is also well established that people without any lack of oxygen in the brain, like in depression or meditation, can experience an 'NDE.' Furthermore, because of some cases of veridical perception during resuscitation, we reached the inevitable conclusion that patients experienced all the aforementioned NDE elements during the period of their cardiac arrest, during the total cessation of blood supply to the brain. Nevertheless, the question of how this could be possible remained unanswered.

A longitudinal study into life changes following NDEs was based on interviews after two and eight years with all patients who had reported an NDE and who were still alive, as well as with a control group of post-resuscitation patients who were matched for age and sex, but who had not reported an NDE. The question was whether the customary changes in attitude to life after an NDE were the result of surviving a cardiac arrest or whether these changes were caused by the experience of an NDE. This question had never been subject to scientific and systematic research with prospective design before. So our Dutch study was also the first to include a longitudinal component with interviews after two and eight years, which allowed us to compare the processes of transformation between people with and without NDEs (van Lommel et al., 2001). The later interviews in our longitudinal study were conducted using a standardized inventory featuring 34 life-change questions (Ring, 1984). Among the 74 patients who consented to be interviewed after two years, 13 of the total of 34 factors listed in the questionnaire turned out to be significantly different for people with or without an NDE. The second interviews after eight years showed that in people with NDEs fear of death in particular had significantly decreased, while belief in an afterlife had significantly increased. Quotation:

"It is outside my domain to discuss something that can only be proven by death. For me, however, this blessing experience was decisive in convincing me that consciousness lives on beyond the grave, and I know now for sure that body and mind are separated. Death was not death, but another form of life" (van Lommel, 2004).

In patients with an NDE we saw a greater interest in spirituality and questions about the purpose of life, as well as a greater acceptance and compassion for oneself and others. The conversations also revealed that people had acquired enhanced intuitive feelings after an NDE, along with a strong sense of connectedness with others and with nature. Or, as many of them put it, they had acquired 'paranormal gifts.' This enhanced intuition is based on interconnectedness with the consciousness of others, and is independent of time (inner knowing of future events or having prognostic 'dreams') and independent of distance (the sense of knowing about an incoming phone call, and of pain, illness, or upcoming death of people, which usually proves to be accurate). The sudden occurrence of this enhanced intuition, or 'nonlocal information exchange,' can be quite problematic, as people suddenly have a very acute sense of others, which can be extremely intimidating (van Lommel, 2010). The typical transformation for only those patients who reported an NDE is a kind of 'objective' proof for this 'subjective' experience, because patients who did not report an NDE did not show the aforementioned transformation. And we know that children below the age of four mostly do not remember their NDE, but still they all show a classical transformation (van Lommel, 2010). This makes it highly probable that for those patients that did not report an NDE, it was due to their not having an NDE, rather than being a result of not remembering an NDE.

The integration and acceptance of an NDE is a process that may take many years, because of its far-reaching impact on people's pre-NDE understanding of life and value system. An NDE could indeed be considered as a spiritual crisis, and it is quite remarkable to see a cardiac arrest lasting just a few minutes give rise to such a lifelong process of transformation. This is why NDEs are also called spiritual transformative experiences, or STEs. For obvious reasons most people feel nostalgic about their NDE because of the unforgettable feelings of peace, acceptance, and love they encountered during the experience, and the feeling of being forced to return back into the body. We identified a distinct pattern of change in people with an NDE and revealed that integrating these changes into daily life is a long and arduous process, because there is at first hardly any acceptance by oneself as well as by others, like doctors, nurses, family members, partners, and friends, which makes the process of coming to terms with the experience so difficult and painful. So the NDE is also a traumatic event, with many years of strong feelings of depression, homesickness, and loneliness.

2. The American Prospective Study on NDEs

Bruce Greyson, who published a prospective study in 116 survivors of cardiac arrest in the USA (Greyson, 2003), found that 15.5% of the patients reported an NDE: 9.5% reported a core NDE, and 6% a superficial NDE with a score of less than 6. He writes that

"no one physiological or psychological model by itself could explain all the common features of an NDE. The paradoxical occurrence of a heightened, lucid awareness and logical thought processes during a period of impaired cerebral perfusion raises particular perplexing questions for our current understanding of consciousness and its relation to brain function. A clear sensorium and complex perceptual processes during a period of apparent clinical death challenge the concept that consciousness is localized exclusively in the brain" (Greyson, 2003).

3. The First British Prospective Study on NDEs

Sam Parnia and Peter Fenwick (Parnia et al., 2001) included 63 patients who survived their cardiac arrest. They found in their study that 11% reported an NDE: 6.3% reported a core NDE, and 4.8% a superficial NDE with a score of less than 6. They write that the NDE reports with veridical perceptions during cardiopulmonary resuscitation (CPR) suggest that the NDE occurs during the period of unconsciousness. This is a surprising conclusion, in their view, because when the brain is so dysfunctional that the patient is deeply comatose, those cerebral structures, which underpin subjective experience and memory, must be severely impaired. Complex experiences as reported in the NDE should not arise or be retained in memory. Such patients would be expected to have no subjective experience, as was the case in the vast majority of patients who survive cardiac arrest, since all centers in the brain that are responsible for generating conscious experiences have stopped functioning as a result of the lack of oxygen (Parnia et al., 2001).

4. The Second British Prospective Study on NDEs

Over a period of four years, Penny Sartori (2006) carried out an even smaller study into NDEs in 39 survivors of cardiac arrest in the UK. She found that 23% reported an NDE: 18% reported a core NDE, and 5% a superficial NDE with a score of less than 6. She concludes that "according to mainstream science, it is quite impossible to find a scientific explanation for the NDE as long as we 'believe' that consciousness is only a side effect of a functioning brain." The fact that people report lucid experiences in their consciousness when brain activity has ceased is, in her view, "difficult to reconcile with current medical opinion."

Some Striking Elements of an NDE

To get a better idea about what patients can sometimes experience during cardiac arrest, I would like to reconsider certain striking and typical elements of an NDE.

Out-of-body Experience

During an out-of-body experience (OBE), people can have veridical perceptions from a position outside and above their lifeless body. Therefore, an OBE is scientifically important because doctors, nurses, and relatives can verify the reported perceptions, and they can also corroborate the precise moment the NDE with OBE occurred during the period of CPR. It is important to mention here that until now it has been impossible to induce a real out-of-body experience with veridical perception from a position outside and above the body by any method whatsoever (Penfield, 1975), despite incorrect suggestions about this possibility in the medical literature while just describing bodily illusions (Blanke et al., 2002, 2004; Blanke & Metzinger, 2008; de Ridder et al., 2007). In a recent review of 93 corroborated reports of potentially verifiable out-of-body perceptions during NDEs, it was found that about 90% were completely accurate, 8% contained just some minor error, and only 2% were erroneous (Holden, 2009). This proves that OBEs cannot be a hallucination, i.e. experiencing a perception that has no basis in "reality," like in psychosis, neither can it be a delusion, which is an incorrect assessment of a correct perception, nor an illusion, which means a misapprehension or misleading image. Moreover, one needs a functioning brain to experience a hallucination, delusion, or illusion, and during cardiac arrest the function of the brain has been lost.

This is the report of a nurse of a Coronary Care Unit (van Lommel, et al., 2001):

"During night shift an ambulance brings in a 44-year old cyanotic, comatose man into the coronary care unit. He was found in coma about 30 minutes before in a meadow. When we go to intubate the patient, he turns out to have dentures in his mouth. I remove these upper dentures and put them onto the 'crash cart.' After about an hour and a half the patient has sufficient heart rhythm and blood pressure, but he is still ventilated and intubated, and he is still comatose. He is transferred to the intensive care unit to continue the necessary artificial respiration. Only after more than a week in coma do I meet again with the patient, who is by now back on the cardiac ward. The moment he sees me he says: 'O, that nurse knows where my dentures are.' I am very, very surprised. Then the patient elucidates: 'You were there when I was brought into hospital and you took my dentures out of my mouth and put them onto that cart, it had all these bottles on it and there was this sliding drawer underneath, and there you put my teeth.' I was especially amazed because I remembered this happening while the man was in deep coma and in the process of CPR. It appeared that the man had seen himself lying in bed, that he had perceived from above how nurses and doctors had been busy with the CPR. He was also able to describe correctly and in detail the small room in which he had been resuscitated as well as the appearance of those present like myself."

It is important to mention that most neuroscientists are quite reluctant to accept the possibility of veridical perception from a position outside and above the lifeless body, because this could be the decisive evidence that conscious perception is possible outside the body, and this is why these perceptions are called just anecdotes. The majority of those materialist scientists want to have more 'objective' proof, and of course most NDE researchers will agree. This is why in several NDE studies hidden signs or targets have been put close to the ceiling in resuscitation rooms, coronary care units, and intensive care units with the purpose that these hidden signs, not visible from the bed, could be an objective proof for veridical perception. With such a study design patients should be able to perceive details of their resuscitation and of these hidden signs from a position outside and above their lifeless body during their CPR, and later these perceptions should be corroborated by doctors, nurses, or relatives. But until now there has been no published case where patients during CPR have perceived this hidden sign, despite perceiving veridical details of their resuscitation previously unknown to them. What could be a plausible explanation for this impossibility to 'prove' the reported perception during OBE by a hidden sign? This lack of 'objective proof' could be caused by so-called 'in-attentional blindness,' also known as 'perceptual blindness' (Mack & Rock, 1998; Simons & Rensink, 2005). This is the phenomenon of not being able to perceive things that are in plain sight. It can be a result of having no internal frame of reference to perceive the unseen object, or it can be caused by the lack of mental focus or attention caused by mental distractions. This in-attentional blindness is the failure to notice a fully visible but unexpected object because attention was engaged on another task, event, or object, because we humans have a limited capacity for attention and intention at any particular time (Most et al., 2005; Chun & Marois, 2002). Only if we have the intention to decide where to place the attention we will perceive consciously the event or object we focus upon. Studies of in-attentional blindness demonstrate that people fail to report having noticed an unexpected object (Koivisto & Revonsuo, 2008). The information from the unexpected object is filtered from awareness by the time people are asked about it. Evidence for in-attentional blindness comes mostly from relatively simple laboratory tasks (Simons & Chabris, 1999), but the phenomenon likely has many daily analogues. For example, automobile accident reports frequently report driver claims that they "looked but failed to see" the other vehicle. Recent evidence suggests that talking on a cell phone, for example, dramatically increases the probability of missing an unexpected object (Scholl et al., 2003). Based on the many corroborated cases of veridical perception from a position outside and above the body during NDEs, it seems obvious that perception really can occur during OBEs, and that missing a hidden target during an OBE must be the result of a lack of intention and attention for this unexpected hidden object, because patients are too surprised to be able to 'see' the resuscitation of their own lifeless body from above during their cardiac arrest or surgery (van Lommel, 2010).

Life Review

During a so-called holographic life review, the subject feels the renewed experience of not only every action or word, but also of every thought from one's life, and one realizes that we apparently seem to be inseparably connected to others. Because one is connected with the memories, emotions, and consciousness of another person in the past, we experience the consequences of our own thoughts, words, and actions to that other person at the very moment in the past that they occurred. These people understand now what in some religions and cultures is known as the cosmic law that everything one does to others will ultimately be returned to oneself. Patients survey their whole life in one glance; time and space do not seem to exist during such an experience ('nonlocality'). Instantaneously they are where they concentrate upon, and they can talk for hours about the content of the life review even though the resuscitation only took minutes. Quotation:

"All of my life up till the present seemed to be placed before me in a kind of panoramic, three-dimensional review, and each event seemed to be accompanied by a consciousness of good or evil or with an insight into cause or effect." "Not only did I perceive everything from my own viewpoint, but I also knew the thoughts of everyone involved in the event, as if I had their thoughts within me. This meant that I perceived not only what I had done or thought, but even in what way it had influenced others, as if I saw things with all-seeing eyes. And so, even your thoughts are apparently not wiped out. And all the time during the review the importance of love was emphasized. Looking back, I cannot say how long this life review and life insight lasted, it may have been long, for every subject came up, but at the same time it seemed just a fraction of a second, because I perceived it all at the same moment. Time and distance seemed not to exist. I was in all places at the same time, and sometimes my attention was drawn to something, and then I would be present there" (van Lommel, 2004).

Conscious Return Into The Body

Some patients can describe how they consciously returned into their body after they had come to understand that "it wasn't their time yet" or that "they still had a task to fulfill." This conscious return into the body is experienced as something very oppressive. They regain consciousness in their body and realize that they are "locked up" in their damaged body, meaning again all the pain and restriction of their disease. Quotation:

"And when I regained consciousness in my body, it was so terrible, so terrible...that experience was so beautiful, I never would have liked to come back, I wanted to stay there.....and still I came back. And from that moment on it was a very difficult experience to live my life again in my body, with all the limitations I felt in that period" (van Lommel, 2004).

Neurophysiology in Cardiac Arrest

The aforementioned elements of an NDE were experienced during the period of cardiac arrest, during the period of apparent unconsciousness, and during the period of clinical death. But how is it possible to explain these experiences during the period of temporary loss of all functions of the brain due to acute lack of oxygen in the cortex and the brainstem (pan-cerebral anoxia)? We know that patients with cardiac arrest are unconscious within seconds. Through many studies with induced cardiac arrest in both human and animal models, cerebral function has been shown to be severely compromised during cardiac arrest, with complete cessation of cerebral blood flow immediately following ventricular fibrillation (Gopalan et al., 1999), and with the clinical findings of the sudden loss of consciousness and of all body reflexes, caused by the loss of function of the cortex, and also with the abolition of brain-stem activity (all brainstem reflexes) with the loss of the gag reflex, of the corneal reflex, and fixed and dilated pupils (van Lommel, 2010). And also the function of the respiratory center, located close to the brainstem, fails, resulting in apnea (no breathing). But how do we know what exactly happens in the brain when the heart stops? The brain accounts for only 2 to 3% of overall body weight, but it uses 15 to 20% of the body's total energy supply, primarily for maintaining the membrane potential (the electric charge across a cell membrane) of the nerve cells, or neurons. Total loss of oxygen supply (anoxia) causes a functional loss of all cell systems and organs in the body. However, in anoxia of only some minutes' duration (transient anoxia), this loss may be temporary, but in prolonged anoxia cell death occurs with permanent functional loss. Some cells respond better to anoxia than others. Neurons respond badly, because their sole source of energy is glucose. Unlike the muscle cells in our body, our brains do not store glucose in the form of glycogen as a ready supply of cell energy. The parts of the brain that are most susceptible to anoxia are the neurons in the cerebral cortex, and in the hippocampus and thalamus, which form an important link between the brainstem and cerebral cortex (Fujioka et al., 2000; Kinney et al., 1994). The total loss of oxygen supply reduces these structures to utter chaos and wipes out their connections. Synapses are the junctions that enable communication between neurons, and when these synapses stop functioning cooperation and coordination between neuronal networks in the brain is no longer possible (van Lommel, 2013). However, a functioning system for communication between neural networks with integration of information seems essential for experiencing 'waking' consciousness, and this does not occur during deep sleep or anesthesia (Ferrarelli et al., 2010), let alone during cardiac arrest. It seems needless to state again that during cardiac arrest a non-functioning brain with a flat line EEG does not implicate that the brain is dead, nor that all neuronal networks must have died: during clinical death, which is the period of complete cessation of cerebral perfusion during cardiac arrest, there is a transient loss of all functions of the cortex and brainstem until adequate circulation and blood pressure are successfully restored by defibrillation.

During Cardiac Arrest the Blood Flow to the Brain Comes to an End

A cardiac arrest will result in a total loss of oxygen supply and a build-up of carbon dioxide (CO_2) in the brain within seconds. The moment the blood flow to the brain comes to an end ('no-flow'), the supply of glucose and oxygen is prevented and a neuron's first symptom will be the inability to maintain its membrane potential, resulting in the loss of neuronal function (van Dijk, 2004). This acute loss of electrical and synaptic activity in neurons can be seen as the cell's inbuilt defense and energy-saving response and is called a 'pilot light state.' The moment the electrical functions of neurons cease, the remaining energy sources can be deployed very briefly for the cell's survival (van Lommel, 2010). In the case of short-term oxygen deficiency dysfunction can be temporary and recovery is still possible, because the neurons will remain viable for a few more minutes in patients with normal body temperature, although under (local) hypothermia it takes a bit longer until irreversible neuronal cell death occurs (Parnia, 2013). We know of this phenomenon of temporary functional loss without cell death in patients with an acute myocardial ischemia, where a temporary and regional contractile dysfunction of the heart is called 'stunning' of the myocardium. Stunning is the reversible reduction of contraction of myocardial cells, or a period of nonfunctioning myocardium without cell death. During a cardiac arrest the entire brain is deprived of oxygen (anoxia), resulting in the loss of consciousness, of all body and brainstem reflexes, and of respiration. This period of 'clinical death' can be reversible, i.e. temporary, if CPR is initiated within five to 10 minutes. This situation cannot be remedied during the resuscitation procedure itself ('low flow'), but only after the cardiac rhythm has been reestablished through defibrillation (van Lommel, 2010). A delay in starting adequate resuscitation may result in the death of a great many brain cells and thus in brain death, and most patients will ultimately die. The survival rate to hospital discharge of patients with an out-of-hospital arrest is only 9.6% (McNally et al., 2011). A study carried out at a coronary care unit has shown that patients whose resuscitation was started within one minute had a 33% chance of survival, compared to only 14% for those who, due to extenuating circumstances, were only resuscitated after more than a minute after the onset of unconsciousness (Herlitz et al., 2000).

Effective CPR (Low Blood Flow) Prolongs the Viability of the Brain

Several studies have shown that external heart massage during CPR cannot pump enough blood to the brain to restore brain function. As far as we know, nobody has ever regained consciousness during external resuscitation of the heart. It always requires defibrillation to reestablish the cardiac rhythm. Without restoration of normal cardiac rhythm and of normal blood pressure, and so without the resumption of cardiac output following successful defibrillation, a long duration of CPR is considered an indication of poor outcome and high mortality, because CPR alone cannot ultimately prevent the irreversible damage of brain cells (Peperby et al., 2003). Adequate CPR can, however, prolong the period of viability of the neurons, especially when external or local cerebral hypothermia is applied (Parnia, 2013). During CPR, blood supply to the brain is 5-10% of its normal value (White et al., 1983), and during external heart massage the systolic blood pressure will usually reach approximately 50 mmHg, with an average of 20 mmHg because of the low diastolic pressure. The maximum average blood pressure during proper resuscitation is 30 to 40 mmHg (Paradis et al., 1989), which is still far too low for the blood to deliver enough oxygen and glucose to the brain. The administration of certain medication during resuscitation can increase blood pressure a little (Paradis et al., 1991), but it will remain well below normal. Furthermore, in the absence of a normal blood supply, the brain cells are likely to swell (edema), which results in increased pressure in the brain (intracranial pressure), and also an increase of cerebral vascular resistance occurs. This is why it was found in animal studies that it actually requires a higher than normal blood pressure to maintain adequate cerebral perfusion and to supply the brain with sufficiently oxygenated blood and to enable the removal of carbon dioxide (CO_2) (Fisher & Hossman, 1996). During resuscitation, blood gasses (oxygen [O_2] and CO_2) are sometimes measured in peripheral arteries to determine the severity of the oxygen deficiency in the blood. However, normal levels of oxygen and carbon dioxide do not guarantee that enough arterial blood, and thus enough oxygen, will reach the brain during resuscitation (van Lommel, 2013).

To summarize, from several studies we know that proper resuscitation, with adequate external heart massage and mouth-to-mouth respiration or respiration via a mask, will produce minimal blood flow ('low-flow') to the brain, which increases the chances of recovery of brain function after the cardiac arrest has been successfully treated with defibrillation. By this minimal cerebral blood flow, the no longer functioning neurons will be able to survive for a longer period of time in the minimal energy state ('pilot light state'), also called 'hibernation' or 'ischemic penumbra' of the brain (Coimbra, 1999), because it prolongs the period of reversibility (viability) before irreversible neuronal cell death and brain death will occur (van Lommel, 2013).

A Flat Line EEG During Cardiac Arrest

Of course, quite often the question arises: how do we know for sure that the electroencephalogram (EEG), the registration of the electrical activity of the cortex, has become flat in those patients with cardiac arrest, and how can we study this? In normal circumstances no attempts are made to register an EEG during cardiac arrest, because this takes far too much time, and patients need to be successfully resuscitated and defibrillated as soon as possible. But there have been some reports in which the electrical activity of the brain was measured during cardiac arrest, for example during surgery. Following the cardiac arrest ('no-flow'), the EEG flat-lined after an average of 15 seconds and remained flat despite external resuscitation ('low flow') (Hossmann & Kleihues, 1973; Moss & Rockoff, 1980; Clute & Levy, 1990; Losasso et al., 1992). A persistent flat-line EEG during external CPR has also been shown in animal studies (Birchner et al., 1980). Monitoring of the EEG has shown that in patients during induced cardiac arrest for threshold testing of an implantable cardioverter defibrillator (ICD) the first ischemic changes are detected an average of 6.5 seconds after circulatory arrest. Ischemic changes in the EEG show a decrease of power in fast activity and in delta activity and an increase of slow delta I activity, and sometimes also an increase in amplitude of theta activity, progressively and ultimately declining to iso-electricity. But more often, initial slowing and attenuation of the EEG waves is the first sign of cerebral ischemia. With prolongation of the cerebral ischemia, progression to a flat-line EEG always occurs within 10 to 20 (mean 15) seconds from the onset of cardiac

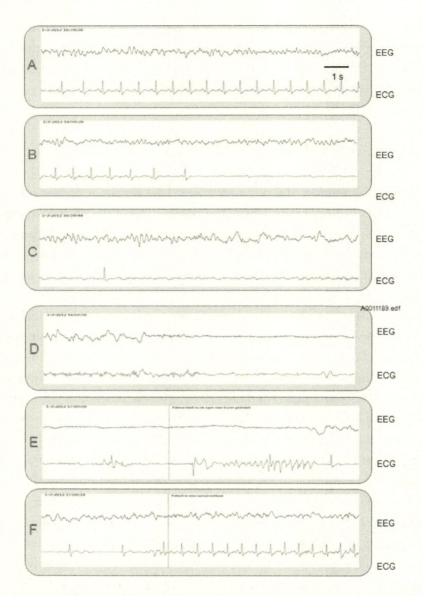

Figure 1. (A-F). EEG and ECG registration during asystole = cardiac arrest. *With the courtesy of prof. M. van Putten, neurophysiologist at the University of Twente*

arrest (Clute & Levy, 1990; Losasso et al., 1992; de Vries et al., 1998; Parnia & Fenwick, 2002), and the EEG remains flat during the cardiac arrest until cardiac output has been restored by defibrillation (Fisher & Hossman, 1996; Marshall et al., 2001). In tests on animals, auditory evoked potentials, or measures of brain-stem viability, can no longer be induced, which means that the reaction caused in a normal functioning brain-stem by sound stimulation is no longer produced (Brantson et al.,1984; Gua et al., 1995).

See Figure 1 (A-F). It is extremely rare that a simultaneous registration of the electrical activity of the heart (ECG) and of the cortex of the brain (EEG) during cardiac arrest could be monitored. But such a simultaneous registration of an ECG and EEG is shown here. A patient was referred because of sudden periods of unconsciousness. During this registration (of 60 seconds, each strip is 10 seconds) a spontaneous cardiac arrest (asystole) with loss of consciousness occurred (B). Due to the lack of oxygen in the brain (anoxia) the EEG starts to change after about 10 seconds (C), and after 18 seconds (D) the registration shows a flat-line EEG. About 30 seconds after the onset of cardiac arrest, a short period of ventricular tachycardia (VT) arises during 4 seconds (E), after which normal heart rhythm gradually recovers, and the EEG normalizes some seconds later. The patient received a pacemaker, after which he remained complaint-free.

Recently a transient and global surge of synchronized gamma oscillations was registered in the EEG of nine rats within the first 30 seconds after induced cardiac arrest, always declining to an isoelectric EEG after 30 seconds, and it was concluded that this coherent activity could be a neural correlate for NDEs (Borjigin et al., 2013). The authors even stated: "This study provides the first scientific framework for the NDEs as reported by many cardiac arrest survivors". However, all of the nine rats exhibited the same coherent patterns in the EEG, while only 10-20% of humans undergoing cardiac arrest report NDEs and, surprisingly, the authors do not refer to the studies with EEG registration in humans with induced cardiac arrest, where these coherent activities have never been registered, and always a flat line EEG was seen within 10-20 seconds after cardiac arrest (see Figure 1). And of course, it cannot be known if these rats were having any experience whatsoever. So we should be extremely cautious before drawing any conclusion about human NDEs: it is one thing to measure brain activity in rats during cardiac arrest, and quite another to relate that to human experience. Additionally, in most human cases the cardiac arrest lasts much longer than 30 seconds, when the EEG in humans (as well as in rats) is flat-lined, and some of these patients with cardiac arrest reported NDEs with corroborated verifiable elements (OBEs) anchoring the experience to later stages of cardiac arrest. As mentioned before, many NDEs also occur under non-threatening conditions which do not involve cardiac arrest or brain injury.

Post-anoxic Reperfusion Injury of the Brain

In those cases where the cardiac arrest lasts longer than 37 seconds, the EEG will not normalize immediately after cardiac output has been restored. Despite maintaining normal blood pressure in the period following resuscitation, this normalization ultimately depends on the duration of the cardiac arrest, and on the application of (local) hypothermia to diminish anoxic cerebral edema. After a complicated resuscitation with persistent past-anoxic coma, it can take hours to days for the EEG to get back to normal (Mayer & Marx, 1972; Smith et al., 1990). We know that the longer the cardiac arrest, the greater the brain damage, the longer the post-anoxic coma and the longer the EEG remains flat or highly irregular. Moreover, normalization of the EEG may actually create an overly positive impression of the recovery of the brain's metabolism, because following restoration of the heartbeat and blood circulation, oxygen uptake in the brain may be reduced for a considerable period of time, which is caused by this so-called post-anoxic reperfusion injury (Losasso et al., 1992; Mayer & Marx, 1972; Buunk et al., 2000). Also, in animal studies with induced cardiac arrest, the post-arrest cortical hypoperfusion-syndrome is prolonged with cortical flow remaining below 20% of normal up to 18 hours post arrest (White et al., 1983).

It seems rational to assume that all 562 survivors of cardiac arrest in the four prospective studies on NDEs should have had a flat-line EEG, because no patient had ever been resuscitated within 20 seconds (van Lommel, 2010). Patients with an acute myocardial infarction who suffer a cardiac arrest in the coronary care unit will usually (and hopefully) be successfully resuscitated within 60 to 120 seconds. At a nursing ward, however, this will take at least two to five minutes. And in the event of a cardiac arrest at home or in the street (a so-called 'out-of-hospital' arrest), it will take at best five to 10 minutes for a patient to be successfully resuscitated, but usually longer, resulting in the death of nearly 90 (82-98)% of these patients with an out-of-hospital arrest (McNally et al., 2011; Lombardi et al., 1994; de Vreede-Swagemakers et al., 1997).

During Cardiac Arrest, an Enhanced Consciousness Can Be Experienced

Based on the findings and conclusions of the aforementioned four prospective studies in survivors of cardiac arrest, there are good reasons to assume that consciousness does not always coincide with the functioning of our brain: enhanced consciousness, with unaltered self-identity, can sometimes be experienced separately from the body. It is important to mention that the quite often proposed objection by neuroscientists that a flat-line EEG does not rule out any brain activity, because it is mainly a registration of electrical activity of the cerebral cortex, misses the mark. The issue is not whether there is any non-measurable brain activity of any kind whatsoever, but whether there is measurable brain activity of the specific form, and in different neural networks, as regarded by contemporary neuroscience as the necessary condition of conscious experience, the so-called neuronal global workspace (Cho et al., 1997; Dehaene et al., 1998). And, as mentioned before, it has been proven in several empirical studies in patients with induced cardiac arrest that there was no such measurable and specific brain activity during cardiac arrest (see Figure 1). Additionally, research drawing on magnetic resonance imaging (fMRI) and PET scans has shown that the joint and simultaneous activity of the cerebral cortex and brainstem with their shared pathways (hippocampus and thalamus) is a prerequisite for conscious experience (van Lommel, 2010). As stated before, exactly these parts of the brain—the neurons in the cerebral cortex, the hippocampus and the thalamus—are most susceptible to oxygen deficiency (Fujioka et al., 2000; Kinney et al., 1994). A flat-line EEG is also one of the major diagnostic tools for the diagnosis of brain death, and in those cases the objection about not ruling out any brain activity whatsoever is never mentioned. Moreover, although measurable EEG activity in the brain can be recorded during deep sleep (no-REM phase) or during general anaesthesia, no waking consciousness is experienced, because there is no integration of information and no communication between the different neural networks (Massimini et al., 2005; Alkire & Miller, 2005; Alkire et al., 2008). So even in some circumstances where brain activity can be measured sometimes no ('waking') consciousness is experienced.

The Assumption that the Brain Produces Consciousness Should Be Questioned

'The brain is the messenger to consciousness'.
Sir John C. Eccles (1903–1997, Australian neurophysiologist, Nobel prize 1963)

Scientific studies into the phenomenon of NDEs highlight the limitations of our current medical and neurophysiological ideas about the various aspects of human consciousness, and the relationship between consciousness and memories on the one hand and the brain on the other. With our current medical concepts it seems indeed impossible to explain all aspects of the subjective experiences as reported by patients with an NDE during a transient loss of all functions of the brain, because the prevailing paradigm holds that memories and consciousness are produced by large groups of neurons or neuronal networks. According to the never proven assumption that consciousness is produced by and localized in the brain, the experience of an extremely lucid consciousness during the period of cardiac arrest should not be possible. Such patients would be expected to have no subjective experience at all, because, as was mentioned before, it has been scientifically proven that during clinical death the brain has a transient loss of all functions of the cortex and brainstem, and also a loss of all activities in the EEG has been registered within 10-20 seconds after the onset of cardiac arrest. Furthermore, even blind people have described veridical perceptions during out-of-body experiences at the time of their NDE (Ring & Cooper, 1999). Despite these findings and conclusions, some possible 'materialist' explanations like anoxia, hypoxia, and high CO_2 have been proposed in the past to understand the cause and content of an NDE. But these theories should be dismissed, as will be explained in the next paragraphs.

Anoxia (Total Lack of Oxygen)

For most neuroscientists and philosophers, the most common explanation for NDEs is still an extremely severe and life-threatening total lack of oxygen (anoxia) of the brain. This should result in the experience of a tunnel by anoxia of the retina, in the blockage of N-methyl-D-aspartate (NMDA) receptors in the brain, and in the release of endorphins, a kind of morphine produced by the body itself, causing hallucinations and a sense of peace and bliss (Woerlee, 2003; Blackmore, 1993). This theory seems inapplicable, however, because an NDE is actually accompanied by an enhanced and lucid consciousness with memories, which should not be possible during anoxia of the brain, and even to experience hallucinations one requires a functioning brain. Moreover, a hallucination is an observation that is not rooted in reality, which is not consistent with descriptions of out-of-body experiences that are open to verification and corroboration by witnesses. NDEs are also reported under circumstances such as an imminent traffic accident (a 'fear-death' experience), during a depression, meditation, or isolation (van Lommel, 2010), or as a 'shared-death' experience (Moody & Perry, 2010), neither of which involves anoxia nor oxygen deficiency. Moreover, in the recently published four prospective studies on NDEs in survivors of cardiac arrest it was found that the lack of oxygen by itself could not explain the cause and content of NDEs (van Lommel et al., 2001; Greyson, 2003; Parnia et al., 2001; Sartori, 2006).

Hypoxia (Oxygen Deficiency)

In the case of oxygen deficiency in the brain (hypoxia, or deprivation of adequate oxygen supply), as can be seen in low blood pressure (shock), heart failure, or asphyxia, the result is not unconsciousness but confusion and agitation. Brain damage after waking from a coma is also associated with confusion, fear, agitation, memory defects, and muddled speech (van Lommel, 2013). A period of unconsciousness, sometimes accompanied by some kind of atypical memories, can occur after fainting induced by hyperventilation, followed by a so-called Valsalva maneuver. The latter involves trying to push air from the body with the mouth and nose closed, which slows the heartbeat and lowers blood pressure, and results in a short-lived oxygen deficiency in the brain (Lempert et al., 1994). Also a study of fighter jet pilots is often cited as a possible explanatory model for NDEs (Whinnery & Whinnery, 1990). Having been placed in a centrifuge, these pilots experienced momentary oxygen deficiency in the brain when the enormous increase in gravity caused their blood to drop to their feet. Fighter jet pilots can indeed lose consciousness, and often experience convulsions, like those seen in epilepsy, or tingling around the mouth and in the arms and legs, as well as confusion upon waking. Sometimes they also experience some elements that are reminiscent of an NDE, such as a kind of tunnel vision, a sensation of light, a peaceful sense of floating without veridical perception, or the observation of brief, fragmented images from the past (Whinnery & Whinnery, 1990). These recollections, however, consist of fragmented and random memories, unlike the panoramic life-review during NDEs. They seldom see images of living persons, and never of deceased people (van Lommel, 2013). Also, the 'classical' transformation after an NDE, as reported in the longitudinal Dutch study, is never reported in these cases. So the effects of periods of hypoxia in the brain have usually been wrongly compared with an NDE.

High CO_2

In the past, NDE-like experiences have been mentioned in people by inducing high carbon dioxide levels (hypercarbia) in the brain (Meduna, 1950). And even recently it was suggested that real NDEs could be caused by high levels of CO_2 in patients during out-of-hospital cardiac arrest. In a study in 52 survivors of cardiac arrest, 21% of them reported an NDE, and a significant correlation was found between higher amounts of CO_2 in the exhalation air (end-tidal CO_2) and with higher arterial blood pressures of CO_2 (Klemenc-Ketis et al., 2011). However, this study included only patients with an out-of-hospital cardiac arrest, where arterial blood samples were taken only in the first 5 minutes after hospital admission, meaning that most of them already had heart rhythm and blood pressure after successful CPR outside the hospital. The main conclusion in this study was that high levels CO_2 in the blood were associated with a slightly higher incidence of NDEs, but this does not explain why the majority of patients with high CO_2 still did not report an NDE. The conclusion that high CO_2 levels could explain the cause of an NDE seems to be preliminary at best: it was obviously forgotten that a correlation with the occurrence of an NDE is something totally different from causation.

The Relation Between Consciousness and Brain Function

"Consciousness, the subjective experience of an Inner self, poses one of the greatest challenges to neuroscience. Even a detailed knowledge of the brain's workings and neural correlates of consciousness may fail to explain how or why human beings have self-aware minds."

David J. Chalmers (1966, Australian Philosopher)

In the last few decades, extensive research has been done by neuroscientists to localize consciousness and memories inside the brain, so far without success. One of the most important questions is how a non-material activity such as concentrated attention or thinking can correspond to an observable (material) reaction in the form of measurable electrical, magnetic, and chemical activity at a certain place in the brain by EEG, MEG (magnetoencephalography), and PET scan, and in the form of increased blood flow by fMRI. Neuroimaging studies have shown these aforesaid activities, with specific areas of the brain becoming metabolically active in response to a thought or feeling. However, although providing evidence for the role of neuronal networks as an intermediary for the manifestation of thoughts (neural correlates), these studies do not necessarily imply that those cells also produce the thoughts. A correlation doesn't elucidate anything about cause or result. And how should "unconscious" matter like our brain "produce" consciousness, while the brain only is composed of atoms and molecules in cells with a lot of chemical and electrical processes? Direct evidence of how neurons or neuronal networks could possibly produce the subjective essence of the mind and thoughts is currently lacking. We cannot measure what we think or feel, because neural activation is simply neural activation; it only reflects the use of structures (van Lommel, 2010).

Materialistic science starts principally from a reality that is only based on physical, observable data. This so-called material reality should be provable, measurable, and reproducible, which is impossible for subjective experiences in our consciousness. We should be aware that, besides external and so-called objective observation, there are subjective, not observable, and not demonstrable aspects in our consciousness like thoughts, feelings, inspiration, and intuition. We can only measure neural correlates of consciousness, and these measurements do not explain anything about the production nor about the content of consciousness. Based on totally different neuroscientific research, Alva Noë writes in his recent book:

"All scientific theories rest on assumptions. It is important that these assumptions be true. I will try to convince the reader that this startling assumption of consciousness research that consciousness is a neuroscientific phenomenon and that it happens in the brain is badly mistaken. Consciousness does not happen in the brain. What determines and controls the character of conscious experience is not the associated neural activity. That is why we have been unable to come up with a good explanation of its neural basis."

He proposes that the brain's job is that of facilitating a dynamic pattern of interaction among brain, body, and world. It seems fair to conclude that current knowledge does not permit us to reduce consciousness to activities and processes in the brain: the explanatory gap between the brain and consciousness has never been bridged, because a certain neuronal state is not the same as a certain state of consciousness (Noë, 2009).

Several Models for the 'Mind-Brain' Relationship

A majority of contemporary western scientists who carry out research into consciousness, such as neuroscientists, psychologists, and philosophers, still have the opinion that there is a materialist and reductionist explanation for consciousness. But up to now there are no uniform scientific views about the relationship between consciousness and the brain (Chalmers, 1996). The well-known philosopher Daniel Dennett still believes, and many with him, that consciousness is nothing other than matter (Dennett, 1991), and that our subjective experience that our consciousness is something purely personal and differs from someone else's consciousness is merely an 'illusion.' According to these materialist scientists, consciousness originates entirely from the matter that constitutes our brain. If this were true, then everything we experience in our consciousness would be nothing but the expression of a machine controlled by classical physics and chemistry, and our behaviour the inexorable outcome of nerve cell activity in our brain. Obviously the notion that all subjective thoughts and feelings are produced by nothing other than the brain's activity also means that it is an illusion to believe in free will. This viewpoint has serious implications for concepts such as moral responsibility and personal freedom.

But, besides several materialistic concepts about the 'mind-brain' relationship, an 'interactionistic-dualistic' model has also been proposed, where consciousness and the brain are totally different entities with different fundamental properties, but somehow are able to interact with each other (Popper & Eccles, 1977). And also the concept of 'phenomenalism' or 'immaterial (or neutral) monism' should be mentioned, which is sometimes also called 'panpsychism' or 'idealism.' According to this latest model all material, physical systems should have a form of subjectivity at a fundamental level, and intrinsic properties of the physical world should be themselves phenomenal properties. If so, then consciousness and physical reality are deeply intertwined. This view acknowledges a clear causal role for consciousness in the physical world, and so consciousness should be regarded as a fundamental property of the universe (Chalmers, 2002). Why and where consciousness originates will probably remain a mystery forever, because presumably the answer to this question is unknowable. Consciousness is not visible, not tangible, not perceptible, not measurable, and not verifiable. We are not able to objectively prove nor measure the subjective content of our consciousness, like our thoughts or feelings.

Summarizing the Findings and Conclusions From Empirical Studies on NDEs

In summarizing the findings and conclusions of the aforementioned four NDE studies, as well as by listening (in an open-minded fashion) to thousands of people who were willing to share their NDEs with us, one can conclude that at present more and more experiences are reported by serious and reliable people who, to their own surprise and confusion, have experienced an enhanced consciousness independent of their physical body. These experiences have been reported in all times, in all cultures, and in all religions (van Lommel, 2010). In several prospective empirical studies it has been proven that an enhanced and clear consciousness can be experienced during the period of cardiac arrest (clinical death), when global cerebral function can at best be described as severely impaired and at worst non-functional (van Lommel et al., 2001; Greyson, 2003; Parnia et al., 2001; Sartori, 2006). And based on these prospective studies on NDEs in survivors of cardiac arrest, one has to come to the conclusion that current scientific views fail to explain the cause and content of an NDE (van Lommel, 2010; van Lommel et al., 2001; Greyson, 2003; Parnia et al., 2001; Sartori, 2006). Additionally, it seems indeed scientifically proven that during cardiac arrest no activity of the cortex and the brainstem can be measured, and also the clinical findings point out the transient loss of all functions of the brain (Clute & Levy, 1990; Losasso et al., 1992; de Vries et al., 1998; Parnia & Fenwick, 2002). All scientists who performed prospective studies on NDEs came to the same conclusion: lack of oxygen by itself cannot explain the cause and content of NDEs (van Lommel et al., 2001; Greyson, 2003; Parnia et al., 2001; Sartori, 2006). And this view is also supported by the fact that an NDE can be reported by people who did not have life threatening illnesses but were in fear of death, in depression, or in meditation (van Lommel, 2010; Greyson et al., 2009; Carter, 2010). In studying the function of the brain it has been proven that under normal daily circumstances, during deep sleep, and during general anaesthesia, a functioning network and a co-operation between many different centers of the brain are prerequisites for the experience of our waking consciousness (Ferrarelli et al., 2010; Massimini et al., 2005; Alkire & Miller, 2005; Alkire et al., 2008). This is never the case during a cardiac arrest (Clute & Levy, 1990; Losasso et al., 1992; de Vries et al., 1998; Parnia & Fenwick, 2002).

Obviously, research on NDEs in survivors of cardiac arrest clearly questions the purely materialistic paradigm in science.

The Concept of Nonlocal Consciousness

'The stream of knowledge is heading toward a non-mechanical reality; the universe begins to look more like a great thought than like a great machine'.

Sir James H. Jeans (1877-1946, English physicist, astronomist, and mathematician)

When empirical scientific studies discover phenomena or facts that are not consistent with current scientific theories, these new facts must not be denied, suppressed, or even ridiculed, as is still quite common. In the event of new findings, the existing theories ought to be elaborated or modified and, if necessary, rejected and replaced. We need new ways of thinking and new forms of science to study consciousness and acquire a better understanding of the different aspects and effects of consciousness. In my opinion, current science must reconsider its assumptions about the nature of perceptible reality, because these ideas have led to the neglect or denial of important areas of consciousness (van Lommel, 2010).

It is indeed a scientific challenge to discuss new hypotheses that could explain the reported interconnectedness with the consciousness of other persons and of deceased relatives, to explain the possibility to experience instantaneously and simultaneously a review and a preview of someone's life in a dimension without our conventional body-linked concept of time and space, where all past, present, and future events exist and are available, and the possibility to have clear and enhanced consciousness with persistent and unaltered self-identity, with memories, with cognition, with emotion, with the possibility of perception outside and above the lifeless body, and even with the experience of the conscious return into the body. In quantum physics, nonlocality or action at a distance is the direct, or instantaneous (i.e. independent of time) transfer of information about objects that are separated in space (i.e. independent of distance). In some articles (van Lommel, 2004, 2006, 2013) and in my recent book (van Lommel, 2010) I describe a hypothesis in which our endless consciousness with declarative memories finds its origin in, and is stored in, a nonlocal realm as (potentially scalar) wave-fields of information, and the brain only serves as a relay station for parts of these wave-fields of consciousness to be received into or as our waking consciousness. The latter relates to our physical body. These informational fields of our nonlocal consciousness become available as our waking consciousness only through our functioning brain in the shape of measurable and changing electromagnetic fields in the EEG. But these electromagnetic fields are not identical with our consciousness; they are just the measurable activities as the result of neural correlations in the brain. In this concept, the function of the brain should be compared with a transceiver—a transmitter/receiver—or interface, exactly like the function of a computer.

In trying to understand this concept of interaction between the invisible nonlocal realm and our visible, material body, it seems appropriate to compare it with modern worldwide communication. We are not consciously aware of the vast amounts of electromagnetic fields that constantly, day and night, exist around us and even permeate us, as well as permeating structures like walls and buildings. At each moment we are invaded by hundreds of thousands of telephone calls, by hundreds of radio and television programs, and by innumerable websites. We only become aware of these electromagnetic informative fields ("the cloud") at the moment we use our mobile telephone or by switching on our radio, television set, or laptop computer. What we receive is neither inside the instrument, nor in the components, but thanks to the receiver, the information from the electromagnetic fields ("the cloud") becomes observable to our senses and hence perception occurs in our consciousness (van Lommel, 2013). For instance: the images and music we hear and see on television are transmitted to our television set. And if we damage one or more components within the television set, we may induce a distortion or even lose the image and sound of the television program, but this does not mean that the program was produced by the television set. The same television program can still be received by another television set. This can be compared with the function of our brain: damage or disruption of specific areas of the brain may result in changes or loss of consciousness (coma), but this does not prove that consciousness should be a product of brain function. In my opinion, it seems that different neuronal networks act as an interface for different aspects of our consciousness, and the function of neuronal networks should be regarded as receivers and conveyors, not as retainers of consciousness and memories. This view is highly compatible with the concept of 'phenomenalism' or 'immaterial (or neutral) monism' (Chalmers, 2002). In this aforementioned concept consciousness is not rooted in the measurable domain of physics, our manifest world. This also means that the (potentially scalar) wave aspect of our indestructible consciousness in the nonlocal realm is inherently not measurable by physical means. However, the physical aspect of consciousness, which presumably originates from the wave aspect of our consciousness through collapse of the wave function ("objective reduction"), can be measured by means of neuroimaging techniques like EEG, fMRI, and PET scan. According to this view, there is a kind of biological basis of our waking consciousness, because during life our physical body functions as an interface or place of resonance. But there is no biological basis of our whole, endless, or enhanced consciousness, because it is rooted in a nonlocal realm. Our nonlocal consciousness does not reside in our brain and is not limited to our brain. So our brain seems to have a facilitating rather than a producing function: to experience consciousness.

It is quite interesting to mention that the assumption that our brain acts as a transceiver and not as a producer of consciousness is in striking concurrence with the view that was expressed over one century ago. Already in 1898 the psychologist William James wrote that the brain's role in the experience of consciousness is not a productive, but a permissive or transmissive role; that is, it admits or transmits information. In his view, consciousness does not originate in this physical world, but already exists in another, transcendental sphere; access to aspects of consciousness depends on the personal 'threshold of consciousness,' which for some people is lower than for others, and which allows them to experience various aspects of enhanced consciousness. James draws on abnormal experiences of consciousness to support his theory:

"The whole drift of my education goes to persuade me that the world of our present consciousness is only one out of many worlds of consciousness that exist, and that those other worlds must contain experiences which have a meaning for our life also." He stated: "The total expression of human experience, as I view it objectively, invincibly urges me beyond the narrow 'scientific' bounds," and he also writes about "the continuity of consciousness" after physical death" (James, 1898).

Other scientists and philosophers shared one century ago the same view (Myers, 1903; Bergson, 1896).

Concluding Remarks

I incline to the idealistic theory that consciousness is fundamental, and that the material universe is derivative from consciousness, not consciousness from the material universe.
Sir James H. Jeans (1877-1946, English physicist, astronomist, and mathematician)

Since the publication of the aforementioned prospective studies on NDEs in survivors of cardiac arrest, with strikingly similar results and conclusions, the phenomenon of the NDE can no longer be scientifically ignored.

According to these empirical studies on NDEs and the evidence from neurophysiological studies during cardiac arrest, the current materialistic view of the relationship between the brain and consciousness held by most physicians, philosophers, and psychologists seems to be too restricted for a proper understanding of this phenomenon. By making a scientific case for consciousness as a nonlocal and thus ubiquitous phenomenon, this view can contribute to new ideas about the relationship between consciousness and the brain. As mentioned before, there are now good reasons to assume that our consciousness does not always coincide with the functioning of our brain: enhanced consciousness with persistent and unaltered self-identity and with the possibility of perception can apparently be experienced independently from the lifeless body.

I am aware that this idea of a nonlocal consciousness can be little more than a stimulus for further study and debate, because at present we lack definitive answers to the many important questions about our consciousness and its relation with brain function. I have no doubt that in the future, too, many questions about consciousness and the mystery of life and death will remain unanswered. However, the findings and conclusions of recent NDE research may not only result in a fundamental change in our ideas about the mind-brain relationship, but also may result in a fundamental change of one's opinions about death, because of the almost unavoidable conclusion that at the time of physical death enhanced consciousness will continue to be experienced in another realm, in which all past, present, and future is enclosed. As someone with an NDE wrote to me: "*Death is only the end of our physical aspects.*" We should acknowledge that research on NDEs cannot give us the irrefutable scientific proof of this conclusion, because survivors of cardiac arrest did not quite die, but they all were very close to death, and without a functioning brain. But, as stated before, it has been scientifically proven indeed that during NDEs enhanced consciousness was experienced independently of brain function. Without a body we still can have conscious experiences, we still are conscious beings. The conclusion seems compelling that endless or nonlocal consciousness has existed and always will exist independently from the body. For this reason, we indeed should seriously consider the possibility that death, like birth, may only be a transition to another state of consciousness, and that during life the body functions as an interface or place of resonance.

To quote Henri Bergson (1859-1941, French philosopher, Nobel prize literature 1927):

"The more we become accustomed to this idea of a consciousness which overflows the organ we call the brain, then the more natural and probable we find the hypothesis that the soul survives the body" (Bergson, 1914).

The view of a nonlocal consciousness also allows us to understand a wide variety of special states of consciousness (van Lommel, 2010), not only near-death experiences, but also mystical and religious experiences, deathbed visions (end-of-life experiences), shared death experiences, peri-mortem and post-mortem experiences (after death communication, or nonlocal interconnectedness with the consciousness of deceased relatives), heightened intuitive feelings and prognostic dreams (nonlocal information exchange), remote viewing (nonlocal perception) and perhaps even the effect of consciousness on matter (nonlocal perturbation), like in meditation, in mindfulness-based cognitive therapy, and in the placebo-effect, where in EEG, fMRI, and PET scan studies functional and structural changes in the brain are demonstrated following changes in consciousness, which could be attributed to neuroplasticity (van Lommel, 2010; Benedetti et al., 2005; Beauregard, 2007).

It often takes an NDE to get people, and even physicians, to think about the possibility of experiencing consciousness independently of the body (Alexander, 2012) and to realize that presumably consciousness always has been and always will be, that everything and everybody is connected in higher levels of our consciousness, that all of our thoughts will exist forever, and that death as such does not exist. Only if we are willing and able to ask open questions and abandon preconceptions will studies into NDEs have the possibility of helping the scientific community to rethink some unproven assumptions about consciousness and its relation with brain function. To quote J. Robert Oppenheimer (1904-1967, American theoretical physicist) (Barnett, 1949): *"There is no place for dogma in science. The scientist is free, and must be free to ask any question, to doubt any assertion, to seek for evidence, to correct any errors.*" As stated before: we need a new, post-materialist science to include all subjective and transpersonal aspects that may occur in our consciousness, and to reconsider our currently widely accepted ideas about the mind-brain relation.

Statement: This chapter is mainly based on my book *Consciousness beyond Life* (van Lommel, 2010), and on my article 'Nonlocal Consciousness' (van Lommel, 2013).

References

Alexander, E. (2012). *Proof of Heaven. A neurosurgeon's journey into the Afterlife.* New York, Simon & Schuster paperbacks.

Alkire, M. T., & Miller, J. (2005). General anesthesia and the neural correlates of consciousness. *Prog. Brain Res.*, 150, 229-244.

Alkire, M. T., Hudetz, A. G., & Tononi, G. (2008). Consciousness and anesthesia. *Science*, 322 (5903), 876-880.

Barnett, L. (1949). J. Robert Oppenheimer. *Life, International Edition*, 7(9), 58.

Beauregard, M. (2007). Mind does really matter: Evidence from neuroimaging studies of emotional self-regulation, psychotherapy, and placebo effect. *Progress in Neurobiology*, 81(4), 218-236.

Benedetti, F., Mayberg, H. S., Wager, T. D., Stohler, C. S., & Zubieta, J. K. (2005). Neurobiological Mechanisms of the Placebo Effect. *The Journal of Neuroscience*, 25 (45), 10390-10402.

Bergson, H. (1896). *Matière et Mémoire*. Translation: Paul, N.M., Palmer, W.S. (1994). *Matter and Memory*: New York: Zone Books.

Bergson, H. (1914, September 27). Quote from interview in *New York Times*.

Birchner, N., Safar, P., & Stewart, R. (1980). A comparison of standard, 'MAST'-augmented, and open chest CPR in dogs: a preliminary investigation. *Critical Care Medicine*, 8 (3), 147-152.

Blackmore, S. (1993). *Dying to Live: Science and the Near-Death Experience.* London: Grafton – An imprint of Harper Collins Publishers.

Blanke, O., Landis, Th., Spinelli, L., & Seeck, M. (2004). Out-of-body experience and autoscopy of neurological origin. *Brain,* 127, 243-258.

Blanke, O., & Metzinger, Th. (2008). Full-body illusions and minimal phenomenal selfhood. *Trends in Cognitive Science,* 13 (1), 7-13.

Blanke, O., Ortigue, S., Landis, T., & Seeck, M. (2002). Stimulating illusory own-body perceptions. The part of the brain that can induce out-of-body experiences has been located. *Nature,* 419, 269-270.

Borjigin, J., Lee, U., Liu, T., Pal, D., Huff, S., Klarr, D., Sloboda, J., Hernandez, J., Wang, M. M., & Mashour, G. A. (2013). Surge of neurophysiological coherence and connectivity in the dying brain. *Proceedings of the National Academy of Sciences,* 110 (35), 14432-14437, www.pnas.org/cgi/doi/10.1073/pnas.1308285110.

Brantson, N. M., Ladds A., Symon, L., & Wang, A. D. (1984). Comparison of the Effects of Ischaemia on Early Components of the Somatosensory Evoked Potential in Brainstem, Thalamus and Cerebral Cortex. *Journal of Cerebral Blood Flow Metabolism,* 4 (1), 68 – 81.

Buunk, G., Hoeven, J. G. van der, & Meinders, A. E. (2000). Cerebral blood flow after cardiac arrest. *Netherlands Journal of Medicine,* 57, 106-112.

Carter, Ch. (2010). *Science and the Near-Death Experience. How Consciousness Survives Death.* Rochester, USA: Inner Traditions.

Chalmers, D. J. (1996). *The Conscious Mind. In search of a Fundamental Theory.* New York/Oxford: Oxford University Press.

Chalmers, D. J. (2002). Consciousness and its Place in Nature. In: *Philosophy of Mind: Classical and Contemporary Readings.* New York/Oxford: Oxford University Press. Also at: http://consc.net/papers/nature.html.

Cho, S. B., Baars, B. J., & Newman, J. (1997). A Neural Global Workspace Model for Conscious Attention. *Neural Networks,* 10 (7), 1195-1206.

Chun, M. M., & Marois, R. (2002). The dark side of visual attention. *Current Opinion in Neurobiology*, 12 (2), 184–189.

Clute, H., & Levy, W. J. (1990). Electroencephalographic changes during brief cardiac arrest in humans. *Anesthesiology*, 73, 821-825.

Coimbra, C. G. (1999). Implications of ischemic penumbra for the diagnosis of brain death. *Braz J Med Biol Res*, 32 (12), 1479-87.

de Ridder, D., van Laere, K., Dupont, P., Menovsky, T., & Van de Heyning, P. (2007). Visualizing Out-of-Body Experience in the Brain. *New England Journal of Medicine*, 357 (18), 1829-1933.

de Vreede-Swagemakers J. J. M., Gorgels A. P. M., Dubois-Arbouw W. I., van Ree J. W., Daemen M. J. A. P., Houben L. G. E., & Wellens H. J. J. (1997). Out-of-Hospital Arrest in the 1990s: A Population-Based Study in the Maastricht Area on Incidence, Characteristics and Survival. *Journal of the American College of Cardiology*, 30 (6), 1500-1505.

de Vries, J. W., Bakker, P. F. A., Visser, G. H., Diephuis, J. C., & Van Huffelen, A. C. (1998). Changes in cerebral oxygen uptake and cerebral electrical activity during defibrillation threshold testing. *Anesth Analg*, 87, 16-20.

Dehaene, S., Kerszberg, M., & Changeux, J. P. (1998). A neuronal model of a global workspace in effortful cognitive tasks. *Proc Natl Acad Sci USA*, 95, 14529–14534.

Dennett, D. (1991). *Consciousness explained*. Boston, London: Little, Brown and Co.

Ferrarelli, F., Massimini, M., Sarasso, S., Casali, A., Riedner, B. A., Angelini, G., Tononi, G., & Pearce, R. A. (2010). Breakdown in cortical effective connectivity during midazolam-induced loss of consciousness *Proc. Natl. Acad. Sci. USA*, 107 (6), 2681-2686.

Fisher, M., & Hossman, K. A. (1996). Volume expansion during cardiopulmonary resuscitation reduces cerebral no-reflow. *Resuscitation*, 32, 227–40.

Fujioka, M., Nishio, K., Miyamoto, S., Hiramatsu, K. I., Sakaki, T., Okuchi, K., Taoka, T., & Fujioka, S. (2000). Hippocampal damage in the human brain after cardiac arrest. *Cerebrovasc Dis,* 10 (1), 2-7.

Gallup, G., & Proctor, W. (1982). *Adventures in Immortality: A Look Beyond the Threshold of Death.* New York: McGraw-Hill.

Gopalan, K. T., Lee, J., Ikeda, S., & Burch, C. M. (1999). Cerebral blood flow velocity during repeatedly induced ventricular fibrillation. *J Clin Anesth,* 11(4), 290-295.

Greyson, B. (1983) The Near-Death Experience Scale: construction, reliability, and validity. *Joural of Nervous and Mental Disease,*171: 369-375.

Greyson, B. (2003). Incidence and correlates of near-death experiences in a cardiac care unit. *General Hospital Psychiatry,* 25, 269-276.

Greyson B., Williams Kelly E., & Kelly E. F. (2009). *Explanatory Models for Near-Death Experiences.* In: Holden J. M., Greyson B. & James D. (Eds.), *The Handbook of Near-Death Experiences. Thirty Years of Investigation..* pp. 213-234. Santa Barbera, CA: Praeger/ ABC-CLIO.

Gua, J., White, J. A., & Batjer, H. H. (1995). Limited Protective Effects of Etomidate During Bainstem Ischemia in Dogs. *Journal of Neurosurgery,* 82 (2), 278 – 84.

Herlitz, J., Bang, A., Alsen, B., & Aune, S. (2000). Characteristics and outcome among patients suffering from in-hospital cardiac arrest in relation to the interval between collapse and start of CPR. *Resuscitation,* 53 (1), 21-7.

Holden, J. M. (2009) *Veridical perception in near-death experiences.* In: Holden, J.M., Greyson, B. & James, B. (Eds.), *The Handbook of Near-Death Experiences. Thirty Years of Investigation.* pp. 185-211 Santa Barbara, CA: Praeger / ABC-CLIO.

Hossmann, K. A., & Kleihues, P. (1973). Reversibility of ischemic brain damage. *Arch Neurol,* 29(6), 375-84.

James, W. (1898) *Human Immortality.* Boston, MA: Houhton Mifflin.

Kinney, H. C., Korein, J., Panigraphy, A., Dikkes, P., & Goode, R. (1994). Neuropathological findings in the brain of Karen Ann Quinlan. The role of the thalamus in the persistent vegetative state. *N Engl J Med*, 330 (26), 1469-1475.

Klemenc-Ketis, Z., Kersnik, J., & Gremc, S. (2010). The effect of carbon dioxide on near-death experiences in out-of-hospital arrest survivors: a prospective observational study. *Critical Care*, 14, R56.

Koivisto, M., & Revonsuo, A. (2008). The role of unattended distractors in sustained inattentional blindness. *Psychological Research*, 72, 39 - 48.

Lempert, T., Bauer, M., & Schmidt, D. (1994). Syncope and Near-Death Experience. *Lancet*, 344, 829-830.

Lombardi G., Gallaghan E. J., & Gennis P. (1994). Outcome of Out-of-Hospital Cardiac Arrest in New York City. The pre-hospital arrest survival evaluation (PHASE) study. *JAMA*, 271, 678-683.

Losasso, T. J., Muzzi, D. A., Meyer, F. B., & Sharbrough, F. W. (1992). Electroencephalographic monitoring of cerebral function during asystole and successful cardiopulmonary resuscitation. *Anesth Analg*, 75, 12-19.

Mack, A., & Rock, I. (1998). *Inattentional blindness*. Cambridge, MA: MIT Press.

Marshall, R. S., Lazar, R. M., Spellman, J. P., Young, W. L., Duong, D. H., Joshi, S., & Ostapkovich, N. (2001). Recovery of brain function during induced cerebral hypoperfusion. *Brain*, 124, 1208-1217.

Massimini, M., Ferrarelli, F., Huber, R., Esser, S. K., Singh, H., & Tononi, G. (2005). Breakdown of Cortical Effective Connectivity during Sleep. *Science*, 309 (5744), 2228-2232.

Mayer, J., & Marx, T. (1972). The pathogenesis of EEG changes during cerebral anoxia. In: Drift, Ed. van der, *Cardiac and Vascular Diseases/Handbook of Electroencephalography and Clinical Neurophysiology*, Vol. 14A, part A, pp. 5-11, Amsterdam: Elsevier.

McNally, B., Robb, R., Mehta, M., Vellano, K., Valderrama, A.L., Yoon, P.W., Sasson, C., et al. (2011). Out-of-Hospital Cardiac arrest Surveillance—Cardiac Arrest Registry to Enhance Survival (CARES), United States, October 1, 2005 – December 31, 2010. *Centers for Disease Control and prevention. MMWR*, 60 (8), 1-19.

Meduna, L. T. (1950). *Carbon Dioxide Therapy: A Neuropsychological Treatment of Nervous Disorders.* Springfield: Charles C. Thomas.

Moody, R. A. Jr. with Perry, P. (2010). *Glimpses of Eternity. Sharing a Loved One's Passage from this Life to the Next.* New York: Guideposts.

Moss, J., & Rockoff, M. (1980). EEG monitoring during cardiac arrest and resuscitation. *JAMA*, 244(24), 2750-1.

Most, S. B., Scholl, B. J., Clifford, E., & Simons, D. J. (2005). What you see is what you set: Sustained inattentional blindness and the capture of awareness. *Psychological Review*, 112 (1), 217-242.

Myers, F. W. H. (1903). *Human Personality and its Survival of Bodily Death.* (2 volumes) London: Longmans, Green.

Noë, A. (2009). *Out of our heads. Why you are not your brain, and other lessons from the biology of consciousness.* New York: Hill and Wang, A division of Farrar, Straus and Giroux.

Paradis, N. A., Martin, G. B., & Goetting, M. G. (1989). Simultaneous aortic jugular bulb, and right atrial pressures during cardiopulmonary resuscitation in humans: insights into mechanisms. *Circulation*, 80, 361-8.

Paradis, N. A., Martin, G. B., & Rosenberg, J. (1991). The effect of standard and high dose epinephrine on coronary perfusion pressure during prolonged cardiopulmonary resuscitation. *J Am Med Assoc*, 265, 1139-44.

Parnia, S. (2013). *Erasing Death. The science that is rewriting the boundaries between life and death.* New York: Harper Collins.

Parnia, S., & Fenwick, P. (2002). Near-death experiences in cardiac arrest: visions of a dying brain or visions of a new science of consciousness. Review article. *Resuscitation*, 52, 5-11.

Parnia, S., Waller, D. G., Yeates, R., & Fenwick, P. (2001). A qualitative and quantitative study of the incidence, features and aetiology of near death experience in cardiac arrest survivors. *Resuscitation*, 48, 149-156.

Penfield, W. (1975). *The Mystery of the Mind*. Princeton: Princeton University Press.

Peperby, M. A., Kaye, W., Ornato, J. P., Larkin, G. L., Nadkarni, V., Mancini, M. E., Berg, R. A., et al. (2003). Cardiopulmonary resuscitation of adults in the hospital: a report of 14720 cardiac arrests from the National Registry of Cardiopulmonary Resuscitation. *Resuscitation*, 58 (3), 297-308.

Popper, K., & Eccles, J. C. (1977). *The Self and Its Brain*. New York: Springer.

Ring, K. (1980). *Life at Death: A Scientific Investigation of the Near-Death Experience*. New York: Coward, McCann & Geoghegan.

Ring, K. (1984). *Heading Toward Omega: In Search of the Meaning of the Near-Death Experience*. New York: Morrow.

Ring, K., & Cooper, S. (1999). *Mindsight. Near-Death and Out-of-Body Experiences in the Blind*. Palo Alto, Ca: William James Center for Consciousness Studies.

Sartori, P. (2006). The Incidence and Phenomenology of Near-Death Experiences. *Network Review (Scientific and Medical Network)*, 90, 23-25.

Schmied, I., Knoblaub, H., & Schnettler, B. (1999). *Todesnäheerfahrungen in Ost- und Westdeutschland. Eine empirische Untersuchung*. In: Knoblaub, H.,& Soeffner, H.G. (Eds.), *Todesnähe: Interdisziplinäre Zugänge zu Einem Außergewöhnlichen Phänomen*. (pp. 65-99). Konstanz: Universitätsverlag Konstanz.

Scholl, B. J., Noles, N. S., Pasheva, V., & Sussman, R. (2003). Talking on a cellular telephone dramatically increases 'sustained inattentional blindness'. *Journal of Vision*, 3(9), 156, 156a.

Simons, D. J., & Chabris, C. F. (1999). Gorillas in our midst: sustained inattentional blindness for dynamic events. *Perception*, 28 (9), 1059–1074.

Simons, D. J., & Rensink, R. A. (2005). Change blindness: past, present, and future. *Trends in Cognitive Sciences*, 9 (1), 16-20.

Smith, D. S., Levy, W., Maris, M., & Chance, B. (1990). Reperfusion hyperoxia in the brain after circulatory arrest in humans. *Anesthesiology*, 73, 12-19.

van Dijk, G. W. (2004). Hoofdstuk 3: Bewustzijn, In Meursing, B.T.J., Kesteren, R.G. van (Eds.), *Handboek Reanimatie*. Tweede herziene druk. Utrecht, the Netherlands: Wetenschappelijke Uitgeverij Bunge. pp. 21-25. [Chapter 3: Consciousness, in *Handbook Resuscitation*. Second revised edition].

van Lommel, P. (2004). About the Continuity of our Consciousness. *Adv Exp Med Biol*. 550, 115-132. In: Machado, C., & Shewmon, D.A. (Eds.), *Brain Death and Disorders of Consciousness*. New York: Kluwer Academic/ Plenum Publishers.

van Lommel, P. (2006). Near-Death Experience, Consciousness and the Brain: A new concept about the continuity of our consciousness based on recent scientific research on near-death experience in survivors of cardiac arrest. *World Futures, The Journal of General Evolution*, 62, 134-151.

van Lommel, P. (2010). *Consciousness Beyond Life. The Science of the Near-Death Experience*. New York: Harper Collins. Translation from: Van Lommel, P. (2007). *Eindeloos Bewustzijn. Een wetenschappelijke visie op de bijna-dood ervaring*. Kampen, Ten Have.

van Lommel, P. (2013). Nonlocal Consciousness. A concept based on scientific research on near-death experiences during cardiac arrest. *Journal of Consciousness Studies*, 20, 7-48.

van Lommel, P., Van Wees, R., Meyers, V., & Elfferich, I. (2001). Near-death experiences in survivors of cardiac arrest: A prospective study in the Netherlands. *Lancet*, 358, 2039-2045.

Whinnery, J. E., & Whinnery, A. M. (1990). Acceleration-induced loss of consciousness. *Arch Neurol*, 47, 764-776.

White, B. C., Winegan, C. D., Jackson, R. E., Joyce, K. M., Vigor, D. N., Hoehner, T. J., Krause, G. S., & Wilson, R. F. (1983). Cerebral cortical perfusion during and following resuscitation from cardiac arrest in dogs. *Am. Journal of Emergency Medicine,* 1 (2), 128-138.

Woerlee, G. M. (2003). *Mortal Minds. A biology of the soul and the dying experience.* Utrecht, the Netherlands: De Tijdstroom.

Chapter Twelve

Consciousness and the Brain: What Does Research on Spiritual Experiences Tell Us?

Alexander Moreira-Almeida, MD, PhD[21]

Introduction

The relationship between consciousness/mind and the brain is one of the oldest and most challenging philosophical and scientific problems. This topic, called "the mind-brain problem," has been subject to intense discussion since, at least, ancient Greece. In order to simplify a long and nuanced debate, there are essentially two major positions: materialist and non-materialist perspectives of mind. The materialist/physicalist perspectives assume that mind/consciousness is the product of chemical and electric activity of the brain. The non-materialist/non-physicalist perspectives defend the view that mind cannot be reduced to brain activity and has its own reality (Moreira-Almeida & Araujo, 2015).

Supporters of the "mind as a brain product" perspective usually base their position on a materialist view of the universe (including human beings) and on empirical data from neuroscience (Moreira-Almeida et al., 2018). We will now briefly discuss these two main arguments often presented to support materialist perspectives of mind.

---

[21] *This chapter is partially based on the paper "Implications of spiritual experiences to the understanding of mind-brain relationship". Moreira-Almeida, A. Asian J Psychiatry. 2013; 6(6):585-9 and on the book "Exploring frontiers of the mind-brain relationship". Moreira-Almeida, A. & Santos, F. S. (Eds). New York: Springer, 2012.*

Materialism Is Not Essential to Science

It is usually assumed (explicitly or implicitly) that scientific activity requires or has proved materialism (the view that all the universe, everything that exists, including human nature, can ultimately be reduced to/explained by matter, i.e. physical forces or particles). Non-materialist perspectives of the universe and human nature are often presented as anti-scientific, superstition, or bigotry. It is repeatedly assumed that materialism is a scientific fact, an undeniable consequence of scientific discoveries, and/or an essential assumption for rationality and scientific activity (Araujo, 2012; Haught, 2005; Moreira-Almeida et al., 2018; Wallach & Reich, 2005).

However, materialism is a metaphysical assumption. This is a conceivable assumption, but not a scientific fact or an assumption essential to perform science. In fact, basically all founders of modern science (e.g. Francis Bacon, Giordano Bruno, Johannes Kepler, Robert Boyle, Galileo Galilee, Isaac Newton) did not accept materialism. On the contrary, they often saw a deep spiritual meaning in the universe and perceived their scientific enterprises as a sacred quest. In exploring the universe or creation, they would be understanding more, and glorifying, the creator (Haught, 2005; Harrison, 2010; Numbers, 2009). Non-materialist perspectives of mind were also defended or at least considered by several founders of scientific psychology such as Wilhelm Wundt (Araujo, 2016) and William James (Sech et al., 2013; Sommer, 2014).

Essentially, all of the major scientific advancements do not require a metaphysical materialism. In the last century it was common to conflate science with a materialist worldview, including its implications for ethics, meaning (or lack thereof) of life, free will, etc. This unwarranted extrapolation of scientific findings has been called "Materialist Scientism," an ideology that has been misguidedly presented as science (Araujo, 2012; Wallach & Reich, 2005).

In addition to materialism, other metaphysical assumptions about the universe have also been proposed. Among them is the view that, in addition to matter, the universe has another fundamental component that cannot be reduced to matter: mind or consciousness, also called spirit, soul, or psyche. Several authors have defended an expanded naturalism, which would include mind in addition to matter as the fundamental "stuff" of the universe (Beauregard et al., 2014). For example, to quote two contemporary influential philosophers of mind:

"Perhaps the natural order is not exclusively physical ... My guiding conviction is that mind is ... a basic aspect of nature ... there is independent support for the step to such an enlarged conception of reality" (Nagel, 2012, pp. 15-16).

"It is often held that even though it is hard to see how materialism could be true, materialism must be true, since the alternatives are unacceptable. As I see it, there are at least three prima facie acceptable alternatives to materialism on the table [interactionist dualism, epiphenomenalism, and panprotopsychism], each of which is compatible with a broadly naturalistic (even if not materialistic) worldview, and none of which has fatal problems. So given the clear arguments against materialism, it seems to me that we should at least tentatively embrace the conclusion that one of these views is correct. Of course all of the views (...) need to be developed in much more detail, and examined in light of all relevant scientific and philosophical developments, in order to be comprehensively assessed. But as things stand, I think that we have good reason to suppose that consciousness has a fundamental place in nature" (Chalmers 2003, pp. 41-42).

Materialist and non-materialist metaphysical assumptions are conceivable ones, and both can guide scientific programs. It is essential to keep intellectual humility and recognize we still do not have a full knowledge of the universe and of all its components.

Neuroscience Does Not Imply Materialism

Too often, it is stated or implicitly assumed that neuroscience proves that brain produces mind. Usually, three sorts of empirical findings are presented as supporting this conclusion: neural correlates of mind activity, brain injuries causing alterations in personality or mind functioning, and brain stimulation generating some mental experience. However, as stated more than a century ago by William James (1898), one of the founders of scientific psychology in the USA, these findings can be easily accommodated to both physicalist and non-physicalist views of mind. According to non-materialist perspectives such as interactionist dualism, the brain is a tool or filter for mind manifestation (such as a TV set is a tool for the exhibition of a TV program produced elsewhere, not inside the TV set). If the brain is an instrument for mind manifestation, there would be correlations between brain function and mind activity. In the same way, the damage or stimulation of the tool (the brain) would influence how mind would function or express itself. But it does not imply that mind is just a product of brain activity, which has been acknowledged by the leading neuroscientists quoted below. The misuse of neuroscience in conflating mind with brain has been exposed by the Nobel laureate neuroscientist John Eccles:

"There is a general tendency to overplay the scientific knowledge of the brain, which, regretfully, also is done by many scientists and scientific writers. For example, we are told that the brain 'sees' lines, angles (…) and that therefore we will soon be able to explain how a whole picture is 'seen' (…). But this statement is misleading. All that is known to happen in the brain is that neurons of the visual cortex are caused to fire trains of impulse in response to some specific visual input." (Popper & Eccles 1977, pp. 225)

More recently, a philosopher and a neuroscientist also complained that:

"contemporary neuroscientists tend to ascribe the same range of psychological attributes to the brain (commonly, although not uniformly, conceived to be identical with the mind). (…) The ascription of psychological – in particular, cognitive and cogitative – attributes to the brain is (…) a source of much (…) confusion. (…) the great discoveries of neuroscience do not require this misconceived form of explanation." (Bennett & Hacker 2003, pp. 3-4).

The neurosurgeon and neuroscientist Wilder Penfield, pioneer of in vivo studies of human brain stimulation during brain surgeries with wakeful patients, concluded after decades of research:

"There is no place in the cerebral cortex where electrical stimulation will cause a patient to believe or to decide. (...) none of the actions that we attribute to the mind has been initiated by electrode stimulation or epileptic discharge. (...)

"For my own part, after years of striving to explain the mind on the basis of brain-action alone, I have come to the conclusion that it is simpler (and far easier to be logical) if one adopts the hypothesis that our being does consist of two fundamental elements" (Penfield, 1978, pp. 77-80).

In addition, several materialist philosophers and neuroscientists recognize that they cannot provide a reasonable explanation about how brain would generate mind. However, they often state that neuroscience is advancing so much that in the near future it will be able to fully explain how mind is produced by the brain. This was called "promissory materialism" by the philosopher Karl Popper, who stated that it:

"is a peculiar theory (...) a historical (or historicist) prophecy about the future results of brain research and of their impact. This prophecy is baseless. No attempt is made to base it upon a survey of recent brain research. The opinion of researchers who, like Wilder Penfield, started as identity theorists, but ended as dualists is ignored. No attempt is made to resolve the difficulties of materialism by argument. No alternatives to materialism are even considered" (Popper, 1977, pp. 97).

Promissory materialism is a rhetorical strategy with "recurrent patterns of analogies and metaphors, besides an old rhetorical strategy of appealing to a distant future, in which all the problems will be solved" (Araujo, 2012, p. 3). It has been used by materialists at least since the 18th century, but its prophecy have never been fulfilled (Araujo, 2012).

In summary, the usual neuroscience findings about brain correlates and mind changes caused by brain damage or stimulation do not necessarily imply physicalism, since they also can be accounted for by non-materialist perspectives. It is therefore essential to look for other empirical data in order to advance the understanding of the mind-brain problem and to engage in better testing and discriminating between materialist and non-materialist views.

Potential of Spiritual Experiences to Advance Discussion of the Mind-Brain Problem

Defining "spirituality" is a very controversial task, but it is often assumed, based on its etymology, that it relates to the spiritual, to the transcendent, to the non-material aspects of the universe (Hufford, 2010; Moreira-Almeida & Koenig, 2006). This is the definition used in this chapter. The belief that there is a non-material component of the universe and in the essence of the human being is a belief shared by many, if not most, spiritual traditions in the world. Based on this, it is not surprising that spiritual experiences (SEs) often involve altered states of consciousness, reports of anomalous experiences and of consciousness beyond the body. Some authors argue that SEs are the source of beliefs in a spiritual realm (Hufford, 2010; Walach & Reich, 2005; Walach, 2015).

SEs often are, prima facie, suggestive of some mind activity beyond the brain/body (e.g.: out of body experience, apparitions near the time of death, contact with non-bodily entities). Exactly because of this "anomalous" characteristic, SEs can potentially be very important to test the different views regard the mind-brain problem, physicalist and non-physicalist ones. SEs are human experiences that have been reported in all cultures throughout time, and they should be submitted to rigorous scientific investigation, not neglected.

William James thought spiritual/psychic experiences could be easily explained by non-materialist perspectives of mind (which he called the "transmission model"), but are very hard to accommodate within materialist views (which he called the "production model"):

"The transmission theory also puts itself in touch with a whole class of experiences that are with difficulty explained by the production theory. I refer to those obscure and exceptional phenomena reported at all times throughout human history, which the 'psychical researchers' (…) are doing so much to rehabilitate; such phenomena, namely (…) premonitions, apparitions at time of death, clairvoyant visions or impressions, and the whole range of mediumistic capacities (…). All such experiences, quite paradoxical and meaningless on the production theory, fall very naturally into place on the other theory. We need only to suppose the continuity of our consciousness (…)" (James, 1898, pp. 298-299).

However, probably because SEs do not fit well into materialist frameworks, they are often neglected and/or understood necessarily as a cognitive or perceptual distortion. William James tells an interesting story about scientists' resistance to investigate the topic:

"I invite eight of my scientific colleagues severally to come to my house at their own time, and sit with a medium for whom the evidence already published in our Proceedings [of the Society for Psychical Research] had been most noteworthy. Although it means at worst the waste of the hour for each, five of them decline the adventure. (…) I advise another psychological friend to look into this medium's case, but he replies that it is useless, for if he should get such results as I report, he would (being suggestible) simply believe himself hallucinated. (...) This friend of mine writes ex cathedra on the subject of psychical research, declaring (I need hardly add) that there is nothing in it (...) and one of the five colleagues who declined my invitation is widely quoted as an effective critic of our evidence" (James, 1901, p. 216).

Due to SEs' challenging and anomalous character, they need be submitted to comprehensive and rigorous scientific scrutiny. Science should not be afraid or avoid any phenomena in the universe; rather, it must take into consideration all sorts of human experiences, including SEs. This is especially true when a scientific field is in a pre-paradigmatic period, using the terminology of Thomas Kuhn (1970). This is the case regarding the mind-brain problem: there is no widely accepted paradigm that can explain all the observations and guide future research.

The recognition that we are in a pre-paradigmatic phase in the exploration of the mind-brain problem would enable us to pursue a more fruitful investigation. It is worthwhile to remember that the scientific skills required to work in a pre-paradigmatic phase are different from those required during a paradigmatic phase, a period called "normal science" by Kuhn. Fruitful work in pre-paradigmatic or revolutionary periods requires a more open-minded approach and not too strong of a commitment to any of the paradigm candidates. It would also require enlarging as much as possible the diversity of the empirical base and avoiding rushed rejection of hypotheses (Chibeni & Moreira-Almeida, 2007; Moreira-Almeida & Santos, 2012).

Throughout history, scientific revolutions often occurred when brilliant scientists took into account a wide range of previously unknown or dismissed phenomena. Galileo with his telescope and Charles Darwin during his five-year long journey aboard the *Beagle* gathered an enormous mass of empirical evidence that was not available to most scientists at that time. The trip and the telescope allowed Darwin and Galileo to face a huge broadening of the empirical base, a base that could no longer be explained by the biological and astronomical established paradigms at their times. The end of these stories is well known to us. The same happened with classical physics, which, more than a century ago, seemed to be able to explain the whole of nature. Such certainty made the eminent physicist Lord Kelvin state in 1900, a few years before Einstein developed relativity theory: "There is nothing new to be discovered in physics now, all that remains is more and more precise measurement." In fact, classical physics is very efficient at explaining most of the physical phenomena happening in our daily lives. However, when the study of microscopic particles and extreme velocities began, classical physics' limitations became evident, giving birth to the scientific revolution of modern physics (Greyson, 2007; Moreira-Almeida & Santos, 2012).

Studies on consciousness need to enlarge and diversify the range of studied phenomena. SEs seem to be a much needed privileged venue to advance our understanding of the mind-brain problem, because they may be influential in empirically testing materialist and non-materialist perspectives of mind (Beauregard et al., 2014; Cardeña et al., 2000; Eysenck & Sargent, 1993; James, 1909; Kelly et al., 2007; Moreira-Almeida & Santos, 2012). In the decades around the transition between the 19th and 20th centuries, many high level scientists investigated in depth the implications of SEs for the mind-brain problem. Some examples are William James, Frederic W. H. Myers, Alfred Russell Wallace, Cesare Lombroso, Oliver Lodge, Pierre Janet, C. G. Jung, Theodore Flournoy, and William

McDougall. This list also includes the Nobel laureates Charles Richet, Pierre and Marie Curie, J. J. Thomson, Henri Bergson, and Lord Rayleigh. Studies on SEs such as trance experiences were seminal to the development of concepts such as subliminal/unconscious mind, dissociation, and hysteria (Alvarado, 2012; Crabtree, 1993; Moreira-Almeida, 2012). Until recently, these previous scientific studies of SEs were traditionally presented in a distorted and dismissive way, as "inherently 'irrational' and 'unscientific'" (Sommer, 2014, p. 39). However, the current view of the history of science based on careful analysis of primary historiographical sources has provided a much more informed and balanced account of these investigations. It has been shown that these investigations of SEs were much more sophisticated and rigorous, and had a larger impact than previously imagined (Sommer, 2014).

Usually based on materialist or non-materialist metaphysical assumptions, SEs frequently seem to represent some sort of contact with a non-material realm (e.g. spirituality, mind, or consciousness) or as some perceptual or cognitive error. From the materialist perspective, SEs cannot have any ontological reality, since the non-material realm does not exist. On the other hand, according to non-materialist perspectives, SEs might be glimpses of the spiritual/consciousness realm or the transcendent reality. This would explain why SEs are so widespread across cultures and history, and why religions would often be

"ways to communicate and thus preserve spiritual experiences, make them culturally available, and open the way to similar experiences for a broader group of people through symbolizations, rites, religious imagery, and texts. Religion, then, would be or at least could be the form-giving and clothing of spiritual experience, which is not only contingent on historical and cultural contexts but is needed to channel the spiritual experiences and their impact into culturally acceptable and understandable ways of "seeing" the world" (Wallach & Reich, 2005, p. 429).

Based on the hypothesis that the brain is a tool or a filter for mind manifestation, the brain would restrict (or "filter") the access to this transcendent realm, to the domain of spirituality or consciousness. Various spiritual traditions have several ways (e.g. meditation, sensorial deprivation, silence, chanting, etc.) to decrease the brain's filtering activity, which would allow a broader apprehension of the spiritual realm (Kelly, Crabtree & Marshall, 2015).

The mind-brain problem and SEs are very controversial issues that too often raise more emotional than rational reactions, from both materialists and non-materialists. However, a truly scientific enterprise needs to be open-minded and rigorous at the same time. The history of science teaches us that intellectual humility is essential, as well as stringent rational interpretation of a wide range of well-documented empirical observations (Chibeni & Moreira-Almeida, 2007).

Given the evidence available and our limited understanding of mind, non-materialistic perspectives deserve at least the same opportunity of development as the materialistic ones. Intellectual freedom is needed to develop and improve paradigm candidates without suppression by dogmatism and intolerance (Moreira-Almeida & Araujo, 2017). According to the philosopher of science Imre Lakatos (1970), scientific development happens in a kind of Darwinian selection of competing paradigms candidates where the fittest survives:

"It would be wrong to assume that one must stay with a research program until it has exhausted all its heuristic power, that one must not introduce a rival program before everybody agrees that the point of degenerations has probably been reached. (...)

"The history of science has been and should be a history of competing research programs: the sooner competition starts, the better for progress. 'Theoretical pluralism' is better than 'theoretical monism'" (p. 155).

I will now present and briefly discuss some of the sorts of SEs that have been scientifically investigated and which can provide fruitful insights and empirical evidence regarding the mind-brain problem. Several of these SEs are discussed more in depth in other chapters of this book, but here I am presenting the main findings and their more direct implications for the mind-brain problem. Before presenting these empirical findings, it is worth noting that during the second half of the 19th century and for most of the 20th century, SEs were often explained away as symptoms of mental disorders. In this way, SEs were usually considered to be a consequence of brain disorders, psychological defenses, or immature personality (Le Maléfan, 1999; Moreira-Almeida et al., 2005). However, there has emerged a growing body of evidence that SEs are not usually related to mental disorders and that they are often actually related to better mental health (Moreira-Almeida & Cardeña, 2011). A recent systematic review of scientific papers investigating experiences commonly associated with the possibility of the existence of a consciousness independent of the brain found almost 2,000 papers indexed on major mainstream scientific databases. There has been an increase in the number of articles in recent decades, and these papers have been published in academic journals with impact factors similar to those where more mainstream topics are published (Daher et al., 2017).

Meditative States

During deep meditative states, many people experience altered states of consciousness including the loosening of the ego's border and a sense of union with other beings and the universe. This type of SE has been one of the most investigated, especially under neuroimaging techniques. Two misunderstandings have been pervasive regarding neuroimaging investigations of SEs: a) the "God spot": the idea that there is a specific brain region (usually in the temporal lobe) responsible for SEs, and; b) the assumption that showing a certain type of brain activation during an SE or brain stimulation raising an experience similar to an SE implies that the brain is the ultimate cause of the SE. Regarding the first assumption, scientific data show that SEs are complex and multidimensional phenomena related to several different brain areas involved in a variety of functions (Beauregard, 2012; Beauregard & Paquette, 2006; Edwards et al., 2012). The second conjecture is related to the fallacy of conflating association with causation. In addition, producing a given experience by brain stimulation does not mean that this experience is always merely a brain phenomenon, with no external reality. Although certain brain areas have been associated with hearing and even produce auditory experiences when stimulated, this obviously does not mean that there is no auditory experience based on an external source (Hageman et al., 2010).

In addition to demonstrating the brain correlates of several consciousness states, the study of meditative states, as voluntarily induced mind states that influence brain states, is a privileged venue to investigate top-down (mind over brain) causation (Beauregard, 2012).

End-of-Life and Near-Death Experiences

End-of-life experiences (ELEs) and near-death experiences (NDEs) provide valuable opportunities to study the mind-brain problem. Since the dying process often involves a progressive impairment of brain function and death may be defined as the stopping of brain functioning, the investigation of the relation between these brain changes and consciousness may be very informative to improve our understanding of the mind-brain problem.

NDEs are a type of SE that have received a lot of academic and lay attention in the last decades (Sleutjes, Moreira-Almeida, & Greyson, 2014). Probably of most interest in NDEs are the claims that conscious and spiritual experiences happen during clinical death. If mind is just a product of brain activity, when brain functioning is impaired or stopped, consciousness should be disturbed or ceased. Several authors, who do not usually do empirical studies of NDEs, have argued that all NDE features could be explained by brain activity and psycho-cultural factors (Lester, 2005; Mobbs & Watt, 2011). However, most of those who have conducted the largest empirical studies on NDEs argue that these factors cannot explain all NDE features and that NDEs suggest some sort of consciousness beyond the brain (Athappilly et al., 2006; Fenwick, 2012; Greyson, 2007; Parnia, 2007; Parnia et al., 2014; van Lommel, 2011). Prospective studies with hundreds of cardiac arrest survivors have found that NDEs could not be explained by medication use, religious belief, fear of death, or cognitive dysfunction (Greyson, 2003; Parnia et al., 2001; Parnia et al., 2014; van Lommel et al., 2001). Experiences induced by hypoxia, drug use, and brain stimulation seem to have some similarities with NDEs, but they seem to be more dissimilar than similar. There is a large controversy about whether the memories related to NDEs refer to what has happened during cardiac arrest or any time before or after it. There are several anecdotal reports of NDE patients describing things that happened during their cardiac arrest, a period when they are supposed to have no conscious experience and no memory. There are also reports of accurate descriptions of the environment made by blind people who claim they had been able to "see" the room during an NDE (Fenwick, 2012; Holden, 2009; Parnia et al., 2014; van Lommel, 2011).

More recently, several studies have been published on ELEs, which are defined as "a set of phenomena which occur in the last few days/weeks of life and are associated with the process of dying" (Santos & Fenwick, 2012, p. 174). During ELEs, patients often report several SEs that occur in clear consciousness and seem to be different from confusional states and drug-induced hallucinations (Fenwick et al., 2010). Another intriguing phenomenon related to ELEs is "terminal lucidity," defined as an "unexpected return of mental clarity and memory shortly before death in patients suffering from severe psychiatric and neurologic disorders" (Nahm et al., 2009, 2012). Scientific studies of these experiences related to the dying process have just started, and they seem to represent promising lines of research regarding the mind-brain problem, since they offer cases of unexpected adequate mental function under severe brain damage and/or dysfunction.

Mediumship

Most cultures and spiritual traditions have reports, both currently and/or in their roots, of experiences of contact with spiritual, non-material entities (e.g., gods, angels, demons, ancestors, deceased loved ones) (Bourguignon, 1976). We use the term mediumship to designate this sort of experience. Specific to our discussion regarding the mind-brain problem, the mediumistic experience most relevant is the claim of contact with deceased people. This claim, frequent in several spiritual traditions, implies, at least at face value, survival of some aspect of mind after the brain's death. This is a very prevalent belief worldwide; according to the World Values Survey, 87% of the world's population believes people have a soul and 68% believe in life after death. Among people living in North America and Western Europe, 24% have felt they have gotten in touch with someone who was dead (European Values Study Group and World Values Survey Association).

In the last 150 years there has been a large body of scientific studies on the source of mediumistic experiences and in testing if mediums can actually get some sort of non-ordinary source of information (e.g. telepathy or contacting the departed). These studies were common in the decades of transition between the 19th and 20th centuries and involved many members of the world's scientific elite, including several Nobel laureates (Moreira-Almeida, 2012). William James emphasized the critical importance of investigating mediumship to understand mind (Sech et al., 2015). He himself investigated the subject for more than two decades and regarding one of the most studied mediums in history, he concluded:

"(…) a universal proposition can be made untrue by a particular instance. If you wish to upset the law that all crows are black, you must not seek to show that no crows are; it is enough if you prove one single crow to be white. My own white crow is Mrs. Piper. In the trances of this medium, I cannot resist the conviction that knowledge appears which she has never gained by the ordinary waking use of her eyes and ears and wits. What the source of this knowledge may be I know not (…); but from admitting the fact of such knowledge I can see no escape" (James, 1896).

Mediumship has already contributed to our understanding of mind, specifically in the exploration of dissociative states and the subconscious mind, but academic interest in mediumship waned during most of the 20th century (Almeida & Lotufo Neto, 2004; Alvarado et al., 2007; Crabtree, 1993). However, in the last few decades there has been some resurgence of scientific studies on mediumship published in academic journals. These studies usually have put emphasis on methods to control for fraud, chance, sensory leakage, and cold reading as explanations for the information provided by mediums. A lot has already been written about methods to investigate this sort of phenomenon (Beischel, 2007/8; Kelly, 2010). Some of these studies have found negative results (Jensen & Cardeña, 2009;

O'Keeffe & Wiseman, 2005) and others have positive findings (Beischel & Schwartz, 2007; Kelly & Arcangel, 2011).

Most mediumistic communications do not provide challenging evidence, but there are well-documented cases where veridical information known to the deceased personality but unknown to the medium were provided by the medium under controlled circumstances. Some mediums got especially high scores for accuracy, providing several specific pieces of information that were recognized by blinded sitters (Moreira-Almeida, 2012).

In addition to randomized and blind studies, it is also useful to perform in depth qualitative analysis of a single or a set of mediumistic communications attributed to a given personality, since they may reveal significant personal details useful to investigate the possibility of personality survival. Our group (NUPES - Research Center in Spirituality and Health, School of Medicine, Federal University of Juiz de Fora, Brazil) recently published a case study investigating the fit and accuracy of mediumistic letters produced by the most prolific Brazilian medium, Chico Xavier (1910–2002) (Rocha et al., 2014). We investigated 13 letters allegedly written by the same deceased personality (J.P.), an engineering student who drowned when he was 24 years old. A special emphasis was put on determining the accuracy of objectively verifiable items of information provided by the letters and the likelihood of Xavier's access to the information via ordinary means of information (i.e. fraud, chance, information leakage, and cold reading).

Xavier, who never obtained material profits from his mediumship, used to perform weekly sessions where hundreds of mourning relatives from all over Brazil sought his help, hoping to obtain a "psychographed" letter (i.e., a letter written by the medium allegedly under the influence of a deceased personality). It is estimated that Xavier produced 10,000 of these letters during his life. Relatives usually, after waiting in a long line, exchanged a few words with Xavier. After that they waited, seated in a large room while Xavier, for about three hours, wrote the letters uninterruptedly at a table in front of the audience. While writing the letters, Xavier had no direct exchange with the sitters. In each session, Xavier used to write an average of six letters.

40 days after J.P.'s death, his parents and his sister travelled 400 km to see Chico Xavier. They had never met previously and, after waiting in the queue, the only thing the sister said to Xavier was that she had lost her brother, that her parents were devastated, and that they would like to receive some news from him or even a letter. She stated definitively that they did not say any names or give any other information to Xavier. At that session, they received the first letter and, in the next five years, they received a total of 13 psychographed letters. In the first letter, there were 16 items of verifiable information, including three first names ("Sueli," "Jair," and "Elvira"), one surname ("grandpa Basso"), and one date ("Sunday"—in reference to the day of J.P.'s death). It also included a detailed description of the circumstances of J.P.'s death (being with friends, resuscitation procedures, the absence of the use of alcohol and drugs), and references to past activities of the deceased (studying, teaching classes, and being fond of kissing). All information was confirmed to be correct and accurate.

Out of the set of 13 letters, we identified 99 items of verifiable information; 98% of these items were rated as a "Clear and Precise Fit," and no item was rated as "No Fit." Given the circumstances, ordinary explanations for accuracy of the information were only remotely plausible. There were some pieces of information that were unknown by the relatives present at the sessions, so their accuracy was able to be checked only later, after some search (e.g. the death of a distant aunt, and some "drop in" communications—situations where allegedly a deceased personality, unknown to the medium or sitters, communicates via the medium without the request of relatives or friends). In addition, the letters expressed several of J.P.'s personality traits (e.g. his use of slang, humor, puns, and particular colloquial expressions). As a whole, these results seem to provide empirical support for non-reductionist theories of consciousness (Rocha et al., 2014).

Our group also performed a functional neuroimaging study with SPECT (single photon emission computed tomography) with 10 mediums. We compared writing complexity of the produced texts and brain activation patterns during "psychography" (trance writing) and control writing (non-trance, regular writing). Experienced mediums produced texts during psychography with higher complexity scores than during control writing. However, despite this more complex writing, they presented lower activation in several brain areas related to the cognitive processing and writing planning (left culmen, left hippocampus, left inferior occipital gyrus, left anterior cingulate, right superior temporal gyrus, and right precentral gyrus). These findings are consistent with mediums' reports of automatic (non-conscious) writing and their claims that an "outer source" was planning the written content (Peres et al., 2012).

It is worth noting that, throughout the last century, the vast majority of scientists who investigated mediumship in depth ended up convinced that conventional explanations (fraud and unconscious mind activity) could explain part but not all the observed data (Almeder, 1992; Beischel, 2007/2008; Bem, 2005; Braude, 2003; Eysenck & Sargent, 1993; James, 1909; Gauld, 1982; Kelly, 2010; Stevenson, 1977). Naturally, there are researchers who remain skeptical on the need of non-conventional explanations for mediumship (Lester, 2005; O'Keeffe & Wiseman, 2005).

Reincarnation

The belief in reincarnation (the rebirth of a soul in a new human body) has been widespread in many cultures and spiritual traditions (e.g. ancient Egypt and Greece, Buddhism, and Hinduism). The World Values Survey has found that about one third of the world population believe in reincarnation. In the last half-century, some scientists have performed careful investigations on thousands of children who claim to remember previous lives (Haraldsson, 2012). Although more frequent in countries where the belief in reincarnation is more prevalent, these cases have also been found and studied in Europe (Stevenson, 2003) and the Americas (Andrade, 1988; Stevenson, 1983). Most cases of children who claim to remember previous lives do not provide challenging evidence requiring non-conventional explanations. However, there is a substantial body of cases where children have reported alleged memories about a claimed previous life that have been verified as accurate. In some cases, not only the factual information are compatible with a deceased unknown to the children and his/her family, but also habits, likes, dislikes, skills, and even phobias and birthmarks compatible with the mode of death (Haraldsson, 2012; Mills et al., 1994; Schouten & Stevenson, 1998; Stevenson, 2000; Tucker, 2008).

These cases of types of reincarnation have implications for the possibility of the persistence of personality after brain death, which has obvious implications for the mind-brain problem (Haraldsson, 2012; Stevenson, 2000). Based on this, it would be worth expanding the exploration of this sort of SE.

Conclusion

The recent trend of scientifically investigating SEs has already produced interesting and thought-provoking findings that deserve careful further exploration. Scientific studies on SEs have produced a large and diversified amount of empirical data directly relevant to the mind-brain problem. Specifically, SEs are hard to accommodate in strictly materialist accounts of human nature and the universe, suggesting consciousness is a fundamental aspect of nature.

References

Almeder, R. (1992). *Death and personal survival: the evidence for life after death.* Lanham: Rowman and Littlefield.

Almeida, A. M., & Lotufo Neto, F. (2004). A mediunidade vista por alguns pioneiros da área da saúde mental (Mediumship as seen by some pioneers in the area of mental health). *Revista de Psiquiatria Clínica,* 31, 132–141.

Alvarado, C. S. (2012). Psychic Phenomena and the Mind-Body Problem: Historical Notes on a Neglected Conceptual Tradition, In: Moreira-Almeida, A., Santos, F.S. (Eds.), *Exploring frontiers of the mind-brain relationship.* New York: Springer, pp. 35-51.

Andrade, H. G. (1988). *Reencarnação no Brasil.* Matao: O Clarim.

Araujo, S. F. (2016). *Wundt and the Philosophical Foundations of Psychology.* New York: Springer.

Araujo, S. F. (2012). Materialism's eternal return: recurrent patterns of materialistic explanations of mental phenomena, In: A. Moreira-Almeida, F.S Santos, (Eds.), *Exploring frontiers of the mind-brain relationship.* New York: Springer, pp. 3-15.

Athappilly, G. K., Greyson, B., & Stevenson, I. (2006). Do Prevailing Societal Models Influence Reports of Near-Death Experiences? A Comparison of Accounts Reported Before and After 1975. *J Nerv Ment Dis,* 194, 218–222.

Beauregard, M. (2012). Functional Neuroimaging Studies of Emotional Self-Regulation and Spiritual Experiences, In: A. Moreira-Almeida, F.S. Santos (Eds.), *Exploring frontiers of the mind-brain relationship.* New York: Springer, pp. 113-39.

Beauregard, M., & Paquette, V. (2006). Neural correlates of a mystical experience in Carmelite nuns. *Neurosci Letters,* 405: 186-190.

Beauregard, M., Schwartz, G. E, Miller, L., Dossey, L., Moreira-Almeida, A., Schlitz, M., Sheldrake, R., & Tart, C. (2014). Manifesto for a postmaterialist science. *Explore,* 10(5), 272-4.

Beischel, J. (2007/2008). Contemporary methods used in laboratory-based mediumship research. *Journal of Parapsychology,* 71, 37–68.

Beischel, J., & Schwartz, G. E. (2007). Anomalous information reception by research mediums demonstrated using a novel triple-blind protocol. *EXPLORE: The Journal of Science & Healing,* 3, 23–27.

Bem, D. J. (2005). Review of the afterlife experiments. *Journal of Parapsychology,* 69, 173–183.

Bennett, M. R., & Hacker, P. M. S. (2003). *Philosophical foundations of neuroscience.* Malden: Blackwell.

Bourguignon, E. (1976). *Possession.* San Francisco: Chandler and Sharp.

Braude, S.E. (2003). *Immortal remains: The evidence for life after death.* Lanham: Rowman and Littlefield.

Cardeña, E., Lynn, S. J., & Krippner, S. (2000). *Varieties of anomalous experience: Examining the scientific evidence.* Washington: American Psychological Association.

Chalmers, D. J. (2003). Consciousness and its Place in Nature. In: S. Stich and F. Warfield (Eds.), *Blackwell Guide to Philosophy of Mind.* Blackwell.

Chibeni, S .S., & Moreira-Almeida, A. (2007). Remarks on the scientific exploration of "anomalous" psychiatric phenomena. *Revista de Psiquiatria Clínica,* 34 (supl.1), 8-15.

Crabtree, A. (1993). *From Mesmer to Freud: Magnetic sleep and the roots of psychological healing.* New Haven, CT: Yale University Press.

Daher, J. C. Jr., Damiano, R. F., Lucchetti, A. L., Moreira-Almeida, A., & Lucchetti, G. (2017). Research on Experiences Related to the Possibility of Consciousness Beyond the Brain: A Bibliometric Analysis of Global Scientific Output. *J Nerv Ment Dis.,* 205 (1), 37-47.

Edwards, J., Peres, J., Monti, D. A., & Newberg, A. (2012). Neurobiological Correlates of Meditation and Mindfulness, In: A. Moreira-Almeida, F.S. Santos (Eds.), *Exploring frontiers of the mind-brain relationship.* New York: Springer, pp. 97-112.

European Values Study Group and World Values Survey Association. (2006). *European and World Values Surveys Four-Wave Integrated Data File, 1981-2004,* v.20060423. Retrieved from: URL: www.worldvalues-survey.org.

Eysenck, H. J., & Sargent, C. (1993). *Explaining the unexplained: Mysteries of the paranormal.* London: Prion.

Fenwick, P. (2012). Near-Death Experiences and the Mind-Brain Relationship, In A. Moreira-Almeida, F. S. Santos (Eds.), *Exploring frontiers of the mind-brain relationship.* New York: Springer, pp. 143-163.

Fenwick, P., Lovelace, H., & Brayne, S. (2010). Comfort for the dying: five year retrospective and one year prospective studies of end of life experiences. *Arch. Gerontol. Geriatr.,* 51, 173–179.

Gauld, A. (1982). *Mediumship and survival: A century of investigations*. London: Granada.

Greyson, B. (2003). Incidence and correlates of near-death experiences in a cardiac care unit. *General Hospital Psychiatry,* 25, 269-76.

Greyson, B. (2007). Near-death experience: clinical implications. *Rev. Psiquiatr. Clin.,* 34(suppl. 1), 116-125.

Hageman, J. J., Peres, J. F. P., Moreira-Almeida, A., Caixeta, L., Wickramasekera II, I., & Krippner, S. (2010). The Neurobiology of Trance and Mediumship in Brazil. In S. Krippner, & H. Friedman (Eds.), *Mysterious Minds: The Neurobiology of Psychics, Mediums and other Extraordinary People*. Santa Barbara, CA: Praeger (ABC-CLIO), pp. 85-111.

Haraldsson, E. (2012). Cases of the Reincarnation Type and the Mind-Brain Relationship, In A. Moreira-Almeida, F.S. Santos (Eds.), *Exploring frontiers of the mind-brain relationship*. New York: Springer, pp. 215-231.

Harrison, P. (2010). *The Cambridge companion to science and religion*. Cambridge: Cambridge University Press.

Haught, J. F. (2005). Science and scientism: the importance of a distinction. *Zygon: Journal of Religion and Science,* 40, 363–368.

Holden, J. M. (2009). Veridical perception in near-death experiences. In J. M. Holden, B. Greyson, & B. James (Eds.), *The Handbook of Near-Death Experiences*. Santa Barbara, CA: Praeger (ABC-CLIO), pp. 185–211.

Hufford, D. J. (2010). Visionary spiritual experiences in an enchanted world. *Anthropology and Humanism,* 35(2), 142-158.

James, W. (1898). Human Immortality: two supposed objections to the doctrine. In G. Murphy, & R.O. Ballou, (Eds.), *William James on psychical research*. New York: Viking Press, 1960, pp. 279-308.

James, W. (1901). Frederic Myers's service to psychology. In G. Murphy, & R.O. Ballou, (Eds.), *William James on psychical research*. New York: Viking Press, 1960, pp.213-25.

Kelly, E. F., Kelly, E. W., Crabtree, A., Gauld, A., Grosso, M., & Greyson, B. (2007). *Irreducible mind: Toward a psychology for the 21st century*. Lanham: Rowman & Littlefield.

Kelly, E. F., Crabtree, A. & Marshall, P. (2015). *Beyond physicalism: toward reconciliation of science and spirituality.*, Lanham: Rowman & Littlefield.

Kelly, E. W. (2010). Some directions for mediumship research. *J Sci Explor.*, 24, 247–282.

Kelly, E. W., & Arcangel, D. (2011). An investigation of mediums who claim to give information about deceased persons. *J Nerv Ment Dis.*, 199(1), 11-7.

Kuhn, T. (1970). *The structure of scientific revolutions (2nd ed.)*. Chicago: The University of Chicago Press.

Lakatos, I. (1970). Falsification and the methodology of scientific research programmes. In I. Lakatos and A. Musgrave (Eds.), *Criticism and the Growth of Knowledge*. Cambridge: Cambridge University Press, pp. 91-195.

Le Maléfan, P. (1999). *Folie et spiritisme: Histoire du discourse psychopathologique sur la pratique du spiritisme, ses abords et ses avatars (1850-1950)*. Paris: L'Hartmattan.

Lester, D. (2005). *Is There Life After Death? An Examination of the Empirical Evidence*. Jefferson: McFarland.

Mills, A., Haraldsson, E., & Keil, H. H. J. (1994). Replication studies of cases suggestive of reincarnation by three independent investigators. *Journal of the American Society for Psychical Research*, 88, 207-219.

Mobbs, D., & Watt, C. (2011). There is nothing paranormal about near-death experiences: how neuroscience can explain seeing bright lights, meeting the dead, or being convinced you are one of them. *Trends Cogn Sci.*, 15(10), 447-9.

Moreira-Almeida, A., & Araujo, S. F. (2015). Does the brain produce the mind? A survey of psychiatrists' opinions. *Arch Clin Psychiatry*, 42, 74-75.

Moreira-Almeida, A., & Araujo, S. F. (2017). The mind-brain problem in psychiatry: why theoretical pluralism is better than theoretical monism. *Dialogues in Philosophy, Mental and NeuroSciences*, 10, 23-25.

Moreira-Almeida, A. (2012). Research on Mediumship and the Mind-Brain Relationship, In A. Moreira-Almeida, F.S. Santos (Eds.), *Exploring frontiers of the mind-brain relationship*. New York: Springer, pp. 191-213.

Moreira-Almeida, A., Almeida, A. A. S., & Lotufo Neto, F. (2005). History of 'Spiritist madness' in Brazil. *Hist Psychiatry*, 16(1), 5-25.

Moreira-Almeida, A., & Cardena, E. (2011). Differential diagnosis between non-pathological psychotic and spiritual experiences and mental disorders: a contribution from Latin American studies to the ICD-11. *Rev Bras Psiquiatr*, 33 (suppl.1), S21-S36.

Moreira-Almeida, A., Araujo, S. F., & Cloninger, C. R. (2018). The presentation of the mind-brain problem in leading psychiatry journals. *Brazilian Journal of Psychiatry*, 40(3), 335-342.

Moreira-Almeida, A., & Koenig, H. G. (2006). Retaining the meaning of the words religiousness and spirituality: A commentary on the WHOQOL SRPB group's "A cross-cultural study of spirituality, religion, and personal beliefs as components of quality of life" (62: 6, 2005, 1486-1497). *Social Science & Medicine*, 63(4), 843-845.

Moreira-Almeida, A., & Santos, F. S. (2012). *Exploring frontiers of the mind-brain relationship*. New York: Springer.

Nagel, T. (2012). *Mind and Cosmos: Why the Materialist Neo-Darwinian Conception of Nature Is Almost Certainly False*. Oxford: Oxford University Press.

Nahm, M., & Greyson, B. (2009). Terminal lucidity in patients with chronic schizophrenia and dementia: a survey of the literature. *J Nerv Ment Dis.*, 197, 942-4.

Nahm, M., Greyson, B., Kelly, E. W., & Haraldsson, E. (2012). Terminal lucidity: A review and a case collection. *Arch Gerontol Geriatr*, 55, 138-42.

Numbers, R. L. (2009). *Galileo goes to jail and other myths about science and religion*. Boston: Harvard University Press.

O'Keeffe, C., & Wiseman, R. (2005). Testing alleged mediumship: methods and results. *British Journal of Psychology*, 96, 165-179.

Parnia, S. (2007). Do reports of consciousness during cardiac arrest hold the key to discovering the nature of consciousness? *Medical Hypotheses*, 69 (4), 933-7.

Parnia, S., Spearpoint, K., de Vos, G., Fenwick, P., Goldberg, D., Yang, J., Zhu, J., Baker, K., Killingback, H., McLean, P., Wood, M., Zafari, A.M., Dickert, N., Beisteiner, R., Sterz, F., Berger, M., Warlow, C., Bullock, S., Lovett, S., McPara, R. M., Marti-Navarette, S., Cushing, P., Wills, P., Harris, K., Sutton, J., Walmsley, A., Deakin, C. D., Little, P., Farber, M., Greyson, B., & Schoenfeld, E. R. (2014). AWARE-AWAreness during REsuscitation-a prospective study. *Resuscitation*, 85(12), 1799-805.

Parnia, S., Waller, D.G, Yeates, R., et al. (2001). A qualitative and quantitative study of the incidence, features and aetiology of near death experience in cardiac arrest survivors. *Resuscitation*, 48, 149–156.

Penfield, W. (1978). *The mystery of the mind*. Princeton: Princeton University Press.

Peres, J. F., Moreira-Almeida, A., Caixeta, L., Leao, F., & Newberg, A. (2012). Neuroimaging during trance state: a contribution to the study of dissociation. *PLoS One*, 7(11), e49360.

Popper, K. R. & Eccles, J. (1977). *The self and its brain*. Berlin: Springer Verlag.

Rocha, A.C., Paraná, D., Freire, E. S., Lotufo Neto, F., & Moreira-Almeida, A. (2014). Investigating the fit and accuracy of alleged mediumistic writing: a case study of Chico Xavier's letters. *Explore (NY)*, 10(5), 300-8.

Santos, F. S., & Fenwick, P. (2012). Death, End of Life Experiences, and Their theoretical and Clinical Implications for the Mind–Brain Relationship. In A. Moreira-Almeida, F.S. Santos (Eds.), *Exploring frontiers of the mind-brain relationship*. New York: Springer, pp. 165-189.

Schouten, S. A., & Stevenson, I. (1988). Does the socio-psychological hypothesis explain cases of the reincarnation type? *The Journal of Nervous and Mental Disease*, 186 (8), 504-506.

Sech Junior, A., de Freitas Araujo, S., & Moreira-Almeida, A. (2013). William James and psychical research: towards a radical science of mind. *Hist Psychiatry*, 24(1), 62-78.

Sleutjes, A., Moreira-Almeida, A., & Greyson, B. (2014). Almost 40 years investigating near-death experiences: an overview of mainstream scientific journals. *J Nerv Ment Dis.*, 202(11), 833-6.

Sommer, A. (2014). Psychical research in the history and philosophy of science. An introduction and review. *Stud Hist Philos Biol Biomed Sci.*, 48 Pt A, 38-45.

Stevenson, I. (1977). Research into the evidence of man's survival after death: a historical and critical survey with a summary of recent developments. *Journal of Nervous and Mental Disease*, 165 (3), 152-170.

Stevenson, I. (1983). American Children Who Claim to Remember Previous Lives. *Journal of Nervous and Mental Disease*, 171, 742–748.

Stevenson I. (2000). The phenomenon of claimed memories of previous lives: possible interpretations and importance. *Medical Hypotheses*, 54 (4), 652-659.

Stevenson, I. (2003). *European Cases of the Reincarnation Type*. Jefferson: McFarland.

Tucker, J. B. (2008). Children's reports of past-life memories: a review. *Explore (NY)*, 4(4), 244-8.

van Lommel, P. (2011). Near-death experiences: the experience of the self as real and not as an illusion. *Ann N Y Acad Sci.*, 1234, 19-28.

van Lommel, P., van Wees, R., Myers, V., & Elfferich, I. (2001). Near death experiences in survivors of cardiac arrest: A prospective study in the Netherlands. *Lancet*, 358, 2039-45.

Walach, H. (2015). *Secular spirituality: the next step towards enlightenment.* New York: Springer.

Walach, H., & Reich., K. H. (2005). Reconnecting Science and Religion: Toward Overcoming a Taboo. *Zygon: Journal of Religion and Science,* 40, 423–41.

Chapter Thirteen

Reductive materialism explains everything, except for two small clouds

Dean Radin, PhD[22]

Introduction

In April 1900, the British physicist Sir William Thompson, also known by his title, "the Right Honorable Lord Kelvin"[23], gave a lecture to the Royal Society. In it, Lord Kelvin confidently proposed that physics was so successful that it was essentially complete, except for two "small clouds" (Kelvin, 1902). The two clouds would come to be known as the "luminous ether" and the "ultraviolet catastrophe." Both referred to anomalies that did not fit the predominant view of what we now call classical physics, but both were also assumed to be problems that would be solved by tweaking existing theories.

A mere eight months later, German physicist Max Planck presented a wild idea at a meeting of the German Physical Society held in Berlin (Plank, 1901). Planck's idea resolved one of the clouds mentioned by Lord Kelvin and founded quantum theory. Einstein explained the other cloud a few years later.

This unexpected turn of events should remind us why small clouds on the horizon are worthy of close attention. Sometimes they are neatly mopped up through minor revisions of existing ideas. But sometimes they persist for decades or centuries. In such cases the solutions—when they are

---

[22] *Chief Scientist, Institute of Noetic Sciences*
[23] *Lord Kelvin was the first scientist elevated to the United Kingdom's House of Lords.*

eventually discovered—may stimulate a completely unexpected paradigm shift and usher in startlingly new concepts, technologies, and even new forms of civilization. E.g., over the course of the 20th century Lord Kelvin's two clouds transformed the Western world from the industrial age into the atomic and information ages.

Today we are faced with two more clouds, commonly known as qualia and quanta. The first cloud has been a mystery throughout history. The second arose as a consequence of Planck's wild idea. "Qualia" refers to the nature of subjective experience and "quanta" to the fact that quantum objects are exquisitely sensitive to being observed. Both clouds raise questions about the nature and role of consciousness in the physical world, and both are challenges to the scientific paradigm of reductive materialism—the assumption that everything, including mind, consists of matter and energy, and that any system, regardless of how complex (again, including mind), can be completely understood by reducing it into its elementary physical components.

Some neuroscientists insist that qualia is a non-problem because consciousness is an illusory side effect of brain processing (Churchland, 1986; Crick, 1994). Others propose that any physical system as complex as the brain will spontaneously develop conscious awareness through some as-yet unknown process (Tegmark, 2015). Some physicists believe that the quantum observer effect (in physics this is called the "quantum measurement problem") is also a non-problem, because consciousness should play no role in physics, or that it is already solved by concepts like environmental decoherence (Schlosshauer, 2007).

Like Lord Kelvin, many scientists today probably assume that these two "consciousness clouds" will eventually be completely understood in conventional terms. I believe that that sentiment is almost certainly wrong. These clouds have been around for a long time and continue to resist orthodox explanations. Instead of wispy puffs fading away in the light of existing theories, these clouds are actually thunderheads that presage a paradigmatic superstorm. They are the leading edge of a host of related clouds, each more challenging than the last (Schwartz, 2010a). This includes genius, savants, near-death experiences, mediumship, cases of reincarnation, and laboratory studies of psychic phenomena.

All of these phenomena stretch the materialist "brain equals mind" assumption to the breaking point because they suggest that the mind is not inextricably bound to the physical brain.[24] I will briefly mention some of the challenges presented by the first three categories, and then I will focus a bit more on psychic phenomena.

Genius

No one who studies the lives and works of Mozart, da Vinci, Copernicus, Shakespeare, Einstein, or Ramanujan can doubt that genius is real, if rare. Of the estimated 100 billion humans who have ever lived,[25] every now and then someone comes along whose talent is so prodigious that it literally reshapes the course of civilization.

The challenge presented by genius is to imagine how the mind, viewed solely as an aspect of brain processing, could generate world-changing mathematical theorems, breakthrough scientific ideas, hypercreative inventions, masterwork books and musical compositions, etc., apparently arising out of the blue, often unbidden, and fully formed (Schwartz, 2010b; Heilman, 2016). If such ideas arose once in a person's lifetime, perhaps we might dismiss them as a fluke. But true genius is a persistent fount of paradigm-shattering creativity, and that is not easily accommodated by current views of the mind as identical to the operations of a brain that is strictly limited to ideas it has already absorbed (Lingg & Frank, 1973; Pandey, 2001).

---

[24] *At least, not in terms of the brain as a classical physical object, which is how it is viewed in the orthodox neurosciences.*

[25] *http://www.prb.org/Publications/Articles/2002/HowManyPeopleHaveEverLivdoEarth.aspx*

Savants

Autistic savants have little to no social skills and very low IQs, and yet they display supernormal capacities of memory, musical talent, artistic talent, or lightning fast mathematical or calendar calculations (Dossey, 2012; Cowan & Frith, 2009; Welling, 1994). The Academy Award-winning 1988 movie *Rain Man* was based partially on the life of savant Kim Peek, who among other things could correctly and instantly recall every word of the estimated 12,000 books he had read. Psychiatrist Darold Treffert, discussing autistic savants, wrote that "Kim Peek possesses one of the most extraordinary memories ever recorded. Until we can explain his abilities, we cannot pretend to understand human cognition."[26]

Treffert described the case of Leslie Lemke, who "is blind, severely cognitively impaired and has cerebral palsy. Yet he played back Tchaikovsky's Piano Concerto No. 1 flawlessly after hearing it for the first time at age 14." (Treffert, 2010, p. 288) If one were to test normally healthy pianists who had not previously heard this concerto, it is safe to say that precisely none of them would be able to do this.

Treffert also described the even stranger phenomenon of what he termed "acquired savants," in which, as the result of an accident, a normal person suddenly gains savant skills. As an example, he offered the following case:

"A 54-year-old surgeon gets struck by lightning, which he survives. After several weeks of mild memory impairment, he develops an obsessive interest in classical music, which was not present pre-incident. He learns to play the piano but has a recurrent, intrusive, unrelenting tune in his head, which he subsequently transcribes into a major sonata; he now performs professionally. His medical skills remain unaffected" (Treffert, 2010, p. 330).

Then there are the completely inexplicable cases of "sudden savants." These are apparently normal people who suddenly obtain savant skills. As Treffert described:

---

[26] http://www.scientificamerican.com/article/inside-the-mind-of-a-sava-2005-12/

"A 30-year-old attorney who had been trying to learn to play the piano, suddenly, over the course of several seconds, abruptly "knows" the rules of music and plays like an accomplished musician to the absolute astonishment of himself and his friends. A similar epiphany occurs in another young man who suddenly could play guitar like a master musician with no need for formal training or lessons. He now performs professionally" (Treffert, 2010, p. 341).

One theory about autistic savants has been proposed by Allan Snyder (Gobet et al., 2014). He proposes that the brain is essentially a filter that actively reduces the "blooming, buzzing, confusion" of the external world into a few understandable concepts and objects based on one's prior experience (James, 1890, p. 462). Gaining expertise is very useful, but it also constrains what can be perceived and thought about. The brains of autistics do not have these levels of specialization (Vallortigara et al., 2008), allowing them to perceive what normal people overlook. Snyder's research has found that by inhibiting certain areas of the brain with transcranial magnetic stimulation, one can momentarily cause a normal person to demonstrate autistic-type abilities (Snyder et al., 2006).

An intriguing experiment that extended Snyder's research involved patients with frontal lobe lesions (Freedman, et al., 2003). The test investigated the effects of the patients' mental intention on remote physical systems, i.e., a psychic effect. One of the brain-damaged patients was able to demonstrate this effect, repeatedly, suggesting that the abilities of some savants may be far more challenging to the existing scientific worldview than previously supposed.

How the brains of autistic savants work is a major problem for the neurosciences, but perhaps at some point their skills would be explainable via conventional concepts. But how similar skills can arise in *acquired* savants remains a mystery. If due to brain damage, then why does every other aspect of the individual remain normal? Explaining *sudden* savants is even more challenging.

Survival

Other evidence challenging the materialistic assumption of mind-as-brain comes from studies of near-death experience (NDE), mediums, and reincarnation. In the first case, most orthodox interpretations of NDEs are explained as side effects of a failing brain (Greyson et al., 2012). Those explanations are countered by the remarkable vividness and long-lasting memories associated with NDEs, as opposed to the vague memories and dulled cognition associated with brains starved for oxygen (Greyson, 2013). In addition, NDEs can result in dramatic and positive personality changes; this is not the case for those afflicted with hallucinations caused by brain damage (Greyson, 1993). When all of the pro versus con arguments are judged, the preponderance of the evidence suggests that the NDE represents an unusual state of awareness that transcends current models of brain functioning (Khanna & Greyson, 2014).

In the case of mediums, double and triple-blind controlled experiments have shown that mediums can obtain verifiably correct information about their clients (Beischel et al., 2015; Kelly & Arcangel, 2011; Delorme et al., 2013). Such experiments are designed to eliminate all known biases and information leakage paths, including any form of direct or indirect contact between the mediums and the clients. Mediums interpret the information they receive as from coming from the deceased, which may or may not be so, but the fact that the information is correct beyond chance expectation raises a problem for brain-based explanations.

In the case of reincarnation, the challenge involves young children who report memories of previous lives, and where their stories can later be verified as correct (Stevenson, 1983). If there were just a few such cases, the evidence could be dismissed as coincidences. But the literature contains thousands of well-documented case studies conducted by investigators who were well aware of the psychological tendencies and social pressures to embellish cultural beliefs (as e.g., in India) (Tucker, 2008). If the self is identical to the brain and its memories, then how does a child obtain verifiable memories of another person, who, from all objective perspectives neither the child nor anyone else in the family could have known?

Psychic Phenomena

No one questions that geniuses and savant individuals exist, despite having no broadly accepted explanations for their talents. But they are so rare that they are easy to ignore. When it comes to evidence for survival of consciousness, there are strong disagreements over the nature of the evidence. Part of the issue is that much (not all) of the evidence for survival is based on case studies, anecdotes, or is qualitative in nature, and genuine mediums are regarded with suspicion because of con artists who present themselves as mediums, but whose only interest is taking advantage of the grieving. Thus, while there is evidence for these consciousness anomalies, the evidence tends to not carry the same degree of scientific gravitas that is provided by controlled, laboratory-based, experimental evidence.

Here is where claimed psychic phenomena like telepathy, clairvoyance, precognition, and psychokinesis are useful to study. These experiences have been frequently reported by ordinary people throughout history, across all cultures, and at all levels of educational experience. And instead of having to rely (mostly) on anecdotes, a wealth of well-controlled experimental studies can be found in the peer-reviewed scientific literature (Radin, 1997, 2006, 2013).

The accumulated evidence in favor of the existence of psychic abilities was already persuasive to many academics in the 1950s. But by the second decade of the 21st century, the weight of evidence has become overwhelming to all but the most entrenched skeptics. The topic still remains controversial in the academic world, but not because empirical data are lacking. The implications of these phenomena are so difficult to accommodate within a simplistic materialistic paradigm that many just find it easier to imagine that the evidence is flawed rather than their favored paradigm is flawed.

It is beyond the scope of this chapter to do justice to the experimental literature of psychic phenomena because it is so extensive. But to illustrate the kind of evidence that is available, we will briefly review one type of telepathy experiment.

Dean Radin

Testing for Telepathy

Telepathy is the experience of gaining an impression about another person's experience, intentions, thoughts, or emotions without the use of the ordinary senses. Spatial distance between the two parties does not appear to be a factor in telepathic experiences, although emotional distance may be.

How can we rigorously test if a claim of telepathy is genuine versus a host of mundane explanations like coincidence, illusion, confabulation, mental illness, or fraud? Say that your cousin Michelle believes she is in telepathic contact with her husband Fred. Michelle provides examples of spontaneous episodes of apparent telepathy that seem credible, and you know her well enough to accept that she is not telling tall tales. You might begin by asking Michelle to select a playing card from a deck, to mentally "send" that card to Fred, and then see if Fred guesses correctly.

This would be a good example of how *not* to conduct a telepathy experiment. Michelle is likely to pick one of her favorite cards, and given that Fred knows her well, he is more likely than not to guess what she picked. The shared memory between Michelle and Fred makes this design unacceptable.

So you add a new element—random selection of the card. Now Fred cannot guess what Michelle selected because their common memory is no longer a factor. Of course, Fred cannot be allowed to watch Michelle pick the card, because its position in the deck, or Michelle's expression as she picks it, might convey a clue.

So you separate the couple into different rooms and satisfy yourself that they can't communicate in any conventional way. Now you ask Michelle to pick a playing card by throwing a pair of dice and using the resulting number to select a card in a well-shuffled deck, and then you see if Fred guesses the card correctly. This would be a valid test, although you would have to repeat it many times to assess whether Fred's "hit rate" was beyond chance, and you would also have to be rigorous in blocking or preventing any sort of ordinary message from passing between Michelle and Fred.

This type of experimental design was used extensively for decades with playing cards and specially designed "ESP card" decks. Unfortunately, after a short while this task becomes incredibly boring. With boredom comes wandering attention, and then performance on the test quickly declines.

To get around this, you devise a new method. First you prepare 100 pools of four photos, where each photo in each pool is of a real object or scene, each having a clear theme (e.g. ocean, desert, food, animal), and where the colors, shapes, and content of the photos are as unique and different from each other as possible. Now you select one of the prepared pools at random, using a true random selection mechanism, and then you ask Fred—who, again, is strictly isolated from Michelle—to select one of the four photos in the pool, also at random.

Fred now mentally sends the contents of the photo to Michelle for a period of, say, 20 minutes. Meanwhile, Michelle is asked to relax and keep her mind open to any impressions she may gain while holding Fred in mind. Then you have a friend (who knows nothing about the target pool) show Michelle all four photos, one of which is the "target" photo that Fred was attempting to mentally send, along with the three non-chosen decoys.

Say that Michelle correctly selected the actual target. The chances would be one in four, or 25%. Is this evidence for telepathy? Possibly, but maybe it was just dumb luck. Only through many repeated tests with this couple, and other couples, could we assess whether information had been genuinely shared between the "sender" and "receiver."

So you expand the test to include many couples, eventually gathering data from thousands of sessions. In the process you develop increasingly more sophisticated controls to make absolutely sure that the participants can't cheat or introduce biases, that your research assistants can't cheat or inadvertently provide clues to the test couple, that the data are recorded properly, that the randomization procedures are adequate, that the statistical methods used to evaluate the results are simple and appropriate, and so on. All known loopholes are closed.

The above experiment is a simplified description of a popular testing method first designed in the 1970s, called the ganzfeld experiment. The word ganzfeld is German for "whole field." It refers to a mild form of unpatterned, low-level stimulation designed to quickly guide the receiver in the experiment into a pleasant, dream-like, but fully awake state, thought to enhance psychic sensitivity.

Example Session

To illustrate the kind of data that can be generated in a ganzfeld telepathy test, what follows is a description of an actual experiment conducted in our laboratory at the Institute of Noetic Sciences on September 9, 2010. We will call the participants Gail and Tom.

Before they came to the lab, a target pool was created consisting of four photos: (1) a grassy field with yellow and blue flowers; (2) a brown bird's nest containing four golden eggs; (3) the great pyramid of Cheops in Egypt; and (4) a flat asphalt road with a double yellow line going into a distant barren landscape. Each photo was placed in a separate opaque envelope, and neither Tom nor Gail knew anything about the images.

When the test session began, a research assistant escorted Gail into a solid steel, double-walled electromagnetically shielded chamber in our lab, then she carefully taped halved Ping-Pong balls over Gail's eyes, turned on a red light pointed at Gail's face, and gave headphones to Gail that were playing white noise. Gail was asked to keep her eyes open throughout the experiment. The research assistant remained in the laboratory to ensure that Gail was okay with the procedure and to let her out of the shielded room if she requested to leave. Meanwhile, I escorted Tom to another room in the building, handed him a die and asked him to toss it to select one of the four photos in the target pool. He did so. I asked Tom to spend the next 20 minutes mentally sending the target image he had selected to Gail. He was able to hear Gail's voice over a one-way radio (a baby monitor).

What follows is a verbatim transcript of everything Gail spoke aloud during the 20-minute sending period. Each new line indicates a pause, sometimes a few seconds in length and sometimes longer. Keep in mind that Gail had no idea what the target photo was; it could have been anything.

"Keep feeling like looking up at tall, I'm looking up at something tall.

Something about texture. Texture.

I feel like something has a rough texture.

Tall, very tall impression, looking up high.

Feel as if I'm walking around observing something, like when you would walk in an art gallery or in a museum and you would look at something.

Wow.

First I'm feeling like tall trees, and then I'm feeling like tall building.

And then I'm like a Yosemite kind of image of a tall rock or a tall, some kind of a very tall solid stone something.

Seeing browns and grays.

Something like a feeling of walking around, looking up and being in awe, in awe of something.

Monolithic or I don't know what the word is.

I'm getting images of Mount Rushmore, I know you're not supposed to say things. [I advised Gail to avoid naming her impressions.]

Half-dome, like just a big stone.

I sort of feel like I'm walking around in a picture, and I'm giving my hand and we're climbing up.

Or something about going up, there's....

It seems like there's also some kind of a round, tall cylinder, and...something long and gray on the right.

Water fountain.

Stone.

At first I felt very much like I was in a nature, forest type of setting...and now I'm feeling more...

Something about a, like...

A plaza."

That is her entire report. When the sending period ended, Gail was shown the four target images and was asked to select the one photo that best matched her impressions. She confidently selected the photo of the pyramid. And in fact, the target that Tom randomly selected was indeed a pyramid, so in this one test session Gail hit the target. That one hit is not very meaningful from an evidential perspective, because by pure chance Gail could have obtained a hit one in four times. But what do we see when this same type of session is run thousands of times?

Meta-analysis

A meta-analysis is a quantitative statistical method for combining the results of numerous experiments with similar aims and designs. It provides a way to analytically determine if an experiment is repeatable and what the combined results reveal. This technique has proved to be particularly useful in assessing studies in the psychological, social, and medical sciences, because effects in those domains are generally small and highly variable.

Since 1974, six meta-analyses have been performed on all known ganzfeld experiments, both published and unpublished. They include (1) Honorton (1985), who covered 28 studies published from 1974 to 1981; (2) Bem and Honorton (1994), covering 10 studies published from 1983 to 1989; (3) Milton and Wiseman (1999), 30 studies published from 1989 to 1997; (4) Storm and Ertel (2001), 11 studies published from 1982 to 1989; (5) Bem et al. (2001), nine studies published from 1997 to 1999, and (6) Storm, Tressoldi & Di Risio (2010), 20 studies published from 1997 to 2008 (Storm et al., 2010; Honorton, 1985); Milton & Wiseman, 1999; Bem and Honorton, 1994; Bem et al., 2001; Storm & Ertel, 2001).

In each of these meta-analyses, the primary measure was the percentage of correct hits. All of the meta-analyses independently showed statistically significant outcomes. This means that reliably repeatable effects were observed in these experiments by dozens of investigators around the world over four decades. Considering all known ganzfeld sessions, the overall hit rate in a total of 4,196 trials (as of 2010) was 31.5%, as compared to chance expectation of 25%. That 7% over chance may not seem impressive, but from a statistical perspective the odds against chance amount to an astounding 13 billion trillion to 1.

A common critique about this finding is the belief that some of these experiments must have failed, which led the investigators to become discouraged, so they failed to report their study. Such behavior would create a clear bias in the overall hit rate. However, critics who have studied the relevant literature in detail, and who know the investigators who have conducted these studies, agree that this "selective reporting problem" cannot eliminate the overall positive results because the number of missing experiments would be implausibly large.

If one nevertheless insisted that the results *must* be due to selective reporting, then the number of experiments needed to nullify the known results can be estimated, and in this case it conservatively works out to 2,002 studies. That is a ratio of 23 unpublished, unsuccessful studies hidden away in investigators' file drawers for each one of the known studies (Tressoldi et al., 2010).

Because the average reported ganzfeld study had 36 trials, those estimated 2,002 "missing" studies would have required 67 × 36 or 72,072 additional test sessions. To produce that many sessions would have required a determined investigator to run ganzfeld sessions 24 hours a day, seven days a week, for 36 years straight, and for not a single one of those sessions to ever be discovered by any other researcher. In addition, the combined result of all of those hidden sessions would have to average out to flat chance. It is always possible that someone with endless resources, patience, and determination might have taken on that Sisyphean task, but it does not seem very likely.

A New Framework

If the paradigm of reductive materialism does not easily accommodate the multiple challenges of consciousness, as represented by the categories mentioned above, then what paradigm would? In developing new explanatory frameworks, it is important to ensure that we do not blithely throw away previous theories. The new paradigm has to include what is already known to work very well within the old paradigm; otherwise there is little reason to adopt it. Indeed, academics often express the fear that a new paradigm will require them to throw away all of the textbooks that they relied upon for so long. Not surprisingly, there is strong resistance to throwing away knowledge that formed the basis of one's career. So we need a framework that does not enflame that fear.

With that in mind, we need a structure of knowledge that does little to no violence to reductive materialism, and yet does allow for, and even predicts, the various consciousness anomalies. I believe there is such a structure, and surprisingly it only requires an adjustment to a single assumption—from consciousness as an epiphenomenon of brain activity to fundamental.

To illustrate why this relatively simple shift in assumption is compatible with the existing scientific paradigm, imagine knowledge as a pyramid. The bottom layer of the pyramid is, in accordance with a materialistic doctrine, physics. Above that is chemistry, then biology, neuroscience, and psychology at the top. Somewhere in the upper tier of this pyramid conscious awareness is said to magically appear. Reductive materialism assumes that phenomena that naturally fall within each layer of the pyramid permeate all layers above it, but often by being absorbed into and emerging into new forms. Thus, electrons are of central importance in physics, but they also exist in new, more complex structures in chemistry, biology, neuroscience, and so on. Within this paradigm, understanding how conscious awareness can be anything other than brain activity is nearly impossible.

While quantum physics, which is located at the very bottom of the physics layer, allows for nonlocal connections and events that take place outside of spacetime, that that layer is relevant to brain processing is currently a highly contentious idea. As quantum biology matures, perhaps processes that support a "quantum brain" will be found, and that will open a crack toward the idea of nonlocal forms of consciousness. In turn, nonlocal consciousness will lessen the anomalous status of the consciousness clouds.

But a quantum brain still has a problem: it fails to account for qualia. This is why an increasing number of scientists and scholars are beginning to embrace ideas like panpsychism, neutral monism, or idealism. Within those frameworks, conscious awareness does not arise or emerge from lower levels; it just *is*.

And in that spirit, imagine our existing knowledge pyramid placed on a new bottom layer. Let us call that layer *awareness*. This is imagined to be a primordial "substance" that is prior to—i.e. it transcends—spacetime, energy and matter. Physics as we know it, including quantum physics, emerges from this awareness layer, so the power of reductionist explanations remains intact. And just as electrons permeate all layers above physics, consciousness would permeate all levels about itself. From this perspective, genius, savants, and survival and psychic phenomena all begin to make sense because the one feature they all share is a means by which consciousness transcends spacetime. The way that consciousness manifests at each layer in the pyramid differs depending on how it is included in ever-increasing complexity and structures, just like electrons. But its essential nature—awareness unbound by spacetime constraints—remains.

An important feature of this revised knowledge pyramid is that all existing scientific disciplines remain intact. There is no need to throw away any textbooks because within each layer all previously vetted information is still completely valid. We have a new underlying metaphysical assumption upon which everything sits, but for most practical purposes existing disciplinary knowledge will not need to radically change. Indeed, the primary change would be the accommodation of effects that are otherwise excluded because of the assumption that physics, rather than awareness, is the foundation on which science rests.

This model is compatible with all mystical and esoteric traditions (Huxley, 1972). It provides a path for bridging science and spirituality. And there are already possible ways to transition from something "below" or more abstract than physics into known physics. Examples include G. Spencer Brown's book *Laws of Form* (Spencer-Brown, 1972; Blarke & Hansen, 2009) and the burgeoning domain of information physics (Wheeler, 1990; Mezard & Montanari, 2009).

When a new consciousness-based paradigm will be embraced is too soon to say. But whether it will arise seems increasingly certain.

References

Bem, D. J. & Honorton, C. (1994). Does psi exist? Replicable evidence for an anomalous process of information transfer. *Psychological Bulletin*, 115, 4-18.

Bem, D. J., Palmer J., & Broughton, R. S. (2001). Updating the ganzfeld database: A victim of its own success? *Journal of Parapsychology*, 65, 207-218.

Beischel, J., Boccuzzi, M., Biuso, M., & Rock, A. J. (2015). Anomalous information reception by research mediums under blinded conditions II: Replication and extension. *Explore (NY)*, 11 (2), 136-142.

Churchland, P. S. (1986). *Neurophilosophy: Toward a unified science of the mind-brain.* Cambridge, MA: MIT Press.

Clarke, B., &. Hansen, M. B. N. (2009). *Emergence and embodiment: new essays on second-order systems theory.* Durham: Duke University Press.

Cowan, R. & Frith, C. (2009). Do calendrical savants use calculation to answer date questions? A functional magnetic resonance imaging study. *Philos Trans R Soc Lond B Biol Sci*, 364 (1522), 1417-1424.

Crick, F. (1994) *The astonishing hypothesis: the scientific search for the soul New York*, NY: Touchstone.

Delorme, A. Beischel, J., Michel, L., Boccuzzi, M., Radin, D., & Mills, P. J. (2013). Electrocortical activity associated with subjective communication with the deceased. *Frontiers in Psychology*, 4, 834.

Dossey, L. (2012). Fractals and the mind. *Explore (NY)* 8 (4), 213-217.

Freedman, M., Jeffers, S., Saeger, K., Binns, M., & Black, S. (2003). Effects of frontal lobe lesions on intentionality and random physical phenomena. *Journal of Scientific Exploration*, 17 (4), 651-668.

Gobet, F., Snyder, A., Bossomaier, T. &. Harre, M. (2014). Designing a "better" brain: insights from experts and savants. *Frontiers in Psychology*, 5, 470.

Greyson, B., Holden, J. M. & van Lommel, P. (2012). There is nothing paranormal about near- death experiences. *Trends in Cognitive Science*, 16 (9), 445; author reply 446.

Greyson, B. (2013). Greyson, B. (2013). Getting comfortable with near death experiences: An overview of near-death experiences. *Missouri Med*, 110 (6), 475-481.

Greyson, B. (1993). Varieties of near-death experience. *Psychiatry*, 56 (4), 390-399.

Heilman, K. M. (2016). Jews, creativity and the genius of disobedience. *J Relig Health*, 55, pages341-349.

Honorton, C. (1985). Meta-analysis of psi ganzfeld research: A response to Hyman. *Journal of Parapsychology*, 49, 51-92.

Huxley, A. (1972). *The perennial philosophy*. Freeport, N.Y.: Books for Libraries Press.

James, W. (1890). *The principles of psychology*. New York City: Henry Holt and Company.

Kelly, E. W., & Arcangel, D. (2011). An investigation of mediums who claim to give information about deceased persons. *J Nerv Ment Dis*, 199 (1), 11-17.

Khanna, S. & Greyson, B. (2014). Near-death experiences and spiritual well-being. *J Relig Health*, 53 (6), 1605-1615.

Kelvin, R.H.L. (1902). *Nineteenth century clouds over the dynamical theory of heat and light*. London: William Clowes and Sons, Limited.

Lingg, A. M. & Frank, H. (1973). *Mozart, genius of harmony*. Port Washington, N.Y: Kennikat Press.

Mezard, M. & Montanari, A. (2009). *Information, physics, and computation*. Oxford: Oxford University Press.

Milton, J. & Wiseman, R. (1999). Does Psi exist? Lack of replication of an anomalous process of information transfer. *Psychological Bulletin*, 125, 387-391.

Pandey, S. N. (2001). *Millennium perspectives on A.K. Ramanujan.* New Delhi: Atlantic Publishers & Distributors.

Planck, M. (1901). On the law of distribution of energy in the normal spectrum *Annalen der Physik*, 4, 553

Radin, D. I. (1997). *The conscious universe.* San Francisco, CA: HarperOne.

Radin, D., (2006). *Entangled minds.* New York: Simon & Schuster.

Radin, D. I. (2013). *Supernormal.* New York: Random House.

Schlosshauer, M. A. (2007). *Decoherence and the quantum-to-classical transition.* Berlin: Springer.

Schwartz, S. (2010). Nonlocality and exceptional experiences: a study of genius, religious epiphany, and the psychic. *Explore*, 6, 227-236.

Snyder, A., Bahramali, H., Hawker, T., & Mitchell, D. J. (2006). Savant-like numerosity skills revealed in normal people by magnetic pulses. *Perception*, 35 (6), 837-845.

Spencer-Brown, G. (1972). *Laws of form, 1st American ed.* New York: Julian Press.

Stevenson, I. (1983). American children who claim to remember previous lives. *J Nerv Ment Dis*, 171 (12), 742-748.

Storm, L., & Ertel, S. (2001). Does psi exist? Comments on Milton and Wiseman's (1999) meta-analysis of Ganzfield research. *Psychological Bulletin*, 127, 424-433.

Storm, L., Tressoldi, P. E. & Di Risio, L. (2010). Meta-analysis of free-response studies, 1992–2008: Assessing the noise reduction model in parapsychology. *Psychological Bulletin*, 136 (4), 471-485.

Tegmark, M. (2015). Consciousness as a State of Matter. arXiv:1401.1219 **[quant-ph].** arXiv.org

Treffert, D. A. (2010). *Islands of genius: The bountiful mind of the autistic, acquired, and sudden savant.* Jessica Kingsley Publishers.

Tressoldi, P. E., Storm, L. & Radin, D. (2010). Extrasensory perception and quantum models of cognition. *NeuroQuantology,* 8 (4, Supplement 1), S81-87.

Tucker, J. B., (2008). Children's reports of past-life memories: a review. *Explore (NY),* 4 (4), 244-248.

Welling, H. (1994). Prime number identification in idiots savants: Can they calculate them? *J Autism Dev Disord,* 24 (2), 199-207.

Wheeler, J. A. (1990). Information, physics, quantum : the search for links. In: Zurek, W. H., Ed., *Complexity, Entropy, and the Physics of Information,* Redwood City: Addison-Wesley, 354-368.

Vallortigara, G., Snyder, A., Kaplan, G., Bateson, P.,. Clayton, N. S. & Rogers, L. J. (2008). Are animals autistic savants? *PLoS Biol,* 6 (2), e42.

Chapter Fourteen

Reincarnation - Any Evidence For It?

Erlendur Haraldsson, PhD

Introduction

Belief in reincarnation is widespread around the globe, and not only in countries dominated by Buddhism and Hinduism where the belief in reincarnation is a part of the religious dogma. The belief is also substantial in the Christian countries of Europe and the Americas.

The European Values Survey conducted in most countries of Europe in 2006-2007 contained two questions concerning the possibility of an afterlife: "Do you believe in Life after Death?" and "Do you believe in Reincarnation, that is that we are born into this world again?" The data revealed that 44.3% of Europeans believe in life after death and 41.2% do not. 21% believe in reincarnation and 65.3% do not. Particularly interesting is the finding that of those who believe in life after death, 47% believe in reincarnation. That is almost half of those who belief in an afterlife. In short, reincarnation is a major concept among Europeans concerning a potential life after death. In the Americas we find an even greater belief, particularly in South America.

Beliefs are one thing; the factuality of reincarnation is another. Why is the reincarnation belief so persistent? Is there any trace of evidence for it?

In many countries we can find children who claim to remember episodes from a past life. If these alleged memories are specific enough and can be verified, they may prove highly relevant for the question of the mind-brain relationship. They may indicate that memory is not only stored in the brain and that mind can exist without a brain and still retain some of its memories. These possibilities are contrary to what is presently known about memory and its dependence on brain functioning.

Half a century ago Professor Ian Stevenson of the University of Virginia conducted the first studies of "cases of the reincarnation type" (Stevenson, 1997, 2001). Since then, over 2,500 cases have been recorded and investigated worldwide. In the 1980s Stevenson invited the author to make an independent study of some cases. Would he find comparable features as Stevenson?

In the following years the author investigated over 60 cases in Sri Lanka (Haraldsson, 1991, 2000a, 2000b), mostly found in Buddhist families and a few among Christians and Muslims, and 30 cases in Lebanon that were found within the Druze community where belief in reincarnation is widespread (Haraldsson & Abu-Izzeddin, 2002, 2004). A few cases were investigated in other countries. The author has published several detailed accounts of individual cases which can be downloaded from his homepage.[27]

The content of these alleged memories (for brevity's sake, from now on referred to as memories only) varied widely; most children spoke of how they died violently through accidents, murder, or acts of war. They spoke of events that lead to their death, of people they knew, and where they had lived. They spoke of events occurring in or near the area where they had lived. Many suffered from phobias which they associated with the mode of death in the previous life.

Most children start to speak of a past life as soon as they can speak, around the age of two and a half. The number of statements they make varies and are on average around 20. Most of them stop talking about their past life around the time they go to school. Often they want to find their previous home, and sometimes tell where it is. They often say that their present mother is not their real mother. Occasionally they reveal knowledge or skills that they were not known to have learnt. Some have birthmarks or deformities that they relate to their mode of death in the previous life. Psychological studies show characteristics that reveal a post-

---

[27] *https://notendur.hi.is/~erlendur/english/*.

traumatic stress disorder (PTSD), but not in every child (Haraldsson, 2003). A likely explanation for the PTSD are the memories of a violent death which preoccupies up to 75% of these children in early childhood.

How Cases are Investigated

The principal method of inquiry is to interview firsthand witnesses to the child's statements about the previous life, such as parents, siblings, relatives, and playmates, as well as the child. This is to ascertain what statements the child has made and how consistently, on several occasions. The second step is to rule out that the child is talking about events that s/he has learned about from his/her environment. If that is not the case and there is reasonable consensus about the statements, then the case is considered worthy of further investigation. It is important to interview the principal witnesses again after some time to test the reliability of their testimony.

The next question is, can a deceased person be traced whose life events correspond to the statements made by the child? Often a person has already been found who it is believed the child is referring to. It has to be checked to determine if such a correspondence does in fact exist. The family of that person is interviewed and relevant documents obtained, such as birth and death certificates, post-mortem reports, etc., as the case may be. As examples of cases of children with past-life memories, a review of three cases follows.

The Case of Thusita Silva

This case is particularly interesting because the girl's statements were recorded by us before any person was found whose life events corresponded to the events that the girl had been talking about. We met Thusita Silva (pseudonym) in 1991 when she was eight years old and lived in poor conditions near the town of Panadura, Sri Lanka which is south of Colombo. Thusita had been talking about her previous life in Akuressa (a city with a population of about 20,000) for a while when her much older brother went there to check on her story. He failed to verify it and scolded the girl. No further attempts were made to solve the case. A few years later we learned about the case and interviewed the girl, her mother, and her grandmother. By this time she had forgotten some of her earlier memories.

Table 1. Thusita Silva's statements about her previous life. The statements that fit the life of Chandra Nanayakkara are marked with +, those that do not fit with −, and indeterminate statements with ?		
1.	I lived in Akuressa	+
5.	My father's name was Jeedin	−
6.	(my father's name was) Nanayakkara	+
7.	River or stream a little distance away	+
8.	The hanging bridge (wel palama) broke down	+
9.	I fell into the river	+
10.	I drowned	+
11.	I was pregnant when drowned	+
12.	I had a husband	+
13.	Our house was larger than present house	+
14.	Walls were coloured	+
15.	I had a sister's daughter	−
16.	My former father was called appa (present father dada)	?
17.	I had a bicycle	+
18.	Bicycle was yellow	−
19.	I went to work by bicycle	−
20.	I rode the bicycle alone	+
21.	I worked in a hospital	−
22.	I wore a white uniform in hospital with cap and shoes	−
23.	Hospital was some distance from home	+
24.	Mother wore frocks	?
25.	Mother had a sewing machine	+
26.	I had two striped frocks	?
Items reported to T. J. but not E. H.		
27.	Big gate at former house	+
28.	My husband jumped into the river to save me	+
29.	My husband was a postman	−
30.	We had a car	+
31.	I had a brassiere	?
17 correct statements (+), 7 incorrect statements (-), 4 indeterminate (?).		

According to her mother and grandmother she had at the age of two and a half claimed: "I am from Akuressa, my father's name is Jeedin

Nanayakkara." She had lived near a river, and when crossing a narrow footbridge she had fallen into the river and drowned, pregnant at the time. She had a husband and the house she had lived in was larger than the present house. For full list of her statements see Table 1.

In Akuressa we found a Nanayakkara family that lived near a hanging bridge for pedestrians. They told us that their daughter-in-law had been crossing the bridge in 1973 when she fell off the bridge and drowned. Her husband was with her. He jumped into the river to save her but almost drowned himself. In the coroner's office there was a file on the case. Chandra Nanayakkara (born Abeygunasekera) had died in December 1973 "by choking after swallowing water when the deceased fell into the River Nilwala from the suspension bridge." She had been 27 years of age and seven months pregnant, and was with her husband when the accident occurred.

Seventeen of Thusita's 28 statements fit the life of Chandra Nanayakkara; seven were incorrect and four indeterminate. All of Thusita's statements relating to the mode of death fit, namely, the hanging bridge, falling into the river, that she was pregnant, and that her husband was with her. The name of her father was not Jeedin Nanayakkara, but her father-in-law was Edwin Nanayakkara. Women in Sri Lanka often refer to their father-in-law as father. The incorrect statements were about the color of her bicycle, that she had worked in a hospital (her best friend did) and that her husband was a postman (his brother was). Other statements were too general to be of much value (Mills, Haraldsson & Keil, 1994).

Thusita's family claimed to have no connection of any kind with Akuressa and none of them had been there when Thusita spoke most about her previous life. Akuressa is about 50km away from Thusita's birthplace in Elpitiya. She and her family had moved to Panadura when we met her.

Cases like Thusita's in which the child's statements were recorded before any previous person has been identified are of particularly great importance. We can then be sure that the child's statements are uncontaminated. Further recent cases of this kind are the cases of Chatura Karunaratne (Haraldsson, 2000b), Dilukshi Nissanka (Haraldsson, 1991), and a case investigated by Keil and Tucker (2005).

The Case of Pretiba Gunawardana

Pretiba Gunawardana, a strongly built and healthy looking boy, was four years old when we met him and his mother in 1989 at their home in one of the suburbs of Colombo. It was only after we convinced Pretiba's mother that we would not publicize the case in Sri Lanka that she was willing to talk to us.

Pretiba made his first statements about a previous life when he was a little over two years old. He had then suffered high fever for a week. After that he frequently spoke about his memories. He spoke to us without hesitation and insisted that his memories were from a previous life.

Pretiba stated that he had lived in Kandy (using the Sinhalese name, Maha Nuwara), the main city of central Sri Lanka. He said his former name was Santha Megahathenne, and that he had lived at number 28 Pilagoda Road. His car had caught fire, he had been burnt on his right leg, hand, and mouth, had been taken to a hospital and then he "came here" (died). His mother told us that he often mentioned two names: an older brother Samantha and an older sister Seetha. According to his father, later Pretiba often said that he wanted to see them. He talked more about names than events. His statements are listed in Table 1. Pretiba had no unusual behavioral traits that seemed related to his statements.

Table 2. Statements made by Pretiba Gunawardana about his previous life.
1. Often mentions Samantha aya (elder brother).
32. Often mentions Seetha akka (elder sister).
33. Elder sister was married.
34. Mentions Look aya and Look akka (big/elder).
35. Mentioned Dhamman Sadhu, a relative of father's brother.
36. They had a car and a bus.
37. This car had been burned (with much smoke) with him in it.
38. Right hand, leg, and mouth had been burned.
39. Admitted to Nuwara hospital, plaster placed on his body.
40. After that he came to this place (died and was born here).
41. He had been to India and to a Hindu temple (kovil).
42. He had a passport.
43. Mentioned name of Natapati (Nathapathi), visited Natapati Devalaya (kovil) while in India.
44. Brought from India some items for his mother (saris and buttons).
45. He lived at number 28 Pilagoda Road in Nuwara (Kandy).
46. He lived upstairs in a house.
47. His father was old.
48. His father had a car.
49. His father wore eyeglasses.
50. Father had gone abroad and returned.
51. Mentions a fight between snake and katussa.
52. He had a girlfriend but did not like to marry that girl.
53. They had a house with land around it.
54. He had an uncle.
55. They had paddy fields.
56. Balansena worked in the paddyfields.
57. There was a temple near the house.
58. Artworks of elephants at the temple.

We asked him if he would like to go to Kandy. He was quick to answer yes. He claimed he could find his house, but when we asked him if he knew its whereabouts, he replied with no. His father had not been willing to search for the previous personality, and the mother shared the common fear of mothers of such children that she might lose her child to the previous family if that family was found. Pretiba said he also wanted to go to Kandy to collect his things.

The postal authorities told us that there was no Pilagoda Road in Kandy city, nor any village or area by that name in the Kandy district. Inquiries about the name Megahathenne revealed a village by the name of Megahathenne some 15 miles away from Kandy. Inquiries there yielded no information about any person having the characteristics described by Pretiba. No Pilagoda Road was found in that village, and the surname Megahathenne was not found in the 1975 telephone directory for Kandy.

The Parents Accepted Our Request to Take the Boy to Kandy.

A few hours' drive up the scenic road leads through many villages and towns. As we were approaching the bridge over the Mahaveli River at the other side of which is Kandy city, and were driving through a busy street, the boy became quite animated. He spontaneously said, "There is Maha Nuwara," (the Sinhalese name for Kandy) and as we crossed the bridge (one of a few on the way) over the Mahaveli river, he correctly remarked, "This is Mahaveli Ganga" (ganga meaning river). None of us had mentioned this name or indicated that we were about to enter Kandy city. Apart from this, there was no response or comment from Pretiba to indicate any recognition or knowledge of the area. Pretiba could not tell us how to find his old home and expressed no wish to see a particular spot, although he enjoyed the journey and drive around Kandy.

We made enquiries in Kandy and Megahathenne but failed to trace a person that fit Pretiba's statements. It was impossible for us to go through the thousands of admissions every year to the Kandy hospital in the hopes of finding the name of Santha Megahathenne.

Without revealing the boy's identity, the main features of the case were publicized with the parents' permission in an interview with the author on December 11, 1990 in the widely circulated Singalese newspaper *Dinamina* and its English edition *Daily News*. No response came from readers. Despite considerable efforts, no person was found corresponding to Pretiba's statements. His case remained unsolved like so many other cases.

The Case of Wael Kiwan

This case is from Lebanon (Haraldsson & Abu-Izzeddin, 2004). It has some of the common weaknesses found in these cases, but also contains some highly specific statements made by the subject that enabled us to identify a deceased person whose life events closely resembled those that the boy had described.

Wael Kiwan was a healthy and mature boy when we met him in his village some 70 km east of Beirut. His parents reported that at a young age he started to say that his name was Rabih, that he had been a grown-up person, had other parents in Beirut, and wanted to find them. There were further statements: "There was a house with a red brick roof," and "he lived in the Jal al Bahr section of Beirut (that is by the sea) and near a house of Allah Wa Akbar [i. e., a mosque]. He spoke much about the sea and a boat. He would draw a wheel of a boat on paper and say: "I used to stand" and he did a circular movement of his hands to show how he had moved the steering wheel. He said that they had a balcony, from which he used to jump to the street. He made the highly specific statement that he had two homes, one in Beirut, and another one to which he had to travel by airplane.

Wael said to his mother like some children do who speak of a previous life: "My [previous] mother is prettier than you." He often repeated the story about his death; it was sunset, he saw people coming towards him, and they shot him. Wael would also tell him: "If you find it, don't tell them that Rabih has died, because they will cry." In Table 4 are listed the statements that he, according to his parents, made before they started to seriously look for a deceased person that fit his account.

Expanding Science

Wael did not recall his family name, so one day his father, mother, and children sat down with him and mentioned many family names in the hopes that he might recognize one of them. When the name Assaf came up, he said that was his previous family name. Assaf is a rather common name and is carried by Druze, Christians, and Muslims alike.

Wael frequently asked his father to try to find his previous home when he went to Beirut on business. He would get upset when his father returned and had not even tried. Finally, his father told a Druze friend in Beirut, Sami Zhairi, what Wael was saying and he promised to ask around. He learned that there had been a Rabih Assaf living close to the sea in the Jal-al-Bahr district whose life seemed to fit Wael's statements.

Finally Wael's father took him to Beirut. Accompanied by Sami Zhairi they went to the house in the Jal-al-Bahr section. Wael ran into the house ahead of the group, into the apartment on the ground floor, where he saw a picture on the wall and said, "This is my picture." It was a picture of Rabih Assaf. In the apartment was Raja Assaf, the brother of the deceased Rabih (their mother, Munira, was not at home). Raja brought out a photo album and asked Wael to identify people. According to Wael's father he recognized Rabih's father, sister, and a paternal aunt. When they left the house and were driving back home, Wael told his father that he was relaxed now that he had found his previous home. Occasional visits followed and the families kept in contact over the years. After meeting the Assaf family, Wael spoke less about his former life.

Rabih's mother Munira Assaf was at home when Wael came the second time. She told us that he seemed happy to be there but did not recognize her as Rabih's mother, nor his twin sister or brother. Munira did not recall that he recognized any photographs, only that he said: "Yes, yes." She took this to mean that he might know the people in the photographs.

On the first visit to the home of the Assaf family, Wael went to the backdoor and asked about the house with a red roof. Rabih had grown up seeing this house from the kitchen and backyard of the apartment. It had been torn down when Wael visited them. This more than anything else made the family believe that Wael was Rabih reborn.

Munira Assaf's apartment is on the ground floor and has a balcony from which it is easy for a boy to jump to the street. Munira Assaf verified that Rabih had often done that. Wael had repeatedly mentioned a boat. Some 30 meters down and near the end of the short street was a small harbor, now crammed between houses and a huge high-rise apartment building. Munira's husband and sons had no boat but friends, relatives, and neighbors did and Rabih used to go to sea with them. Most of the boats were rowing boats, and a few had motors and a tiller. These small boats did not have steering wheels. However, Rabih might have gotten a ride on a boat with a steering wheel. An old mosque is approximately 100 meters away from Rabih's house on the same street as the harbor, and is the only mosque in the Jal-al-Bahr area.

Wael had stated that he had two homes, one of which you had to go to with an airplane. This fits the fact that Rabih had also lived in the United States. The phrase, "I used to throw an iron to stop the boat" was only reported to us by Wael's aunt Fadia. By iron ("hadideh" in Arabic) Wael probably meant an anchor, a word unlikely to be known by someone living far from the sea.

Rabih's mother did not learn more from Wael about his life as Rabih. However, she was still convinced and accepted him, but also said: "Nothing will bring my son back."

Wael's mother told us that he had given two accounts of his death. The first was that "they" had shot him in his head. The second version was that a group of people had kicked him and hit him until he did not feel anything (hence his parents assumed that he had been killed that way).

Rabih died in South Pasadena, California in 1988. He moved from Lebanon to the USA when he was 21 years old and studied electrical engineering for two years. During the third year he wanted to return to Beirut, was unable to do so because of the civil war in Lebanon, nor did he have money to either stay in California or to return to Beirut. He was depressed, attempted suicide by swallowing pills, and was brought to a hospital and survived. Rabih moved to stay with distant relatives. On January 9, 1988 his paternal cousin, Abboud Assaf, found him dead in his garage. He had hanged himself. This was verified in a telephone interview with him, nor was he aware that a group of people had kicked him and hit him until he did not feel anything. Rabih's mother did not know of any such incident.

Table 3. Statements made by Wael Kiwan according to his parents. The statements that fit the life of Rabih are marked with +, those that do not with −, and indeterminate statements with ?	
1. My name was Rabih.	+
59. I was big (not small).	+
60. I have parents. They are not here, they are in Beirut	+
61. My house is in Beirut near the sea	+
62. My house is near the house of Allah Wa Akbar (mosque).	+
63. There is a house with red brick roof.	+
64. It was sunset and I saw people coming and they shot me.	−
65. A group of people hit me and kicked me until I did not feel anything.	−
66. I was often on a boat out at sea.	+
67. I used to stand and steer the boat with a wheel.	?
68. I would walk from my house to the sea.	+
69. My house is in Jal al Bahr.	+
70. I had two homes, one in Beirut, and one to which I go with an airplane.	+
71. We had a balcony.	+
72. I used to jump from the balcony to the street.	+
73. I used to throw an "iron" to stop the boat. (Only reported by his aunt).	?
74. My [previous] mother is prettier than you.	?
12 verified statements, 2 found incorrect and 3 indeterminate statements.	

The families of Wael and Rabih lived far apart and were complete strangers. That was one of the merits of the case. The principal weakness is that the subject's statements were not recorded until after the two families had met. 12 of the 17 statements Wael made correspond to events in the life of Rabih Assaf. Four items could neither be confirmed nor refuted. The statement that Rabih would stand in the boat holding a steering wheel may have happened, but was certainly not the rule because the small boats on which he often went to sea did not have steering wheels.

An important statement made by Wael does not fit, namely his mode of death. This is the only major discrepancy between Wael's statements and the life of Rabih. Rabih committed suicide, whereas Wael speaks of being shot. If we allow some speculation and fantasy, then the following statement by Wael may carry some significance: "If you find my family, do not tell them that Rabih has died. They will cry." Could it possibly mean that he had some guilt about his mode of death or that he did not want it to be known? In view of the hanging, an "announcing dream" of Wael's mother is also interesting, for she dreamt before Wael's birth, of a grown boy who was sweating and breathing rapidly with difficulty. Could this be related to Rabih's hanging?

Several of Wael's statements fit well with the life of Rabih: the name Rabih, the family name Assaf, that he had lived close to the sea and went to sea on a boat(s), that there was a mosque close to his home, that he would jump from his balcony to the street, had lived in two places, to one of which he had to travel by airplane, and the statement that he made when he first visited the Assaf family, namely that behind his home had been a house with a red roof. These statements are highly specific and unlikely to be due to chance.

Psychological Characteristics of Children With Past-Life Memories

Do children claiming past-life memories differ psychologically from other children? Two studies in Sri Lanka (Haraldsson, 1997; Haraldsson, Fowler & Periyannanpillai, 2000) and one in Lebanon (Haraldsson, 2003) show that they do. Stevenson noticed early on that they frequently suffered from phobias that often seemed related to their past-life memories. This observation was verified in Sri Lanka when such children were compared with peers of the same age and social background. Later this was replicated in Lebanon. Results from two items on the Child Behaviour Checklist can be seen in Table 4.

Table 4. Phobias and fears in subjects and controls in two combined studies in Sri Lanka. Results of two items in the Child Behavior Checklist.

	Subjects (n=57)	Controls (n=57)
Fear situations, places...		
Often	16	4
Sometimes	16	18
Never	21	33
Too fearful or anxious		
Often	12	2
Sometimes	14	8
Never	28	45

The Child Behavior Checklist (CBCL) and the Child Dissociation Checklist (CDC) revealed symptoms that characterize PTSD patients with an identifiable trauma, such as phobias, fears, outbursts of anger, and nightmares. In both Sri Lanka and Lebanon, significant differences in the Problem score on the CBCL and an elevated CDC score indicate that children with past-life memories are often traumatized (see Table 5). Child abuse is a potential cause, but there were no signs of abuse in their short life. Does the cause of the trauma lie in the images/memories of a past life that they report? The fact that 77% of the Lebanon sample, and 76% of the combined Sri Lanka samples, speak of experiences of a sudden violent death makes that explanation more plausible. The mean Problem score for the CBCL is higher for children speaking of violent death (47.38, n=24)[28]

---

[28] *"n" means the number of persons involved in the calculation. t-test is for statistical analyses. p means the likelihood that the results are due to chance; e. g. p=.03 indicates that the likelihood is 3 in a hundred that this result is due to chance.*

than for those who do not (36.00, n=6). A statistical t-test reveals a significant difference between the groups (t=2.43, p=.03, two-tailed) and gives weight to the PTSD argument.

Table 5. Psychological differences between subjects and controls in three studies in Sri Lanka and Lebanon

Child Beh. Checklist Problem Score	Subjects	Controls	Z-value
First Sri Lanka Study	41.33	26.77	3.73**
Second Sri Lanka Study	34.54	17.54	3.80**
Lebanon Study	45.10	27.70	3.73**
Child Dissociation Checklist			
Second Sri Lanka Study	6.59	1.69	3.80**
Lebanon Study	1.47	.23	2.61*

Correlation between CBCL and CDC is .57 (p<.001)			
First Sri Lanka Study	Mean age	9.39 years	12 boys 18 girls
Second Sri Lanka Study	--	7.83	14 boys 13 girls
Lebanon Study	--	10.62	19 boys 11 girls

These children do not confabulate more than other children, are not highly suggestible, do not live in social isolation or in disturbed family relationships, and are apparently not attention-seeking (Haraldsson 1997, 2003). They daydream or get lost in their thoughts more often than other children. Is it because they are preoccupied with their last-life images? Our data cannot answer that.

Discussion

Any explanatory theory of these cases has to account for three findings: memories that have been verified as correct in the absence of a normal explanation, psychological characteristics such as phobias and PTSD, and birthmarks that are found in some cases and fit the wounds of an alleged previous personality. Cases differ greatly and different explanations may apply for different cases.

Normal as well as transcendental/paranormal interpretations have been put forward to explain the cases. They have ranged from criticism of the way the investigations have been conducted, to failing to consider sufficiently how the cases are culturally molded. Published accounts by Stevenson are highly detailed and thorough; for example, the lengthy reports in Stevenson's four volumes on *Cases of the Reincarnation Type* (Stevenson 1975-1983). It is hard to imagine how cultural influences can cause birthmarks as they are formed in the womb before the child is born.

Another criticism concerns the possibility that the correspondence between statements of the children and events in the life of certain deceased persons may be due to chance. This is a serious criticism in view of the many cases that remain unsolved, which is up to 64% in Sri Lanka.

The chance interpretation is made doubtful for some of the most impressive cases, as they contain highly specific statements made by the child. This interpretation also runs into difficulties when applied to birthmark cases, the phobias, and the PTSD found in many children, as they are not known to have been exposed to life-threatening situations.

Could it be that these children are psychically gifted and able to zoom in on facts in the life of a person that lived before they were born? This interpretation runs into difficulty when attempting to explain the psychological aspects and the birthmark cases. And why do these children, who are not known for any particular psychic gifts, zoom back on one particular deceased person?

Then there are transcendental interpretations. Possession is sometimes mentioned, also in countries where belief in reincarnation is dominant, although the reincarnation hypothesis is more widely accepted. It seems to explain rather easily the phobias, PTSD, and the birthmark cases. There is, however, a serious stumbling block: the reincarnation hypothesis runs contrary to our present knowledge of memory's dependence on brain functioning. It is hard to see how the reincarnation concept can be accommodated within the current scientific framework without accepting mind as an independent reality.

The two opposing explanatory models seem irreconcilable without a radical change of the present scientific view. The evidence supporting the reincarnation hypothesis has been growing over the last decades. Even renowned skeptics like the astronomer Carl Sagan wrote: "At the time of writing there are three claims in the (paranormal) field, which in my opinion, deserve serious study", the third being "that young children sometimes report details of a previous life, which upon checking turn out to be accurate and which they could not have known about in any other way than reincarnation" (Sagan, 1966, p. 302).

These cases may have great implications for any theory of the mind-body relationship. The reincarnation hypothesis has to assume that mind and body are two separate entities which are only combined for a certain period of time.

References

Haraldsson, E. (1991). Children claiming past-life memories: Four cases in Sri Lanka. *Journal of Scientific Exploration*, 5, 233-262.

Haraldsson, E. (1997). Psychological comparison between ordinary children and those who claim previous-life memories. *Journal of Scientific Exploration*, 11, 323-335.

Haraldsson, E. (2000a). Birthmarks and claims of previous life memories I. The case of Purnima Ekanayake. *Journal of the Society for Psychical Research*, 64(858), 16-25.

Haraldsson, E. (2000b). Birthmarks and claims of previous life memories II. The case of Chatura Karunaratne. *Journal of the Society for Psychical Research*, 64 (859), 82-92.

Haraldsson, E. (2001). Do Some Children Remember Fragments of a Previous Life? In D. Lorimer (Ed.), *Thinking beyond the brain*. London: Floris Books, 81-94.

Haraldsson, E. (2003). Children who speak of past-life experiences: Is there a psychological explanation? *Psychology and Psychotherapy: Theory Research and Practice*, 76, 1, 55-67.

Haraldsson, E. & Abu-Izzeddin, M. (2002). Development of Certainty about the Correct Deceased Person in a Case of the Reincarnation Type: The Case of Nazih Al-Danaf. *Journal of Scientific Exploration*, 16, 363-380.

Haraldsson, E. & Abu-Izzeddin, M. (2004). Three randomly selected Lebanese cases of children who claim memories of a previous life. *Journal of the Society for Psychical Research*, 86 (875), 65-85.

Haraldsson, E., Fowler, F. & Periyannanpillai, V. (2000). Psychological Characteristics of Children Who Speak of a Previous Life: A Further Field Study in Sri Lanka. *Transcultural Psychiatry*, 37, 525-544.

Haraldsson, E. & Samararatne, G. (1999). Children who speak of memories of a previous life as a Buddhist monk: Three new cases. *Journal of the Society for Psychical Research*, 63(857), 268-291.

Mills, A., Haraldsson, E., & Keil, H. H. J. (1994). Replication studies of cases suggestive of reincarnation by three independent investigators. *Journal of the American Society for Psychical Research*, 88, 207-219.

Sagan, C. (1966). *The demon-haunted world: Science as a candle in the dark.* New York: Random House.

Stevenson, I. (1960). The evidence for survival from claimed memories of former incarnations. *Journal of the American Society for Psychical Research*, 54, 51-71, 95-117.

Stevenson, I. (1975-1983). *Cases of the reincarnation type. Vols. I-IV. Vol. I Ten cases in India (1975); Vol. II Ten cases in Sri Lanka (1977); Vol. III. Twelve cases in Lebanon and Turkey (1980); Vol. IV Twelve cases in Thailand and Burma (1983).* Charlottesville: University Press of Virginia, 1975-85.

Stevenson, I. (1997a). *Reincarnation and biology. A contribution to the etiology of birthmarks and birth defects. Volumes 1 and 2.* Westport, Connecticut: Praeger.

Stevenson, I. (1997b). *Where reincarnation and biology intersect.* Westport, Connecticut: Praeger.

Stevenson, I. (2001). *Children who remember previous lives. A question of reincarnation.* Revised edition. Jefferson, N. C.: McFarland and Co.

Stevenson, I. & Haraldsson, E. (2003). The Similarity of Features of Reincarnation Type Cases over Many Years: A Third Study. *Journal of Scientific Exploration*, 17, 2, 283-289.

Stevenson, I. & Schouten, S. (1998). Does the socio-psychological hypothesis explain cases of the reincarnation type? *Journal of Nervous and Mental Disease*, 186, 504-506.

Tucker, J. R. (2005). *Life before life.* New York: St. Martin's Press.

Chapter Fifteen

On the Psychological Need and Scientific Evidence for a Postmaterialist Expansion of Essential Science

Charles T. Tart, PhD

I have functioned in two primary roles with respect to what we are calling a postmaterialist science. One is as a transpersonal psychologist interested in the consequences of our views of reality and their effects on individuals' and cultures' lives and happiness. The other is as a parapsychologist researching the scientific evidence that shows materialism is inadequate in important ways as a complete view of the universe.

In this chapter, I will first primarily function in the first role and discuss some important but seldom recognized psychological effects that may result from having a totally materialistic worldview. This is especially likely when you think that Science – I capitalize Science here to remind us of its psychological power! – claims to have ***proven*** that a total materialism, a claim widely believed, is the most fundamental truth.

Secondly, I will briefly outline how science has actually shown that we humans sometimes manifest knowledge and actions that simply do not fit into a reductive, materialistic worldview, but point toward a reality that is often called spiritual. This latter discussion, while extremely important, is very abbreviated here due to space limitations. It is covered at length in my book *The End of Materialism: How Evidence of the Paranormal is Bringing Science and Spirit Together* (Tart, 2009).

Lest the forest be lost for the trees, my final conclusions in that book – based on my own half century of research and more than a century of research by others – are that *it is reasonable to be both scientific on the one hand and spiritually oriented in your worldview and style of living on the other hand.* A great deal of discrimination is still required in all areas of life, of course, as we have huge numbers of powerful beliefs that are false or are serious distortions of reality.

Meaning

After 50 years as a psychologist and 75 years as a human being, I'm clear that once our basic physical and social survival needs are met, we need to find *meaning* in life. There can be a lot of variation here; what provides adequate meaning for one person may not be suitable or useful for another person. But common and important sources of meaning come from "religion" or "spiritual experiences." I put those terms in quotes here to remind us that there are huge variations in definition and usage of these terms, but will not continue with the awkward quotes.

By spiritual experiences, I mean events that do not make sense in ordinary material terms, physical terms. These events may just happen to you, either for no discernible reason or perhaps as a result of intentional spiritual practices such as prayer or meditation. Such events intellectually and, usually much more importantly, emotionally convince you at a deeper level than ordinary experience and thinking that there is much more to life than just the material, and that life makes a kind of higher sense. Such noetic experiences point toward ways of living that are more important than the rewards that come from just being comfortable in our material world.

For example, persons might have a kind of "mystical experience" where they feel deeply at one with all life in the universe. They know *beyond any doubt* that the basic principle of the universe is Love, or that there is some kind of higher existence, the realm of spirit or spirits, or god-like beings or God. Such experiences can totally change a person's view of life.

These kinds of experiences were probably the basic foundation of most, if not all, religions. When I say religious in contrast to spiritual in this chapter, I mean the socially organized sets of beliefs about the spiritual and the consequent rules for living, commonly taught to and often conditioned in people as children. For humans, society, ethics, religious beliefs and rules are mixed in with all sorts of cultural beliefs, politics, and morality to stabilize the functioning of society. Usually only a few people have direct, personal spiritual experiences: for many, they just hear about the conclusions that committees of religious people have come to about what life and the spiritual mean. I focus on spirituality and spiritual experience here, not religion.

Meaning from a Scientistic/Materialist Perspective

What is "materialism" or "physicalism?" I use those two terms synonymously in this chapter. Broadly speaking, materialist or physicalist philosophy is a form of philosophical monism, a *positing* – a decision to believe, since you can't prove such an absolute - that *all* of reality can be reduced to one fundamental "substance" in nature, namely physical matter and energies. If anything happens, it happens because of a change in the state of the material world. This basic level was once understood to be the atoms of chemical elements. Now, with further reduction, it's considered to be subatomic particles and fundamental physical forces like gravity and electromagnetism.

What we think of as mental phenomena, consciousness, our inner experience, are considered to arise solely from the complex interaction of such basic physical, material objects and forces. Your understanding of the previous sentence, e.g., is, in principle, totally reducible to a specific electrochemical reaction in your brain, which is further reducible to those basic material elements and forces, and that's the end of the story. There is no more basic "reality" beyond that to understand. Meaning is not material, and therefore has no fundamental existence and is not needed for a complete explanation of reality.

Science over the last few centuries has been focused almost exclusively on the material world, with fantastic results! Scientific understandings and their technological products are an enormous force in life today. One psychological consequence of such great success is that many people, including many scientists, thus think science is inherently materialistic – although it isn't.

Meaning?

What does materialistic science seem to say about our human need for meaning?

This is seldom put so bluntly, as it can be unpleasant for most of us to think about. But let me briefly express what I understand of the widespread, ostensibly *scientific* attitude about the question of meaning directly. I hope that readers will both *think* and *feel* about this.

- Any meaning we may experience is a physically lawful outcome of our biology which, in turn, is based on lawful properties of physics and chemistry.
- Any meaning or lack of meaning, indeed any human experience, comes down to nothing but certain patterns of electrical and chemical actions in the material brain.
- As spiritual experiences have no material reality, any meaning that we attribute to spiritual experiences or religion *per se* is fantasy and nonsense.
- Change the chemistry and electrical pattern and experienced meaning changes.
- One more important conclusion is political and social, but largely implicitly adopted by many practitioners of science and so thought of as *a scientifically validated truth*. Since the way religion has developed has often resulted in a great deal of psychopathology and poor ways of dealing with life, science can also rightly say that a lot of religion and spirituality is associated with psychopathology or is indeed *inherently* psychopathological.

So if you want more meaning in life, is physics and chemistry enough? To accept a worldview where things just happened according to the laws of physics? After matter bumped into itself for a few billion years life formed (for no intentional reason), and evolution mechanically selected[29]

---

[29] *Not "selected" with any intention, of course, it just happened that certain patterns survived better than others.*

for life that could survive? And you are just the result of this meaningless process?

Indeed, spiritual experiences are not only dismissed as meaningless by many of the high social status, scientifically educated people in our society today, spiritual prayer and religious pursuits are usually further considered signs of being ignorant and a loser. This view is reflected in the widely known saying attributed to Karl Marx, "Religion is the opiate of the masses." Exploit the ignorant masses, keep them from rebelling by promising them pie in the sky after they die…

Reasons for Questioning Total Materialism

If you noticed your feelings, not just your thoughts as you read the above, you may be somewhat uncomfortable now. But surely you shouldn't ignore (what seems to be) science just because it makes you uncomfortable?

As touched on in many chapters in this volume, there are many empirical and scientific reasons for questioning a *total* materialism. I've usually been relatively intellectual about such questioning, and that's important. But as I've reminded my students at the (former) Institute of Transpersonal Psychology for years:

Every culture and every person within a culture is a "philosopher, a scientist, a theorist" in that she has a worldview, a set of more or less integrated beliefs as to what the world is like. The "world" includes the physical world, our own selves, other people, and "otherworldly" aspects of reality. Psychological science has documented in detail that your personal and cultural worldview automatically and habitually affects/constructs your thinking and perception in important ways, including what kinds of values and goals make "sense" and how you perceive things. Some actions or ideas are not even seriously thought about, e.g., as they are "obviously" impossible or undesirable. And if apparently "impossible" events happen, considerable conflict may be experienced.

But we are only partially intellectual creatures; the emotional slant of our perceptions is also extremely important, so let me focus more directly on that angle now.

Charles Tart

Practical Consequences of Our Belief Systems

Over the years, I have taught classes and led workshops for thousands of people dealing with our ultimate nature, our psychic and spiritual potentials, and the blocks to realizing such possible potentials. When opportunity allows, I try not to just lecture. I give more experiential exercises to illustrate points and have ensuing discussion periods, since I like to get feedback on whether I'm effectively communicating, or what understandings of mine could be better expressed. I've often been frustrated to see that when I've made a point about the way we limit ourselves, people say they "get it" but they only "get it" at a rather shallow, intellectual level.

They can say the right words, but they don't seem to have any appreciation for the emotional depth or power of some of our culturally imposed limitations. One result is that back in the early 1980s, I devised a group exercise that helps most people see more clearly, at a feeling level, what our materialistic and apparently scientific worldview can do to us. (I usually accompany descriptions of the exercise with a footnote: "Note that this is a learning exercise and does *not* represent the personal opinions of the author." So readers should not think the exercise represents what I actually believe or are the only ways materialistic beliefs can be interpreted or have effects.)

The exercise is an exaggeration of many aspects of psychological and scientific reality, not an accurate report on all its fine nuances. Parts of it don't connect with particular people, and, indeed, it's designed to irritate people in the service of searching for deeper truth. But for most people participating in it, it makes it clearer what our materialistic worldview often does. I call this exercise the Western Creed, although now it's pretty widespread in all modern cultures, not just in the West. I'm going to describe it in some detail so the interested reader can try it with other people as well as themselves to further explore deeper feelings associated with materialism.

For maximum potential impact from the Western Creed exercise, it's best to be part of a group – ideally in a workshop of mine that you volunteered to take – because you believed I'm an authority on these issues. Let's pretend that you are in such a workshop now.

Reading it by yourself like you're going to do here is a greatly diluted form of the exercise. But if you honestly pay attention to your emotional and bodily *feelings*, not only your thoughts while doing it, you may learn some useful things about yourself. You may not like them, but sometimes we have to become sadder in order to become wiser. And you might discover some things about yourself that you like very much. You might also want to get a group of friends together who are curious about these kinds of affairs and lead them in the exercise. The open sharing of feelings afterwards can be very illuminating...

To do the exercise, I ask everyone to give themselves permission to go along with it, to "play the game," as it were. When you play a card game, for example, you're not going to have any fun if you keep the attitude: "These are just some ink patterns on pieces of cardboard, randomized as to order and played by arbitrary rules, with no real consequences." Similarly, for the Western Creed exercise: I ask that you play the game, suspend disbelief, assume that what we're doing has truth value to it, and *not worry about intellectually analyzing it while doing it.*

Of course most of us cannot simply turn off our habits of intellectual analysis, but we can keep bringing our focus back to our body sensations and emotions, thus shifting the balance away from excessive intellectualization. I usually give people a few minutes after the recitation to think about it, and to share their experiences with me and each other. Then I announce that they may, if they wish, focus on intellectually analyzing their responses and intellectually tearing the Creed to pieces so they won't have to pay any further attention to what they felt. Or they can take some notes on what they've learned from their feelings and response.

To begin the recitation itself, I have people line up in neat, orderly rows, stand at attention, and put their right hands on their hearts. This is the way most Americans of my generation pledged allegiance to the American flag in school as children, and while I'm not sure it's that common anymore, it draws on some social conditioning. You were trained to be sincere when doing this. Choose something similar from your cultural background if dominant hand on the heart doesn't mean anything for you. Note too, that while not intended as a commentary on any Christian beliefs *per se*, the overall form of the Western Creed is based on the widespread Nicene Creed to further draw on some people's previous social conditioning. Then I read short phrases from the Western Creed aloud with a brief pause while the group repeats them. Then we sit down in silence for a couple of minutes and reflect.

You can watch a version of this on the web at: http://www.western-creed.com/Tart_ITP.html.

For solitary practice now, I suggest you stand up at attention, put your hand on your heart, hold this book in your other hand and read the Western Creed aloud, slowly and seriously. Pause a few seconds between each statement. If needed, deliberately make your voice tone serious, and play the game. Give primary attention to any emotions or other feelings that come and go in your body, as well as any spontaneous subtle variations in the tone of your voice. Again, *don't particularly think about or analyze it while doing it. You can do that later.*

If you know you're going to be distracted in the next few minutes, you might wait for an uninterrupted time. Otherwise, stand up now and begin the exercise.

THE WESTERN CREED

A Belief Exercise

I BELIEVE - in the material universe - as the only and ultimate reality - a universe controlled by fixed physical laws - and blind chance.

I AFFIRM - that the universe has no creator - no objective purpose - and no objective meaning or destiny.

I MAINTAIN - that all ideas about God or gods - enlightened beings - prophets and saviors - or other non-physical beings or forces - are superstitions and delusions. - Life and consciousness are totally identical to physical processes - and arose from chance interactions of blind physical forces. - Like the rest of life - **my** life - and **my** consciousness - have no objective purpose - meaning - or destiny.

I BELIEVE - *that all judgments, values, and moralities - whether my own or others - are subjective - arising solely from biological determinants - personal history - and chance. - Free will is an illusion. - Therefore the most rational values I can personally live by - must be based on the knowledge that **for me** - what pleases me is Good - what pains me is Bad. - Those who please me or help me avoid pain - are my friends - those who pain me or keep me from my pleasure - are my enemies. - Rationality requires that friends and enemies - be used in ways that maximize my pleasure - and minimize my pain.*

I AFFIRM - *that churches have no real use other than social support - that there are no objective sins to commit or be forgiven for - that there is no divine retribution for sin - or reward for virtue - Virtue **for me** is getting what **I** want - without being caught and punished by others.*

I MAINTAIN - *that the death of the body - is the death of the mind. - There is no afterlife - and all hope of such is nonsense.*

(Returning to instructions for Western Creed Exercise): Now sit down quietly, perhaps close your eyes, and feel any feelings and body sensations you have more closely. If you want to take some notes about them also, that's fine.

Some Reactions to the Western Creed Exercise

I'll mention a few things about typical reactions to the Western Creed exercise, and some of my personal feelings about it. But what *you* personally have noticed and felt is the primary value to draw from having participated.

About 90% of the people who do this exercise find themselves depressed.

This is usually surprising to them, as most of the self-selected people who take my classes or come to my workshops think of themselves as spiritually-oriented people, with a belief system that goes well beyond the materialistic. Yet they discover that many of these materialistic beliefs and some of their possible consequences are indeed part of their personalities, and may be causing turbulence and difficulties in their lives, especially any spiritual aspects of their lives.

A small number of people, maybe 5% or so, feel good and rather relieved after doing the Western Creed exercise. They can stop worrying about their "sins" and shortcomings and failures since they don't matter after all!

As many times as I've led the Western Creed exercise, I still tend to feel depressed after saying it aloud.

As to intellectual analysis of the structure of the Creed, I'm grossly overgeneralizing about the world view materialism could lead to in order to stimulate emotions and observations that might increase people's self-knowledge. People who might describe themselves as materialists vary a great deal on how much of the content above they accept as part of their world view and, of course, probably all of us have many inconsistencies in our personal views. Don't take the creed as some kind of scholarly analysis of consistent philosophies: *it's designed to irritate!* But try not to be intellectual while doing it, you'll miss the emotions and body feelings that may tell you something you didn't know.

Personally, I have nothing against the belief that most things we encounter in our ordinary lives are primarily or exclusively material, and that studying them with the methods of current materialistic science is necessary and very useful. I've done and continue to do a lot of that myself. *I object to the claim, both explicit and implicit, that a materialistic explanation includes everything in reality and thus allows one to automatically reject anything spiritual, without wasting time looking at it in detail.* That is scien*tistic*, not scien*tific*, and can lead in the direction of the kind of beliefs and feelings expressed in the Western Creed. *Scientism* is the term sociologists invented decades ago (Bannister, 1987; Hobbs, 1910) to describe how an apparently scientific attitude becomes rigid and starts to function like a dogmatic religion.

An important aspect of science is the search for truth or, more practically, for theories and explanations with the greatest fidelity to what can be observed, regardless of how we feel about them. There has been very little research on the profound effects various beliefs about the nature of reality can have on people's psyches and therefore their perceptions of the world, themselves, and their actions. I'm not advocating cultivating false beliefs just because they make people feel better. However, it is asking for trouble to ignore psychological consequences that theories and beliefs have, especially those with more power and prestige when thought of as scientific *facts*.

Because beliefs can affect us in ways that have little to do with reality, they are extremely important to understand. But effective belief systems should also align themselves with reality, as we best understand it, for maximum effectiveness. The fact that I personally don't think total materialism is really scientific, or that I don't *like* some of its possible consequences, is not a logical reason to question its validity. The fact that (a) it is poor quality science, scien*tism*, and (b) it is a *philosophy* overgeneralized as an absolute, and (c) it has major psychological and behavioral consequences are valid reasons to question it.

Now in my role as an investigator of parapsychological matters, something I see as a sub-discipline within transpersonal psychology, I turn to a very brief outline of the scientific findings that call for a postmaterialistic expansion of knowledge and especially call for investigation of the "spiritual." The claims of total materialism – that everything can or will be ultimately explained in terms of physical processes, and the spiritual is inherently nonsense – are simply *factually wrong*.

I regret that space limitations require me to be so brief and stick to the basics rather than share some interesting developments.

Science

What is the essence of science?

One of our primary drives as human beings is that we want to understand things, both to simply satisfy our curiosity and to be able to control them for our benefit. I've long distinguished, somewhat simplistically, four traditional ways to better understanding. The *Way of Experience* is where you have some personal, direct experience of things. The *Way of Reason* is where you logically think things through. The *Way of Authority* is where you ask questions and get answers from someone considered an authority. The

Way of Revelation takes account of the fact that sometimes we have what seem to be brilliant understandings when we are in unusual states of mind such as a dream, meditative state, or reverie.

Each of these ways can be very useful, but none of them is sufficient to be science.

We all know people who have had lots of experience in certain areas, yet don't seem to have a good understanding of things. We know authorities who have sometimes been, and often still are, extremely wrong. We know of people who indulge in brilliant reasoning that has led to ridiculous ideas. Revelations, while often extremely satisfying to those who have them, often have nothing to do with the actual nature of the world.

Basic science or – as I prefer to call it – *essential science*, is a dynamic, interacting synthesis of these various ways. I've sketched this dynamic process in Figure 1, below. You typically start out with a primary emphasis on experience, stressing careful observation of what you are interested in, and a commitment to try to improve your ability to observe that area of interest. From these observations you reason and come up with theories, explanations that organize and seem to make sense of the data you've collected.

We know that what seems to be logical completeness, though, may be rationalization or coincidence rather than any deeper truth about something. So essential science insists that *you must make logical predictions from theory that you can then go out and test* by further observation and experiment. A good theory correctly predicts things that haven't been observed before. Authority is involved in that you have colleagues who can make good observations or reason well or test your predictions, so they keep you from being stuck in your own narrow mindsets and biases.

And there is significant scientific work that starts with inspirations that come from unusual states of consciousness, but no matter how convincing and brilliant they seem, they still have to come back to what the actual data are. Does your inspired theory make sense of it? So far, so good. If it's to be a useful and proper scientific theory, does it make testable predictions which, when tested, work out?

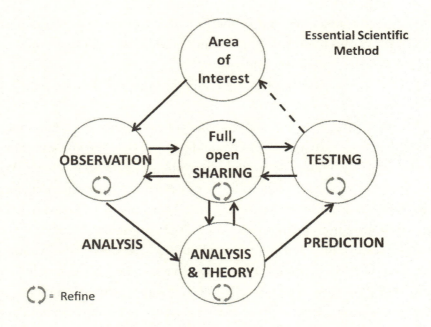

Figure 1: Process of Essential Science

The application of essential science in the last few centuries has resulted in an enormous increase in knowledge and practical technology. As Thomas Kuhn (Kuhn, 1962), noted historian of science pointed out, however, when you get a really good theory that seems to explain everything important in a field, that theory becomes a *paradigm*, a relatively automatic way of thinking about and doing all further work in that field. The positive side of a paradigm is that it makes research efficient and avoids useless lines of research. This kind of "inside the box" thinking is what Kuhn referred to as *normal science*. The negative side, though, is that this tends to lead to a neglect or actual suppression of observations and thinking which do not fit inside the box. This distorts the scientific process.

When we talk about the widely believed modern idea that science has "disproven" the spiritual, this is generally based on the fact that science has been incredibly successful about material things, while being materialistic in its approach. Since ideas about what the spiritual is, or reports of events that seem spiritual in nature don't seem to fit with that materialistic approach, they are automatically ignored or suppressed. The paradigm, largely explicit but also somewhat implicit, of almost all contemporary fields of science is materialism. But as to the automatic rejection of the spiritual, note carefully it's not as if all these spiritual ideas and apparent observations have been carefully and scientifically tested. They just become unfashionable or "impossible" and so are ignored. You might say the spiritual has been deemed "nonmaterial" and so, insofar as anyone thinks science is only about the material, the spiritual has no place in it.

I have never accepted such an unnecessary limitation on the application of essential scientific method. Elsewhere, (Tart, 1972, 1998) I have proposed expanding basic science by carrying it out in various altered states of consciousness and including experiences per se as *data*, to be observed, theorized about, and resultant theories then tested as to their consequences.

This narrowing and conceptual ossification has been a dominant trend in science in general. However, there have been a few people who applied essential science to phenomena we consider to be or are related to the spiritual, topics that do not readily fit into a materialistic framework. This field of science – originally called *psychical research*, now mostly called *parapsychology*, and expanding into the related area of *transpersonal psychology* – is miniscule in terms of people and resources compared to science as a whole. But thousands of observations and rigorous experiments now show that certain things – *psi* manifestations, for example – definitely happen that do not fit into our prevailing materialistic frameworks. Certain other apparent psychic phenomena for which the evidence is not as conclusive also may exist. We will quickly survey the basic findings.

The space limitations in this single chapter keep me from presenting any details on these phenomena, but the interested reader will find more information in my recent book *The End of Materialism: How Evidence of the Paranormal is Bringing Science and Spirit Together* (Tart, 2009). That and many other references in this volume will guide the reader to the relevant scientific literature. Be careful, however, to distinguish the scientific literature of parapsychology from the popular literature where ideas and feelings are given much more weight than actual evidence. I don't mean there's no value in popular literature, but when you're weighing evidence you generally want to give more emphasis to scientifically collected evidence than to what is mainly opinion or limited personal experience. That this popular literature vastly exceeds the small amount of scientific literature demonstrates how important these phenomena are judged to be by people in general.

Mind Does Things The Physical Brain Cannot Do: The Big Five

In reviewing the scope of observations that do not fit with a view that only what is material is ultimately real, I usually divide them into what I call the Big Five. So many high quality experimental verifications, as well as observations of them occurring in everyday life, exist that there should be no reasonable doubt about these parapsychological phenomena. People who still deny their existence are, in my judgment, either ignorant or irrationally prejudiced. I will briefly describe these five and also survey some phenomena I call the Many Maybes. These are apparent parapsychological phenomena that have had a lot less investigation, or are much more complex, so they might turn out to be artifacts or misunderstandings. All of these have enormous implications for our view of reality, and call for intense research in a postmaterialist science.

Basic Parapsychological Experiments Design

The first of the Big Five is what is conventionally called *telepathy*. Many of us have had the experience of suddenly knowing something we couldn't normally know, but turns out to be what someone else was thinking about at that moment. Years ago, for example, I sometimes came home from the university after an unexpected phone call from some old friend I hadn't heard from for many years, let's say Bob Walters, and was planning to tell my wife about it. Before I could say anything, though, she told me about something important related to her day and we talked about it for a while. Suddenly she would say something like, "I wonder whatever happened to Bob Walters; we haven't heard from him in years?"

Of course, in these so called "spontaneous" cases, it's often hard to know what's coincidence and what is not.

Paranormal phenomena are basically about things that are not supposed to be able to happen *given the supposed completeness of our knowledge about the physical world.* As such, parapsychological experiments begin by setting up a situation where we assume we thoroughly understand the physical world and then create conditions that test that knowledge.

You take some target material -- information that needs to be psychically obtained or a physical object or process that we want to be psychically influenced – and shield it from possible physical influences. This shielding can be very simple like putting the target in a locked room.

Shielding can be more elaborate, for example: put the target inside a box, lock the box inside a desk drawer, and have the desk inside a locked room. In addition, the room can be in a different building from where the *percipient,* the person who's supposed to get the information, or the agent is located.

Light rays don't pass through opaque walls, sound waves are greatly attenuated passing through walls and by the square of the distance, so they quickly get lost in the inherent noise level of the air, etc. So, insofar as our knowledge of reality is indeed complete and it's all material, there's no known material energy or substance, no way, to get the target information out of that room.

Then we have to determine what is "coincidence." If a percipient is trying to guess the order of a deck of cards, for example, as was usually the case in the classic era of parapsychological studies, then we know what chance performance is. For ordinary playing cards, for example, a percipient should get 50% correct by chance alone if guessing red or black, 25% correct if guessing suit, etc. Mathematicians long ago developed basic statistical procedures to help us decide whether a given result was unlikely enough that we don't want to just say coincidence but posit some other influence.

Then we have to provide for accuracy of observation and lack of error or bias in assessing the results of the experiment. If it's a simple matter of right or wrong on a given try, such as calling a hidden card red or black, that's a straightforward assessment. You can even have more than one experimenter independently check scoring if you like, or have automatic recording systems. If it's a complex assessment, such as a percipient trying to describe what a distant location or photograph is like, you can balance out subjective bias to a level where it doesn't matter in judging degree of resemblance.

This can be done by a series of studies with different targets and having a judge who is blind as to which description is supposed to go with which target, rate the degree of similarity, and calculate the odds of any particular pattern of ratings occurring by chance. The field of parapsychology pioneered in routinely using the best experimental methodology, double-blind methods, so that experimenters' biases wouldn't matter, and still leads most if not all fields of science in this gold-standard method for reducing/eliminating bias (Sheldrake 1999).

Telepathy

The first of the Big Five is telepathy. The simplest type of laboratory experiment uses a blindly shuffled deck of cards (at least 10 dovetail or riffle shuffles for adequate randomization) as the target material. A person acting as agent or sender looks at each card consecutively for a fixed period and tries to mentally "send" it. A percipient, sensorially isolated from the agent and target material, writes down what she thinks the card is for each trial. The degree of correspondence is later checked. Many telepathy experiments, as with the other Big Five studies, have produced significant results, far more than could be reasonably expected by coincidence alone.

Clairvoyance

The classical laboratory experiment was that a deck of cards was thoroughly shuffled without anyone looking at them. Then either the cards were laid out facedown without looking, or the shuffled deck was just put back in its box. A percipient was then asked to call or write down the order of the target deck of cards. At the time of the percipient's calls, the desired information did not exist in anyone's mind so there was no possible present-time sender. A form of ESP, clairvoyance, that could directly get information about the physical state of the world was ostensibly called for. Recently the remote viewing procedure has been the most popular (and highly successful) way to study and practically use clairvoyance (Targ & Puthoff, 1977; Tart, Puthoff, & Targ, 1979).

Many people believed that telepathy might be possible due to popular ideas about it after the discovery of electrical waves in the brain. They reasoned that telepathy operated by some kind of "mental radio," and so expected that telepathy experiments might work, but not clairvoyance. No radio waves are emitted by cards; yet, in general, clairvoyance experiments have been just as successful as telepathy ones.

Precognition

The third of the Big Five is precognition. A precognition experiment can be either telepathic or clairvoyant. Basically a percipient was asked to write down information about a designated target, for example, the order of a deck of cards, but that information had not yet been created. At a specified *future* time after the response request, an experimenter without looking shuffled a deck of cards very thoroughly a preset number of times. The order of the cards were then compared to the already recorded calls. As with telepathy and clairvoyance studies, too many experiments were statistically significant for precognition to be due to coincidence.

I personally have a difficult time with precognition, as I can't imagine how we can get information from the future, but the data say it happens. Observed data *always* take precedence over what an experimenter thinks or feels in essential science.

Collectively, telepathy, clairvoyance and precognition are referred to as forms of Extra Sensory Perception (ESP). In any particular experiment you may not know which of these psychic abilities is the operative one, so you can talk about General Extra Sensory Perception (GESP.) An experiment that is ostensibly about telepathy may show significant results, for example, because the percipient is clairvoyantly getting information about the cards rather than from the sender. Or the percipient may be precognizing the information.

If the latter idea sounds ridiculous, some of my physicist colleagues who work with parapsychology think precognition is possible, perhaps even expected, given an expanded view of the physical world allowing for quantum effects. But they view clairvoyance or telepathy as impossible since physics does not know of a mechanism for the relevant information to cross space or penetrate physical barriers. They have explained the why of this to me but, not being a physicist, I don't understand the explanation. Since this kind of theory has not led to better control of ESP, I remain interested in it but am somewhat skeptical of its usefulness.

Psychokinesis

Psychokinesis (PK) is a direct effect of wishing/willing for a particular physical outcome when there is no possible – given the assumed completeness of our understanding of the physical world – way for known physical energies to make that outcome happen. In the classic era of parapsychology, for example, many experiments involved a machine bouncing dice around in a spinning wire cage. A trap door controlled by a timer opened and the dice fell onto a table with further bouncing around. An agent at a distance from the table was told something like, "Make threes come up this time." Which die face was the designated target was systematically altered in these studies so any possible physical biases in the dice canceled out.

Cards are almost never used in ESP experiments today since states of computer-like devices are often the targets. Likewise, most PK experiments are now done with computer-like electronic devices that generate numbers at random. The agent is told something like, "Make the red light blink significantly more than the green light for the next half minute." Far too many PK experiments have been successful for the results to be due to chance.

Psychic Healing

Psychic healing refers to the effects of wishing/willing on biological processes. These might be the rate of healing of some systemic illness in a person, rate of healing of deliberately inflicted wounds in an animal, or molecular biological processes at a cellular level. Psychic healing may be a form of PK, or may be something different that deals with living rather than dead matter.

The Many Maybes

There are many other unusual phenomena that seem impossible, but are occasionally reported in everyday life or seem to show up occasionally (but not very reliably) under laboratory conditions. For many of these, there are only a few observations of them happening in everyday life. The quality of these observations is questionable so it's hard to know whether they are misperceptions of ordinary physical events or genuine psychic phenomena.

For others, including the ones I will briefly mention below, there are enough high-quality observations and sometimes experiments that I would describe them as *maybe* being real, *maybe* not: we simply need a lot more research on them. *Insofar as they are real though, they have tremendous implications for our view of reality and human nature.* The ones I'll briefly describe here, and describe in more detail in my *The End of Materialism* book, are: *out-of-body-experiences (OBEs)*, *near-death experiences (NDEs)*, *after-death communications (ADCs)*, *postmortem survival* (as suggested by the phenomena of *mediumship)*, and *reincarnation*. Even if they turn out to be incorrect interpretations of other phenomena, they have been central in the creation of human beliefs about the spiritual and so deserve intense study.

Out-of-Body Experiences (OBEs)

I will discuss this kind of experience at greater length here because of its powerful psychological aftereffects.

Popular and even some scholarly reports often confuse out-of-body experiences (OBEs) and near-death experiences (NDEs). My defining characteristics of an OBE are: (a) you find yourself located somewhere else than where you are certain your physical body is located at that time and, an important qualification, (b) you feel that your state of consciousness during the OBE is clear and much like your ordinary, relatively rational, normal consciousness.

This qualification sharply distinguishes OBEs from dream consciousness. In the latter, you think you're somewhere else but later realize your physical body was in bed sleeping. During dreams, you almost never know that where you *seem* to be located is not where your physical body is *actually* located. Further, in retrospective recall and examination from your waking state, you realize your state of consciousness during a dream was far less clear and rational than during your ordinary waking state.

We can further distinguish OBEs from lucid dreams. In the latter, the dreamers feel their consciousness is as normal as in waking, but they know *at the time* that what they are experiencing is a dream. Lucid dreams are fascinating; I was very pleased when my *Altered States of Consciousness* book (Tart, 1969) reintroduced knowledge of lucid dreams. But lucid dreams typically do not have an ESP component so are not of concern to us here.

OBEs are typically brief, seldom lasting more than a few minutes. There is little good survey data on how common they are. A variety of possible causal conditions may precede an OBE, but often there is no clear particular cause. Sleep or unconsciousness are the most common starting conditions. The aftereffects of OBEs are striking and important, however. Typically, someone who has had an OBE, an experience that to them is *as real or "realer" than ordinary experience*, will say something like: "I no longer *believe* that my mind will survive the death of my body... I *know* it will. I have experienced my mind existing independently of my body."

The realness of an OBE is usually inherent in the experience itself. But it is even stronger when persons experientially go to some physical location during the OBE other than where their physical body is and correctly report something they could not have known ordinarily. This means some kind of ESP is involved. There's been very little experimentation attempting to induce OBEs, although that may be beginning to change.

Unfortunately we are beginning to see studies that claim to explain OBEs *away* as nothing but illusions. Rather than meeting the defining criteria I mentioned above, these studies usually take some isolated aspect associated with OBEs and treat it as if it were a full OBE. It is as if one took rolling over in bed and going to sleep as "sexual behavior." True, that's often one aspect of sexual behavior, but it's very misleading to call the one component the whole.

I demonstrated that OBEs could be studied under laboratory conditions (Tart, 1968) as a result of luckily meeting someone who had had frequent OBEs since she was a child. I will describe this study more fully as it demonstrates how apparently weird and unusual phenomena can be studied under laboratory conditions. She had experienced many OBEs in her life and felt she could continue to do so in laboratory conditions.

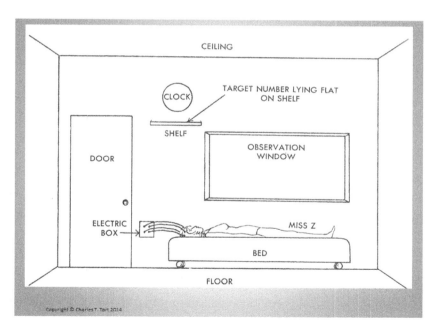

Figure 2: Experimental arrangement to study out-of-body experiences of Miss Z.

Miss Z, the pseudonym I've used to protect her privacy, had several OBEs in my sleep research laboratory. She would awaken, report an OBE, and estimate its duration and how long it took her to awake. She showed a distinctive brainwave pattern during those reported OBE periods but no physical changes that might suggest she was near dying. Figure 2 shows the laboratory arrangement. After she was wired up for physiological measures, she was allowed to go to sleep but asked to wake up and report any OBEs she had. She was also asked to try, while "out," to get in position to read a five digit random number written on a piece of paper on a shelf near the ceiling. On the one occasion when she reported an OBE and had been in position to read that number, she correctly reported it.

Near-Death Experiences (NDEs)

One set of circumstances frequently associated with OBEs and often causal is physiological trauma of the sort that is often fatal, including cases where a person appeared to be physically dead for a period of time. Sometimes a doctor had certified that the person had died. This is the Near-Death Experience (NDE).

Most, but not all, NDEs begin with an OBE. Typically, persons feel they are floating above an accident or surgical scene, look down at their body, and see accident bystanders or doctors. A few NDE cases report accurate and unexpected observations of the physical scene around the body, although not as precisely as my study with Miss Z found. Of course, it may not occur to you to study details of the scene when you've gone through great trauma, believe you have died, and may even have heard a doctor pronounce you dead! This is especially so if it looks like you can go on to a state of incredible love and bliss, a common aspect of NDEs.

What distinguishes an NDE from an ordinary OBE is that, during a NDE, perceptions and consciousness functioning do not remain like those occurring in ordinary consciousness. The NDEr finds herself or himself in some kind of altered state of consciousness with unusual perceptions and understandings. These noetic understandings are difficult, if not impossible, to adequately communicate later after returning to ordinary consciousness and embodied life.

As with OBEs, those who have had NDEs are almost always convinced they will survive bodily death. Usually of more immediate importance, they know that the insights gained during their NDE will require drastic life changes to live in accordance with what they now deeply know. One of the most common insights, for example, is that the person has not learned to love, and must return to ordinary life to learn this vital lesson.

NDEs now occur much more frequently than they did in the past because of the development of modern medical resuscitation techniques. Death that was indeed final a few decades ago can now sometimes be reversed as medical technology constantly improves. An NDEr, for example, may show no pulse, blood pressure, or detectable brain activity for several minutes before revival. An estimate made decades ago is that some 8 million people, at least, have experienced an NDE.

If you read scholarly literature about the "soul," much effort is expended on linguistically deriving the word from old words for breath or air. Given scholarly and scientific prejudice against taking spiritual and psychic experiences seriously, it's safe for scholars to stay abstract like this. However, OBEs and NDEs have been reported in all cultures. These experiences may be, in part, where ideas that we have a soul and survive death came from.

After Death Communications (ADCs)

People have long described experiencing what they called ghosts, spirits, and apparitions. Some of these are vague and fleeting, and are dismissed soon after occurring as not real by those experiencing them. But many are powerful and impressive to the experiencers, and are taken as evidence for the reality of some kind of postmortem survival. Sometimes it seems as if these experiences are deliberately produced from the "other side" of death as a form of communication, often with the intent of reassuring still-living loved ones that the deceased person is okay.

Thus, the modern acronym ADC, after-death *communication*, implies intention from the post-death state to communicate. When looked at by non-experiencers, many of these reports aren't very evidential for survival, and may well be hallucinations. But a significant number require more serious consideration. ADCs are not something it would be easy to do deliberate experiments on, but regardless of materialistic attitudes about their impossibility, they keep happening to people.

An ADC with a prominent psychology professor involving his recently deceased wife, e.g., led him to comment:

"To me these experiences are real. So real they have changed my life. My depression was gone, absolutely lifted, after the second instance. I have never looked back. I know she lives on somewhere and that life after what we call death is far too important a topic to leave for softheaded people to think about.

"Now from a hardball scientist who teaches multivariate statistics, research methods, and one who wrote computerized diagnostic software, I have joined the paranormal set. I am sure that some of my colleagues think I have indeed gone round that bend when they hear about my public talks and workshops exploring the issues as we in the sciences are prone to do." (Tart, 2009, pp. 250-253).

Some ADCs include the imparting of important information about the deceased, such as where important missing papers are stored and information unknown to the person having the experience. So some kind of ESP may be involved.

Postmortem Survival in an Afterlife

The most direct evidence suggesting possible postmortem survival comes from studies with spiritualist mediums. A medium is someone who believes he or she can serve, usually in a special session termed a *séance*, as an intermediary to convey messages to and from whatever aspect of people survives death. In the classical days of studying mediumship – it was much more widespread in the Western world from mid-1800s through mid-1900s – many mediums went into "trances."

Mediums usually remembered nothing after coming back to normal. During their ASC, they believed they were temporarily controlled by a guiding spirit so they (mediums) could perform their role as a communications intermediary.

Such deep-trance mediums are rarer nowadays. Contemporary mediums usually remain in pretty much an ordinary state of consciousness (it hasn't been studied in detail) while getting visual and auditory images of what the deceased spirits want to communicate.

People who go to a mediumistic séance usually have recently lost a loved one and, even if skeptical, hope for reassurance that their loved one still exists and is happy. They almost always get this. In terms of the evidential value for *proving* that the deceased person still exists, the quality of the information is often low, consisting too often of generalities that would fit anyone, for example, "Your loved one said she always loved you more than you could ever know."

However, sometimes the information the ostensible deceased spirits give to prove their identity is quite specific and could not have been known to the medium by ordinary means. Occasionally this comes about through deliberate fraud on the part of the medium for, like any human activity, there is money to be made by fleecing the gullible. But there have been many excellent cases where there's no question about the honesty of those involved.

For some who have studied mediumship, there is more than enough evidence to convince them that we survive death in some form and go on to a more spiritual life. Some are impressed by the specificity and correctness of the identifying information. Others wonder if the information could come from the unconscious use of telepathy or other forms of ESP on the mediums' part to pick this useful information out of the mind of the person who has come to the séance.

Perhaps the most amazing thing about mediumship is that – as with the question "Do we survive death in some form?" – *we have left it as a matter of uninformed belief or disbelief*, rather than supporting comprehensive scientific research on the subject. For two decades, for example, I have hosted an online discussion group among the few scholars and scientists who have published contributions to understanding mediumship and answering the question of whether we survive. Yet, while I'm considered something of an authority on the subject of possible survival, I've had almost no time to study it directly. Most of the experts on my discussion forum are in a similar situation. This is very strange and sad.

Postmortem Survival as Reincarnation

Many have heard about apparent past lives being recalled as a result of hypnotic regression. While a few of these cases are fairly impressive (Bernstein, 1956), they have two major problems. First, a hypnotized person is very suggestible and wants to please the hypnotist, so can easily create false memories, believed by them unquestioningly during the hypnotic state, about an imagined previous incarnation.

The second is that in modern times most adults have read or seen historical documentaries. As such, they have a general knowledge about what things were like, so a false reincarnation memory can be pretty historically authentic. It's very difficult in today's world to determine with certainty that a person producing such memories under hypnosis has not been exposed to the relevant historical information at some time in their life.

The most impressive cases arguing for reincarnation are those of young children, roughly between three and seven, who spontaneously recall a past life. Generally such cases begin with the child making unusual remarks, such as "We don't eat that kind of food," or "I want to go home and be with my wife." Then the child goes on to provide more specific details. Psychiatrist Ian Stevenson, now deceased, of the University of Virginia, was an outstanding pioneer in systematically collecting cases of childhood memories (Stevenson, 1974).

When possible, he investigated whether records of a deceased person with the specific described characteristics could be found when there was no plausible normal way for the child to have known about this person's life. It's much easier to know what information young children have been exposed to than adults.

Stevenson's research is carried on today by several colleagues at the Division of Perceptual Studies at the University of Virginia Medical School. The last time I checked, they had about 2500 solved cases, plus a couple of thousand more that were still being worked on. "Solved" in the sense that records of a deceased person were found that fit the child's memories well. In many of these the amount of information from the child was accurate and unusual. This makes, at minimum, an argument that the possibility of reincarnation should be thoroughly investigated, not dismissed because of a commitment to total materialism.

There are also some especially impressive cases where, for example, a child remembers being killed by a gun shot in a purported prior existence. The child has unusual birthmarks: a small round scar on his chest and a much larger and ragged scar on his back. Past medical records show that the person in the alleged previous life was indeed shot and died as the child remembers. The entry wound to the chest would indeed leave a small round scar with a larger and ragged scar corresponding with the exit wound.

Working Conclusions

I call the following *working* conclusions, *not* final, as I try to remember that what I think we know scientifically is provisional, well worthwhile, but always subject to possible revision as new data are collected.

With regard to human nature, we can frame the points I have made here as good news and bad news. The good news is that the scientific method, coupled with a philosophy of total materialism, and applied intensely to the material world has resulted in an enormous amount of progress in understanding and dealing with that world. We can, and in many ways are, creating a better world for human beings. For example, we understand immensely more about how the physical structure of the body and nervous system shapes our mental as well as physical nature.

The bad news is that the results of science and technology are too often used for harm: harm to others, to life in general, and to our planet. There's nothing I see in a *totally* materialistic view that logically *requires* the powerful values and ethics needed to deter such negative uses. Further bad news: religion and spirituality have been major sources of positive values and ethics. However, total materialism – which has become identified with being scientific *fact* rather than an intellectual strategy – has made many people believe that all religion and spirituality are nothing but fantasies and imaginings, and often pathological ones to boot. Thus ethics and values stemming from them can be seen as meaningless outcomes of mindless evolution, not something inherently true and important.

Being part of a tribe that protected and supported each other had survival value so that tendency was genetically selected for. But that's just a physical result, not an independent moral imperative. That easily becomes, "Treat others in your tribe well, that's a good investment, but people outside your tribe don't matter much." As I cautioned in introducing the Western Creed exercise, this is an example of a world view that *can* be drawn from total materialism and has important consequences. But this is not an impartial and scholarly overview of all possible world views and their consequences.

I want to emphasize that last point, as I find I am often misunderstood on this issue. I am not theorizing that all people who have a totally materialistic approach to life are bad, far from it! All sorts of values and behavior and justifications go with all sorts of world views. We humans are not very consistent. But I am pointing out that a totally materialistic world view can make it easier to rationalize and justify self-interest and dismiss other values.

Religion and spirituality are not infallible solutions to problems of ethics and morality, of course; we humans can twist any religion and spirituality to nasty ends. But they have been and could continue to be a valuable source of ethics and compassionate motivation – *especially if they are intelligently refined*, a major goal of transpersonal psychology.

As just one example of possibilities with major world outcomes, there is a classical kind of mystical experience that some scholars (Forman, 1999) have termed the *unitive experience*. People have experienced, at the deepest level they have ever felt, that *they are one with all living things* and the universe. Naturally, then, their welfare cannot be separated from the welfare of all.

Those who have had unitive experiences strive to act in considerate and compassionate ways to other life and people. They do this – not because they're *supposed to* or have been socially *conditioned to*, or threatened with Hell if they don't – but because it's the obviously sensible thing to do once they've deeply realized the unity of all life. It's a goodness that's just natural from the inside, not something that is demanded, conditioned or coerced.

But total materialism – a *philosophy* thought to be scientific fact – dismisses such a mystical experience as a major malfunctioning of the brain. Scientism posits that consciousness is nothing but electrochemical actions in your brain; there is no real connection with other life or the rest of the universe other than what is mediated by physics and chemistry. Someone suffering in a distant place has no direct effect on your consciousness. Your happiness is ultimately a matter of the electrical and chemical patterns within your brain and body. So what's sensible is to take care of your own electrochemical balance and be happy. Other people and other life are quite secondary.

The Western Creed has helped many people see how deeply a philosophy of total materialism has penetrated their automatic ways of thinking about and perceiving reality, and some of the alienating consequences it has for them. Such insights do not automatically make us wiser or more compassionate. But changing toward a desired direction is generally more effective if we know where we're starting from, what the obstacles are, and there's something real to go toward.

There's no doubt that religious and spiritual views can make people feel better for psychological and social reasons even if, as total materialists argue, those views are fantasies. I have briefly reviewed how we actually have extensive and rigorous scientific data to show that the mind cannot be reduced to just brain functioning. These data show that sometimes:

a) we can have a more direct perception of other people's thoughts and feelings (telepathy)
b) we can have a more direct way of knowing what's going on in the world (clairvoyance)
c) we can affect our world (psychokinesis and psychic healing)
d) these phenomena can sometimes transcend ordinary physical time (precognition)

Those Big Five psi phenomena make a strong case that we are not *just* electrochemical reactions isolated with our skulls. We are something more.

There is also scientific evidence, but of a more varied and not so certain quality – the Many Maybes – that for some suggests and for some proves:

e) our minds can sometimes operate independently of the body (OBEs and NDEs)
f) some aspects of mind may survive bodily death (OBEs, NDEs, ADCs, postmortem survival as evidenced by mediumship, and reincarnation).

The idea of spiritual growth becomes much more real when these phenomena are taken into account rather than simply considered to be pleasant fantasies. I am not arguing that existing religions and spiritual disciplines know all about this "something more." I see them as attempts to deal with the occasional experiences that give people tastes and hints about that something more, but then get distorted and immersed in social and political issues and may become pathological, as well as a source of important values. What might we become if we:

- developed a *science* of spirituality?
- applied disciplined observation and theorized and tested the consequences?
- showed a willingness to alter our views as needed?
- honestly exchanged our observations and thinking instead of fighting senseless wars over who has the True Faith?

It's possible. I hope we will do it. Will it be Truth? Or perhaps just the best we can do within the human condition, but a lot better than destructive scientism and sectarianism.

Summing Up

We need meaning in our lives. Our need for meaning in life isn't satisfied by believing existence is a meaningless accident after physical particles just happened to bump into each other for a few zillion years. The first part of this chapter, especially the Western Creed, may have given you some deeper emotional, as well as intellectual, insight into how we need post-materialist meaning. Let's continue to investigate the material aspects of the world as best we can. But that's not enough.

I am not arguing that we should accept without question any ideas or beliefs labeled "spiritual" or "religious." Many of them are factually false, and some are psychologically toxic, whatever may have been their origin or social value when first they began circulating. Many have been subverted by various individuals and groups seeking power over others and are best discarded. This advice applies not to just religious and spiritual ideas, of course, but all ideas. We need to refine our ideas and know more about which ones usefully reflect reality and which do not.

Although essential science isn't the only useful way of acquiring knowledge, it is an excellent way to cross-check ideas, beliefs, theories, and philosophies against what can be observed and experienced. When essential science is applied to psychic phenomena, as briefly outlined in the second part of this chapter, a picture of some real aspects of human nature – including what is meant by "spiritual" – begins to emerge. What we know to date is undoubtedly a partial and probably distorted picture, but it's only been a very short time in history that we've studied psychic aspects of our nature in a scholarly and scientific way.

I have high hopes that parapsychology, as a basic science of what's psychically possible, and transpersonal psychology, as a science of what the spiritual might mean and how it could be usefully applied, may eventually make real and health-promoting spiritual experiences possible for most people. I have hope for a world in which many people are naturally kind to others because they have experienced a form of deep unity based on what are, to them, *real connections.*

References

Bannister, R. (1987). *Sociology and Scientism: The American Quest for Objectivity*. Chapel Hill: University of North Carolina Press.

Bernstein, M. (1956). *The Search for Bridey Murphy*. New York: Doubleday.

Forman, R. (1999). *Mysticism, Mind, Consciousness*: SUNY Press.

Hobbs, A. (1910). *Social Problems and Scientism*. Harrisburg, Pennsylvania: Stackpole.

Kuhn, T. (1962). *The Structure of Scientific Revolutions*. Chicago: University of Chicago Press.

Sheldrake, R. (1999). How widely is blind assessment used in scientific research? *Alternative Therapies, 5*(3), 88-91.

Stevenson, I. (1974). *Twenty Cases Suggestive of Reincarnation* (2nd ed.). Charlottesville, VA: University of Virginia Press.

Targ, R., & Puthoff, H. E. (1977). *Mind Reach: Scientists Look at Psychic Ability*. New York: Delacorte Press/Eleanor Friede.

Tart, C. (1968). A psychophysiological study of out-of-the-body experiences in a selected subject. *Journal of the American Society for Psychical Research, 62*, 3-27.

Tart, C. (1969). *Altered States of Consciousness: A Book of Readings*. New York: John Wiley & Sons.

Tart, C. (1972). States of consciousness and state-specific sciences. *Science, 176*, 1203-1210.

Tart, C. (1998). Investigating altered states of consciousness on their own terms: A proposal for the creation of state-specific sciences. *Ciencia e Cultura, Journal of the Brazilian Association for the Advancement of Science, 50*(2/3), 103-116.

Tart, C. (2009). *The End of Materialism: How Evidence of the Paranormal is Bringing Science and Spirit Together*. Oakland, CA: New Harbinger.

Tart, C., Puthoff, H., & Targ, R. (Eds.). (1979). *Mind at Large: Institute of Electrical and Electronic Engineers Symposia on the Nature of Extrasensory Perception.* New York: Praeger.

Chapter Sixteen

Science, Soul, and Death

Marilyn Schlitz, PhD
John H Spencer, PhD

Those who tackle philosophy aright are simply and solely practicing dying, practicing death, all the time, but nobody sees it.[30]

Plato

We at least know that all of the consciousness we have experienced in our lives cannot be destroyed; it's stored somewhere.[31]

Rudy Tanzi, PhD

Introduction

What is death? What, if anything, happens after we die? And how does the act of seeking answers to these questions affect our daily lives?

We have been reflecting on such questions throughout history, with answers being offered from both religion and philosophy. Such answers have ranged from total nihilism to eternal peace in heaven, to utter contempt for even bothering to think about such things.

Modern science has been relatively slow to give these types of questions the serious attention they deserve. However, some researchers, especially those who have rejected materialism, have begun to build bridges between ancient spiritual insights and modern scientific theory. Indeed, it would not be an exaggeration to say that the postmaterialist approach to science is leading to what historian of science Thomas Kuhn would refer to as a *paradigm shift* (Kuhn, 1970). But the fundamental shift is not actually

---

[30] *Plato. (Trans. 1999). pp. 466-467. Phaedo, 64a.*
[31] *Quoted in Schlitz, 2015.*

in science (at least not solely within science): it is more of a philosophical shift with extraordinary implications for science, and for society as a whole.

Philosophical Paradigms and Societal Shifts.

As Kuhn clarified, new approaches and questions emerge when paradigm shifts occur. The competing paradigms can be disruptive, as they may not be at all compatible. These shifts are disruptive, because competing paradigms are often incommensurable and not easily reconciled. This has certainly been the case with respect to materialism, the view that only physical stuff or matter is real. Materialism has falsely been assumed to be a scientific fact when, in reality, it is a philosophical (or metaphysical) view about the nature of reality.

It is often very challenging for scientists (or for any of us) to let go of their personal beliefs, even when confronted with scientific evidence—such as the resistance to various aspects of quantum physics, even among some of those who were pioneering this new scientific understanding. How much more difficult, then, to uproot our false beliefs when what is required is not so much looking at evidence but, rather, pushing ourselves into far deeper rational reflection in order to understand and release our false beliefs.

As is well known, some people in the past who challenged the ruling religious paradigm were labeled heretics and burned at the stake. Today, scientists who challenge the dominant materialist paradigm may not be burned alive, but they have sometimes been ostracized from their community of scientists or medical professionals, or they and their work have been the targets of smear campaigns.

There is significant irony here. First, many of the greatest pioneering physicists who brought us quantum physics denied materialism and instead (directly or indirectly) endorsed Platonism, which, among other key points, claims that *nonphysical* laws underpin physical reality. Second, there is no scientific experiment that could ever prove that materialism is true. And third, *ad hominem* attacks (and smear campaigns) are not at all scientific.

While many transpersonal experiences such as near-death and out-of-body experiences have been reported by people of all ages and across cultures, paradigm wars know no historical boundaries, and mainstream materialist science has often dismissed such claims as fraud, delusion, or nothing more than epiphenomena (a type of byproduct) of the brain. But it is not very rational to claim that so many people throughout history have all been lying or deluded, especially when their experiences share so many similar features, and when they claim that such transpersonal experiences have seemed more real to them than their experiences in daily life.

Indeed, Erwin Schrödinger, one of the founding pioneers of quantum physics, writes that "the mystics of many centuries, independently, yet in perfect harmony with each other (somewhat like the particles in an ideal gas) have described, each of them, the unique experience of his or her life in terms that can be condensed in the phrase: DEUS FACTUS SUM (I have become God)" (Schrödinger, 1967, p. 93). Clearly Schrödinger had no problem with accepting such transpersonal or mystical experiences.

It also makes little sense to claim that such experiences can be explained by epiphenomenalism, "the view that mental events are caused by physical events in the brain, but have no effects upon any physical events" (http://plato.stanford.edu/entries/epiphenomenalism). Mental events or properties, which on the materialist account emerge from physical events or causes, must themselves either emerge as something physical or as "something" nonphysical. If they emerge as something nonphysical, then materialism is defeated, and then there would be many challenging questions to consider, such as what the nonphysical "things" emerge into, where they are, how they are related back to the physical, and how something physical that has no awareness or consciousness somehow suddenly produces awareness and consciousness.

If they emerge as something physical, then they should be able to be measured completely, which is to say that all our inner thoughts and experiences, whether we are conscious of them or not, should be able to be displayed objectively for all others to experience physically in the same way that we experience them internally. Apparently, this has not yet happened, but perhaps someday it will (Berkeley News, 2011; Guardian, 2015) If it ever did occur, if we really could see what others see inside their own minds in the same (or relatively similar) way they see inside their own minds, this would be quite extraordinary, but it still would not mean that materialism is true.

In any case, it takes only the most basic self-observation to realize that our mental states and our beliefs can have a direct impact on our physical bodies. If you believe Joe stole your bike, then you will probably be angry at him, which means you will experience a variety of physical / emotional states. But when you realize that Joe didn't in fact steal it, your belief changes, and then your anger dissipates. It seems difficult to deny that your mental state had an effect on your physical body in such a case.

Even if all internal experiences could be accurately revealed in an objectively physical way to others, there are still other problems the materialists must face. For example, there is still the question of the experiencer, the very essence of whatever it is that is experiencing anything in the first place. This essential experiencer, or essential self, must in some way remain unified through all the endless variety of transitory experiences, and such relatively stable unification would require some sort of separation from the experiences. If there were no separation whatsoever, then there would simply be a flow of events, because there would be no one—no entity, essence, soul, mind, or consciousness—to be aware of these events.

This question of unification cannot be facilely dismissed. Even the eighteenth century skeptical philosopher David Hume admitted that he could not explain such unity: "but all my hopes vanish, when I come to explain the principles that unite our successive perceptions in thought or consciousness" (Hume, 1826, p. 55).

Schrödinger offers an interesting perspective on why it is so difficult to pinpoint the experiencer or observer in our scientific investigations: he writes that "the reason why our sentient, percipient and thinking ego is met nowhere within our scientific world picture can easily be indicated in seven words: because it is itself that world picture. It is identical with the whole and therefore cannot be contained in it as a part of it" (Schrödinger, 1967, p. 138.).

Additionally, any awareness of anything implies that there must be some sort of separation from the physical events that we are aware of, and that anything that can be self-aware must necessarily be nonphysical.

These are significant claims, and you may find more detail in Spencer's *The Eternal Law* (2012). Here we will note only one interesting point of general agreement or convergence between science and religion.

As the First Vatican Council (1869-1870) states: "since he [God] is one, singular, completely simple and unchangeable spiritual substance, he must be declared to be in reality and in essence, distinct from the world" (Tanner, 1990, p. 805). And for those who think that great scientists are somehow above all this apparent nonsense, Schrödinger even went so far as to argue that consciousness is universal and singular: 'there *is* only one thing and what seems to be a plurality is merely a series of different aspects of this one thing, produced by a deception (the Indian MAJA)" (Schrödinger, 1967, p. 95 (original emphasis).

Although all these questions benefit greatly from a consideration of all the relevant data from the various physical and social sciences, they are ultimately rooted in philosophy. Therefore, the initial or fundamental paradigm shift is of a philosophical nature. Until we put in the required philosophical effort, we are not going to maximize the power and potential implementation of the emerging postmaterialist science, or of any new paradigm.

In this emerging postmaterialist paradigm, there is a mutual interdependence to be found between science and spirituality. There are no quick divides or easy points of separation. As Kuhn observed decades ago, while scientists are experts in charting the course of our physical nature, they carry within them their own metaphysics, (which is a technical term in philosophy that generally refers to our attempt to offer a comprehensive rational account of the most fundamental aspects of all reality). Social psychologists have established that the values and beliefs of all of us, scientists included, inform our worldviews in key ways, below the threshold of conscious awareness. As the paradigm shifts, so do our metaphysical assumptions, at least if we are shifting with the new paradigm.

However, while we need to do the work in our minds to reject false or harmful beliefs, this individual process is also served or hindered by the society in which we live. First, although we should never ignore the importance of individual thought—someone achieving a new insight or making a new discovery on their own—we equally cannot dismiss the fact that all individuals are part of society as a whole, in one way or another. For example, Max Planck was the only one (so far as we know) who had the key insight that would lead to the development of quantum physics, but the data that he used in his reflections were based on the work of numerous individuals. Furthermore, a society that fosters objective scientific research is more likely to provide the place for extraordinary discoveries made by individuals, while also enabling (hopefully) beneficial applications. Therefore, a sociological perspective is also vital in facilitating the potential opportunities for paradigm shifts.

In general, social transformation follows the same basic pattern as individual transformation, where both paths tend to be more fractal than linear. Transformation can be messy. The breakthroughs that are emerging today are appearing at the intersections of worldviews, disciplines, and ways of knowing and being. The shift that is upon us represents a new ontology, or model of reality, beyond the senses and into expanded realms of being. While paradigm shifts can be quite unsettling, and even frightening, to those who cling to the previous paradigm (and we all struggle with letting go of old patterns and beliefs), we should ideally be open to embracing such shifts, provided that they are actually offering us a more accurate representation of reality.

Ideally, a new worldview should offer many unexpected possibilities and opportunities, and ideas that were previously dismissed are reconsidered in a new light. Science aims to explain reality, so far as possible. Therefore, it should not dismiss the transpersonal or mystical experiences of so many people as if they were nothing more than neurochemical malfunctions. Trying to *explain away* uncomfortable evidence is not the same thing as offering an *explanation*.

The Soulful Revolution in Science

If consciousness were not real, then you would have a difficult time explaining how you were reading and understanding this sentence. Let's take it as granted, therefore, that consciousness is real. But then we have to ask:

what *is* consciousness? Is it the same as mind? As soul? Is it nothing more than your brain, and isn't your brain connected to the rest of your body, directly or indirectly? If consciousness is in the brain, or just *is* the brain, then how many different consciousnesses do we have? It would seem like quite a large number, since the brain can be broken down into ever smaller parts, all the way down to subatomic particles. And then we are back to the issue of unification, because we would then have to explain how all these parts are unified into some kind of functional whole.

Interestingly, the scientific study of consciousness was once a strictly taboo topic, but it has now become a spark that is shifting scientific, academic, religious, and social discourse. For example, in 1950 there were about 23 articles published on consciousness, whereas in the year 2000 there were approximately 11,480 (Solso, 2003). Scientific investigation has its limits, both pragmatic and intrinsic, but how can there be any topic that science considers taboo? And it certainly doesn't follow that just because something may not fall under the lens of scientific investigation that it, therefore, must be unreal.

Although it is vitally important to consider all the subtle similarities and differences between the meanings of the terms "mind," "soul," or "consciousness," this is a topic that is far too vast for such a short chapter. For our purposes, we can consider the essential core of what they are all pointing to or presupposing in one way or another, which is that there is some fundamental core or undefiled nature that we are in essence, and there does not seem to be any sufficient reason not to refer to that core as "soul."

Schrödinger also agreed with psychiatrist Carl Jung that "all science...is a function of the soul, in which all knowledge is rooted" (Schrödinger quoting Jung in Schrödinger, 1967, p. 129). Even if Schrödinger would have preferred the word "mind" or "consciousness," he does not shy away from Jung's use of the word "soul." In either case, they are both referring to the same thing—the very subject of awareness, the nonphysical locus of all experience, the self or being or consciousness that 'I am.' While it may be beyond the limits of science to directly access soul, it is not at all scientific to deny its reality. Soul, in this sense anyway, is presupposed by the possibility of being able to do science in the first place.

Many cultures throughout history have held to the worldview that when we die, something else lives on. How do these views match the physical model that currently defines mainstream Western science? In what ways does the postmaterialist science of consciousness address experiences of extended awareness, near-death experiences, communication with the deceased, and reincarnation? Bridging insights from both inner (intuitive) and outer (rational) ways of knowing may well help us move into a new view of human possibility, now and after we die. As spirituality and science intersect, what emerges is an evidence-based spirituality that is a new worldview for the twenty-first century, but one that is rooted in ancient spirituality/philosophy.

Rudolph E. Tanzi, PhD, is one of several key scientists helping to drive this emerging worldview. His work combines impeccable scientific credentials with a deep spiritual practice. Tanzi is Joseph P. and Rose F. Kennedy Professor of Neurology at Harvard Medical School, and directs the Genetics and Aging Research Unit at Massachusetts General Hospital, where his research centers on the genetic causes of Alzheimer's disease.

Tanzi also believes that consciousness extends beyond the body. He is committed to establishing links between physical and nonphysical reality. His views on consciousness and what may lie beyond bodily death are both unconventional and provocative.

During an interview for the film and book by Schlitz, *Death Makes Life Possible* (2015), Tanzi offers several key insights. For example, he notes that, scientifically, we do not know for certain whether or not identity or self-awareness can survive death, but that there are many key questions in this area of thought that scientists have no idea how to answer, and so they often try to simply wave them away. Tanzi continues:

"The other side of the coin that most neuroscientists don't want to talk about is, where is consciousness? Where are memories? When you think about the past, where were they [the memories] stored? We don't have an answer for that in neuroscience. I ask students, I ask other professors this all the time. They say—it's all this hand waving—"You know, it's in your neural network." I'm like, "Where exactly?" "Oh, in the synapses." No, the synapses fire. [They fire] to recall the memory, but where's the actual memory? Where's my mother's face if I see it? What's the thumb drive of the brain that stores the jpg of my mother's face? We have no idea.

"Then the question becomes, is it stored here [pointing to his head], but not as a unified mass, which you would need for identity? Or is it actually coalescing as a global energy within a unified mass that we can call identity. And for lack of a better word, we have the word *soul*. The soul is then the keeper of the identity. The consciousness you experienced over your life stays intact. I believe that. That's more of a spiritual belief right now than a scientific belief. But I trust my intuition more than anything, and my intuition says yes, this is probably the case" (Schlitz, 2015).

For Tanzi, another scientist who uses the word "soul", who we are is not defined solely by our physical experience. This may be surprising to hear from someone who has forged his career in mapping the molecules and mechanisms of awareness through our brains and bodies. In his unique way, he has found a worldview that offers an integration of what he knows from his scientific training and his own intuitive or inner ways of knowing. Tanzi, like other postmaterialist scientists, is suggesting that who we are transcends our brains and bodies. This idea points us toward new connections between personal experience and the soul as keeper of our identity. Death, within this worldview, is another phase in our ongoing transformation. This is a compelling idea that characterizes this twenty-first-century scientist, and it offers an emerging new paradigm for us all.

There are many other contemporary scientists who hold similar views, such as Lothar Schäfer, a retired professor from the University of Arkansas, where he taught physical chemistry for forty-three years. One of the harbingers of this new worldview, Schafer is optimistic that science is reaching a new way of understanding consciousness. Like Tanzi and other postmaterialist scientists, he speaks about wholeness as the core of reality, countering the materialist and reductionist worldview that reduces the world to its parts while pretending there is no whole. While he made his career in physical chemistry, measuring, manipulating, and explaining the microscopic world, he sees the basis of matter as nonmaterial and the universe as interconnected.

"All things are connected," he explains, "Not in the empirical world, but in their nonempirical roots.

"The argument is this: if the universe is wholeness, everything comes out of it, everything belongs to it, including our consciousness. In that case, consciousness is a cosmic principle. The only chance you have that your consciousness survives when you die is that there is some consciousness outside. What may be in us is perhaps not our consciousness, but a cosmic consciousness" (Schäfer, quoted in Schlitz, 2015)

In discussing his own cosmology, Shafer acknowledges that a personal transformation linked his views of death with his scientific worldview. When he was younger, he was frightened about death. Today he finds nothing frightening about it. Not that he has any clear opinion on what happens after; still, he believes that "there is a cosmic mind with which we are connected. If there is a cosmic mind, it would be strange if it wasn't connected with ours" (Quoted in Schlitz, 2015). Schafer's comments echo those made by another pioneering founder of quantum physics, Wolfgang Pauli, who believed that there is a "cosmic order independent of our choice and distinct from the world of phenomena" (Pauli, in Jung and Pauli, 1955, p. 152).

Stuart Hameroff, MD, is an anesthesiologist, as well as a professor and the director of the Center for Consciousness Studies at the University of Arizona. For many years, he has been seeking to understand the nature of consciousness and how it relates to the brain. His particular passion is the potential for quantum physics to explain the furthest reaches of consciousness.

In his interview with Schlitz (2015), Hameroff explains his own views on the subject of consciousness and life after death. In particular, he articulates a model he developed in collaboration with Sir Roger Penrose, the famed British mathematical physicist. In Hameroff's view, which he hopes may explain the survival of consciousness after bodily death, microtubules are a key to consciousness. These protein structures are the body's scaffolding, out of which our skeletal system takes form. These structures are tubular and so, he says, can act as a kind of conductor for quantum events to occur in the body—and beyond. While such views are somewhat controversial, Hameroff also discusses more conventional but equaling startling data.

Hameroff relates a case study by an intensive-care specialist at George Washington University in Washington, D.C. He explains that the palliative care physician, Lakhmir Chawla, and his colleagues (2009), were treating patients who were dying. These patients and their families had elected to withdraw life support so that the patients would die peacefully. During this time, there were brain monitors on the patients. Hameroff describes what happened:

"When they started out, [the patients] had a level of physiological activity that was below what we would consider conscious in anesthesia. But there was some activity. As the heart stopped, and the blood stopped flowing, and the blood pressure pretty much went to zero, this number dwindled down to about zero, and the heart stopped. But then, in seven out of seven cases that Chawla studied, there was a sudden burst of brain activity that turned out to be gamma synchrony. This is a correlate of consciousness, that lasted anywhere from ninety seconds to twenty minutes, in one case" (Quoted in Schlitz, 2015).

Since the patients died, we cannot say for certain whether or not they actually had something like a near-death or out-of-body experience, but the evidence suggests that it is possible. At the very least, even after the stopping of the heart, there was still measurable activity correlated with consciousness. Something was certainly happening.

For those who are interested in exploring in greater detail these and other related issues, please see Schlitz (2015) and Spencer (2012). But for the stubborn skeptic, it seems that no amount of empirical evidence from numerous scientists will ever be sufficient. Such parochialism is certainly not scientific, and the accusation that postmaterialists are peddling pseudoscience not only reflects skeptics' own false understanding of science (perhaps making *them* the genuine pseudoscientists), but also forces them to say that many of the greatest pioneering physicists throughout history were all pseudoscientists, too.

There are numerous further examples that could be provided of scientists who have thought in similar ways, but let us end this chapter with one who is generally less well known. In his other paper in this anthology, "The Reality of One (and Zero)," Spencer notes that Kurt Gödel, one of the greatest pioneering logicians in history and an intellectual giant, (Yourgrau, 2005, p. 56; Collins, 1998, p. 727-728) held some extraordinary philosophical views, only two of which we shall mention here. Gödel believed that "materialism is false" and that "the world in which we live is not the only one in which we shall live or have lived" (Gödel, quoted in Wang, 2001, p. 316). The skeptics want to say that rejecting materialism or believing in some form of reincarnation is not logical, but they are unlikely to be able to match the logical rigor of a mind such as Gödel's.

To be clear, we are not making the claim that just because Gödel, Schrödinger, or any other pioneering scientist rejected materialism or believed in existence beyond bodily death that, therefore, those views are true. But what we are claiming is that those skeptics who wish to say that these views are false need to contend with such extraordinary scientific and logical minds who are in complete disagreement with them.

The Practice of Death

We have seen only a brief sample of the growing number of scientists who give serious consideration to the possibility of life or existence beyond physical death. This may be a great source of comfort to many people, and be repugnant to those who hold to a materialistic metaphysics. It does seem odd, however, to assume so quickly that surviving bodily death is necessarily comforting. After all, if you were a really horrible person in life, the thought of continuing after death may not be so comforting, given the possibility of punishment for horrible acts committed during life.

In any case, whether or not you believe in any sort of afterlife, and whether or not you accept all, part, or none of the ideas and evidence presented in this anthology, it is still extremely likely—even more likely than having to pay taxes—that you will die someday. And even the most devoted materialists cannot claim to know absolutely that nothing happens after death. After all, they (in this life anyway) have never died before, so how could they (or anyone) know for certain, absolutely, one way or another? How could they know whether or not the act of dying is something most pleasant and beautiful or something most horrifying and dreadful? Perhaps at the moment of death, we experience a slowing down of time, approaching or even reaching an eternal moment, or at least the experience of an eternal moment. And what then?

There are various spiritual traditions that teach us to reflect on death and on our mortality in order to help us live more fully in the now, to help us find the true purpose for our being here in the first place, and to fulfill that purpose as best we can. It is unfortunate, however, that the West has very much rejected its own philosophical tradition going back to Plato, Pythagoras, ancient Egypt, and beyond. The essential purpose of philosophy—the love of wisdom—was, as Plato stated clearly, the practice and preparation for death. Contemporary academic philosophy is generally so far removed from such esoteric (and practical) teachings that Plato would likely recognize much of it as little more than sophistry, and perhaps not even very good sophistry at that.

How amazing it would be for society to facilitate postmaterialism, and to provide the support and resources that would better enable us to tackle these sorts of profound questions, bridging modern science and ancient wisdom from around the world.

We are living in a time of enormous change. The new science of consciousness speaks to the emergence of a new paradigm that focuses on the power and potential of our minds. Postmaterialist scientists have innovative ideas about the nature of reality—ideas informed by both their scientific training and their own spiritual beliefs and practices. New discoveries supporting the possibility that our essential identity may exist independently of space and time can give us a fresh new understanding of who we are—and what we may become beyond death.

This new worldview offers an expanded understanding of self that bridges both our physical and our metaphysical beliefs. We are finding new ways of understanding life as part of a nonlocal, interconnected universe that exists outside of linear space and time. The view of reality that is emerging in the twenty-first century is dynamic, inclusive, and in some ways beyond words. As the contributions in this unique volume demonstrate, just as this paradigm shift impacts science, it is also impacting society at large. In particular, a new worldview about death and the afterlife is impacting our system of healthcare, where death is often viewed as the enemy that must be conquered. As we transition to a new worldview that invites in the fullness of life in all its brilliant facets, we may create a new vision for our human nature. And in doing so, we may find new paths to healing our collective fear of death.

References

Auyong, D., Klein, S., Gan, T., Roche, A., Olson, D., & Habib, A. (2010). Processed electronencephalogram during donation after cardiac death. *Anesthesia and Analgesia*, 110, 5, 1428-32.

Berkeley News. (2011). (http://news.berkeley.edu/2011/09/22/brain-movies/)

Chawla, L, Akst, S., Junker, C., Jacobs, B., & Seneff, M. (2009). Surges of electroencephalogram activity at the time of death: a case series. *Journal of Palliative Medicine*, 12 (12), 1095-1100.

Collins, R. (1998). *The Sociology of Philosophies: A Global Theory of Intellectual Change*. Cambridge: The Belknap Press of Harvard University Press.

Guardian. (2015). https://www.theguardian.com/science/occams-corner/2015/apr/09/will-neuroscientists-ever-be-able-to-read-our-minds).

Hameroff, S. & Penrose, R. (1996). Orchestrated reduction of quantum coherence in brain microtubules: a model for consciousness. *Mathematics and Computers in Simulation*, 40 (3), 453-80.

Hume, D. (1826). *The Philosophical Works of David Hume, Vol. 11*. London: Adam Black and William Tait.

Jung, C. G. & Pauli, W. (Trans. 1955). *The Interpretation of Nature and the Psyche* [Jung: 'Synchronicity: An Acausal Connecting Principle' (Trans. R. F. C. Hull); Pauli: 'The Influence of Archetypal Ideas on the Scientific Theories of Kepler' (Trans. P. Silz).] London: Routledge & Kegan Paul.

Kuhn, T. S. (1970). *The Structure of Scientific Revolutions,* 2nd edition. Chicago: University of Chicago Press.

Plato. (Trans. 1999). *The Great Dialogues of Plato* (Trans. W. H. D. Rouse). NY: Signet Classic reprint.

Schlitz, M. (2015). *Death Makes Life Possible.* Sounds True: Boulder.

Schrödinger, E. (1967). *What is Life? & Mind and Matter.* Cambridge: Cambridge University Press.

Solso, R. (2003). *The Psychology of Art and the Evolution of the Conscious Brain.* Cambridge, MA: MIT Press.

Spencer, J. H. (2012). *The Eternal Law: Ancient Greek Philosophy, Modern Physics, and Ultimate Reality.* Vancouver, BC: Param Media.

Tanner, N. P. (Ed.). (1990). *Decrees of the Ecumenical Councils*: Volume Two *Trent to Vatican II.* Sheed & Ward and Georgetown University Press.

Wang, H. (2001). *A Logical Journey: From Gödel to Philosophy.* Cambridge, MA: MIT Press.

Yourgrau, P. (2005). *A World Without Time: The Forgotten Legacy of Godel and Einstein.* Allen Lane, *an imprint of* Penguin Books.

Chapter Seventeen

Towards a Postmaterialist Society (Back to Plato)

Neal Grossman, PhD

"These are frightening men you're talking about"[32]

Plato

In the past, when I taught metaphysics, I would impress upon my students that there is no connection between being a materialist and being materialistic. The former involves a belief system that asserts that all real things are constituted by matter, and whatever is not so constituted is unreal. The latter involves a psychological attitude, or value system, according to which the acquisition of material goods (wealth and status) motivates and defines how one lives one's life. It is quite possible, I would tell my students, to be a philosophical materialist without also being materialistic with respect to the conduct of their lives. Many individuals who define themselves as materialists are very kind and caring human beings, not at all selfish in their personal lives, strive to make this world a better place for all, and do not worship the gods of wealth and status.

I now believe that I was mistaken, not with respect to the fact that many who profess faith in materialism are altruistic in their behavior, but rather with respect to the claim that there is no connection between materialism and being materialistic. There is a connection, and it is a logical one. If, as is the case, so-called materialists are able to behave decently and

---

[32] Plato, *Sophist* 246b. Plato is mocking the materialists, those who believe *"that anything they cannot squeeze in their hands is absolutely nothing"* [*Sophist* 247c].

even altruistically, it is in spite of their faith in materialism, not because of it. Materialists, of course, do not identify their beliefs as "faith-based." For the materialist, it is always the "other" belief systems that are based on faith, not his or her own. But materialism is as faith-based as fundamentalist religion, because (i) there is no evidence that supports it and (ii) much evidence that has falsified it. For a thorough presentation of the evidence that has falsified materialism, see *Irreducible Mind* (Kelly et al., 2007).

To believe in something that has been shown to be false requires much irrational faith, together with astounding ignorance of the empirical evidence that has demonstrated its falsity. This ignorance is what allows them to sustain their faith. In fact, many materialists go out of their way to avoid becoming informed of data that would falsify their beliefs, in much the same way that one might expect a fundamentalist Christian to avoid acquainting herself or himself with the facts of geology and paleontology. Sixty years ago, the British philosopher C.D. Broad, who investigated parapsychological research and took it seriously, said of his colleagues, "If, like most contemporary Western philosophers and scientists, I were completely ignorant of, or blandly indifferent to these phenomena, I should, like them, leave the matter there. But I do not share their ignorance, and I am not content to emulate the ostrich" (Broad, 1962). His remarks are as true today as they were in his time. With respect to the data that falsifies materialism, ignorance, arrogance, and denial are still the tools of contemporary academics.

But, getting back to our topic, the logical connection between materialism and being materialistic is obvious. If everything is just matter, if all we are are atoms and particles in motion, then there is no possibility of accounting for the most important things in life: kindness, compassion, altruism, love, to say nothing of spiritually transformative experiences—for if one desires to live consistently with the religion of materialism, one ought to desire and pursue only those things that the religion says are real, that is, things that are material in nature and hence can be "squeezed in their hands," such as wealth, possessions, and status. Whatever cannot be quantified as some sort of material good is unreal, and one ought not to waste one's time pursuing such imaginary fantasies as loving-kindness.

Unlike individuals who may identify as materialists, our present capitalist society is quite consistent with respect to being a logical consequence of materialist ideology: only the pursuit of material goods constitutes a "good life," hence the pursuit of wealth and status as a means to acquire such goods. The true materialists of our culture are not academics (who love argument and discussion much more than they love money, and hence do not actually live their professed value system), but the Wall Street bankers and corporate executives, who seek nothing but money. They are true sociopaths, and as Plato said, quite "frightening" indeed,[33] as they are able to harm millions of people without any twinge of conscience. Adherence to materialist ideology explains the singular lack of compassion and loving-kindness in the institutions of our present culture. For, of the many and varied motivating desires within the human being, from greed on the one hand to altruism on the other, a materialist society like our own selects mostly for greed, which is why the economic and political aspects of society are controlled by those individuals who are motivated by greed, rather than by those who are motivated by kindness and compassion. But according to Spinoza, greed and ambition are "species of madness" (Spinoza, B., *Ethics*, part 4, prop. 44, scholium), and to the extent that Spinoza is correct, we have allowed the world to be run by individuals who have become mad through their greed for wealth and status. In our present social order, the lunatics are indeed running the asylum.

Closely associated with materialist ideology in practice is another metaphysical belief system, called atomism. Atomism holds that the real world is constituted by independently existing units, whose interactions constitute the entire material realm of being. Putting the two together, we get materialist reductionism, the official religion of academia, which holds that all things, including consciousness, can be reduced to the motions of these fundamental units of matter. We note in passing that atomism is empirically false, as the field theories of the 19th century, and relativity and

---

[33] *If you want to get really frightened about materialism, read, or rather do, "The Western Creed" in Charles Tart's contribution to this volume. Those who have internalized this belief system and live accordingly (the Wall Street sociopaths, not the academics) are indeed, as Plato said, frightening human beings.*

quantum theory of the 20th century, support wholism, not atomism. According to our best theories about the nature of matter there are no fundamental units of matter, and everything is deeply interconnected with everything else, such that the entire physical universe comprises a single unbroken whole (Bohm, 1985). Such deep inconsistencies seem to have eluded the notice of academic materialist reductionists, who are wedded to a false 18th century theory of matter, according to which the fundamental units are easily imaginable, like billiard balls or marbles, having precise spatio-temporal definition, and of course, can be squeezed in one's hands.[34]

However, although atomism applied to the material world is certainly false, the more pernicious nature of atomism occurs in Western religions and theologies, which hold that minds or souls, although not reducible to matter, are nevertheless all separate from and independent of one another; hence the belief that some souls may be separated off from others and sent to hell permanently. This is a vicious belief system that allows for, condones, and even encourages the most extreme forms of cruelty and violence now in evidence all over the world. But the atomism of Western religions is contradicted by the data emerging from 130 years of research. The worldview emerging from and supported by this empirical data asserts

---

[34] *Because academic materialist reductionism—"fundamaterialism", as I like to call it—has been and still is so influential, I want to linger with this theme for another footnote. To believe in materialist reductionism requires that one be not only (i) ignorant of the empirical data that shows beyond a reasonable doubt that consciousness is not produced by the brain and (ii) ignorant of the fact that our best theory about the nature of matter (quantum mechanics) implies that Atomism is false, but also be ignorant of the fact that a major interpretive strand of the quantum theory holds that the theory itself requires that consciousness exist as an independent variable. This is referred to as the "problem of measurement". (See the writings of von Neumann, Wigner, and Stapp for the details). It seems to me that materialist reductionists, if they were intellectually honest, would feel some need to address the fact that our best theory about the nature of matter appears to support neither atomism nor materialism. But the fundamaterialists do not feel a need to do so, any more than the creationists feel any need to address the facts of geology. This is why I said that materialist reductionists are wedded to an 18th century concept of matter.*

that consciousness is a fundamental existent, perhaps *the* fundamental existent, and also that the individual consciousness we experience ourselves as being is so intrinsically connected with other individual consciousness so as to constitute a single "One Mind" (Dossey, 2014). This is Plato's "World Soul," which creates both the world and our experience of it. The term "panentheism" is sometimes used to describe a worldview of this type.

Now, it is not my intention here to discuss metaphysics per se. Rather, I wish to explore the following question: just as greed-based capitalism is a social order that follows logically from a materialist metaphysical belief system, what is the new social order that follows from empirical findings that strongly suggest (i) consciousness is not created by the brain and (ii) individual minds, such as our own, are intrinsically connected so as to form a single One Mind, of which we are all essential components?[35] What follows from the empirical fact, established by science beyond a reasonable doubt, that our physical brains do not create the very consciousness we experience as ourselves? If human consciousness is not self-caused, and is not caused by the physical brain, then what, or perhaps who, causes this consciousness to come into being? And more importantly, for the purposes of this chapter, is the question: what follows from (i) and (ii) above with regard to a possible social order that embraces and is in harmony with our emerging "postmaterialist science?"

From the fact that consciousness is not created by the brain, it follows that consciousness—that is, our minds—did not begin to exist when the brain was formed. It also follows that it will not cease to exist when the brain dies. So the mind, prior to associating with a body and "becoming" what we are now experiencing as our (embodied) "selves" or "personalities," exists in its own right. Considerable insight into the nature of non-embodied existence may be gleaned by studying the near-death experience (NDE) in depth. These reports confirm in great detail Plato's claim that

---

[35] *The first statement (i) is an empirical fact for which the evidence is so strong that only those who are studiously ignorant of the evidence can deny it. The second statement (ii) is the most probable "grand" hypothesis, or world-view, that accounts for all the data.*

the body acts as a damper to the mind's native intelligence.[36] NDErs (and mystics) report being more awake, more conscious, more real, and more of who they really are, when out of the body than when in it. So the embodied consciousness, the personality, is experienced as "less real" than the non-embodied consciousness. The embodied consciousness emanates, so to speak, from something greater than itself. I will arbitrarily use the words "personality" and "ego" to refer to embodied consciousness, and with some reluctance use the word "soul" to refer to the greater reality we experience ourselves as being when not embodied. The soul is of course the greater of the two, and the personality is embedded in the soul, perhaps in a way similar to how the "self" in a dream is embedded in the mind of the dreamer.

If we were to ask a materialist to say something about the relationship between our present personality and the forces or causes that create the personality, the resulting story would say a lot about the development of the brain of the individual. Some combination of genetics and environment caused the present personality to come into being. But no meaning or purpose plays any role in the story. We do not "choose" our genetic makeup, and we do not "choose" our upbringing, so the major causal factors necessary for creating the unique individual personality that we are has nothing to do with us. We are the result of processes that merely "happened" to us, or that merely "happened" to generate us. And of course, because there is no deep meaning or purpose to our existence, the only "meaning" to be found in embodied life lies in chasing after material goods.

The empirical data that establishes as fact that consciousness is not created by matter offers a much different response to questions pertaining to the relationship between the present personality and its cause(s). Using data from NDE research, especially the life review (see following), and the

---

[36] *"The body confuses the soul and does not allow it to acquire truth and wisdom whenever it (the soul) is associated with it (the body)"*, Plato Phaedo 66a (parenthesis mine). *"if we are ever to have pure knowledge, we must escape from the body and observe matters in themselves with the soul by itself"* (Phaedo 66e)

claim that the non-embodied state is "realer than real," as well as data from reincarnation cases (especially the "in-between" state), together with data from research mediums, it appears that there is intention and purpose underlying the lives, the personalities, of each and every human being. In sharp contrast to materialism, it is not by mere accident that we are the unique individuals that we are. The soul, it appears, exercises some choice with regard to the specific individuals who are our parents, knowing in advance the environmental conditions that come with the choice of parents. So the soul intends, if you will, to manifest as us, and selects for parents and environmental conditions that will bring about its intentions.

But why? Notice that this question cannot even be raised under a materialist worldview. The atoms and physical forces that create the body and constitute its very being have no "purpose" whatsoever. But if the personality is intentionally created by a consciousness that is greater than itself, and if this personality is actually a part of, or embedded in, the larger creating consciousness, then questions of meaning and purpose necessarily arise. No student of the NDE can fail to notice, perhaps with a bit of dark humor, that many if not most NDErs are quite reluctant to return to their bodies, and are often quite upset upon finding himself or herself still embodied. So why can't they stay? Why are they sent back? And to take this query to its logical extreme, why were we compelled to take on physical form in the first place? There is quite a bit of data on the first two questions (I count as "data" what people report—one report is an "anecdote," but thousands of reports constitute "data"). NDErs state that they are sent back because there is more for them to do here, that it is not their time. So our individual lives have intrinsic meaning and purpose, and it is reasonable to conclude that there is reason and purpose underlying the soul's "decision" to manifest as us.

Now what, if anything, follows from this with regard to society as a whole? Materialism, we have said, leads quite logically to the kind of social order we have today, a social order that selects for greed and ambition, since only individuals who are so motivated have any chance of "succeeding" as our society defines "success." Another "measure" of our society's true values would be the "pay" offered to those in the helping professions, versus the "pay" offered to those in business and finance, professions entirely dedicated to the pursuit of greed and personal ambition. Those who have only the gambler's talent—the ability to lie with a straight face—receive the most remuneration, which accurately reflects the values of this materialist culture. But if our personality is caused by our soul, or by a consciousness greater than our personality, and it is caused not randomly but intentionally, then what conclusion does that lead to? Is it ever the case, we ask, that non-embodied consciousness would create a personality, or an aspect of itself, with the intent that the created personality spend its so-called life chasing after wealth and status? Of what use are such things to the soul? "For what shall it profit a man, if he shall gain the whole world, and lose his own soul?" The "man," the embodied consciousness, cannot of course "lose" the soul of which he is a part. But he can lose his sense of connectedness with the larger consciousness that has manifested as his human form, and can come to believe that he is only the human form; he can come to value only what aggrandizes the form, and forget the values of knowledge-seeking and compassion that motivated the soul to manifest as a human body/personality in the first place.

The soul, or the consciousness that creates us, can have no motivations that pertain to the yet-to-be-created body and personality. Souls do not compete with one another, since, as NDErs report, they experience directly their interconnectedness with all other souls, so as to constitute a single "One Mind." To reverse the old joke, no one has ever been told by the "Being of Light" that the reason they have to go back to their body is to make more money or gain more status. On the contrary, NDErs tell us that the "reasons" for which they are sent back all fall under the headings of knowledge and love, and many studies show that the most profound after-effect of the NDE is that greed and status-seeking fall away from the personality, replaced by knowledge-seeking and compassion, as motivators. We note that it is precisely this—that our greed-based status-seeking materialist social order is the opposite of the values of love, compassion, and knowledge that NDErs experience while out-of-body—that causes them so much stress upon returning. The question we are asking might be put as follows: what might a social order look like that would be in harmony with what NDErs experience, a social order based on knowledge and love?

It might be objected that a social order based on knowledge and love is impossible, because humans, like other animals, are by nature greedy and competitive. But the only thing humans are "by nature" is mortal. Cooperation is as easily observed among animals as competition, and a new-born human is infinitely malleable by its culture. Those in whom selfishness and status-seeking reign tend to believe that everyone else is just like them, and have constructed ideologies according to which their own status-seeking and greed-based behaviors are just what Darwin's "survival of the fittest" demands. But this is untrue. There are, to be sure, plenty of individuals who dedicate their lives to the pursuit of status and wealth. But it is also true that there are individuals who, despite being raised in a culture that idolizes greed and ambition, are nevertheless kind, compassionate, and altruistic. What might a social order look like that selects for the latter human motivations, instead of the former?

Thus far my argument has been mostly conceptual: from the fact that consciousness is not produced by the brain, it follows that the particular form of consciousness that we experience as our very self is caused, not by matter, nor by itself, but by another form of consciousness. This "creating" form of consciousness, which I sometimes refer to as the soul, has the usual characteristics associated with consciousness: awareness, meaning, intent, intelligence, joy, and love. I then argued that, because the soul is not material, its motivation or purpose in creating, or manifesting as, the human form, cannot possibly have anything to do with material acquisition, except what is necessary to keep the body functioning properly. To the extent, therefore, that a soul upon becoming human becomes obsessed with thoughts of material acquisition, it has deviated from its original purpose in manifesting as human. A social order that is in harmony with the fact that consciousness is not created by the body—a postmaterialist social order—will have no place for greed and ambition.

Less strongly established by empirical data, but established nonetheless, is panentheism, which holds that individual souls are not atomic units of consciousness that exist independently of one another, but instead are perhaps like droplets of water condensing from a common source. Western religions, except for their mystical components, are deeply atomistic in nature, denying that all minds are intrinsically connected so as to constitute a single "One Mind," which is the panentheistic hypothesis. If it is the case that all individual minds taken together constitute a single One Mind, then the Golden Rule is a logical consequence. In the deeper mystical and near-death experiences, one experiences oneself as the manifesting consciousness that manifests not only as his or her unique human form, but also as the form of all other beings. All manifested forms are as important and as "divine" as one's own, and any attitude other than one of loving-kindness towards all created forms is inconsistent with panentheism and the experience of deep interconnectedness. A social order based on the Golden Rule is the only kind of society consistent with our emerging postmaterialist science; it is also the only kind of social order that, at this present time, will allow consciousness to continue manifesting in human form. For the Earth has reached its limit with respect to the amount of greed it can support, and if humanity continues along the materialists' path of greed and status-seeking, the planet will no longer be able to support human life. Materialism at present has zero survival value.[37] A postmaterialist philosophy, if it is to be worth anything, must, like postmaterialist science, be in harmony with empirical data. Let's take a look at some of this data that favors a panentheistic worldview.

Traditional theism holds that God creates us ex nihilo, out of nothing. Panentheism holds that God creates us ex Deus, out of Himself. Well, perhaps we should leave the word "God" out of this and refer instead to the consciousness that creates us. Quite literally, our individual minds are "part of" the mind of the creating consciousness itself. A few well-chosen quotes from deep NDEs make this point very well:

"…..we are aspects of the one perfect whole, and as such are part of God, and of each other" (Ring, 2006, p. 299).

---

[37] *Everyone knows that the current course of human behavior is unsustainable, hence suicidal. But no one seems able to trace the causes to the materialist ideology permeating all aspect of present culture, least of all the materialists themselves.*

"And it became very clear to me that all the higher selves are connected as one being, all humans are connected as one being, we are actually the same being, different aspects of the same being" (Ring, 2006, pp. 287-88).

"I realized that the entire universe is alive and infused with consciousness. Everything belongs to an infinite whole. We're all facets of that Unity—we're all One"(Moorjani, 2012, p. 70).

"In my (NDE) experience, I became the Source—I existed in everything and it all existed within me—I became eternal and infinite" (Moorjani, 2012, p. 67).

It would be difficult to find a clearer statement of panentheism than the above quotes.

I argued above that because we are created by consciousness, there is meaning and purpose to our lives, and this meaning and purpose can have nothing to do with material acquisition. The following statement expresses this very concisely: "God told me there were only two things that we could bring back with us when we died …..LOVE and KNOWLEDGE …. So I was to learn as much about both as possible" (Ring, 2006, p. 296). And this is more or less the universal testimony of NDErs. There is a purpose in being human, a purpose that has nothing to do with material acquisition and status-seeking, and everything to do with growing in our ability to love and understand. A postmaterialist social order will have to be in harmony with these values. Children will be raised according to these values rather than the values of greed and self-aggrandizement. Needless to say, capitalism will have to go the way of feudalism, monarchy, slavery, and other social orders that have outlived their usefulness.

Ken Ring is among the few scientists with the courage to highlight the moral implications of the NDE. The Golden Rule, he concludes, is not a mere "precept for moral action." Rather, the Golden Rule "is actually the way it works…if these accounts in fact reveal to us what we experience at the point of death, then what we have done unto others is experienced as done unto ourselves" (Ring, 2006, p. 162). Let's take a look at a few accounts that lead to this conclusion.

"Everything I had ever said or done, or even thought, was right there......I rethought every thought, I re-experienced every feeling, as it happened, in an instant. And I also felt how my actions, or even just my thoughts, had affected others. When I passed judgment on someone else, I would experience myself doing that. Then I would change places in perspective, and experience what that judgment had felt like for them to receive from me......Multitudinous actions or thoughts, derived from my own meanness, unkindness, or anger, caused me to feel the consequent pains of the other people.....And I felt their pain for the full length of time they were affected by what I had done. Because I was in a different dimension where time can't be measured as we know time to exist on earth, it was possible to know all of this and experience it all at once, and with the ability to comprehend all of this information" (Ring, 2006, p. 158).

"....it showed me not only what I had done, but even how what I had done had affected other people ......because I could feel those things ......not even your thoughts are lost ....Every thought was there" (Ring, 2006, p. 159).

"All of a sudden....my life passed before me ......What occurred was every emotion I have felt in my life, I felt. What my life had done so far to affect other peoples' lives, using the feeling of pure love that was surrounding me as the point of comparison. And I had done a terrible job. God, I mean it! ....Looking at yourself from the point of how much love you have spread to other people is devastating" (Ring, 2006, p. 159).

"I remember one particular incident.....when as a child I yanked my little sister's Easter basket away from her, because there was a toy in it that I wanted. Yet in the review, I felt her feelings of disappointment and loss and rejection. What we do to other people when we act unlovingly! Everything you have done is there in the review for you to evaluate (and) when I was there in that review there was no covering up. I was the very people that I hurt, and I was the very people I had helped to feel good ....It is a real challenge, every day of my life, to know that when I die I am going to have to witness every single action of mine again, only this time actually feeling the effects I've had on others" (Ring, 2006, p. 159).

"It was an opportunity to see and feel all the love I had shared, and more importantly, all the pain I had caused. I was able to simultaneously re-experience not only my own feelings and thoughts, but those of all the other people I had ever interacted with. Seeing myself through their eyes was a humbling experience" (Ring, 2006, p. 160).

"Mine was not a review, but a reliving. For me it was a reliving of every thought I had ever thought, every word I had ever spoken, and every deed I had ever done; plus, the effect of each thought, word, and deed on everyone and anyone who had ever come into my environment or sphere of influence, whether I knew them or not.....No detail was left out. No slip of the tongue or slur was missed. No mistake or accident went unaccounted for. If there is such a thing as hell, as far as I am concerned, this was hell" (Ring, 2006, p. 160).

As I mentioned before, one or two such accounts may be dismissed as "anecdotes." But when such accounts are multiplied a hundred fold, a thousand fold, ten thousand fold and more, then they constitute data that must be taken seriously. It is quite obvious that our present capitalist social order is deeply inconsistent with these data.

The details of what a postmaterialist society might look like are of course beyond the scope of this chapter. Indeed, they are beyond the scope of any chapter that could be written at this time. But, following Plato, we can say this much now: in our new society, spiritual wisdom on the one hand, and political and economic power on the other hand, must coalesce in the same individuals. Who, we might ask, shall we put in charge of governing and managing the wealth and finances of our society (playfully assuming, for the moment, that the decision is up to us)? Should it be people who are very wealthy? Should it be people who are very popular? Or should it be, perhaps, people with advanced degrees from Harvard Business School? Our present disastrous social order shows quite clearly that none of the above provides the requisite skills for governing. What qualifications, then, must an individual have in order to govern properly?

Let's develop the point by analogy, in the manner of Plato. Every area of human endeavor recognizes that there is special knowledge, talent, training, and skills relevant to the specific area. Whether we consider art, music, and sports, or science, medicine, and engineering, or carpentry, plumbing, and cooking, we recognize that each area requires talent, education, skills, and much training before anyone can be considered as proficient in that area. Why, asked Plato some 2,400 years ago, do we make an exception for politics and economics? Why do we as a society collectively behave as if money-making (greed) and status-seeking (ambition) were the only, or best, qualifications required of those who seek political and economic power? If we could step back from our current situation (capitalism) a little bit, is it not insane for society to trust its economic well-being to those among us who are most greedy? Is it not equally insane to give political power to those who are most ambitious? Since when have greed and ambition been demonstrated to produce individuals who are fit to be the "guardians" (Plato's term) of the collective wealth of society? Clearly, from any sane perspective, allowing individuals who are mentally ill—as Spinoza would say, who are suffering from the "madness" of greed and ambition—to rule is like putting the fox in charge of guarding the henhouse. This experiment has been done, and the results are absolute disaster. Allowing greed and ambition to rule and control the wealth of the Earth is leading directly and unambiguously to the destruction of the Earth's ability to support life, and nothing could conceivably be more disastrous for humanity than our extinction.

I know that economists and other apologists for our current system will rave about the importance of the "profit motive," without which, they believe, no one would do anything; but their arguments must now be seen as hollow, for two main reasons. (i) The so-called profit motive, a consequence of materialism, is leading to the destruction of the human race. Therefore, if the human race is to survive, the profit motive must disappear. But just as importantly, (ii) the major premise of economists, that the "profit motive" is necessary to motivate people to get off their butts, so to speak, is empirically false. Most people, even those who have not had an NDE, are not motivated by the desire to profit over others. They—or rather, we—are motivated by desires such as curiosity, kindness, helping others, and developing and expressing our talents and abilities. These, I submit, are the real motivators of human behavior. Only individuals who are already somewhat mentally ill will fall for all this "profit motive" nonsense. And those who have had a deep NDE know something about this that it is important for us to learn. In the context of the life review, we experience the "other" as our "self." As Ken Ring has clearly shown, this is not merely some vague empathy for the other, but an experience of actual identity with the "other." The profit motive instructs us to seek advantage over the other. But since the "other" is experienced as our very self, the profit motive becomes a logical impossibility, since there is no "other" and it is logically impossible to gain advantage over our self. The profit motive is thus formally inconsistent with the life review, because in the latter there is no "other" over whom one could "profit."

We know that capitalism will very soon come to an end, either by destroying the Earth's capacity for life, or by being replaced by an economic/political system that will allow the planet to continue supporting human life. Since I am an optimist, I shall consider the second option. We are seeking for someone who will conduct and manage the affairs of our whole society. What is the appropriate qualification for the job of leadership? What is the education, the training, required in order to trust an individual with such responsibility? I think that perhaps, at long last, the world is ready to seriously consider Plato's answer to this question. Is it not now obvious? Clearly, the individuals we put in charge of managing our economy and governing our society must be free from greed and ambition, and must "desire nothing for themselves that they do not also desire for others" (Spinoza, B., *Ethics*, part 4, prop.18, scholium). Where might we find such people? Read again the above quotes in which NDErs describe themselves as being every person with whom they interacted. Could one who has had such an experience ever misuse political or economic power? Clearly not. Plato might say that one who is to become a ruler must first have caught a vision of the Form of the Good. Or equivalently, we might say that the most important qualification for becoming a leader is that one has experienced directly the interconnection of all beings—or, what is the same thing, that one has experienced directly the knowledge of the union between his own mind and the One Mind that has created both himself and all other minds. This is the knowledge of mystics and (deep) NDErs, and only such knowledge removes all temptation to abuse power and authority.

And this is really the point of Plato's *Republic*: worldly power and spiritual enlightenment must come together in the same individuals. As Plato puts it: "Until philosophers rule as kings or those who are now called kings and leaders genuinely and adequately philosophize, that is, until political power and philosophy entirely coincide...cities will have no rest from evil, nor, I think, will the human race" (Plato, *Republic*, 473d). The passage is well known, but Plato's concept of the "Philosopher-king" is not well understood, especially by academics. The word "philosopher," as Plato uses it, has nothing to do with those who are called by that name in academic institutions.[38] For Plato, a philosopher is a lover of wisdom, and wisdom is the state of consciousness enjoyed by the gods; that is, it is a state of consciousness that does not involve the body. Plato is quite explicit about this. Comparing the experiences of the embodied soul with the non-embodied soul, he states, "When the soul makes use of the body to investigate something, be it through hearing or seeing or some other sense, it is dragged by the body to the things that are never the same ("physical" things), and the soul itself strays and is confused and dizzy, as if it were drunk. But when the soul investigates by itself (i.e. without the body) it passes into the realm of what is pure, ever existing (eternal), immortal and unchanging, and being akin to this, it always stays with it (the eternal) whenever it is by itself and can do so; then the soul rests from its wanderings (in the physical realm) and dwells with it (the eternal) unchangingly, for it (the soul) is dealing with what is unchanging, and its experience then is what is called wisdom" (Plato, *Phaedo*, 79 c, d) (parentheses mine).

Notice that, for Plato, the word "wisdom" refers to the soul's experience when released from its association with a body, and the philosopher, then, is one who desires for herself or himself this state of consciousness. Now, the majority of academic "philosophers" today are materialists/

---

[38] *In Book Six of the Republic, Plato severely criticizes those who are called "philosophers" but do not practice philosophy, that is, are not seekers of wisdom. His criticisms are as appropriate today as they were in his time.*

atheists who believe that consciousness is entirely produced by the physical brain. Hence they most definitely do not seek for themselves a state of consciousness (non-embodied) that they believe does not exist. So no materialist can satisfy Plato's definition for being a philosopher.[39] But mystics and NDErs would count as philosophers for Plato, for they have been outside the cave, have experienced the real, and are ever-seeking to align their human consciousness experience with what lies beyond the shadows of the cave.[40] NDErs understand what Plato means when he refers to embodied consciousness, compared with the heightened reality of non-embodied consciousness, as wandering around "confused and dizzy, as if drunk." It is to such individuals, and only to such individuals, that a sane society will entrust its politics and economics, for the empirical data show quite clearly that the experience of being absorbed into the light, and the unconditional love thereof, removes the motivations of greed and ambition from the mind of the experiencer.

Until now, such experiential knowledge has been quite rare, available only to some spiritual teachers and advanced monks. But today, many individuals have had spiritually transformative experiences, and as medical technology continues to advance, many more will be brought back from so-called death, and will have had the experience of consciousness, per se, unencumbered by a body. There will be no shortage of individuals who, because they have themselves seen and "become" the light of the creating

---

[39] *It will be a while, I think, before academic philosophy finds its way back to Plato. But the same data that has created the need for a postmaterialist science has also created a need for a postmaterialist philosophy, so I am confident that things will eventually change. Meanwhile, Plato has much to offer those who are convinced that materialism is false. His fundamental insight that spiritual wisdom and temporal power must be joined, if humanity is to be saved, is the most profound idea of our time. Also, for those who have had an NDE, Plato's poignant description of the difficulties involved in coming back to the body is remarkably accurate. See Republic, (516e – 518a).*

[40] *Allegory of the Cave summary: https://web.stanford.edu/class/ihum40/cave.pdf*

consciousness, are now qualified to hold positions of leadership in our post-materialist world.

How might all this come about? For it is quite unlikely that those who currently hold economic and political power will themselves become lovers of wisdom.[41] Indeed, greed and status-seeking are addictions, in that the more one has of these things the more one needs in order to get the same "high" from acquiring them. They are no more able to relinquish their addiction to money-making than an alcoholic can relinquish his craving for drink. Neither should we hold our collective breath waiting for our universities, professional organizations, and other institutions of research to announce that science has established the reality of spirit, and that henceforth we should all start loving one another. For our universities, as institutions of our culture, necessarily reflect and transmit the values of the culture's materialist paradigm. Our universities have done, and are doing, whatever they can to impede this research, rather than promote it. Nevertheless, through the media, the results of our research are reaching a much wider audience. For example, when the details of the life review become common knowledge, people will know that it is impossible to gain advantage by harming another, and greed and ambition, which necessarily harms others, will fall away. Those of us who are students of the NDE will doubtless have already noticed this within ourselves.

One of Plato's major themes is that the outer social order mirrors the inner psychological order, and vice versa. A "just" individual is one who is ruled by her or his higher emotions and desires; a "just" society is one that is ruled by the most morally developed of humans. As individuals, we have the power to move things along, so to speak, by looking within, examining our own emotions and desires, and identifying those of our own desires that fall under the general headings of greed and ambition. If, for example, we notice that we are seeking status and desire to "get ahead" of others, then we might reflect that those "others" we wish to get ahead of will feel hurt (as we would feel if someone "got ahead" of us). So the desire to get ahead necessarily involves hurting others, and as Ring has emphasized, it

---

[41] *Plato himself got into trouble on this point. See his 7th letter for the details.*

is in the nature of things that in the life review we will feel the hurt we caused. These and similar reflections may be sufficient to relinquish "getting ahead" as a motivation.

This, or something like this, is what Socrates must have meant at his trial, when he stated: "the unexamined life is not worth living" (Plato, *Apology* 38a). I think Socrates' injunction will be satisfied if, while contemplating any course of action, we ask ourselves, "how will this play out in my life review?" And if enough individuals examine themselves in this way, change their inner life accordingly, and talk about it with others,[42] the outer social reality will follow suit. That is my hope.

References

Bohm, D. *(*1985). *Wholeness and the Implicate Order.* London: ARK Paperbacks.

Broad, C.D. (1962). *Lectures on Psychical Research: Incorporating the Perrott Lectures, Given in Cambridge University.* New York: Humanities Press.

Curley, E. (1994). *A Spinoza Reader: Ethics.* Princeton: Princeton University Press.

Dossey, L. (2014). *One Mind: How Our Individual Mind is Part of a Greater Consciousness And Why It Matters,* Carlsbad, CA: Hay House.

---

[42] *This last point is important. There are powerful taboos in our materialist society against discussing such experiences with others. Our recent cultural experience that culminated in legalizing gay marriage came about largely because gay people increasingly came out of the closet. At some point, every straight person realized that they had friends and family members who were gay, and resistance dropped away. The "spiritual" closet is perhaps even larger than the gay closet was. If enough people who have had spiritually transformative experiences dropped their fear of ridicule and came out of the closet to friends and family, then everyone would realize that they personally know someone who has had such an experience. At this point, perhaps, it would become acceptable to talk openly about such experiences in our culture, and our culture would necessarily change as a result.*

Kelly. E. F., Kelly, E. W., Crabtree, A., Gauld, A., Grosso, M., & Greyson, B. (2007). *Irreducible Mind: Toward a Psychology for the 21st Century*. Lanham, MD: Rowman & Littlefield.

Moorjani, M. (2012). *Dying to be Me*. Carlsbad, CA: Hay House.

Plato. (2002). *Plato: Five Dialogues*, (Grube, G.M.A., Transl.) Cambridge: Hackett Publishing.

Plato. (1974). *Republic*. (Grube, G.M.A., Transl.) Cambridge: Hackett Publishing.

Plato (1993). *Sophist*. (White, N.P., Transl.) Cambridge: Hackett Publishing.

Ring, K. (2006). *Lessons From the Light*. Needham, MA: Moment Point Press, p 299.

Chapter Eighteen

Kundalini Awakenings: Expanding Science to Encompass a Postmaterialist Perspective

Marjorie Hines Woollacott, PhD

Introduction

Despite the frequency of their occurrence, spiritually transformative experiences (STEs) are one of the least discussed and therefore hidden phenomena in our culture. Research has shown that these STEs can occur under a variety of circumstances, including among others, during meditation or other intense spiritual practices, during a near-death experience (NDE), spontaneously, and as a result of ingestion of psychedelics. Since in the majority of cases these experiences appear to have an energetic aspect to them many researchers believe that STEs are a form of *kundalini* awakening (KA). Regardless of how they are named, it is clear that STEs occur with surprising prevalence. A Gallup poll (2002) asked individuals to rate the statement, "I have had a profound religious experience or awakening that changed the direction of my life," on a scale from 0 to 5. Zero represented "does not apply at all" and 5 represented "applies completely." Amazingly, 41 percent of Americans (i.e., about 80 million adults) responded that the assertion *completely* applied to themselves. Even 25% of the individuals who reported having no religious preference responded that the statement fully applied to them.

Ironically, despite their prevalence, these types of experiences are rarely subjected to scientific scrutiny and are not often part of media and public discourse. As a result, individuals who have these types of experiences typically have no frame of reference in which to understand, assimilate, and integrate the experience into their lives in a beneficial way. In addition, the prevailing materialist scientific and medical opinion places them in a framework in which these experiences are considered a pathological manifestation of an impaired brain. Thus the individual seeking help following such an experience is often diagnosed as mentally ill. This diagnosis leads to treatments aimed at "curing" the pathology through medication and or therapy.

One contributing factor to this concealment of the phenomenon is the currently pervasive materialist world view that pervades science and academic research, which considers these experiences to be, from a permissive point of view anecdotal or unsubstantiated, and from the extreme conservative medical view, to be pathological. This has led many individuals who have had these experiences to deny the phenomenon, even to themselves, as they assume it may have been at best only their imagination, or at worst, a sign of psychosis. There are many differences in interpretation of these phenomena between the lenses of materialist and postmaterialist science, including explanations of their physiological basis and transformative effects, which will be discussed in this chapter.

A growing number of scientists and clinicians are embracing an alternative postmaterialist framework that considers these experiences as both a normal and essential phenomenon to the process of individual and human growth. These two opposing frameworks have a profound impact at both an individual and societal level. In the first framework, such experiences are considered pathological phenomena and therefore of no real benefit to the individual or society. In contrast, the second framework views such experiences as an important catalyst for transformation at both the individual and societal level. We may not yet fully understand the scientific nature of these experiences, but whatever the ontological status of these spiritually transformative awakenings may be, they are perceived as real by the individuals who experience them, and thus merit inclusion in both scientific and medical inquiry.

Historical Background

As historical information on the experience of energetic or *kundalini* awakening is not readily available in western culture, a brief background of the origin of the concept is provided. I will first describe the origin of the concept in India, followed by mention of similar concepts in other cultures. Texts discussing the mystical process of the awakening of what is called the *kundalini* energy appeared in India beginning in about the fifth or sixth centuries C.E. (White, 1996; Brooks & Bailly, 1997; Muller-Ortega, 1997; Shantananda, 2003). According to these texts, universal consciousness during the process of creation, as an expression of its own enjoyment and free will, limits and conceals its true nature and becomes the finite self, present within all beings. In this process it takes the role of the energy that gives life to sentient beings (Muller-Ortega, 1997). This aspect of the universal consciousness, which is said to exist within each human being, is referred to as the *kundalini*.

The *kundalini* is described as having two forms, an outer form, which is considered to be the force that gives rise to the universe and governs the body's physiological processes, and an inner form, considered to be the force underlying the awakening of each human's spiritual awareness. Tantric texts such as the *Tantraloka* state that at a certain point in each person's evolution, the *kundalini* is awakened through the phenomenon of cosmic grace, and the ignorance of their true nature is removed (Muller-Ortega, 1997). According to the texts, the awakening occurs in different forms or levels of intensities according to the quality of preparedness of the individual seeker.

After the energy is awakened these texts describe a process of transformation and purification that is accompanied by the flow of this energy through subtle energy centers of the body (chakras), typically described as positioned along the spinal column from the base of the spine to the crown of the head. This purification process is said to be accompanied in many cases by spontaneous bodily movements, called kriyas (Brooks & Bailly, 1997; Wallis, 2008). The final goal of the process is an experience of expansive or unity awareness, accompanied by equanimity, joy and peace (Muller-Ortega, 1997).

Though this energy is termed *kundalini* in the Indian traditions, in China, this vital energy of the body is called *chi;* in Japan it is *ki*; the Hebrew tradition speaks of the *shekinah*; and the Christian tradition refers to it as the Holy Spirit. African tribesmen, the !Kung, are known to dance for long periods to activate or "heat up" the energy they call *n/um* so that a transcendent experience, the *!Kia,* can be awakened (Sannella, 1987). It is interesting that this concept was also present in Greek literature and mentioned by Plato. Plato describes the transmission of the enlightened state of consciousness from Teacher to student. He says, "Acquaintance with it must come rather after a long period of attendance on instruction in the subject itself and of close companionship, when, suddenly, like a blaze kindled by a leaping spark, it is generated in the soul and at once becomes self-sustaining" (Plato: Letters: VII 341cd).

It is important to note that different cultures and spiritual traditions describe this energetic awakening in various ways. Some individuals may think that because their own experience did not reflect the classic description (e.g., energy shooting up the spine), it was not an energetic or kundalini awakening. In fact, as you will see in the research below, within the variety of possible experiences there appear to be key elements of the awakening, which can include a sense of energy moving through and around the body, associated with a sense of joy and of enhanced connection with other beings in the universe. This is also accompanied by a new understanding of the nature of consciousness, with a sense that it is fundamental to who we are.

Research on Energetic Spiritual or *Kundalini* Awakening

As discussed earlier, research on energetic spiritual or *kundalini* awakenings reveals that they can be triggered by a number of different circumstances, including meditation or other intense practices, and NDEs (Greyson, 2014; Woollacott et al., 2020; Taylor, 2012). Two research groups, including Greyson (2000) and Sanches and Daniels (2008) have developed *Kundalini* Scales (Greyson: the Physio-Kundalini Syndrome Index (KI); Sanches and Daniels: the Kundalini Awakening Scale), based on the hypothesis that *kundalini* awakening may be a typical underlying aspect of mystical experiences that result in transformational changes in an individual's life.

Supporting this concept, Greyson and Khanna (2014) showed that participants who had experienced an NDE underwent clear beneficial behavioral transformations associated with this energetic awakening. More recently Taylor and colleagues (Taylor, 2012; Taylor and Egeto-Szabo, 2017) have studied what they call awakening experiences, which include intensified, expanded awareness, and feelings of expansion or well-being, similar to what is described in *kundalini* awakenings. Interestingly, they have found that intense emotional experiences, such as depression and despair, could trigger these types of energetic awakenings. Taylor proposes that a period of depression or despair may lead to a dissolution of attachments involving one's self-image and concepts concerning life and the world, which give rise to the egoic sense of self. Taylor proposes that when there is increasing detachment from the sense of ego and these concepts begin to dissolve, one is close to a state of liberation from the challenges in life and this contributes to the energetic awakening and feelings of expanded awareness.

Our Research on Kundalini Awakening

Building on these previous studies our research group (Woollacott, Park & Kason, 2020) has performed a larger scale study on individuals within the general population to better understand the phenomenology of spiritually transformative energetic awakenings as well as their subsequent behavioral and physiological transformative effects.

We collected detailed descriptions of both the physical experiences and changes in conscious awareness of persons having any type of STE/KA (e.g., spontaneous energetic awakenings, those occurring through NDEs, and through spiritual practices). We used a detailed questionnaire created by members of the Kundalini Research Network (KRN) with both quantitative data sections and open-ended survey questions. The data are from a subset of questions within Questionnaire, with the quantitative data determined from 342 individuals, while the verbal descriptions (qualitative data) were taken from appropriate descriptions within the entire questionnaire. The mean age of participants was 49 ± 12 yrs. (Woollacott et al., 2020).

On average, subjects reported that the experience of energetic awakening was very mystical, including feelings of expansion (conscious awareness leaving the body or expanding beyond the body), and an experience of being surrounded by light or love. Some samples of the experiences reported include:

1. [This was] my very first meditation. I was instructed in transcendental meditation in 1973. I transcended, following my TM instructors teaching instructions. I meditated 20 minutes. I came out of the building into the summer sunshine and I saw the world totally differently. The sky was bluer the sun was brighter, the birds were louder, the grass greener – it was "as if" a veil a screen had been lifted and I could see forever into the universe clearly…no stress –I was "one" with the sky, the clouds, the whole universe. It grew stronger every day.

2. The experience came quite suddenly one evening while in my room preparing for bed. It was as though I was aware of a non-physical being of "energy" or light, emerging from one corner of the room. As I approached it – it also seemed to come nearer to me until "we" merged. At that moment I felt as though every cell in my body was "on fire" or "charged" in a way unknown or unfelt before… The "being" and I were ONE. I was able to see and know things beyond the scope of experience and knowledge of my 15 years. I seemed to "hear" inaudibly – as though knowledge and vision were transferred directly into my mind from this source. I felt incredible peace and joy: a sense that all worked out in the universe – despite the ostensible appearance. [I] had somewhat of a global, universal awareness. I consider my mystical experience the most "singular" event regarding what's real – that I've ever had.

3. While meditating, two times felt something rush up spine, also felt heat below belly. Once while meditating, great vibrations through body. I stopped meditating because it scared me. (Woollacott et al., 2020)

Though these experiences represent only a small sample of the total reported, several recurring themes were found. The STE/KA could occur spontaneously, either when awake or during the night, in the middle of sleep. STE/KAs could also occur during meditation, both in initial exposure to the practice or as a result of intense meditation practice, or in the presence of a master of meditation. And individual may also be initially elated or frightened by the new unexpected experiences. However, over time individuals noted that the experience led to beneficial life transformations including a profound sense of joy, peace and expansive awareness.

One of the questions asked of participants was "What was your experience of the energy?" Table 1 shows the responses in order of frequency of appearance, regarding the nature of this energy in general (e.g., unusual flows of energy in and around the body).

Table 1. General Experiences of the Kundalini Energy		Percent
1	Unusual flows of energy through or around the body	85%
2	Unexplained vigorous body jerks or spasms	76%
3	Body shaking or vibrations	72%
4	Feelings of head and/or body expansion	70%
5	Hot flashes/heat intolerance	67%
6	Unexplainable mood and energy swing	66%
7	Night sweats	60%
8	Spontaneous Yogic breathing	51%
9	Spontaneous Yogic postures	49%

Examples of these experiences include: Category 1. I noticed energy trickling (tickling) its way all along the spine moving up and coursing through everywhere in my body – the sensation is especially pleasant in the head/scalp, etc.

Category 4. Unusual in that my body drops away. There is an expansion, a oneness, with all of creation.

Category 9. Kundalini creates spontaneous asanas, flowing postures a la Tai Chi or classical Eastern dance.

Triggering Events for Kundalini Awakening

While some individuals reported that STE/KA experiences occur spontaneously, many others reported triggering events. Respondents were thus asked to check activities that occurred just prior to their STE/KA. Individuals were free to check more than one activity as a trigger; thus the combined percent of responses is greater than 100. Table 2 shows the results from the individuals in the sample who responded to this question (n=148), listing the top 11 elements out of 22 total.

	Table 2. Triggers for 1st Kundalini Experience	Percent
1	Thinking about or concentration on spiritual issues	41%
2	The presence of a spiritually developed person	34%
3	Intense meditation	30%
4	Intense prayer	25%
5	Near-death experience	21%
6	Reading spiritual material	21%
7	Sleep	20%
8	Music	13%
9	Severe physical illness	12%
10	Breathwork or pranayama	10%
11	Yoga	9%

Examples of verbal descriptions include: 1. (*thinking about or concentration on spiritual issues*): "[I experienced a] rush of energy, tingling, sense of being with God accompanying [the] blessing following [my] first communion." 2. (*reading spiritual material*): "I was in the middle of reading Muktananda's *Where are you going?* When I started spontaneously repeating "God is Love" over and over as I was filled with bliss and unconditional love."

Transformational Changes

Transformational changes are also a key component of an STE/KA and have been the subject of a number of research studies. For example, with regard to NDEs, Janet Schwaninger and her colleagues in a controlled prospective clinical study examined life transformation in a group of cardiac arrest patients after an NDE (Schwaninger et al., 2002). Each participant was asked to rate life changes in a number of categories (such as desire to help others, feelings of self worth, sense of sacredness of life, ability to express love for others) on a scale from 1 to 5 (1 meaning it had strongly increased, 5 strongly decreased). Participants with an NDE had scores that ranged from 1.4-1.6, meaning these qualities had strongly increased in their lives, in direct contrast to the non-NDE control group.

In counterpoint, to determine the transformative effects of ingestion of the hallucinogenic, psilocybin, a study by Stephen Ross and colleagues (Ross et al., 2016) performed a randomized controlled trial with terminal cancer patients who had high anxiety levels concerning their cancer and the end of life. Participants were guided through the psilocybin experience in a meditative clinical setting with professional guides. Though the original aim of the study did not include evaluation of mystical experiences associated with energetic awakenings (the aim was to determine changes in anxiety/depression), they noted that 64% of the participants rated the experience as either the singular or top five most *spiritually significant*, or the singular or top five most *personally meaningful* experience of their entire lives.

What are verbal expressions of this highly significant life transformation? In a similar study by Barrett and Griffiths (2018), there is a verbal description of the experience of one participant. He shared, "I was gone... or I should say this earthly part of me was. It was still on the couch in some sort of suspended animation awaiting my return. I was in the void. This void had a strange and indescribable quality to it in that there was nothing to it but this feeling of unconditional and undying Love. It felt like my soul was basking in the feeling of this space. I have no idea how long this lasted. Time and space did not exist there ...it was all different manifestations of this Love feeling I found myself wrapped in (p. 397).

Are these transformations similar to transformations triggered by a *kundalini* awakening? There are certainly many similarities. The experience narrative above suggests that it was associated with a new relationship with spirituality, and the feeling that this was more real than any previous experience. The participant had a sense of unity and interconnectedness with all of life. and the experience of unconditional and undying love.

Finally, in the study previously mentioned by Woollacott, Park and Kason (2020) we specifically aimed to explore a broad spectrum of transformational changes associated with the STE/KA. Participants were asked to respond on a 5 point Likert scale from marked to slight decrease, through no change, to slight and marked increases when exploring changes in a variety of areas of their life, including changes in sensory sensitivity, creative and healing and psychic abilities, and values/beliefs.

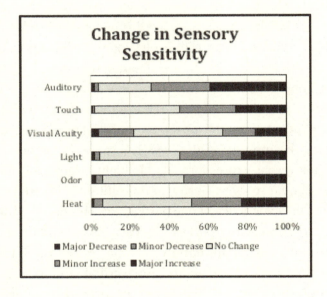

Figure 1.

In Figure 1 you see changes in sensitivity to different types of sensory stimuli. Note that participants indicated that they experienced a substantial increase in sensitivity (32-69%) to auditory, visual, touch and olfactory information, as well as an increase in sensitivity to heat.

Certain types of transformation are often dismissed by health care professionals as being unable to substantiate. However, changes in psychic abilities have been previously reported for persons who have undergone NDEs (Nouri & Holden, 2008). Figure 2 shows that these changes also are perceived to occur by persons undergoing not only NDEs but many other types of STEs; as you see in the figure the changes include transformations in creativity, capacity to heal, psychic abilities and impact on electronic devices. Note again, the substantial increases in each of these abilities post KA/STE.

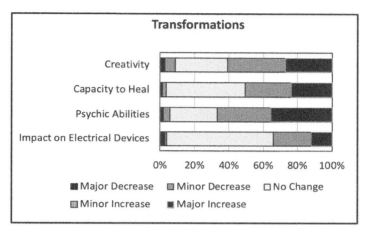

Figure 2.

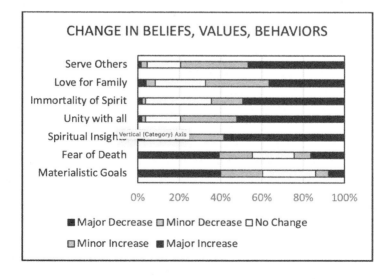

Figure 3.

The Time Frame for Transformation

Research results indicate that, in the case of NDEs and other spiritual awakenings, transformation is a dynamic process that includes an immediate change in the individual's deepest being, where he/she understands that consciousness is fundamental and eternal. This immediate transformation is often characterized as the "seed" of transformation. This new "seed" of understanding then plays itself out over time in the individual's outer life. Thus there is also a long-term aspect of STE transformation.

We examined the long-term transformations (over the past 5-10 year period) in beliefs, values, and behaviors as you see in Figure 3. Note that there were strong increases in values and behaviors that enhance interactions with others, such as serving others, love for family a belief in the immortality of the spirit and a sense of unity with others, along with accompanying spiritual insights. In contrast there were substantial decreases in fear of death and materialistic goals.

Comments that accompanied these quantitative responses included:
- [I have] a great urge to give of healing help to my fellow man.
- I believe we are all united no matter color, creed, etc. I am more tolerant of others, but I do not feel religious in a "church" sense.
- [The experiences] showed me even more the limitations of material life. [They] gave me insights about conditioning, the cage of the ego.

The last question within the questionnaire asked individuals to note whether they had discussed their experience with a health care professional and if the answer was yes, was the response satisfactory. Only 46% had discussed this with a professional. It may not be unexpected that participants were least satisfied (80%) with health care professionals trained in traditional medicine and most satisfied (20%) when talking to professionals familiar with NDEs, trained holistically, or trained in Jungian therapy. One person stated: [The doctor] didn't really think things like this happen – [he said,] "it is only your imagination." A woman said, "I was encouraged strongly by my MD husband to see a psychiatrist. When he suggested I admit myself to the psychiatric hospital I had clear guidance from within to accept the advice. As a nurse who had worked with psychiatric patients

I was not fearful. I stopped talking about what I was experiencing, went along with the system and was discharged in 8 days" (Woollacott et al., 2020).

The Value of Discussing STE/KAs Within a Postmaterialist Context

It is interesting that there are many scientific articles on the topics of meditation, yoga and other tools that come from spiritual traditions related to topics such as on stress reduction and increased mental function; however peer-reviewed research on energetic or *kundalini* awakenings and their transformative effects are rare. It is likely that this is related to the nature of experience, which does not fit into the current materialist model of the nature of consciousness. Nor is its exploration easily adaptable to traditional means of scientific experimentation.

However, it is perhaps surprising that results from the above studies of persons experiencing energetic awakenings across a variety of contexts confirm historical accounts of the *kundalini* awakening process that from a materialist medical perspective have been judged as simply anecdotal. These accounts were typically reported in texts from tantric and yogic traditions, case studies, and in broader studies of NDEs. (Krishna, 1993; Brooks & Bailly, 1997; Muller-Ortega, 1997; Singh, 1980; Wallis, 2008; Greyson, 2000). The verbal reports from the research studies discussed above support these historical accounts, indicating that the general characteristics of the energetic awakening are experienced as very mystical. For example, individuals in our study experienced a sense of heightened perception (the sky was bluer, the sun brighter), and a sense of unity, accompanied by joy and expansive love ("I was filled with bliss and unconditional love. I was one with the whole universe."). In comparison, a tantric text described the results of the kundalini awakening as "blissful" and an experience "in which there is no division or limitation" (Shantanana, 2003).

Though we and others have documented the prevalence of *kundalini* energetic awakenings in the general population, this phenomenon is not discussed in medical research and training; it is also rarely discussed in the media and public conversation in western culture. In consequence, persons experiencing an energetic awakening usually have no reference or context in which to place the experience and thus integrate it into their lives in a fully beneficial way. As many cohorts within our culture, including but not limited to scientists, academics and health care professionals, often view such experiences as pathological or irrelevant to individual growth, their capacity to respond appropriately to these individuals is limited. One reason for including discussion of STE/KAs within a postmaterialist context is that it allows both the experiencer and their health care professionals to understand that the experience is not abnormal or pathological, but, in fact, can be viewed as a highly beneficial growth process. This issue is not limited to STE/KAs; it also includes our culture's refusal to discuss death. This simply highlights the need to have open dialogues on many subjects that are considered "taboo" in our culture, in order to explore and normalize these areas of experience.

Possible Neural Correlates of the Energetic Awakening

Recent studies on the functional correlates of various brain networks has indicated that the wide-ranging narrative or Mind Wandering Network of the brain, described by many researchers as the Default Mode Network (DMN), is the source of our notion of self and our identification with our role in the world (Carhart-Harris & Friston, 2010). The components of the DMN include areas of the medial prefrontal cortex, the posterior cingulate cortex, the precuneus, the inferior parietal lobe, and the lateral temporal cortex.

A growing number of neuroscientists (Barrett & Griffiths, 2018; Brewer et al., 2011; Woollacott & Shumway-Cook, 2020) have proposed that transformative experiences like those described above, which produce a sense of unity, joy and expansiveness are associated with ego-dissolution, i.e., with an experience of the border between one's self and the external world dissolving. In fact, Barrett and Griffith's studies show a high correlation between a sense of unity consciousness and reduced activity and decoupling of the DMN.

In additional studies, Judson Brewer's team from Yale University School of Medicine, has demonstrated significant reductions in two primary nodes of the DMN during meditation, when comparing trained meditators to a control group (Brewer et al., 2011). These results indicate that the brain definitely becomes quieter in meditation – as the narrative part of the brain is silenced. What is the significance of this quieting of the DMN?

Woollacott and Shumway-Cook have hypothesized that during mystical experiences such as those found in STE/KAs, a disruption of the activity in the DMN quiets the narrative mind; this results in a diminishing of the normal filtering process of the brain, thus enabling an expanded awareness of subtler perceptions that are normally filtered out. In fact, changes in the DMN which were found by Brewer et al. (2011) during meditation have also been seen in Psilocybin studies (Barrett and Griffiths (2018).

Results from the meditation and psilocybin studies demonstrate very similar neural effects, with both showing reduction of the activity in the DMN. They also show that the reduction in this activity is directly correlated with an individual's increased sense of unity consciousness and ego-dissolution.

Though these studies are interesting, one might also ask if this phenomenon extends to the expansive state of awareness experienced in NDEs. Brain imaging is not feasible during an NDE related to cardiac arrest. However, available EEG data that have been previously collected during NDEs show that the entire cortex, including the DMN, is deactivated (van Lommel et al., 2001; Woollacott & Shumway-Cook, 2020).

Kundalini Awakening, the Filter Theory and Mystical Experiences

One might ask why a reduction in the activity of the DMN of the brain could actually be associated with a *kundalini* awakening and the concomitant mystical experiences of unitive consciousness. This hypothesis is based on an analysis of the Filter Theory, which was first proposed by psychologists in the late 1800s, including William James (1958; 1902). It is also a part of modern psychological theory (Broadbent, 1958). Research suggests that neural networks in the brain filter or limit incoming information to reduce the processing demands on the brain. A number of brain networks serve as attentional filters, reducing the immense amount of information continually inundating the senses. As the brain has a limited processing capability, these attentional filters underlie our ability to function successfully throughout our lives (Woollacott & Shumway-Cook, 2020).

We propose that the DMN serves as one of the filters, since it persistently restricts awareness and sustains attention on the ongoing self-referential narratives of the brain (Woollacott & Shumway-Cook, 2020). It can be conceived as a reducing valve mechanism, that normally confines the contents of a vaster awareness within narrow limits defined by the requirements of day-to-day life (Kastrup and Kelly, 2018; Swanson, 2018). It is possible that during STE/KAs, when the DMN is substantially reduced, filtering is lessened, and with this, awareness expands to include perceptions of mystical phenomena. Many research articles have verified that with cardiac arrest and a flatlined EEG some persons perceive events around them from a perspective outside of the body. A possible interpretation of these data is that during an NDE with cardiac arrest and flat EEG, filters that typically inhibit wider more inclusive states of awareness are not functional.

An alternative explanation to this hypothesis, from a materialist perspective could be that that reduced activity and connectivity in the brain's key connector hubs, which include the DMN, would allow what could be called a state of unconstrained cognition. This could result in other brain areas being released to interact in new ways and thus contribute to a brain-produced mystical experience such as that of unity awareness. Our hypothesis is an alternative to that view; however, it is possible that elements of both hypothesized mechanisms contribute to STE/KAs. In this way, lowered activity in the DMN, may release other parts of the brain to interact in new ways and also lessen the filtering mechanisms of the brain, allowing a wider perception.

Summary and Conclusions

In summary, we believe that the data from a variety of sources show that STE/KAs are verifiable phenomena experienced by a substantial portion of the general population. The characteristics of STE/KAs include unusual flow of energy within and around the body, a sense of great joy, of love, and a sense of unity with all. There is often an immediate shift in the understanding of the basis of reality, described by one person in this way. "[It was] a dramatic life-changing experience which left me with an absolute knowledge that we do not die and are definitely spiritual beings, something I had not previously believed" (Woollacott et al., 2020). In addition there are typically substantial longer-term beneficial transformations in sensitivity, psychic and healing abilities as well as beliefs and values. One person shared that they were aware of a sense of unity consciousness, that is, a feeling of the oneness of all creation.

In spite of this, the phenomenon is rarely studied by academics in general and scientists in particular, and experiences are seldom shared with others by the experiencers. A number of factors contribute to this, including 1) the prevalence of a materialist world view by physicians and scientists, which tends to see these experiences as either imagined or pathological, and 2) the tendency of experiencers to downplay the validity of their experience, possibly because it doesn't duplicate standard descriptions of intense mystical energetic awakenings. One example of this comes from the author of one of our chapters, Dr. Neal Grossman. He shared with me, after reading the journal article cited above on Kundalini awakenings (Woollacott et al., 2020).

"After reading your paper I was able to re-assess an experience I had as a mild kundalini awakening, involving Plato. I was 16 years old, exploring the Boston Public Library, picked up a big book with Plato's name on it, and the book spontaneously opened to the Allegory of the Cave. As I read it, my body started to shake and tremble, chills up and down the spine, and tears flowed freely. I remember now, with humor, trying to suppress the experience, because I was in a public space and there were other people around. But I could not control it. I understood the Allegory perfectly and completely, even though I would have identified as an atheist/materialist at the time. Later, when I studied Plato formally at the university, I was dismayed that none of my professors understood Plato's allegory, including Plato scholars. I now wonder if it was the *kundalini* experience that cemented the understanding in my mind, and forever made materialism an impossible option for me" (Grossman, personal communication, July 26, 2020).

Neal Grossman also noted that he did not share the information with anyone until about 40 years later, when he shared it with a well-known philosopher, Huston Smith, who was quite taken by it, and mentioned it in later writings. Grossman said to me,

"You are right about academics being uncomfortable sharing personal experiences. But I think, at least in my own case, there has been some sort of denial involved......I believed that spiritual experiences (STEs) happened to other people, but that my over-active academic left brain permanently bars me from such experiences. But now, looking back on my life, I can see in my past several other experiences of a similar nature. So I now suspect that we left-brain academic types may have had more STEs than we remember or admit."

We hope that these data on the nature of STE/KAs and this final example for contemplation will lead to increased discussion of these topics by both experiencers, scientists, academics, health care professionals, and the general public. Hopefully, these discussions will lead to a "normalization" of this phenomenon, so that it can be understood as a highly beneficial part of the human growth process. We believe that the postmaterialist world view has a great capacity to move the science exploring STE/KAs forward. It offers both a framework for understanding the phenomenon and the methodology for examining its potential source and subsequent transformational effects.

References

Barrett, F. S., & Griffiths, R. R. (2018). Classic hallucinogens and mystical experiences: Phenomenology and neural correlates. *Current Topics Behavioral Neuroscience, 36*, 393–430.

Brewer, J. A., Worhunsky, P. D., Gray, J. R., Tang, Y. Y., Weber, J., & Kober, H. (2011). Meditation experience is associated with differences in default mode network activity and connectivity. *Proceedings of the National Academy of Sciences USA, 108*(50), 20254–20259.

Broadbent, D. E. (1958). *Perception and communication.* Pergamon Press.

Brooks, D. R., & Bailly, C. R. (1997). Kundalini: Awakening the divinity within. In: *Meditation Revolution.* South Fallsburg, NY: Agama Press.

Carhart-Harris, R. L. & Friston, K. J. (2010). The default-mode, ego-functions and free-energy: A neurobiological account of Freudian ideas. *Brain, 133*(Pt 4), 1265–1283. https://doi.org/10.1093/brain/awq010

Gallup, G. H. (2002). Religious awakenings bolster Americans' faith.https://news.gallup.com/poll/7582/religious-awakenings-bolster-americans-faith.aspx/; 2002; Accessed 10 January 2020.

Greyson, B. (2000). Some neurophysiological correlates of the physio-kundalini syndrome. *Journal of Transpersonal Psychology,* 32,123-134.

Greyson, B. (1993). Near-death experiences and the physio-kundalini syndrome. *Journal of Religious Health,* 32, 277-290.

Greyson, B. (2014). Congruence between near-death and mystical experience. *International Journal for the Psychology of Religion, 24*, 298–310.

Greyson, B., & Khanna, S. (2014). Spiritual transformation following near-death experiences. *Spirituality in Clinical Practice, 1*, 43–55.

James, W. (1958). *The varieties of religious experience.* Mentor. (Original work published 1902).

Kastrup, B. & Kelly, E. F. (2018). Misreporting and confirmation bias in psychedelic research: What do images of the brain under psychedelics really tell us about its relation to the mind? *Scientific American*, Blog, Sept. 3, 2018.

Krishna, G. (1993). *Living With Kundalini*. Boston: Shambhala.

Muller-Ortega, P. E. (1997). Shaktipat: The initiatory descent of power. In: *Meditation Revolution*. South Fallsburg, NY: Agama Press.

Plato. (1966). Plato in Twelve Volumes, Vol. 7, Letters (Bury, R.G., Transl.) Cambridge, MA: Harvard University Press.

Ross, S., Bossis, A., Guss, J., Agin-Liebes, G., Malone, T., Cohen, B., Mennenga, S. E., Belser, A., Kalliontzi, K., Babb, J., Su, Z., Corby, P., & Schmidt, B. L. (2016). Rapid and sustained symptom reduction following psilocybin treatment for anxiety and depression in patients with life-threatening cancer: A randomized controlled trial. *Journal of Psychopharmacology, 30*(12), 1165–1180. https://doi.org/10.1177/0269881116675512.

Sanches, L., & Daniels M. (2008). Kundalini and transpersonal development: Development of the Kundalini awakening Scale and a comparison between groups. *Transpersonal Psychology Review*, 12, 73-83.

Sannella, L. (1987). *The Kundalini Experience. Psychosis or Transcendence?* San Francisco: Integral Publishing.

Schwaninger, J., Eisenberg, P. R., Schechtman, K. B., & Weiss, A. N. (2002). A prospective analysis of near-death experiences in cardiac arrest patients. *Journal of Near-Death Studies, 20*, 215–232. https://doi.org/10.17514/JNDS-2002-20-4-p215-232.

Shantananda, Sw. (2003). *The Splendor of Recognition: An Exploration of the Pratyabhijna-hrdayam, a Text on the Ancient Science of the Soul*. South Fallsburg, NY: SYDA Foundation.

Singh, J. (1980). *The Doctrine of Recognition. A translation of the Pratyabhijnahrdayam*. Albany, NY: SUNY Press.

Swanson, L. R. (2018). Unifying theories of psychedelic drug effects. *Frontiers in Pharmacology*. https://doi.org/10.3389/fphar.2018.00172

Taylor, S. (2012). Transformation through suffering: a study of individuals who have experienced positive psychological transformation following periods of intense turmoil. *J Humanistic Psychology*, 52, 30-52.

Taylor, S., & Egeto-Szabo, K. (2017). Exploring awakening experiences: a study of awakening experiences in terms of their triggers, characteristics, duration and after-effects. *J Transpersonal Psychology*, 49, 45-65.

Wallis, C. (2008). The descent of power: possession, mysticism and initiation in the Shaiva theology of Abhinavagupta. *Journal of Indian Philosophy*. 36, 247–295.

White, D. G. (1996). *The Alchemical Body*. Chicago: University of Chicago Press.

Woollacott, M., Park, R., & Kason, Y. (2020). Investigation of the phenomenology, physiology and impact of spiritually transformative experiences –kundalini awakening. *Explore*. https:/doi.org/10.1016/j.explore.2020.07.005

Woollacott, M. & Shumway-Cook, A. (2020). The mystical experience and its neural correlates. *Journal of Near-Death Studies* 38.1, 3-25.

Appendix

Expanding Matter: A New Postmaterialist take on Quantum Consciousness

Emmanuel Ransford

PART 1
Two Ways of Behaving, Two Kinds of Causation

Causation is a great idea. Without it, we could hardly make any *rational* sense of the world. It is little wonder, then, that science rests heavily on it. For some, like the French scientist Pierre-Simon de Laplace a few centuries ago, everything in the world, big and small alike, was under its unrelenting sway. Today, however, quantum randomness suggests otherwise. It is a core feature of the smallest specks of matter. This randomness shows in the spontaneous decay of a radioactive atom, for which we can only figure out a *likelihood* of occurrence over a given time interval. The exact moment of this event is unknown, and indeed *unknowable*. Roughly speaking, when the atom decays, its nucleus "jumps" from an ill-defined (or fuzzy) energy state to a clear-cut (or sharp) one.

Quantum randomness also shows when the spin of an electron prepared with no definite value, as if smeared-out or "fuzzy," is measured. The measurement brings about a sharp and definite spin value,[43] one that can't be foretold and that didn't even exist before. Generally speaking,

---

[43] *This value can either be "spin up" or "spin down", with respect to a given direction. It is also the measurement outcome. (The spin is an intrinsic angular momentum of elementary particles.)*

measuring an electron shrinks it, from a fuzzy to a sharp state[44]. These dramatic evolutions—that of the decaying atom and that of the measured electron—are sudden and random. They are a far cry from the smooth, well-behaved and wave-like behavior that runs the quantum show the rest of the time.

Conventional wisdom has it that quantum randomness, insofar as it is genuine, is causation-free. I strongly beg to differ however, since random events don't necessarily fly in the face of causation. A lack of *deterministic* causation does not, as such, entail a lack of causation. The reason for this is that causation and *deterministic* causation are not one and the same, and the possibility of *non-deterministic* causation cannot be swatted away. It can't be ruled out offhandedly, and it ought to be fully acknowledged. Now, being non-deterministic, this "lesser" kind of causation is random-looking. It is therefore not too much of a stretch to assume—as I do—that it lies at the heart of quantum randomness and pulls its strings.

Both *deterministic* and *non-deterministic* causation share the same birth right, whereby core causation exists in two major strains. The first one is forced upon things from the outside. I call this deterministic strain of causation exo- or **out-causation**. Obviously enough, the fall of an apple under the pull of gravity and the thawing of ice under the sun are out-causal. The second strain goes by the name of endo- or **in-causation**. An in-causal evolution or behavior wells up from inside. Strange though it sounds, it is even, in a way, *chosen*. This is precisely what makes it non-deterministic. In-causation is creative, and is redolent of the controversial notion of free will. The thought here is that planning ahead, deciding to

---

[44] *This attribute of the state (its fuzziness or sharpness) relates to the physical aspect being measured (e.g. fuzzy or sharp spin, fuzzy or sharp position, fuzzy or sharp energy, etc.). A fuzzy state and a sharp one are respectively, in quantumspeak, a superposed state and an eigen one. If an electron is prepared in an initial state that is already sharp, the formal measurement isn't a true one, for want of an actual quantum threat (see below). It will therefore elicit no quantum leap. Please do notice that in this paper, I use the electron as a symbol of any elementary particle (be it a proton, a photon, a muon, a neutrino, a Higgs boson, etc.).*

Expanding Science

smile or whistle on whim and actually doing it, is somehow to behave in-causally.[45]

To recap, out-causation is causation from without whilst in-causation is causation from within. In the real world, out-causation feeds determinism whereas in-causation comes across as random. It drives quantum randomness. Determinism and randomness are therefore the hallmarks of the two major strains, "in-" and "out-", of causation. Don't get me wrong however: I'm specifically talking about *quantum* randomness. I am *not* saying, nor am I implying, that wherever randomness arises in the world out there, in-causation is behind it.

Holomatter Means Wholeness

By adding a dash of (random-looking) in-causation to quantum objects, we turn ordinary matter into **holomatter** (*holo* is the Greek root for "whole"). This notion is consistent with the fact that electrons and other subatomic particles display both deterministic and random features. By the same token, they follow two alternative evolution laws. The first one is wave-like and deterministic—it is plainly out-causal. Physicists ascribe to it a slew of other features. The second law, on the other hand, is sudden and random. I assume it to be in-causal. It plays out in quantum jumps, wave collapses, (measurement-triggered) wave function reductions, decays of unstable systems, inelastic collisions, and many more. For simplicity's sake, I'll use the umbrella word of "jump" or "leap" to refer to any of these events.[46] They

---

[45] *Admittedly, our biological brain also plays a significant part here. It 'downsizes', but doesn't remove entirely, our inner decision-making agency—our free will, as it were.*

[46] *The deterministic (out-causal) law is overwhelmingly prevalent. It has some additional characteristics, such as: smoothness, unitarity (a mathematical property) and a proneness to quantum fuzziness. This fuzziness refers to mingled, or superposed, quantum states. As for the random (in-causal) law, its additional characteristics are: discontinuity, non-unitarity, quantum sharpness creation, and more (most strikingly, it is nonrelativistic too). A jump always shrinks a quantum object from a fuzzy to a sharp state.*

happen rather seldom, and last virtually no time. Some types of jump are much less obvious than the conspicuous leap of an electron in an atom.

Incidentally, an electron that undergoes a quantum jump looks point particle-like. This is on two grounds, namely: for one, its sudden jump typically shrinks the electron to a point-like sharpness and, for two, it involves no waves (waves, being smooth, wouldn't allow such a discontinuous shape-shifting event).

Let me define as **holoparticle** any elementary particle whose in-causal component is explicitly taken into account. A holoparticle is a particle of holomatter. If a hint of in-causation really dwells within ordinary matter as I surmise, then holomatter is matter in its fullness or wholeness. Actually, it deals with wholeness twice over, because (holo)particles have an unwavering duty to remain whole. Whatever the circumstances, an electron, a photon, or any (holo)particle in its wave-like motions cannot be ripped apart into independent shreds or subunits.[47] It has to remain whole, no matter what, or else it will altogether disappear (e.g. by being absorbed). I call **quantumhood**[48] this mandatory and rock-solid wholeness. It is an all-or-nothing affair, whereby you can have a whole particle or no particle at all, but never anything in between.

Quantumhood can be threatened, such as when a "fuzzy" electron is hard-pressed by a detector to split up in two independent halves, each half-electron being in a different, and sharp or well-defined, position or spin state. Such a **quantum threat** forces a reaction. It elicits a quantum jump or leap that shrinks the whole electron into either one of the two sharp states. This dramatic event wipes the quantum threat out. This suggests that jumps are nature's weapons of choice to enforce quantumhood (more on this can be found in Part 2).

---

[47] *These shreds or subunits (or indeed, sub-wave packets) are deemed independent if they lose their ability to interfere mutually.*

[48] *Quantumhood can be defined with respect to the wave interference that takes place within a wave packet. Because of it, physicists never find, say, 142.37 or 20.615 electrons or photons in their experiments—they only ever find whole numbers (for example, 142 or 20) of them. When the environment is too threatening, an electron or a photon will suddenly disappear; it will typically be absorbed as a whole.*

To figure out how these things may work concretely, just fancy that you're about to cut a potato in two halves, with a twist however: your potato is a magic one, and it cannot be split (this is quantumhood-for-magic potatoes!). Accordingly, the potato will thwart all your efforts to cut it. How? A smart and easy way to pull off this trick would be for it to shrink—or "jump"—to one side of your threatening knife so that, try as you would, its blade would never cut anything but the air.

Detectors and detecting devices beget quantum threats. This is what they are about. If they belong to a measuring apparatus, they threaten quantumhood in, say, the electron to be measured. The latter reacts by "jumping." This is the same story again: the quantum jump shrinks the electron in one shot, from its fuzzy (and threatened) initial state to a sharp (and threat-free) one.[49] This shrinking occurs instantly. It leads to a definite measurement outcome, brought about by the sharp end-state.

Let's recall the main ideas here: the principle of quantumhood is a principle of wholeness that bears on the (holo)electron and on any (holo)particle more generally. It precludes them, as they move about in their deterministic and wave-like fashion, from being torn into bits that would no longer interfere mutually. This principle is iron-clad. Nature enforces it by means of the (wave-less) quantum jump.

Our Meaningful and Sentient Universe

With the foregoing, I hope that quantum jumps—whether prompted by measurements or not—become less of a riddle. They are simply quantumhood-enforcers.[50] At this point I want to share with you something about the great British physicist Paul Adrien Maurice Dirac. In his book *Nature Loves to Hide* (2012), Shimon Malin reveals that Dirac, whom he met

---

[49] *I hope that I have made it clear that the initial fuzzy state feeds the quantum threat while the sharp end-state is "threat-less" or "threat-free".*

[50] *I believe that with holomatter and its hidden in-causal dimension, we can better understand not only the quantum leap, but also the weird—and thus far unexplained—property of quantum entanglement (see more on this in Part 2).*

once, told him that a collapse of the quantum wave—a collapse is a quantum jump by another name—occurs because "Nature makes a choice" (Malin, 2012, p. 127). Then Malin, upon asking "When does nature make a choice?" got this answer from Dirac: "When there is no longer a possibility of interference." It seems to me that the first pronouncement—*nature makes a choice*—rings like an implicit endorsement of in-causation. As for Dirac's second pronouncement—nature makes a choice *when there is no longer a possibility of interference*—it goes straight to the heart of quantumhood. I therefore suspect that Dirac almost hit upon the holomatter idea. However, as far as I know, he did not follow through, or communicate, on his insights.

This being said, we can proceed one step further and consider the following: *because* we have a subjective mental life, we can willfully decide to do this or that as we go about our daily lives. This inspires me to assume that in-causation, loosely speaking, is bound up with a subjective content that might, in turn, relate to some kind of awareness.[51] It goes without saying that the latter would be vanishingly dim at the level of an electron. This claim may at first sound wild and far-fetched, and even shockingly over-the-top. Yet, sentience is a genuine feature of reality, and mainstream science notoriously fails to *really* account for it. This is why I feel free to think out of the box of received wisdom.

Incidentally, a new concept of information can be developed from here. This supral information, as I call it, owes much to the quantum phenomenon of entanglement which, for holomatter, is a straightforward effect of an in-causal bonding of elementary particles. I dub this bonding **supralness** (more on this in Part 2). I suspect that this supral information, which is subjective,[52] underpins our qualia, these felt contents of our experience (e.g. the redness of red).

---

[51] *This implies, against materialism, that awareness or sentience stands on its own, and is even, somehow, a core feature of the world.*

[52] *It is also hidden (like the in-causal dimension of holomatter) and non-local (owing to supralness). See more in Part 2. The systematic study of the subjective contents of the supral information, as it relates to its structural characteristics, can be dubbed suprology (this new field of research would draw on topology, combinatorics, graph theory, and other branches of mathematics).*

Expanding Science

To conclude, holomatter and subjective in-causation, if they hold water, seem poised to shed new light on the mind-body problem and on the enigma of the conscious brain (more on this in Part 2, yet again). They also give some weight to the idea that our universe, somehow and within limits, is a sentient one. This is an exciting idea, one that gives meaning to our otherwise silent, mineral, and seemingly pointless world.

PART 2
More Than Meets the Eye

Plainly enough, quantum physics is about matter. Less obviously, perhaps, it's about lumps and jumps. These lumps are fuzzy bundles of interfering waves that, physicists have found, make up elementary particles.[53] Jumps, on the other hand, are discontinuous leaps. They occur sporadically in particles, and last no time—blink and you'll miss them. A particle that jumps is no longer a lump. It's something else (no one knows exactly what). Jumps are events such as quantum leaps and transitions, radioactive decays, and wave function collapses. They also lie at the heart of the photoelectric, Compton, and tunnel effects.[54] All these microscopic events, and many more, share key features. They are sudden, irreversible, wave-less, particle-like, nonrelativistic, and non-unitary. Most strikingly, they are random and discontinuous. This randomness is puzzling. *Why should nature occasionally drop determinism?* It turns out that quantum jumps are necessarily random *because* they serve a purpose—which, I believe, hasn't been fully appreciated yet (more on this later).

---

[53] *These elementary particles are also called subatomic or quantum particles. They are very different from classical particles, and some have aptly christened them "wavicles" on account of their baffling wave-and-particle nature.*

[54] *In the photoelectric effect, a metal gives out electrons when illuminated by, say, a blue (but not a red) light. In the Compton effect, a photon has its wavelength increased after being scattered by a charged particle. In the tunnel effect, a quantum particle tunnels through a barrier that it couldn't cross classically. These effects cannot be explained by classical physics.*

Before I carry on, let me recall that science is firmly rooted in an attitude of critical openness—unlike ideology, which is mired in likes and dislikes. Openness means that no scientist worth her salt would dismiss a possible assumption offhandedly, just because she doesn't like it or because it "sounds crazy." When addressing an unresolved issue, she ought to leave no stones unturned, seek out all the options, and put them squarely on the table. Then "criticality" takes over. It is down to implementing a suitable procedure aimed at weeding out the irrelevant options or assumptions.

Randomness-wise, at least three options are available. One, labelled **H1**, is that of chance pure and simple. According to this option, quantum randomness is hollow. Were it a box, it would be an empty one. We can name this hypothesis lack of cause, or a-causation. However, the box of quantum randomness could be full instead. This option branches out into **H2a** and **H2b**. **H2a** holds that the box contains some hidden determinism[55] while **H2b** assumes nondeterministic causation. We can name the latter endo-causation or in-causation, and reframe determinism as exo-causation or out-causation. Let me define these concepts:

- **In-causation** (or endo-causation) is any causal law that stems from within. This inward or endogenous causation can therefore be tweaked on a whim or "at will" as it were, as though by some decision-making agency.[56] This makes it random.
  - **Out-causation** (or exo-causation) is any causal law that comes from without. This outward or exogenous causation is out of reach and cannot be tampered with. It is therefore unchanging and deterministic. Indeed, any determinism is out-causal.

The three assumptions entail different things for our hypothetical box of quantum randomness. Namely:

H1   The box is empty   (*a-causation*)

H2a The box is full and contains a hidden determinism (*out-causation*)

---

[55] **H2a** *leads to the so-called hidden variable theories of quantum physics.*
[56] *At the quantum level, this putative "agency" is exceedingly rudimentary at best.*

H2b The box is full and carries a nondeterministic kind of causation (*in-causation*)

As far as I know, only **H1** and **H2a** have been considered in earnest by physicists, leaving **H2b** by the wayside. Our tendency to conflate *deterministic* causation and causation *tout court* has certainly played a part, by (wrongly) implying that a lack of determinism is tantamount to a lack of causation. However, critical openness demands that we take **H2b** into consideration. It gives a nondeterministic, because in-causal, content to the box of randomness. With **H2b**, there's more to quantum randomness than meets the eye.[57]

Where will this take us? Let's find out.

Seeds of Awareness

In assumption **H2b**, matter is not what it's made out to be. It becomes **holomatter,** which, unlike plain matter, possesses an extra in-causal dimension. It turns out that this extra dimension is overwhelmingly dormant, or latent. This makes it well nigh invisible, and it goes unnoticed. Here would be the reason why it has been all but ignored thus far. At times, however, the in-causal dimension pops out of its latency, almost instantly. It then pulls the strings of quantum randomness. (As we will soon see, it does so on behalf of nature's consistency.)

By virtue of this insight, electrons and the like become particles of holomatter, or holoparticles. They are made up of two components, or parts: one is out-causal and hence deterministic, the other is in-causal and hence random. We can call **outdown** the "lower" out-causal part and **inup** the "upper" in-causal parts (*see drawing*). Both coexist within a holoparticle.

---

[57] Interestingly, in-causation pushed to its limit becomes what I call "ur-causation". **Ur-causation** is sheer in-causation. It is in-causation stripped of any hint of out-causation: ur-causation is totally free from any limiting (deterministic) constraint. Intriguingly, it points to a transcendent level of reality by its unique and "otherworldly" properties. (My books *L'origine quantique de la conscience* and *La conscience quantique et l'au-delà* explore this issue at some length.)

They cannot be wrung apart, much like the two sides of a coin. (*The drawing nevertheless separates them, for simplicity's sake.*)

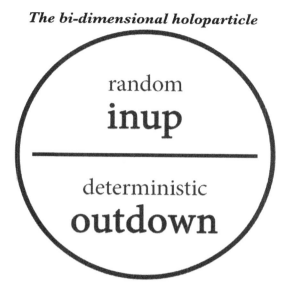

A holoparticle has two parts. In the drawing, the upper one is the inup. It comes across as random because it is in-causal, or faintly "self-willed." The other one, down or below, is the outdown. It is out-causal and hence deterministic.

Now, the outdown and the inup are active in turns. When they are active, they single-handedly drive the dance of the (holo)particle. The outdown has the lion's share of activity. When it holds its sway, the particle behaves like a wave—or, rather, it looks like a bunch of interfering waves lumped together. On the other hand, the inup is nearly always resting or latent. When it kicks off in its active (and exceedingly short-lived) mode, the inup elicits a quantum jump, whose outcome is random and particle-like.

We thus have a straightforward rule of thumb to determine which part of the (holo)particle is active at any time: *When we have a lump, the outdown is active. When we have a jump, the inup is active.*[58]

Determinism is objective, and so is the deterministic outdown. But what about the inup? I suspect it to be subjective, because in-causation arguably goes hand in hand with some decision-making ability. (Don't get me wrong: I'm not "psychologizing" the holoparticle. I write "decision-making" to avoid a neologism, but in the present context it should be clear that what I mean is a far cry from our human decision-making.) Furthermore, I believe that the "self-willedness" of in-causation is akin to a core feature of psychism[59] and consciousness—the one commonly known as free will.

Self-willedness and in-causation are somehow akin to free will, which is currently a highly controversial notion. As a matter of fact, recent experiments show beyond doubt that our free will is definitely less—*much less*, perhaps—than we spontaneously think it to be. A host of factors, unbeknownst to us, constrain some, if not most, of our "free" choices and decisions. The way our brains are hard-wired is one of these factors. However, if free will is down, it is not out yet, and the jury is still out. Dismissing it is a matter of personal ideology, and not of science, since some facts strongly bear it out.[60]

---

[58] *A lump is wave-like whereas a jump shrinks the particle to a point-like, and hence particle-like, end-state (as explained later). Together they would underlie the alleged wave-particle duality of quantum mechanics.*

[59] *By "psychism" I mean the whole gamut of sentience—be it conscious awareness or any subliminal, subconscious, or unconscious state. Incidentally, because of the two contents of holomatter, one objective and the other subjective, the postmaterialist approach based on it is neither monistic nor dualistic, but is rather a kind of oxymoronic "dualistic monism", as I wrote in "Peeking at the Conscious Brain: New Clues, New Challenges", ANPA WEST Journal (J. of the Western Chapter of ANPA), Vol. 5, No 2, 6-26, Winter 1995.*

[60] *It is not possible to address properly the controversy of free will in a few sentences. Again, I have discussed this issue and mentioned some facts that clearly back the freedom of will in my books L'origine*

Coming back to the inup, we may think of it as a "seed of awareness" lurking in any speck of matter, or particle, in the universe. This idea may sound fairly wild and outlandish at first, and we may find it hard to wrap our mind around it. Let's nevertheless take it in as a mere *possibility* and see what comes next.

Don't Mess Around with Quantumhood

Quantumhood is an all-important, but so far overlooked, feature of the quantum world. It is so important that it trumps everything else at its level and, no matter what, it always get the upper hand. Quantumhood reaches far and deep into the roots of reality—but what is it exactly? Here's its definition:[61]

Quantumhood *is an all-or-nothing affair, whereby we may find 3 or 17 electrons, but never 2.98 or 17.263 of them. It is a "straitjacket" forced upon micro-objects. At times, quantumhood can be challenged and threatened. Such is the case when, through an appropriate setup, we insist on splitting an electron into two separate, and not-mutually-interfering, bits; e.g. 0.38 of it here, 0.62 there.*

Quantumhood means wholeness. It means wholeness of quantum micro-objects, and it is grounded in quantum wave interference. The trouble is, this "interferential wholeness" or "wave wholeness" can be threatened. Here's how: Have a photon hit a half-silvered mirror, whereupon it will evolve into two half-photons flying wide apart.[62] Next, have one of them hit a photodetector, and bingo—you have pulled off a quantum threat, since you managed to threaten quantumhood. It is so because, should the detector absorb this half-photon, the remaining one would now stand on its own and the photon-wide wave interference would be gone. This would shatter the photon wholeness, which is exactly what quantumhood is up

---

quantique de la conscience, La conscience quantique et l'au-delà; and, more recently, in Huit leçons essentielles sur la science quantique.

[61] *This definition is adapted from E. Ransford, Panpsychism, the Conscious Brain, and Beyond, which makes up chapter 12 of the book Science and the Primacy of Consciousness, R. Amoroso et al (eds.), The Noetic Press, 2000. (By the way, quantumhood arguably implies quantization.)*

[62] *One of them is reflected, the other is transmitted.*

Expanding Science

against.[63] However, the mere spatial splitting of the photon into its two halves neither threatens nor violates quantumhood, because waves are wont to stretch indefinitely. This provides ample room for the far-out parts, or tail-ends, of the waves of each half-photon to overlap and keep interfering together, however remote they both seem to be. Thus, *seeming* photon-splitting notwithstanding, the photon-wide interference remains in good working order. We should never take the spatial splitting of photons and the like at face value.

This point involves the quirks and twists of quantum waves, which differ from classical waves; they interfere mutually if (and only if) they belong to the same (holo)particle, and they vanish instantly whenever a jump takes place. This very point, I believe, is of paramount importance for getting the hang of what the quantum world is up to.

Quantumhood has teeth. It bares its fangs under a quantum threat; but fangs are woefully inadequate to cope with a quantum threat (that is, as we recall, to cope with any situation in which the wave wholeness of a particle is in danger of being lost). This is where in-causation comes in handy. Here's how: When a quantum threat looms large for, say, an electron, this somehow triggers a wake-up call for its inup. Then the inup snaps into its active mode, eliciting a quantum jump. This sudden and game-changing event shrinks the electron down to size, which now looks point-like. The whole point of this dramatic shrinking is that the quantum threat occurred *because* the electron was too fuzzy, much like a smeared-out lump. This fuzziness feeds the quantum threat, while the "shrunk down" final sharpness of the particle washes the threat away.

The message here is that a jump is nature's way to shape-shift an initially fuzzy (and therefore threatened) quantum particle into a pin sharp (and accordingly threat-free) end-state.[64] The jump happens because it is a fuzziness-buster: it is nature's silver bullet to enforce quantumhood. This

---

[63] Let me add that a quantum measurement is always carried out by threatening quantumhood in the object to be measured (it does so by means of a detector).

[64] Recall that in quantum-speak, fuzzy and sharp states are dubbed the superposed and eigen states respectively.

"leaping fix" is incredibly smart. It is driven by the inup, and it is so efficient that no quantum threat will ever checkmate quantumhood—you can bet on it.

How is it that the electron's fuzziness feeds the quantum threat? To get the hang of this, let's compare an electron (and any holoparticle, for that matter) to a loaf of bread. Take a loaf and, in order to cut it in two halves, a knife. When you cut it, you just do it with no further ado. It is that easy because there is no quantumhood, and therefore no quantum threats, for loaves of bread. Were it not so, the loaf could not and would not be cut, however hard one might try. Here's what may happen instead: The loaf would suddenly shrink, as by a jump of sorts, either to the right or to the left of the knife, and the knife would end up having nothing to cut but the air. This shows that the threat (of being cut) depends on the bread being on both sides of the knife. Plainly enough, "being on both sides" plays the part of the electron's fuzzy state whilst being shrunk "to the right or to the left" plays the part of the electron's sharp end-state. One feeds the threat, the other is threat-free.[65]

We now gather why the jump is random: given the same initial fuzzy state (which is present on both the right and the left), there are two possible end-states (right only and left only), and no deterministic process can ever decide which one will appear. I believe that this randomness isn't blind, aimless, and empty. It doesn't come out of thin air. I believe that the "decision" to shrink either to the right or to the left arises precisely from the in-causal part, or inup. Quantum randomness is jump-based and serves a purpose. It is about shape-shifting quantum objects so as to ward off quantum threats. This is why I suspect quantum randomness to be in-causation caught in the act.[66]

---

[65] *Of course, the knife may assume another position to create a new threat: the loaf, fuzzy again in this different context, would likewise "jump" towards a new shrunk and sharp end-state. (This highlights the fact that the fuzziness and sharpness of quantum objects are not intrinsic to them; they are context-dependent.)*

[66] *Because of various (out-causal) rules and constraints, the physical outcomes of in-causal initiatives are constrained, to the effect that quantum randomness is probabilistic.*

A case in point is a photon that will end up hitting a photosensitive screen, over which its waves are initially spread out. This state is fuzzy. It feeds a quantum threat by putting the photon in danger of being shredded and then absorbed by tiny bits, according to its spreading on the screen. Quantumhood flatly rules such an outcome out, and it will never materialize. As we know, a jump is therefore in order. It pops out instead, and swiftly shrinks the photon to a pin sharp end-state that's random. In this new garb, the photon is fit to be absorbed—as a whole, in one shot, and in a single spot. Upon being absorbed by the screen, it creates and leaves a small dot on the screen, a dot that can all too easily be misinterpreted as evidence that the photon, at times at least, is a point-particle.

The dot is nothing but the tell-tale sign that a jump has occurred. It's the upshot of a shape-shifting jump, the very one that led to the highly localized absorption of the photon. Incidentally, the observer doesn't play an important role in this affair, other than provoking a quantum threat for the incoming photon by means of the photosensitive screen, or of any detecting device belonging to a measuring apparatus.

Quantum jumps, I believe, are in the business of quantumhood-enforcement. This is the key.

As an aside, let me add that the jump hails from the in-causal dimension of reality, which is overtly nonmaterial and, as such, doesn't have to comply with the laws of the (material) out-causal dimension—that of Einstein's relativity included. It is no wonder, then, that it is nonrelativistic. In much the same way, it may account for most of the other odd features of quantum jumps or leaps, which would no longer be odd indeed. We may see now how the holomatter hypothesis manages to explain and remove much of the quantum weirdness.

Desperately seeking the deed

The "psychic," subjective, or mental dimension of reality seems hard—if not outright impossible—to reconcile with its physical dimension. The properties shared by neural behaviour and conscious experience, if anything, are few and far between. On the other hand, there's a lingering suspicion that if psychism and the mind were truly nonmaterial, the mind-body interaction would go against the laws of physics. Furthermore, the neural correlates of our mental states and the causal connections found between some chemicals and our thoughts and feelings are strongly suggestive of a material origin of the mind.

Can holomatter bring fresh ideas to bear on these issues, and is there any room for a possible mind-body interaction within its framework? If so, can we then pin down this matter-psychism interaction, and will it violate physical laws? These are daunting questions. They *have* to be addressed and answered if holomatter is to be of any use. For simplicity's sake, I call the core mind-body interaction the **deed**. It would underpin the sensory-motor interplay that plays out in the animal kingdom. We seem hopelessly clueless about the deed; but things look much brighter if we surmise that ordinary matter is out-causal while psychism is in-causal. Then there's an obvious lead: to pin down the deed, look straight inside any elementary particle. Look no further than the electron, and find out whether and how its inup and its outdown twitch and jolt each other. Recall that the inup and the outdown are active in turns, so that one of them is always off and resting. This implies that they can only interact *indirectly*, if at all.

The core mind-body interplay—and hence the inup-outdown interplay—could tentatively be understood as follows:

- A jump is how the 'psychic' part of the electron tweaks its matter part. It does so by picking an end-state out of a range of possible ones.
- Conversely, a quantum threat is how the matter part of the electron impinges on its 'psychic' part. It does so by triggering a jump that will lift the 'psychic' part out of its latency.[67]

When the jump is over, matter makes its comeback where this jump left off. Here, 'matter' specifically means the electron's out-causal part, or outdown. Now, the electron can again be described as a bundle of quantum waves, or "lump," but it bears the material footprint of the 'psychic' dimension. This footprint relates to the shape-shifting produced by the in-

---

[67] *Recall that a jump is inup-driven and occurs when the inup becomes active and, obviously, is no longer latent. (We'll soon see that quantum jumps can at times be shared, and that this sharing is down to an in-causal bonding between particles.)*

causal "choice" that dramatically shrunk the electron, and even destroyed and absorbed it perhaps, as the jump took place.

The deed is no mystery. We gather that if holomatter holds any water, it is etched in the makeup of elementary particles—and it was hiding in plain sight all along! We failed to spot it because we mistook holomatter for plain matter. The deed and its two components, quantum threats and jumps, are clearly *not* incompatible with the laws of physics—instead, they are written into them. Incidentally, threats and jumps have more to do with the sensory side and the motor side of the mind-body dialogue respectively.

This is not the whole story yet, and other levels of complexity are needed to account for the richness and diversity of the mind-body dialogue as we experience it. That we investigate now—tentatively again.

Togetherness on the Sly

The quantum world, as we've just seen from the holomatter perspective, provides a candidate for the core matter-psychism interaction, or deed. It kindly gives another candidate for the blending of in-causal parts. This "in-blending," which I call **supralness**, raises the hope that wide-scale, or truly "macro-psychic," entities may appear. Aren't our minds such "macro-psychic" entities? The M-P-S diagram below shows graphically what interactions may arise between two particles of holomatter, supralness being one of them.[68] Let me define it:

Supralness is an endo-causal binding, or blending, of (holo)particles. It weaves in-causal ties, which may be called **supral links**, between particles. It is instantaneous and distance-blind—this is little wonder, as it is in-causal and hence nonmaterial and nonrelativistic. It is the root cause of entanglement.

Quantum entanglement is stealthy. It binds subatomic particles, be they near or far, as if by some wild and invisible bonds that would instantly

---

[68] *These (holo)particles, being bi-dimensional, can interact in more ways than they would were they made of plain matter only.*

correlate the outcomes of their *shared* quantum jumps and, consequently, the results of their measurements, too.⁶⁹ This is quite puzzling, to say the least. Entanglement is a well-established but poorly understood property whereby, say, two electrons remain tied together, or correlated, after they have interacted, regardless of their distance. With it, quantum physics is really about lumps, jumps—and (supral) links as well.

The M-P-S diagram

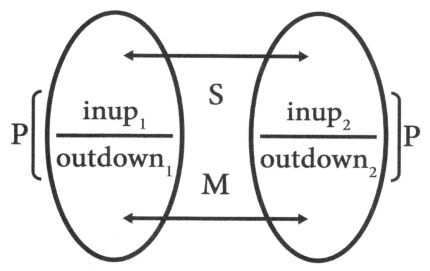

As we saw above, supralness blends the in-causal parts, or inups, of particles.⁷⁰ It spawns invisible threads or links that run between entangled

---

[69] *The results of quantum measurements are brought about by quantum jumps, which are themselves triggered by the measurement process (and more accurately, by its detector, whose job is to threaten quantumhood in the particle to be measured).*

[70] *This in-causal binding, or "in-blending," is nature's stunning trick to keep track and, when required, uphold some shared conservation laws. The trouble with these laws is that they start off in a suspended and virtual state. They cannot be enforced at once, because of quantum fuzziness. (I explain this concept at some length in two of my books, viz. L'univers quantique enfin expliqué and Huit*

particles. These (supral) links, exemplified by **S** in the drawing below, weld the inups and result in their unification. This endo-causal unification can be either partial or total. It shows when the inups become active, and brings about the correlations of entanglement.

Each holoparticle has a deterministic outdown and a random inup. We can therefore write: $\mathbf{h_1}$ = (outdown$_1$, inup$_1$) and $\mathbf{h_2}$ = (outdown$_2$, inup$_2$). This bi-dimensionality allows varied interactions, namely **M**, **P**, and **S**. **M** is a *material* interaction between outdown$_1$ and outdown$_2$. It is fully deterministic. **P** is an interaction between *either* inup$_1$ and outdown$_1$ *or* inup$_2$ and outdown$_2$. It is inup-driven, and therefore random. (I call it a *paral* interaction.) **S**, finally, is an interaction between inup$_1$ and inup$_2$. (I call it a *supral* interaction.) It binds or "in-blends" them together, thereby correlating their in-causal initiatives or "choices."[71]

If entanglement is a straightforward consequence of supralness, it makes sense and we readily gather why it flouts the rules of ordinary matter (and, more accurately, those of the out-causal dimension). Interestingly enough, supralness creates a new type of information. This **supral information**, as I name it, is easy to grasp. Take a handful of beads, and threads to bind them. With these, free your creativity and make objects shaped into stars, pears, flowers, butterflies—whatever you desire. These shapes or patterns bring structure, *and hence information*, to your bead-and-thread treasure trove. They encode and store data: one shape encodes the information "star," another the information "pear," the next one the information "flower," and so on.

Quite generally, any medium endowed with structure can store data, and the in-causal dimension of holomatter is such a medium. So, if we take particles and supral links instead of our beads and threads respectively, we

---

leçons essentielles sur la science quantique. The latter explains why quantum indistinguishability is another source of supralness, along with shared conservation laws.)

[71] Furthermore, **M** is smooth, wave-like, reversible, relativistic, and unitary; **P** arises when the particle's inup snaps out of its resting state (a quantum jump is then in order); **S** is instantaneous—so is **P**, by the way—and distance-blind. Finally, no "cross-interaction" seems to exist between inup$_1$ and outdown$_2$, or between inup$_2$ and outdown$_1$.

likewise conclude that the in-causal dimension can code and store information. This information belongs to the in-causal dimension, and so is altogether invisible, non-local, and subjective. Indeed, *"The complexity and variety of this supral information is virtually boundless: think of all the patterns that can be wrought by linking a basketful of beads with threads!"* (Ransford, 1999).

Now, storing data means *memorizing* data, and the storage capacity of this "supral memory" is truly amazing. We may wonder, "Has it anything to do with what the brain specialists call our declarative memory?"[72] We may call **suprel** a unit of supral information. Think of it as a few beads and threads arranged in a simple pattern where the beads, again, are holoparticles and the threads are supral links. *"A suprel is an elementary bit, or unit, of a brand-new type of information which is embedded in supralness. It is encoded in supral patterns [...]"* (Ransford, 1999). Of course, a suprel is invisible, non-local and subjective, since it belongs to the supral information.

Quantum Consciousness and Brain Consciousness

Supralness (or entanglement) has a unique knack. It knits or "in-blends" (holo)particles into in-causal wholes. These wholes, as we know, are "psychic" in nature. It's not too much of a stretch to assume that, given the right circumstances, they become aware.[73] If so, then supralness has the potential to take the mind-matter dialogue to new levels of richness and complexity—at least if by "mind" we refer to *quantum* conscious entities.

---

[72] *Our declarative memory deals with our mental recollections, the ones that we can recall consciously. It doesn't include the memory of, say, biking, piano playing, and other acquired motor skills and habits.*

[73] *This assumption rests on some additional notions, including that of paralgen. A **paralgen** is an alleged micro-device that kindles holomatter out of its usual matter state and into its paral state. Crudely put, a paralgen "wakes up" the in-causal content of holoparticles. It therefore elicits quantum jumps. (More on this notion in chapter 12 of the book Science and the Primacy of Consciousness, R. Amoroso et al (eds.), The Noetic Press, 2000, or in my papers "Panpsychism, the Conscious Brain, and Our Mind-body-soul Nature", and "Peeking at the Conscious Brain: New Clues, New Challenges", published in the ANPA WEST Journal (J. of the Western Chapter of ANPA), Vol. **5**, No 2, 6-26, Winter 1995.*

But why should (ordinary) *brain* consciousness be radically different from *quantum* consciousness? I expect them to be quite similar in essence. (This does not imply anything specific about the soul, which does not belong to the same level of reality.)

If jumps are driven by inups and if entanglement stems from supralness as I propose, they both involve the subjective in-causal dimension of holomatter and are therefore central to the quantum consciousness idea. Jumps stir the inups out of their silent, and presumably non-conscious, latency. Because of this, they can be seen as "sparks of consciousness"—and very fleeting ones at that. In the same vein, a suprel can be thought of as a "pixel of the mind." It would be akin to a letter of the language of our subjective experience. I thereby suspect that suprels underpin our qualia and subjective states.[74] On this insight, our inner mental lives may hugely benefit from supralness and from the global—and universe-wide—tapestry that it weaves, through its many supral links, in the in-causal dimension of reality.

Now, the whole idea of *brain-consciousness-as-quantum-consciousness* is easy to grasp through the light bulb metaphor. If a light bulb emits only a few photons at a time, it hardly generates any light at all since this light is much too dim to be seen. When, on the contrary, it yields huge quantities of photons (as it normally does), it produces a visible light. This is obvious enough. Now think "brain" instead of "light bulb" and "consciousness" instead of "light." A light bulb that gives off few photons at a time becomes a brain where not so many jumps occur at a time. Too few sparks of consciousness won't add up to a full-blown conscious state. Expect this state to be dim and slightly above non-consciousness instead. It could be dream-like or anything of that ilk. It would take vast and consistent streams of entangled jumps to achieve true consciousness, much like a visible light arises from huge flows of photons.

I thereby suspect that suprels underpin our qualia and subjective states. I also suspect them to be cooked up by neurons working tightly

---

[74] *Qualia are the subjective contents of experience, viz. the felt redness of red. (Mathematically speaking, suprels are topological and combinatorial entities.)*

together, particularly in response to specific stimuli. An attractive possibility for the brain's suprel-churning loci is the vertically oriented columns, or cylinders, found in the neocortex.[75] Interestingly, some of these elementary patterns of cells organized and stacked in columns are found in areas where sensory information is processed. Imagine these specialized modules of neurons working together to produce, say, "red color" suprels here and "high-pitched sound" or "sweet smell" suprels there.

Two examples of suprels

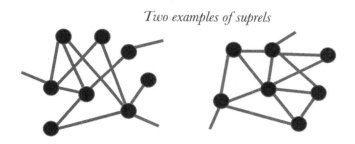

A suprel is a unit (bit) of supral information; which is altogether hidden, nonlocal, and subjective. It is a pattern wrought from beads (*the holoparticles*) bound by threads (*the supral links*). This pattern may encode specific data, and more often than not, it belongs to a much broader supral network. The drawing above shows two examples (artist's view) of such patterns.

As an aside, let me recall that it may seem today that *"the evidence is building up that we can explain everything interesting about the mind in terms of interactions of neurons."*[76] If to "explain" means to find the neural correlates of conscious events, this statement is undoubtedly true. Science can arguably explain a great deal with these correlates, which address the so-called third-person aspect of mental events. Deep-learning algorithms built on neural networks can even emulate them. Let's not get carried away, however; knowing everything about these correlates does not help us to understand, let alone crack, the conundrum of the conscious brain. It merely dances

---

[75] *These vertical cylinders, or cortical columns as they came to be known, were discovered by Vernon B. Mountcastle.*

[76] *Here I quote philosopher Paul Thagard, of the University of Waterloo in Ontario.*

around the "hard problem" of brain consciousness, and of how some physical stimuli end up as qualia. Thus, if to "explain" is to unlock the mystery of the first-person experience, science falls short. It even fails entirely. Perhaps, though, science will fare better in the future. I believe that by adding in-causation to its explanatory framework, it would narrow down its current explanatory gap.

Related Issues and Open Questions

As regards brain-based awareness, what I suggest here is that our organ of sentience pulls off its conscious trick by binding (or "in-blending") countless sparks of the mind together, which would flow in huge and continuous streams. These "sparks" are particles undergoing quantum jumps. Still we may wonder, *"How could the conscious brain have anything to do with quantum quirks and features?"* After all, our thinking organ is macroscopic, and macroscopic objects are known to be ruled by classical physics. The thing is, long-lasting macroscopic quantum states are well nigh impossible. The warm and messy wetware of the brain, with its throngs of jiggling atoms and particles, with its swarms of ions and droves of molecules, make them highly unlikely. However, there is still a glimmer of hope for the quantum brain. There are strong hints that the alleged impossibility of macroscopic quantum states is far from watertight, and there is mounting evidence that some biological processes—photosynthesis, olfaction, and enzyme action, to name but a few—involve long-lived quantum states at the macro-level.

Brain-wise, promising avenues are being explored by some research scientists. Matthew Fisher is one of them.[77] Observing that life had billions of years to learn how to exploit the quantum rules through its exquisite molecular machinery, Fisher is convinced that *"the brain uses quantum mechanics."* To make his point, he zeroes in on a molecule called the Posner cluster which, he argues, allows for long-lived quantum effects. Fisher

---

[77] *Fisher's approach is presented in the Annals of Physics, vol. 362, 593-. Another attempt, championed by Stuart Hameroff and Sir Roger Penrose, is based on brain microtubules. (These are building blocks of the cytoskeleton, viz. the cell's skeleton.)*

suggests that the brain's extracellular fluids *"could be awash with highly entangled Posner clusters"* that would *"go inside the neurons, contributing to the way cells signal, respond and start to form thoughts and memories."* Fisher's approach is very exciting. It shows that one should think twice, perhaps, before dismissing the idea that the brain can routinely handle long-lasting quantum states. This is new, and this is good news for the holomatter approach outlined here (no link with Fisher's approach).

To conclude, it appears that the in-causal assumption on which holomatter rests kills two birds with one stone. First, it connects the dots of quantum weirdness in a way that dissipates most of it, since, jumps and entanglement do make sense with in-causation. They serve a purpose. The second "bird" is the vexing mind-body problem and, more broadly, the riddle of the conscious brain. Here, again, in-causation sheds a new explanatory light. (Of course, this light is purely speculative at this stage.) Most significantly, holomatter—through what I call the deed—seems poised to articulate a postmaterialist solution to the mind-body problem.[78]

Other issues to be explored are the link between free will and in-causation, the role of supralness in brain sensory integration and mental binding, the relationship between suprels, qualia, and our declarative memory, and much more. Much work needs to be done before we can seriously contemplate a "holo-theory" of the conscious brain. Needless to say, it will have to take into due account the remarkable and fast-expanding knowledge of brain and cognitive sciences.

Let me add that in-causal interconnectedness is the rule in our entangled universe. All of life—sentient life, especially—is woven into a wider supral fabric. This fabric stores countless suprels, whose subjective data are available near and far. They make a rich tapestry and turn the universe into a gigantic hologram. This is akin to theosophy's Akashic records, to the collective unconscious introduced by C. G. Jung, and to the morphogenetic fields championed by Rupert Sheldrake, who contributed a chapter to this book. Moreover, holomatter provides a framework for such

---

[78] *We recall that the deed is twofold, which reflects the fact that the psychism-matter interplay is a two-way road. It's two-in-one: both a (sensory-side) quantum threat and a (motor-side) quantum jump wrapped up together.*

nonconventional phenomena as telepathy and mediumship. This is because supral links are telepathic bonds at heart. Some of them lend invisible and boundless wings to our psychism. They expand our minds non-locally. With supralness, the sky's the limit. Thanks to it, our minds are not brain-bound—they reach to the stars![79]

My main and last take-home message is this: science has nothing to lose, and potentially much to gain, to acknowledge the *possibility* of in-causation. After all, in-causation may hold the key to two daunting puzzles: that of quantum weirdness and that of brain consciousness.

Can the idea of in-causation wash? I hope the future will tell.

References

Malin, S. (2012). *Nature Loves to Hide*. World Scientific.

Ransford, E. (1999). Panpsychism, the Conscious Brain, and Our Mind-body-soul Nature, *The Noetic Journal*, 2(3), 323-332.

---

[79] *Dean Radin, Gary E. Schwartz, Stephan A. Schwartz, Rupert Sheldrake, Russell Targ, and other researchers argue forcefully about such a non-locality of the mind, with compelling evidence to back their claims.*

About the Authors

MARIO BEAUREGARD, PH.D., is a neuroscientist currently affiliated with the Department of Psychology at the University of Arizona. His groundbreaking work on the neurobiology of emotion and mystical experience has received international media coverage. Dr. Beauregard is the author of *Brain Wars: The Scientific Battle Over the Existence of the Mind and the Proof That Will Change the Way We Live Our Lives*.

«»

NATALIE L. DYER, PH.D., is a Research Scientist with Kripalu Center for Yoga & Health and Connor Integrative Health Network. She completed her PhD in Neuroscience at Queen's University and her Postdoctoral Fellowships in Psychology at Harvard University and at Harvard Medical School. She has published multiple scientific papers and presented her research to diverse audiences throughout North America and Europe. Natalie is also an energy medicine practitioner and teacher, incorporating Japanese Usui Reiki and North American, European, and Tibetan shamanism into her practice.

«»

LARRY DOSSEY, M.D., is an internal medicine physician, former Chief of Staff of Medical City Dallas Hospital, and former co-chairman of the Panel on Mind/Body Interventions, National Center for Complementary and Alternative Medicine, National Institutes of Health. He is executive editor of the peer-previewed journal *Explore: The Journal of Science and Healing*. He is the author of 12 books on the role of consciousness and spirituality in health, most recently *One Mind: How Our Individual Mind Is Part of a Greater Consciousness and Why It Matters*, which have been translated into dozens of languages. He lectures around the world.

AMIT GOSWAMI, PH.D., is a theoretical quantum physicist and retired full professor from the University of Oregon's Department of Physics. He is the author of *The Self-Aware Universe*, in which he pioneered the idea of "science within consciousness" and elucidated the famous observer effect in quantum physics. Amit was featured in the film What the Bleep Do We Know!?, and is the author of nine other books based on his research in quantum physics and consciousness.

《〇》

ISABELLE GOULET, PH.D., is a cellular and molecular biologist specializing in epigenetics and cancer biology. In the course of her research, she came to the realization that truly innovative health advances would require a daring new perspective on human biology. She started to seek out nonconventional practices to gain a more holistic understanding of the healing processes of the human body and began her training in healing practices rooted in aboriginal traditions. She founded SCIENTIVE to explore, through research and hands-on experience, the body's natural ability to heal.

《〇》

NEAL GROSSMAN, PH.D., is a recently retired associate professor of philosophy at the University of Illinois at Chicago. His interests have been far ranging, from the Philosophy of Science, especially quantum mechanics, to Spinoza, Plato, mysticism, and now, survival research. He has published two books: (i) *The Spirit of Spinoza: Healing the Mind*, is a readable presentation of Spinoza's remarkable system of spiritual psychotherapy. And (ii) *Conversations With Socrates and Plato: How a Postmaterialist Social Order Can Solve the Challenges of Modern Life and Insure Our Survival*.

ERLENDUR HARALDSSON, PH.D., is a Professor emeritus of psychology at the School of Health Sciences in the Psychology Department of the University of Iceland. Dr. Haraldsson is an active researcher, publishing over 70 technical papers and several books, including *The Departed Among the Living: An Investigative Study of Afterlife Encounters* and *Modern Miracles: The Story of Sathya Sai Baba: A Modern Day Prophet*. He is also the co-author of *At the Hour of Death: A New Look at Evidence for Life After Death* and author of the forthcoming *Indridi Indridason: the Icelandic Physical Medium*, and has appeared in the BBC Documentary In Search of the Dead.

《〉》

EMILY R HAWKEN, PH.D., is an American-born Canadian physiologist and neuroscientist. Emily currently lives and works in Kingston/Canada where she researches the relationship between the brain and the world to better understand the human experience. As an early career researcher, Emily has published over 30 peer reviewed clinical and cellular/molecular neuroscience papers. Emily is driven by curiosity and dedicated to raising her three children.

《〉》

ALEXANDER MOREIRA-ALMEIDA, M.D., PH.D., is Associate Professor of Psychiatry in the School of Medicine (Universidade Federal de Juiz de Fora) and Founder and Director of the Research Center in Spirituality and Health, Brazil. He is Chair of the WPA (World Psychiatric Association) Section on Religion, Spirituality and Psychiatry and Coordinator of the Section on Spirituality of the Brazilian Psychiatric Association. He is the editor of *Exploring Frontiers of the Mind-Brain Relationship*, and is also a co-founder of the Campaign for Open Sciences to promote the movement toward a Postmaterialist Science.

DEAN RADIN, PH.D., is Chief Scientist at the Institute of Noetic Sciences and Associated Distinguished Professor at the California Institute of Integral Studies. He has held appointments at AT&T Bell Labs, Princeton University, University of Edinburgh, and SRI International, and is the author or coauthor of over 200 technical and popular articles, four dozen book chapters, and four books, including the best-selling *The Conscious Universe* (1997), *Entangled Minds* (2006), the 2014 Silver Nautilus Book Award winner *Supernormal* (2013), and *Real Magic* (2018).

«»

EMMANUEL RANSFORD worked as an economist After graduating from France's Ecole Polytechnique. However, he soon became interested in the mind-body problem, and he felt that this conundrum could only be solved through quantum physics. This led him to view matter in a different light, as something alive rather than inert. As his holomatter approach to the conscious brain was too unconventional to be accepted by mainstream science, Emmanuel developed this approach independently. He is the author of several books and papers, mostly in French, on this topic, such as *L'Univers Quantique enfin Expliqué (The Quantum Universe Explained at last...)*.

«»

MARILYN SCHLITZ, PH.D., is a social anthropologist, researcher, writer, and charismatic public speaker. She currently serves as President Emeritus and Senior Fellow at the Institute of Noetic Sciences. For more than three decades, Marilyn has been a leader in the field of consciousness studies. Her research and extensive publications focus on personal and social transformation, cultural pluralism, extended human capacities, and mind body medicine. She recently wrote and produced a feature film (called Death Makes Life Possible) with Deepak Chopra on the topic of death and dying, and how engaging that topic in a deep and meaningful way informs the way we live our lives. Schlitz is currently Dean of the Institute of Transpersonal Psychology at Sofia University in Palo Alto, Ca.

LORNE SCHUSSEL, PH.D., M.S. is a Clinical Psychologist, Postdoctoral Fellow and Research Director of the Contemplative Science and Post Materialism Lab at Columbia University, Teachers College. He is visiting faculty at the Spirituality Mind Body Institute and formerly Project Director of the Contemplative Neuroscience and Connectivity Project. His research focuses on the utilization of novel mind-body practices, human connectivity, contemplative neuroscience, and integrating clinical biomarkers (epigenetic, HR, EEG) into clinical research. Dr. Schussel developed a psychological healing practice known as "The Best Self Visualization Method" which has been cited in the New York Times, ABC-online, and the Huffington Post. Lorne has recently taught the technique to appointed state judges as visiting faculty at the California State Judicial College for a course on mental health and employee burnout.

«◊»

GARY E. SCHWARTZ, PH.D., is a professor of psychology, medicine, neurology, psychiatry, and surgery at the University of Arizona and director of its Laboratory for Advances in Consciousness and Health. He served as the Founding President of the Academy for the Advancement of Postmaterialist Sciences. His books include *The Afterlife Experiments*, *The Sacred Promise*, and *Super Synchronicity*.

«◊»

RUPERT SHELDRAKE, PH.D., best known for his hypothesis of morphic fields and morphic resonance, is a biologist and author of more than 85 technical papers and 11 books, including *Morphic Resonance: The Nature of Formative Causation* and *Science Set Free: 10 Paths to New Discovery* (called *The Science Delusion* in the UK). He was a Fellow of Clare College, Cambridge, where he was Director of Studies in biochemistry and cell biology, and was also a Research Fellow of the Royal Society. He is currently a Fellow of the Institute of Noetic Sciences, in California, and of Schumacher College, in Devon, England. He is also a co-founder of the Campaign for Open Sciences to promote the movement toward a Postmaterialist Science.

《◊》

JOHN H SPENCER, PH.D., was awarded his degree from the University of Liverpool, specializing in the Philosophical Foundations of Quantum Physics. He is the multiple award-winning author of *The Eternal Law: Ancient Greek Philosophy, Modern Physics, and Ultimate Reality*, which is endorsed by Prof. Sir Roger Penrose and Dr. Ervin Laszlo. He is also a contributing co-editor of *The Beacon of Mind: Reason and Intuition in the Ancient and Modern World*, and contributor to various publications.

《◊》

CHARLES T. TART, PH.D., is one of the founders of the field of transpersonal psychology. He has had more than 250 articles published in professional journals and books, and is the author of *The End of Materialism: How Evidence of the Paranormal Is Bringing Science and Spirit Together* and *Mind Science: Meditation Training for Practical People*. He is an Emeritus Core Faculty Member at the Institute of Transpersonal Psychology (now called Sofia University) in Palo Alto, California, and Professor Emeritus of Psychology at the Davis campus of the University of California. Charles is also a co-founder of the Campaign for Open Sciences to promote the movement toward a Postmaterialist Science.

《◊》

PIM VAN LOMMEL, M.D., is a cardiologist who has studied near-death experiences (NDEs) for more than thirty years. In 2001, he and his fellow researchers published a study on NDEs in the renowned medical journal The Lancet. The article caused an international sensation as it was the first scientifically rigorous study of this phenomenon. He is the author of the bestseller *Consciousness Beyond Life: The Science of the Near-Death Experience*.

MARJORIE WOOLLACOTT, PH.D., is Professor Emeritus of Human Physiology and Neuroscience at the University of Oregon. Her research has been funded by the National Institutes of Health and includes both research in rehabilitation medicine and alternative forms of therapy such as tai chi and meditation. She is president of the Academy for the Advancement of Postmaterialist Sciences (AAPS), the Research Director of the International Association of Near Death Studies (IANDS), and has written more than 200 peer-reviewed research articles—several of which were on spiritual awakening and meditation, the topic that motivated her to write her latest book, *Infinite Awareness: The Awakening of a Scientific Mind*.

Index

Academy for the Advancement of Posmaterialist Sciences (AAPS), i, ii
Achterberg, Jeanne, 209
acquired savants, 314
Across the Frontiers (Heisenberg), 90–91
after death communications (ADCs)
  about, 372–73
  deathbed communications, 15
  materialism denying, 60
  mediums. *See* mediumship research
  percentage who have, 297
  skepticism, true versus pseudo, 40–50
afterlife
  belief in, 297, 330
  letter-writer Chico Xavier, 299–300
  mediums providing evidence, 373–75
  reincarnation. *See* reincarnation
Alexander, Eben, 70
alternative medicine, 67–69, 73–74, 168–70
Apology (Plato), 414
AQUA (Automated Query and Analysis) software for HPP study, 36–38
Aristotle retarding science, 90
Aspect, Alain, 98
astral projection, 102
atheism and materialism, 135, 138
atomism, 399–401
atoms
  Bell's theorem, 98
  bio-photons, 100–101, 103–4, 104–6
  choices made by, 17, 148, 454
  entanglement. *See* quantum entanglement
  experiences of subatomic particles, 146, 149
  Fröhlich's mind journeys, 107
  Heisenberg on material objects, 91
  holomatter. *See* holomatter
  matter at atomic level, 86, 91
  one object is many, 92
  panpsychism, 142
  Pauli cosmic clock dream, 106
  quantum mechanics. *See* quantum mechanics
  Whitehead on experiences, 146
autistic savants, 314, 315
awareness
  paradigm foundation, 324
  quantum consciousness, 446–49, 458–60

subject-object split, 161, 164
Beauregard, Mario
  International Summit organizer, ii
  this anthology, iv
  Toward a Postmaterialist Psychology, 73
Being of Light, 10, 404
belief (spiritual)
  health relationship with, 62–63
  materialism's effects on worldview, 353–59
  mind-brain. *See* mind-brain via spirituality
  postmaterialist benefits, 63, 67
belief systems and personal conduct
  atomism, 399–401
  faith required for materialism, 398
  Golden Rule postmaterialism, 405–9
  life review in near-death experience, 407–9
  materialism and material goods, 398–99, 402
  materialist leadership, 410
  materialist social order, 403–5, 405
  mind separate from brain, 401
  One Mind, 400, 401
  panentheism, 400, 405–7
  personality formation, 402–3
  postmaterialism, 401
  postmaterialist leaders, 409–11, 413–15
  postmaterialist social order, 404–9
  souls embodied versus non-embodied, 411
  souls manifesting our current selves, 402–5
Bell's theorem, 98
Bergson, Henri, 144, 275
bio-photons
  about, 100–101
  dream states, 105
  geo-magnetic activity and, 105
  neural connectivity, 103–4
  quantum brain connectivity, 104–6
Birth and Rebirth (Eliade), 65
blind people's near-death experiences, 263, 296
body influenced by mind, 7
Bohm, David, 149
Bohr, Niels, 28, 163
Bókkon, István, 101, 105

Bourey, Alan D. (*The Case for Truth*), 51
brain
   bio-photons, 100–101, 103–4, 104–6
   BRAIN initiative, 116
   carbon dioxide levels and near-death experiences, 266
   cardiac arrest injury, 255, 261
   clinical death definition, 242
   creating mind as fact, 119, 123, 287, 312
   creating mind as flawed idea, 16, 58, 70, 204, 263, 266–68
   Decade of the Brain, 116
   EEG. *See* EEG
   filter function of, 16, 58–60, 293, 431
   filter function of autistics, 315
   frontal lobe lesions and psi, 315
   materialist brain knowledge, 118–21
   materialist versus postmaterialist theories, 100–101
   memory location, 175, 240, 266, 389
   messenger to consciousness, 263, 268
   mind existing separately from, 124, 150–51, 262, 269, 401
   mind influencing, 6
   mind-brain models, 268
   mind-brain via spirituality. *See* mind-brain via spirituality
   oxygen levels and near-death experiences, 264–65
   perception and memory, 160
   thinking outside the box, 124–27
   thoughts within structure of, 266–68
   trance writing brain activity, 300
   transceiver for mind, 19–20, 58, 271–73, 287
Brenner, Sydney, 135
Bridges system, 72
Bringing Spiritually Oriented Psychotherapies into the Health Care Mainstream (Richards et al.), 72
Broad, C. D., 221, 398
Brown, G. Spencer (*Laws of Form*), 325
Burt, Cyril, 59
Bush, George W., Sr., 116
Cabot, Richard, 206
Call for an Open, Informed Study of All Aspects of Consciousness, A (Cardeña), 72
Campaign for Open Science website, iii
cancer
   carcinoma interconnectivity, 104
   genetic influences, 187
   mice receiving healing with intent, 213
   nonlocal communication, 217
   predicting outcomes from genes, 196
capitalism, 409–11
cardiac arrest
   anoxia, 264, 269
   brain injury from, 255, 261
   carbon dioxide levels, 266
   CPR for brain viability, 256–57
   EEG flat line, 258–61, 261, 269
   enhanced consciousness during, 239, 243, 248, 249, 250, 262, 263, 269, 296–97, 432
   hypoxia, 264, 269
   near-death experiences. *See* near-death experiences (NDEs)
   neurophysiology in, 254
Careña, Etzel (A Call for an Open, Informed Study of All Aspects of Consciousness), 72
Cartesian dualism, 139
Case for Truth, The (Bourey & G. E. Schwartz), 51
Cases of the Reincarnation Type (Stevenson), 345
causation
   deterministic and non-deterministic, 439–40
   in-causation, 439–40, 445, 452
   in-causation and subjective content, 442–43
   out-causation, 439–40, 445
   quantum randomness and, 438–40
cellular nature and origin, 163–64
Chaban, Victor V., 217
chakras
   kundalini awakenings, 419
   science within consciousness, 160, 170–73
Chalmers, David
   consciousness fundamental, 17, 268
   neurons and self-awareness, 266
   subjective experience problem, 135, 160
choices
   atoms making, 17, 148, 454
   experience as consciousness choosing, 159
   free will, 448

holoparticle in-causal initiatives, 454, 456
in-causation and quantumhood, 442
clairvoyance tests, 365–66
Cliness, David, 177
clinical death definition, 242
cognitive psychology, 140
communication with the dead. *See* after death communications
complementary and alternative medicine (CAM)
   about, 67–69
   institutes and conferences, 73–74
   science within consciousness, 168–70
complex systems
   geese migration example, 192–93
   gene expression, 192–93, 195
   human body as, 193
   modeling, 195, 196
consciousness
   brain as filter, 16
   brain creating as fact, 119, 123, 287, 312
   brain creating as flawed idea, 16, 58, 70, 204, 263, 266–68
   connecting outer and inner experience, 98
   cosmic consciousness within, 391
   creator of Mental Universe, 126–27
   fundamental, 1, 400
   materialist philosophies, 140–42
   mind as. *See* mind
   nonlocal consciousness, 162–63, 270–73, 275, 276
   not destroyed, 382
   quantum. *See* quantum consciousness; science within consciousness
   science within. *See* science within consciousness
   soul creating, 405
Consciousness beyond Life (van Lommel), 276
Consciousness Explained (Dennett), 138
Copernican Revolution paradigm shift, 5, 96
creativity, 173–74
Crick, Francis, 135, 138
dark matter, 136
Darwinism, 165–66
de Quincey, Christian, 147
death
   about, 382
   clinical death definition, 242

communication after, 40–50, 60, 297, 372–73
consciousness in patients after, 392
fear of and NDE occurring, 241, 245, 264, 269
fear of promoted by materialism, 61
fear of relieved by postmaterialism, 70
flat-line EEG as brain death, 262
life after. *See* afterlife; reincarnation
life after belief percentage, 297, 330
materialist paradigm shifts, 383–87
microtubules for consciousness survival, 391
near-death experiences. *See* near-death experiences
neurophysiology of cardiac arrest, 254
practice of death, 382, 393–95
souls. *See* souls
spiritual experience and mind-brain, 296–97
terminal lucidity, 297
Death Makes Life Possible (Schlitz), 389
deathbed communications (DBCs), 15
Declaration for Integrative, Evidence-Based, End-of-Life Care that Incorporates Nonlocal Consciousness (S. A. Schwartz et al.), 72
deed of mind-body interaction, 453–54
Default Mode Network (DMN), 430–31, 431–32
Dennett, Daniel, 86, 138, 268
depression
   after-death communication dispelling, 373
   kundalini awakenings, 421
   near-death experiences from, 241, 245, 247, 264, 269
Descartes, René, 139
dharma, 177
Dirac, Paul Adrien Maurice, 442
distant healing. *See* telecebo response
Distant Mental Interactions with Living Systems (DMILS), 212–13
DNA
   genes. *See* gene expression
   non-coding sequences, 189
   science within consciousness, 164
domain of potentiality, 155
Dotta, Blake, 104
double-slit experiment wave function collapse, 126
dream states
   bio-photons during, 105

cosmic clock dream of Pauli, 106–7
human mind and global field, 105
Jung analyzing Pauli's, 106
dual nature of light, 27
dualism, 137, 158–60
duration implying consciousness, 144–45
Dyer, Natalie L. (Trent)
this anthology, iv
Toward a Postmaterialist Psychology, 73
Dyson, Freeman, 17, 149
Eberhard's theorem, 162–63
Eccles, John C., 263, 288
Eeden, Frederik van, 243
EEG (electroencephalogram)
cardiac arrest injury of brain, 261
flat line and enhanced consciousness, 262, 432
flat line as brain death, 262
flat line during cardiac arrest, 258–61, 261, 269
NDE flat-lined yet perceptions, 11, 254
people physically separated but connected, 103–4, 162
telecebo effects, 210
ego self, 160
Einstein, Albert
quantum mechanics and relativity, 122
Reason manifesting in nature, 88
spirit manifest in laws of universe, 55
electromagnetic spectrum, 196
electrons having experiences, 149
elementary particles. *See* atoms
Eliade, Mircea (*Birth and Rebirth*), 65
eliminative materialism, 140
End of Materialism, The (Tart), 349, 362
end-of-life care
end-of-life experience definition, 297
nonlocal consciousness incorporated, 72
spiritual experience and mind-brain, 296–97
energy medicine, 67, 168–70
kundalini awakenings, 419–20
Reiki, 68, 73, 168
Therapeutic Touch, 212
enlightenment
experiencing the sacred, 69–70
science within consciousness, 181–82
Entangled Minds (Radin), 210
epiphenomenalism, 140, 384

ESP (extrasensory perception)
about, 8
clairvoyance tests, 365–66
criticism of, 218–21
essential science tests of, 365–67
evidence of postmaterialism, 8–10
fMRI signs of distant healing, 209
intrinsic connectedness, 216–18
intuitive thought, 158, 166, 247
Jung exploding at Freud about, 202
nonlocal quantum consciousness, 162–63
precognition, 203, 366–67, 378
psi phenomena. *See* psi phenomena
telepathy. *See* telepathy
essential science, 359–63
Eternal Law, The (Spencer), 108, 385
evidence of postmaterialism
about evidence, 5
CONSORT criteria of studies, 210
deathbed communications, 15
genius, 313
mediumship research, 13–15, 26, 60, 316
mind beyond space and time, 8–10, 18, 58
mind's power over body, 6–8
near-death experiences, 10–12, 19, 26, 58, 60, 239, 262, 316
postmaterial persons. *See* hypothesized postmaterial persons
psi phenomena, 8–10, 317–21
reincarnation and past-life research, 12–13, 26, 316, 345
savants, 314–15
skepticism, true versus pseudo, 40–50
telecebo effects, 209–12
evidence-based science
essential science for postmaterialism, 359–63
importance of, 27
kundalini awakenings, 420–24
postmaterial persons. *See* hypothesized postmaterial persons
psi phenomena, 317–21
randomized controlled trials, 27, 28, 30–32
soul and science, 387–93
telepathy meta-analysis, 214
evolution
consciousness via, 141, 143, 165
consciousness-based, 166–67

475

genes. *See* gene expression
intrinsic connectedness, 218
morphogenetic fields, 164, 165
neo-Darwinism, 165–66
experience
    brain filtering, 59
    consciousness as stream of, 124
    consciousness connecting inner with outer, 98, 108
    consciousness making choices, 159
    electrons having, 149
    essential science, 360
    experiencer separate from experiences, 385–86
    experiencing the sacred, 69–70
    gene expression and, 197–98
    getting outside the brain, 124
    internal physical or not, 158–60
    materialism versus dualism, 138
    materialism versus postmaterialism, 76
    materialist philosophies, 140
    mental versus physical aspect, 18
    morphogenetic fields, 159
    otherworldly, 105
    panpsychism, 142–47, 268
    postmaterialism, 57, 107
    scientific materialism, 2, 3
    soul as locus of all, 388, 390
    spiritual as mental illness, 59–66, 294, 417
    spiritual providing meaning, 350–51
    studying, 5
    subjective experience, 126, 135, 138, 140
    subjective experience and quantum mechanics. *See* qualia and quanta
Explore journal articles, iii, 47
exterior and interior. *See* interior and exterior
extrasensory perception. *See* ESP
Farhadi, Ashkan, 217
Feinberg, Gerald, 219
Fenwick, Peter, 249
Feynman, Richard, 26, 28
fighter pilot near-death experiences, 264
Fisher, Matthew, 461
fMRI (functional MRI) scanner
    enhanced consciousness during cardiac arrest, 262
    telecebo effects, 209
Freud, Sigmund
    Jung exploding about ESP, 202

psychical researcher in next life, 57
the unconscious, 161
views on ESP, 202, 225
Fröhlich, Herbert, 107–8
frontal lobe lesions and psi, 315
ganzfeld technique, 8, 319, 320
    meta-analysis, 322–23
geese migration complex system, 192–93
gene expression
    complex systems, 192–93, 195
    context influencing, 190
    correcting, 197
    cracking the code of life, 193–97
    environmental information converted by, 197–98
    expression states, 189, 190
    genes mapping destiny, 186
    genes not mapping destiny, 187–88
    Human Genome Project, 186, 188
    non-coding DNA sequences, 189
    predicting outcomes from, 191–92, 195, 198
    protein transcription, 188–90
genius challenging materialism, 313
geomagnetic storms and bio-photon emission, 105
Gödel, Kurt, 84, 392
Golden Rule postmaterialism, 405–9
Grand Design, The (Hawking), 136
Greyson, Bruce, 248
Grossman, Neal, 433–34
Hameroff, Stuart, 391
Hanson, Ronald, 102
Haraldsson, Erlendur, 12
Hawking, Stephen (*The Grand Design*), 136
healing intentions. *See* telecebo response
health
    call for postmaterial approach, 72
    carcinoma interconnectivity, 104
    distant healing. *See* telecebo response
    end-of-life care, 72, 296–97
    energy medicine, 67, 168–70
    future events unconsciously anticipated, 214
    gene expression therapies, 197
    genes predicting outcomes, 191–92, 195, 198
    morphogenetic fields, 160, 168
    past medical event healing intentions, 214
    postmaterialist institutes and conferences, 73–74

science within consciousness, 167
spirituality improving, 62–63, 67
Heisenberg, Werner
   Across the Frontiers, 90–91
   observer collapsing waves of
      possibility, 155
   One, 91
   Platonic Ideas, 90–91
hell as life review at death, 408
Henry, Richard Conn, 124
Hoffman, Donald D., 220
holomatter
   about, 440–43, 444, 462
   creation of, 446–49
   holoparticle, 441
   mind-body interaction, 453–54
   quantum randomness, 438–40, 444–47
   quantum threat, 441–42, 449–51
   quantumhood, 441–43, 449–52
   supralness, 443, 454–58
Hotta, Masahiroi, 99
HPP. *See* hypothesized postmaterial
   persons
Hume, David, 385
Humphrey, Nicholas, 141
Hunter, Lawrence, 194
Huxley, Aldous, 59
hypothesized postmaterial persons
   (HPPs)
   about HPPs, 28
   about the study, 29–30
   automated hardware and software
      system, 30, 33–34
   electromagnetic organization of, 36
   evidence validating, 39
   experimenter consciousness ruled out,
      29
   hardware for HPP RCT, 34–36
   mediumship research, 35, 48
   practical requirements for conducting
      study, 33–34
   randomized controlled trials, 30–32
   skepticism, discernments, 43–53
   skepticism, true versus pseudo, 40–50
   software for HPP RCT, 36–38
   test suite, 38–39
immaterial monism, 268
immaterialism, 88
inner and outer
   all levels of organization, 18
   consciousness and matter, 144
   consciousness connecting, 98
   cosmic consciousness within, 391
   exteriorization across time, 214
   exteriorization of thoughts healing,
      209–10
   exteriorizing emotions, 202, 223–24
   in- and out-causation, 439–40
   Jung's interior feelings exteriorizing,
      203
   materialist perspective, 351, 384–86
   memory in brain versus nonlocal, 175
   mind and body, 145, 204
   soul and science, 389
   telecebo effects exteriorizing, 207–9
Institute of Noetic Sciences, 210
interactionist-dualistic mind-brain model,
   268, 287
interconnection of people
   experiencing the sacred, 69
   interpersonal healing for placebo
      effect, 205
   life review in near-death experiences,
      252
   mind connected to greater field, 104–6
   near-death experiences, 247, 406–9
   One Mind, 400, 401, 404, 405
   physically separated but connected,
      103–4
   telecebo interpersonal healing, 207–9,
      216–18
   Wolfgang Pauli and Carl Jung, 97–98,
      99, 106–7
interconnection of psyche and physis
   Carl Jung and Wolfgang Pauli, 97
   Carl Jung on, 100
   cosmic clock of Wolfgang Pauli, 107
   molecular level, 17
   mysticism of Pauli and Fröhlich, 107–
      9
   participatory universe, 18
   postmaterialist paradigm, 19
   psi phenomena, 18
interconnection of quantum
   entanglement. *See* quantum
   entanglement
interconnection of universe, 391, 394
International Summit on Postmaterialist
   Science, Spirituality, and Society
   (2014), ii, 71
Internet and social media as
   programming tools, 75–76
interpersonal healing for placebo effect,
   205

intuitive thought, 158, 166
  near-death experiences enhancing, 247
Irreducible Mind (Kelly), 397
Isojima, Yasushi, 101
James, William
  brain producing mind, 287
  brain transmitting consciousness, 273
  filter function of brain, 16, 431
  mediumship, 13, 297
  mediumship and colleagues, 291
  non-materialist, 286, 290
  panpsychism, 144
  spirituality and mysticism, 57
  study abnormal to know normal, 239
Jeans, James H., 270, 273
Jefferson, Thomas, 206
Jung, Carl
  banging at Freud, 202
  bangs from tabletop and knifeblade, 203–4
  collective unconscious, 105
  cosmic clock dream of Pauli, 106
  Memories, Dreams, Reflections, 202
  past, present, future as one, 108
  personality types, 158
  Psychology and Alchemy, 97
  science a function of the soul, 388
  unexplainable phenomena, 221
  Wolfgang Pauli and, 97–98, 99, 106–7
Kabat-Zinn, Jon, 66
Kalanithi, Paul, 116
Kelly, E. F. (*Irreducible Mind*), 397
Kelvin, Lord (William Thomson), 292, 311
Kepler Challenge, 52
King, Larry, 50
Klein, Leslie, 53
Kobayashi, Masaki, 101
kriyas, 419
Kuhn, Thomas
  new theories after insecurity, 123
  paradigm shifts, 382, 383
  paradigms as currently accepted, 118
  paradigms can and should change, 4
  pre-paradigmatic scientific fields, 291
  scientific revolution bursting into existence, 125
  Structure of Scientific Revolutions, 4
  theory into paradigm, 361
kundalini awakenings (KAs)
  about, 419–20, 433–34
  Default Mode Network, 430–32
  kriyas, 419

Kundalini Research Network, 421
  neural correlates possible, 430–31
  personal experience, 433–34
  research, 420–21
  research by authors, 421–24
  spiritually transformative experiences, 417–18
  transformation time frame, 428–29
  transformational changes, 424–27
  triggering events for, 424
  value of discussing, 429–30
Laboratory for Advances in Consciousness and Health (University of Arizona), 14
Lakatos, Imre, 294
Lashley, Karl, 175
Laws of Form (Brown), 325
Lemke, Leslie, 314
Li, Tongcang, 102
life after death. *See* afterlife; reincarnation
life review in near-death experiences, 252–53, 407–9
life's nature and origin, 163–64
light
  Being of Light in near-death experiences, 10, 404
  bio-photons, 100–101, 103–4, 104–6
  cellular signaling, 100
  double-slit experiment, 126
  dual nature of, 27
  electromagnetic spectrum, 196
  energy medicine, 67
  photon entanglement, 102
  photons interconnected, 98
Linde, Andrei, 17
locus quantum monad, 176
Maddox, John, 220
Malin, Shimon (*Nature Loves to Hide*), 442
Manifesto for a Postmaterialist Science, iii, 71, 125
Margenau, Henry, 219
Maslow, Abraham, 57
materialism
  about, 1, 85, 135, 351
  atomism, 399–401
  capitalism, 409–11
  creed of, 354–59
  creed of science, 133–34
  definition of, 86
  effects on worldview, 353–59

evidence against. *See* evidence of postmaterialism; qualia and quanta
experiencer separate from experiences, 385–86
failures of, 1–3, 125, 134–37, 155
faith required to believe in, 398
false per Gödel, 84
harms of, 57–62, 65, 121, 376, 418
human need for meaning, 352–53, 379, 402
material acquisition and, 398–99, 402
Materialist Scientism, 286
materialist social order, 403–5, 405
matter as basis of, 85–89, 351
mechanistic dualism rejected, 138
metaphysical basis of, 87
panpsychism, 142–47, 268
philosophies of, 140–42
postmaterialism as end of, ii, iii
programming by. *See* program is changing
promissory materialism, 134, 289
qualia and quanta challenging. *See* qualia and quanta
scientific creed, 133–34
scientific paradigm currently, 118
unconstrained cognition, 432
mathematics
dreams of Wolfgang Pauli, 106
non-materialism of, 91–94
matter
atomic level. *See* atoms
basis as nonmaterial, 390
basis of materialism, 85–89, 351
consciousness as, 268
dark matter, 136
matter is unconscious, 133, 137–39, 148
mind in addition to, 286
mind metaphysically prior to, 88
non-material reality, 88, 89
physics founders as dualists, 139
postmaterialist scientific paradigm, 126
meaning
materialist perspective, 351–53, 379, 402
purpose and meaning of lives, 402, 407
spiritual experiences for, 350–51
mechanistic dualism, 138
medicine
 allopathic versus alternative, 168–70
call for postmaterial approach, 72
carcinoma interconnectivity, 104
complementary and alternative, 67–69, 73–74, 168–70
future events unconsciously anticipated, 214
gene expression therapies, 197
past medical event healing intentions, 214
placebo effect, 205–7
postmaterialist institutes and conferences, 73–74
reductionist paradigm, 118
telecebo effect, 207–9
meditation
internal experiences via, 158
mindfulness meditation, 66
near-death experiences from, 241, 245, 264, 269
research on, 67
spiritual experience, 295–96
mediumship research
about mediums, 373
afterlife evidence, 373–75
brain activation patterns during trance writing, 300
evidence of postmaterialism, 13–15, 26, 60, 316
hypothesized postmaterial persons, 35, 48
letter-writer Chico Xavier, 299–300
mind-brain via spirituality, 297–301
scientists gullible, 41
William James's colleagues' resistance, 291
Memories, Dreams, Reflections (Jung), 202
memory
autistic savant Kim Peek, 314
bio-photon research, 101
brain hierarchy, 160
connection to the past, 146, 150
creed of science, 133, 138
events containing memory of past, 144, 146
location in brain, 175, 240, 266, 389
near-death experiences, 11, 60, 239, 241, 249, 296
near-death experiences requiring, 245
past activities affecting present, 150
past-life. *See* past-life memories

Expanding Science

reincarnation and, 176
resonance theory, 150
mental illness
   materialist brain knowledge, 119
   spiritual experiences as, 63–66, 294, 417
metaphysical basis of materialism, 87
metta, 66
Miller, Lisa, ii
mind
   beyond space and time, 8–10, 18, 58
   brain creating as fact, 119, 123, 287, 312
   brain creating as flawed idea, 16, 58, 70, 204, 263, 266–68
   brain transceiver for, 19–20, 58, 271–73, 287
   brain-mind models, 268
   connection to greater field, 104–6
   evolution of, 165
   existing separately from brain, 124, 150–51, 262, 269, 401
   Fröhlich journeying into subatomic realm, 107
   irreducible, 17
   metaphysically prior to matter, 88
   mind-brain via spirituality. *See* mind-brain via spirituality
   panpsychism, 142–47, 268
   power to influence brain and body, 6–8
   quantum psycho-physical parallelism and, 158–60
   scientists on mental events affecting physical world, 2
   self-referential nature of, 124
   telecebo effect from interpersonal healing, 207–9
   thoughts as quantum objects, 159
   unconscious mind, 148–49, 161
Mind and Cosmos (Nagel), 143
mind-brain via spirituality
   end-of-life and near-death experiences, 296–97
   meditative states, 295–96
   mediumship, 297–301
   mind-brain models, 268
   neuroscience not implying materialism, 287–89
   reincarnation, 301
   science beyond materialism, 286–87
   spiritual experiences studied as science, 290–95

mindfulness meditation
   about, 66
   internal experiences via, 158
   mindfulness-based stress reduction, 66
   research on, 67
   spiritual experience, 295–96
mind-matter interaction (MMI) experiments, 9
morphogenetic fields, 159, 160, 164, 168
Nagel, Thomas (*Mind and Cosmos*), 143
Nature Loves to Hide (Malin), 442
near-death experiences (NDEs)
   about, 10, 239–41, 371–72
   Being of Light, 10, 404
   blind people describing perceptions, 263, 296
   brain producing conscious assumption, 263
   carbon dioxide levels, 266
   cardiac arrest blood flow to brain, 255
   cardiac arrest CPR, 256–57
   cardiac arrest EEG flat line, 258–61, 261, 269
   cardiac arrest neurophysiology, 254
   clinical death definition, 242
   conscious return into body, 253–54
   description of, 241–43
   enhanced consciousness while unconscious, 239, 243, 248, 249, 250, 262, 263, 269, 296–97, 432
   evidence of postmaterialism, 10–12, 19, 26, 58, 60, 239, 262, 316
   fear of death after, 246
   fear of death causing, 241, 245, 264, 269
   Golden Rule and, 405–9
   kundalini awakenings, 420–21, 424
   life after death and, 176
   life review, 252–53, 407–9
   materialist turned postmaterialist, 70
   mind-brain models, 268, 401
   nonlocal consciousness, 270–73, 275, 276
   numbers of people experiencing, 241
   out-of-body experiences, 10, 19, 58, 239, 250–52, 250–52, 371
   oxygen levels low, 264–65, 269
   panentheism, 406–7
   prospective studies, 243–49
   purpose and meaning of lives, 402, 407
   returning to bodies, 403, 404

spiritual experience and mind-brain, 296–97
thoughts within brain structure, 266–68
transformational effects of, 241, 243, 246–48
neo-Darwinism, 165–66
neuroscience
  brain does not equal mind, 287–89
  BRAIN initiative, 116
  getting outside the brain, 124–27
  how a new paradigm emerges, 121–24
  kundalini awakenings, 430
  materialism not implied, 287–89
  materialist brain facts, 118–21
  neuroscientist's doubts, 116–17
  nonlocal communication between cells, 217
  qualia as illusory side-effect of brain, 312
  savants challenging, 315
  scientific paradigm currently, 117–18
  scientific paradigm shift, 123–27
Newton, Isaac, 122
Newtonian physics, 122, 123
Nhat Hanh, Thich, 216
nocebo responses, 205, 226
Noë, Alva, 267
nonlocal consciousness
  article on, 276
  near-death experiences, 270–73
  science within consciousness, 162–63
  variety of, 275
Obama, Barack, 116
One, 91–94
One Mind, 400, 401, 404, 405
online resources
  Campaign for Open Science website, iii
  medication or placebo, 206
Oppenheimer, J. Robert, 275
out-of-body experiences (OBEs)
  blind people having near-death experiences, 263
  defining characteristics of, 369–70
  essential science testing of, 369–71
  near-death experiences, 10, 19, 58, 239, 250–52, 371
  near-death experiences as hallucinations, 264
oxygen deprivation in brain, 261
panentheism, 400, 405–7

panpsychism, 142–47, 268
paradigm shift
  consciousness and brain science, 123–24
  current paradigm as reductionist, 118, 124
  Darwinian selection of competing paradigms, 294
  death and survival of consciousness, 383–87
  defining paradigms, 118
  how a new paradigm emerges, 121–24, 125
  mind-brain as pre-paradigmatic, 291
  neuroscience, 123–27
  paradigms from robust frameworks, 117, 122
  paradigms to do science, 120
  power and potential of our minds, 394
  quantum mechanics, 5, 56, 122
  reductive materialism replacement, 323–25
  sciences to postmaterialism, 152, 382
  scientific revolutions, 4–5, 96, 292
  spiritual experience studies, 387–93
parapsychology. *See* psi phenomena
Paré, Ambroise, 205
Parmenides, The (Plato), 93
Parnia, Sam, 249
past-life memories
  case of Pretiba Gunawardana, 334–41
  case of Thusita Silva, 332
  case of Wael Kiwan, 338–41
  evidence of postmaterialism, 12–13
  explanations of, 344–46
  investigation process, 332
  mind transcending death, 60
  mind-brain relationship, 330
  psychological characteristics of children with, 342–43
  PTSD from, 331, 343, 345
  research, 301, 375–76
  research by Ian Stevenson, 331, 375
Pauli, Wolfgang
  Carl Jung and, 97–98, 99, 106–7
  cosmic clock dream, 106–7
  cosmic order, 88, 107, 391
Peek, Kim, 314
Peirce, Charles Sanders, 144
Penfield, Wilder, 288
Penrose, Roger, 159, 391
perception

after death, 11, 239, 248, 249, 250
blind people describing NDE, 263, 296
brain hierarchy, 160
duration implies consciousness, 144
experiencing the sacred and, 70
materialism's effects on worldview, 353
mind entwined with, 150
Persinger, Michael, 103–4
personal unconscious, 161
personality formation, 402–3
personality types of Jung, 158
Phaedo (Plato), 411
phenomenalism, 268
physicalism, 140
physics
    duration implies consciousness, 144–45
    Fröhlich journeying into subatomic realm, 107
    interconnection of psyche and physis, 107–9
    materialism flaws, 136–37
    mystical physicists, 84, 87, 107–9
    mysticism ridiculed, 65
    Newtonian, 122, 123
    non-materialism of mathematics, 91–94
    nothing new to be discovered, 292, 311
    physicists rejecting materialism, 84, 87, 89, 107, 384
    Platonic world of ideas, 89–91
    quantum. *See* quantum mechanics
    Wolfgang Pauli and Carl Jung, 97–98, 99, 106–7
Pizzi, Rita, 217
placebo effect, 205–7
    animals demonstrating, 208
    belief and health, 62
    interpersonal healing for, 205
    nocebo and telecebo comparison, 226
    nocebo responses, 205
    telecebo effect, 207–9
Planck, Max
    consciousness fundamental, 223
    mental events affect physical world, 2
    mind is matrix of all matter, iii
    physical laws, 220
    quantum theory founded, 311, 386
Plato
    Apology, 414

body a damper to mind's intelligence, 401
kundalini awakenings, 420, 433–34
leadership selection, 409–11
matter as basis of materialism, 85–89
men who are frightening, 397
mind metaphysically prior to matter, 88
non-material reality, 88, 89
One, 91–94
Parmenides, The, 93
Pauli's cosmic clock, 106
Phaedo, 411
philosophers, 411
philosophers practicing dying, 382, 394
physicists rejecting materialism, 84, 87, 89
Plato in physics, 89–91
Platonic Ideas, 91, 383
Platonic realism, 88
Republic, 412
Socrates on unexamined life, 414
souls embodied versus non-embodied, 411
World Soul, 400
zero, 93–94
Popper, Karl, 134, 289
post-anoxic reperfusion injury of brain, 261
postmaterialism
    about, ii, 58
    censorship of, 56
    consciousness connecting outer and inner experience, 98
    essential science, 359–63
    experiencing the sacred. *See* spirituality
    international summit, ii, 71
    kundalini awakenings, 429–30
    materialism's end, ii, iii
    postmaterial persons. *See* hypothesized postmaterial persons
    postmaterialist leaders, 409–11, 413–15
    postmaterialist paradigm, ii, 16–20
    postmaterialist social order. *See* belief systems and personal conduct
    program is changing, 55–57
    scientific ridicule, 56, 84, 218–21, 353
postmaterialist paradigm (PMP)
    emergence of, 16–17
    implications of, 19

international summit advancing, ii
key elements of, 17–20
post-traumatic stress disorder from past-life memories, 331, 343, 345
precognition, 203, 366–67, 378
  future health, 214
Priestley, J. B., 221
Principia Mathematica (Whitehead and Russell), 144
Process and Reality (Whitehead), 147
program is changing
  about, 55–57
  complementary and alternative medicine, 67–69
  experiencing the sacred, 69–70
  Internet and social media influence, 75–76
  materialism suppressing change, 63–66
  mindfulness meditation, 66–67
  postmaterialism emerging, 57–62, 70
  postmaterialist institutes and conferences, 73–74
  postmaterialist sciences, 71–73
  seeking the sacred, 62–63, 69
psi phenomena
  about psi, 51
  call for research on, 72
  coincidence check, 364
  criticism of, 218–21
  ESP. *See* ESP
  essential science and, 361–63
  essential science experiment design, 363–65
  essential science tests of, 365–67
  evidence of postmaterialism, 8–10, 317–21
  frontal lobe lesions and, 315
  hypothesized postmaterial persons, 28–32
  mental and physical interconnectedness, 18
  near-death experiences enhancing, 247
  nonlocal consciousness, 162–63, 270–73
  psychokinesis, 8–10, 8, 202, 203–4, 367
  telepathy. *See* telepathy
psilocybin ingestion, 425
psyche and physis. *See* interconnection of psyche and physis

psyche and quantum psycho-physical parallelism, 158–60
psychic healing, 368
psychokinesis (PK)
  about, 8
  essential science tests of, 367
  evidence of postmaterialism, 8–10
  Jung banging at Freud, 202
  Jung bangs from tabletop and knifeblade, 203–4
psychology
  call for postmaterial approach, 72, 73
  cognitive psychology, 140
  essential science and spirituality, 361–63
  essential science method, 359–61, 363–65
  essential science of telepathy, 363–65
  founders non-materialist, 286
  materialism's effects on worldview, 353–59
  meaning from scientific materialist perspective, 351
  meaning from spiritual experiences, 350–51
  positive psychology, 62
  quantum psychology, 177–80
  religion as psychopathological, 352
  spiritual experiences as mental illness, 63–66, 294, 417
  transpersonal psychology, 362
  Western Creed exercise, 354–59
  Wolfgang Pauli and Carl Jung, 97–98, 99, 106–7
Psychology and Alchemy (Jung), 97
PTSD from past-life memories, 331, 343, 345
Puthoff, Harold, 162
qualia and quanta versus materialism
  definitions, 312
  genius, 313
  paradigm shift, 323–25
  physics known except two small clouds, 311–13
  psychic phenomena, 317–21
  reductive materialism challenged by, 312
  savants, 314–15
  supralness underpinning qualia, 443
  survival after death, 316
  telepathy test meta-analysis, 322–23
  telepathy tests, 318–21

quantum consciousness
   awareness, 446–49, 458–60
   brain consciousness and, 458–60
   brain using quantum mechanics, 461
   deterministic and non-deterministic causation, 439–40
   holomatter, 440–43, 444, 462
   holomatter creation, 446–49
   in-causation, 439–40, 445, 452
   in-causation and subjective content, 442–43
   mind-body interaction, 453–54
   out-causation, 439–40, 445
   quantum jumps, 440–43
   quantum randomness, 438–40, 444–47
   quantum threat, 441–42, 449
   quantumhood, 441–43, 449–52
   questions remaining, 461–63
   supral information, 457
   supralness, 443, 454–58
   suprels, 457, 459–60
quantum creativity, 173–74
quantum entanglement
   about, 96–101, 126, 455
   in-causal interconnectedness, 462
   mind connected to greater field, 104–6
   neural entanglement, 102–4
   photon entanglement, 102
   supralness and mind-body, 454–58
   telecebo effect, 216–18
   wave function collapse, 126, 155
quantum mechanics (QM)
   awareness as foundation layer, 324
   Bell's theorem, 98
   brain using, 461
   consciousness explained by, 391
   consciousness within. See quantum consciousness; science within consciousness
   double-slit experiment, 126
   events not objects, 145
   evidence that boggles the mind, 27
   materialism questioned, 2, 136–37, 155
   mental universe, 126
   Newtonian mechanics insecurities, 2, 5, 123
   nonlocal signal-less communication, 155, 159
   observer affects observed system, 2, 126, 136, 155, 312
   observer and primacy of consciousness, 160–61
   observer's role, 155
   paradigm shift, 5, 56, 96, 122
   Planck founding, 311, 386
   quantum entanglement. See quantum entanglement
   quantum jumps, 440–43
   quantum objects, 126, 155, 159
   quantum randomness, 438–40, 444–47
   quantum wave function collapse, 126, 155
   subjective experience and. See qualia and quanta
   suspended between quantum states, 102
   wave-particle duality of objects, 155
   wholism versus atomism, 399
   Wolfgang Pauli and Carl Jung, 97–98, 99, 106–7
quantum psychology, 177–80
   Quantum Psychology Spectrum of Consciouness, 178–79
quantum psycho-physical parallelism
   ecology of the psyche and, 158–60
   nature of the unconscious, 161
   nonlocal quantum consciousness, 162–63
   origin and nature of self, 160–61
   sciences applied to, 157
quantum self, 160
Radin, Dean
   Entangled Minds, 210
   ESP meta-analysis, 214
   quantum entanglement, 216
Rain Man movie, 314
random number generators (RNGs), 9
randomized controlled trials (RCTs)
   drug versus postmaterial, 30–32
   postmaterialism study. See hypothesized postmaterial persons
   science gold standard, 27, 28
reductive materialism. See materialism
Reiki energy medicine, 68, 73, 168
reincarnation
   atheism and materialism, 138
   belief in, 297, 301, 330
   dharma to be fulfilled, 177
   evidence of postmaterialism, 12–13, 26, 316, 345
   mind-brain via spirituality, 301
   nonbiological, robotic, or holographic self, 58
   past-life memories. See past-life memories

science within consciousness, 174–77
Republic (Plato), 412
retro-temporal healing intentions, 214
Richards, P. S. (Bringing Spiritually Oriented Psychotherapies into the Health Care Mainstream), 72
Ring, Ken, 406–9
Russell, Bertrand (*Principia Mathematica*), 144
Sagan, Carl, 26, 50, 346
Samadhi, 66, 181–82
savants challenging materialism, 314–15
Schäfer, Lothar, 390
Schlitz, M. (*Death Makes Life Possible*), 389
Schrödinger, Erwin
  consciousness fundamental, 1, 223
  consciousness universal and singular, 386
  mental events affect physical world, 2
  mystical experiences, 384
  observer in scientific investigations, 385
  quantum entanglement, 96, 98, 216
  science a function of the soul, 388
Schwartz, Gary E.
  Case for Truth, The, 51
  International Summit organizer, ii
  mediumship research, 14–15
  this anthology, iv
  Toward a Postmaterialist Psychology, 73
Schwartz, S. A. (Declaration for Integrative, Evidence-Based, End-of-Life Care that Incorporates Nonlocal Consciousness), 72
science
  biology's big questions, 135
  Campaign for Open Science website, iii
  consciousness. *See* science within consciousness
  CONSORT criteria of studies, 210
  creed of science, 133–34
  essential science and spiritual experience, 361–63, 376–79
  essential science experiment design, 363–65
  essential science method, 359–61
  essential science of out-of-body experiences, 369–71
  essential science of psi phenomena, 365–67
  evidence-based, 27
  founders non-materialist, 84, 87, 108, 286
  genes. *See* gene expression
  human need for meaning, 352–53, 379
  Kepler Challenge, 52
  Manifesto for a Postmaterialist Science, iii, 71
  materialism flaws, 134–37
  Materialist Scientism, 286
  materialistic foundation, 132, 139, 286
  matter as basis of materialism, 85–89, 351
  matter is unconscious, 133, 137–39, 148
  neuroscience. *See* neuroscience
  new theories emerging from insecurity, 123, 125, 292
  non-dogmatic, open-minded, 3, 56, 71, 275
  non-materialism of mathematics, 91–94
  objective truth, 50
  observer affects observed system, 2, 126, 136, 155, 312
  observer in scientific investigations, 385–86
  panpsychism, 142–47, 268
  physics. *See* physics
  Platonic world of ideas, 89–91
  postmaterialism emerging, 71–73, 125, 418
  postmaterialist institutes and conferences, 73–74
  randomized controlled trials as standard, 27, 28
  rational mysticism at root of, 91
  ridicule of postmaterialism, 56, 84, 218–21, 353
  scientific paradigm. *See* scientific paradigm
  scientific revolutions, 4–5, 96, 125, 292
  skepticism, true versus pseudo, 40–50
  soul and science, 387–93
  spiritual experiences should be studied, 291–95
  spirituality compatible with, 70, 349, 386

spiritually transformative experiences, 417
Science Set Free (Sheldrake), 134, 150
science within consciousness (SWC)
    alternative medicine, 168–70
    chakras, 160, 170–73
    consciousness into quantum physics, 156
    consciousness-based evolution, 166–67
    creativity, 173–74
    enlightenment, 181–82
    health as harmony of bodies, 167
    life after death, 174–77
    life's journey, 177–80
    nature and origin of life, 163–64
    nature of the unconscious, 161
    nonlocal quantum consciousness, 162–63
    observer collapsing waves of possiblity, 155
    origin and nature of self, 160–61
    quantum psycho-physical parallelism, 157–60
    questions tackled by, 157
    scientific articles on consciousness, 388
    soul after death, 387–93
    unconscious mind, 148–49, 161
    wave-particle duality, 155
scientific materialism. *See* materialism
scientific paradigm
    awareness as foundation layer, 324
    consciousness and brain science, 123–24
    current, 117–18
    Darwinian selection of, 294
    how a new paradigm emerges, 121–24, 125
    matter as only reality, 135–37
    matter is unconscious, 133, 137–39, 148
    mind-brain as pre-paradigmatic, 291
    neuroscience shift, 123–27
    paradigms defined, 118
    paradigms from robust frameworks, 117
    paradigms to do science, 120
    postmaterialist substrate of reality, 126
    qualia and quanta challenging. *See* qualia and quanta
    sciences shifting, 152
    theory into paradigm, 361

scientism, 358
Searle, John, 140, 141, 159
self
    brain in postmaterialism, 100–101
    interconnection of people, 69
    interconnection of psyche and physis, 107–9
    loss via brain disease, 119
    mind connected to greater field, 104–6
    neural entanglement, 102–4
    origin and nature of, 160–61
    photon entanglement, 102
    psyche and quantum psycho-physical parallelism, 158–60
    quantum entanglement, 96–101
    Schrödinger on self, 98
    Wolfgang Pauli and Carl Jung, 97–98, 99, 106–7
self-referential nature of mind, 124
shamanism
    exteriorizing intention, 222
    misunderstood as mental illness, 63–66
Sheldrake, Rupert
    morphogenetic fields champion, 164, 462
    Science Set Free, 134, 150
Shermer, Michael, 41
skepticism
    discernments, 43–53
    materialist scientific creed as questions, 134
    quotes on, 218
    true versus pseudo, 40–50
Smolin, Lee (*The Trouble With Physics*), 136
Snyder, Allan, 315
Socrates, 414
souls
    atomism separating souls, 400
    consciousness in patients after death, 392
    creating consciousness, 405
    description of, 388, 390
    embodied versus non-embodied, 411
    manifesting our current selves, 402–5
    panentheism, 400, 405
    science and, 387–93
    soul as keeper of identity, 390
Spencer, J. H. (*The Eternal Law*), 108, 385
Spinoza, B., 399, 410
spirituality

atomism applied to, 400
complementary and alternative
    medicine, 67–69
energy medicine, 67
experiencing the sacred, 67, 69–70
God distinct from world, 386
health improved by, 62–63, 67
healthcare incorporating, 72
kundalini awakenings, 419–20
materialism suppressing, 63–66, 291,
    353, 376–79, 418
meditative states, 66–67, 295–96
mind-brain problem via. *See* mind-
    brain via spirituality
near-death experiences enhancing, 247
postmaterialism emerging, 57–62, 70
program is changing, 55–57
religion as psychopathological, 352
religion contrasted with, 350
science compatible with, 70, 349, 386
science founders spiritual, 286
science of the soul, 387–93
science studying for mind-brain, 290–
    95
seeking the sacred, 62–63, 69
spiritual experiences as mental illness,
    63–66, 294, 417
spiritual experiences providing
    meaning, 350–51
spiritual experiences studied by
    essential science, 361–63
spiritual experiences studied for mind-
    brain, 290–95
spiritually transformative experiences,
    417–18
spiritually transformative experiences
    (STEs), 417–18
kundalini awakening, 417
Stapp, Henry P., 217
Stevenson, Ian
    author invited to make independent
        studies, 331
    Cases of the Reincarnation Type, 345
    detail in published accounts, 345
    past life researchers, 12, 375–76
    psychological characteristics of
        children with past-life memories,
        342
Storm, Lance, 214
Strawson, Galen, 142–43
Structure of Scientific Revolutions
    (Kuhn), 4

subatomic particles. *See* atoms
sudden savants, 314–15
Summhammer, Johann, 217
supralness, 443, 454–58
    in-causal interconnectedness, 462
    supral information, 457
    suprels, 457, 459–60
Tanzi, Rudy, 382, 389–90
Targ, Russell, 162
Tart, Charles T. (*The End of
    Materialism*), 349, 362
telecebo response
    consciously applying, 222
    criticism of, 218–21
    everyday applications, 223–24
    evidence for, 209–12
    evidence from DMILS, 212–13
    exteriorization of thoughts healing,
        209–10
    interpersonal healing, 207–9, 216–18
    intrinsic connectedness, 216–18
    Jung exploding at Freud, 202–3
    Jung explosions prior, 203–4
    mental events exteriorizing, 203, 204
    mind interiorized, 204
    nocebo responses, 205
    nonlocal mind, 215
    placebo effect, 205–7
    placebo, nocebo, and telecebo
        comparison, 226
    remote aspect, 208
    telecebo effect, 207–9
    telepathy meta-analysis, 214
    time aspect, 214
telepathy
    about, 151, 318
    clairvoyance tests, 365–66
    criticism of, 218–21
    Freud's views on, 225
    ganzfeld technique, 8, 319, 320
    ganzfeld technique meta-analysis,
        322–23
    meta-analysis, 214
    scientific experiment design, 363–65
    testing for, 318–21, 365
teleportation, 102
terminal lucidity at death, 297
Tesla, Nikola, 59, 105, 106
Therapeutic Touch (TT), 212
Thomson, William (Lord Kelvin), 292,
    311
thoughts as quantum objects, 159

time
  cosmic clock dream of Pauli, 106–7
  duration implying consciousness, 144–45
  healing intentions across time, 214
  Jung beyond limitations of, 108
  matter definition, 86
  memories connecting to the past, 146, 150
  mind not limited to, 8, 18, 58, 150
  number one, 93
  psyche and matter merging in a moment, 108
  Whitehead on processes of matter, 145–47
Toward a Postmaterialist Psychology (Beauregard et al.), 73
transpersonal psychology, 362
Treffert, Darold, 314–15
Trent, Natalie L.
  this anthology, iv
  Toward a Postmaterialist Psychology, 73
Tressoldi, Patricio, 214
Trouble With Physics, The (Smolin), 136
Truzzi, Marcello, 50
Tucker, Jim, 12
Tyson, Neil deGrasse, 50
unconscious mind, 148–49
  future medical events anticipated, 214
  nature of, 161
unconstrained cognition, 432
universal mind prior to matter, 88

universe
  great thought, not great machine, 270
  interconnected, 391, 394
  Mental Universe with consciousness as creator, 126–27
  participatory universe, 18
  spirit manifest in laws, 55
van Lommel, Pim (*Consciousness beyond Life*), 276
Vedral, Vlatko, 216
vitalism, 135
Von Neumann, John, 2
Walmsley, Ian, 102
Ward, Keith, 86
wave-particle duality, 155
Western Creed exercise
  creed, 356–57
  introduction, 354–56
  reactions to, 357–59
Whitehead, Alfred North
  concrete facts, 90
  Platonic world of ideas, 90
  Principia Mathematica, 144
  Process and Reality, 147
  processes of reality, 144–47
wholism versus atomism, 399
Wigner, Eugene, 2
Woollacott, Marjorie, iv
Wundt, Wilhelm, 286
Xavier, Chico, 299–300
Yin, Zhang-Qi, 102
Zerhouni, Elias, 218
zero, 93–94

Made in the USA
Coppell, TX
26 January 2023